Christianity in the Caribbean

Christianity in the Caribbean

Essays on Church History

Edited by Armando Lampe

UNIVERSITY OF THE WEST INDIES PRESS
Barbados • Jamaica • Trinidad and Tobago

The University of the West Indies Press
1A Aqueduct Flats Kingston 7 Jamaica W I

ISBN 976-640-029-6

05 04 03   5 4 3 2

CATALOGUING IN PUBLICATION DATA
Lampe, Armando
    Christianity in the Caribbean : essays on church history / Armando Lampe.
    p.cm
    Includes bibliographical references and index.

    ISBN 976-640-029-6
    1. Christianity – Caribbean Area. 2. Caribbean Area –
    Church history. 3. Church and state – Caribbean Area –
    History. 4. Slavery and the church – Caribbean Area.
    I. Lampe, Armando.

    BR640.C57 2001   279.9729 dc-20

Book design and text composition by Jenni R. Anderson, Spanish Town, Jamaica
Cover design by Robert Harris
Body text in 10.5 on 13pt Gilde with Optane display type

Printed in Jamaica by Stephenson's Litho Press Ltd

Contents

Preface

The present work is fairly limited in scope, focusing on only one of the religions practised in the Caribbean. It is a collection of essays on themes related to the history of Christianity and society in the Caribbean. In the first essay, Meier examines rights of the people and the mission of the Catholic Church from the sixteenth century to the mid seventeenth century. The other studies address the following themes: the institution of slavery and the Christian religion from the seventeenth to the nineteenth centuries (Hunte and Lampe), the decolonization process and the Catholic Church in the nineteenth century (Hurbon), and the relationship between churches and military dictatorships in the twentieth century (Wipfler and Tschuy).

It is not possible to separate this book from other Commission of Studies on Latin American Church History (CEHILA) publications on the Caribbean. The first was published in Portuguese: *Escravidao negra e História da Igreja na América Latina e no Caribe*, edited by J.O. Beozzo (Petrópolis 1987). The second appeared in French: *Le phénomène religieux dans la Caraïbe: Guadeloupe-Martinique-Guyane-Haïti*, edited by Laënnec Hurbon (Montréal 1989). The, third was published in Spanish: CEHILA, *Historia General de la Iglesia en América Latina*. Tomo IV: Caribe (Chetumal-Salamanca 1995). From this publication, we selected the chapters of the present work, which were originally written in other languages, and I take full responsibility for any short-comings that may exist in the translation of these essays into English.

Acknowledgments

No project of this kind can be undertaken without the cooperation of others. I owe profound gratitude to Enrique Dussel and Samuel Silva Gotay. I am indebted to the University of Quintana Roo. My sincere gratitude goes to the co-authors of this book. And last but not least, my thanks go to The University of the West Indies Press for producing this material.

Abbreviations

ABC	American Baptist Convention
ABHMS	American Baptist Home Mission Society
CBOC	Convención Bautista Occidental
CBOR	Convención Bautista Oriental
CCEC	Cuban Council of Evangelical Churches (Consejo Cubano de Iglesias Evangélicas)
CCLA	Committee on Cooperation in Latin America
CEHILA	Commission of Studies on Latin American Church History
CWS	Church World Service
IE	Iglesia Episcopal
IM	Iglesia Metodista
IMC	International Missionary Council
IP	Iglesia Presbiteriana
MECS	Methodist Episcopal Church, South
MSC	Movimiento Social Cristiano
OAS	Organization of American States
OP	Order of Preachers
PCUS	Presbyterian Church in the United States (South)
PCUSA	Prebyterian Church in the United States of America (North)
PECUSA	Protestant Episcopal Church in the United States of America
SBC	Southern Baptist Convention
SET	Seminario Evangélico de Teología

JOHANNES MEIER

The Beginnings of the Catholic Church in the Caribbean

Due to religious reforms in Spain at the end of the fifteenth and at the beginning of the sixteenth centuries, the mission and the foundation of the church in the West Indies required suitable personnel. As early as 1511–12, the dioceses of Santo Domingo, Concepción de la Vega and Puerto Rico were established with specially chosen bishops and competent cathedral chapters. The political officials of the church carefully examined the moral qualification of the priests and brothers who were to be sent there. Strict criteria were used in the selection and nomination of bishops. From as early as that period, interesting personalities such as Alessandro Geraldini in Santo Domingo (1516–24) and Rodrigo de Bastidas of Coro/Venezuela (1531–41) and Puerto Rico (1541–67) were known. The long nomination process was regulated by the law of patronage, and the Roman Curia exercised minimal influence. This complicated procedure and the vast distances involved caused bishops to be absent from their American dioceses for long periods. On the island of Santo Domingo, the ratio between resident and absentee bishops was 2:1. By 1620, the Caribbean had a fully developed church hierarchy which functioned almost intact until late into the eighteenth century.

The dioceses of the Caribbean enjoyed little prestige. Only on rare occasions were resident bishops of Spanish dioceses transferred to them. It was much more frequent for bishops to be transferred out of the Caribbean. Several archbishops of Santo Domingo were determined to other dioceses of more prestige such as Bogotá, Quito, Cuzco or La Paz. San Juan de Puerto Rico and Santiago de Cuba were among the least preferred. The mission of the bishops was to direct and administer the dioceses as well as look after the common good of the clergy and the spiritual needs of the faithful. The bishops could hardly have reflected on their special obligations towards the Indians, who quickly disappeared from the Greater Antilles. Moreover, the bishops failed to show sufficient zeal towards the slaves. After the Council of Trent (1545–63) and the Junta Magna (1568), an obvious intensification of the spiritual direction of the dioceses could be observed. Indeed, regular and systematic pastoral visits were undertaken by the bishops. This development reached its peak at the beginning of the seventeenth century. At that time, the three dioceses of the Caribbean were governed by Bishops of the Order of Preachers (OP): Agustín Dávila y Padilla, Santo Domingo (1599–1604); Martín Vázquez de Arce, Puerto Rico (1599–1604); and Juan de las Cabezas Altamirano, Santiago de Cuba (1602–10). The situation stabilized in the seventeenth century: the Christendom of Spanish America had found its identity; even the Caribbean, a region on the periphery of the Spanish-speaking world, shared in the spirit of the "Siglo de Oro".

The Indigenous Peoples

The native Caribbean population at the outset of the conquest

When Columbus reached the American continent in 1492, it was inhabited by 57 million people, one-eighth of the world's population at that time.[1] The Indios or indigenous people, as they were referred to by the Europeans, belonged to different nations and had achieved different levels of cultural awareness. The Caribbean islands, the first region colonized by the Europeans, were inhabited mainly by three groups: the Ciboneys, the Tainos and the Caribs. They originated in the Orinoco Basin and migrated from there to inhabit different Caribbean islands. First came the Ciboneys, a few centuries before Christ, then the Tainos, during the first century of our era, and finally the Caribs, around the year 1000.[2]

At the end of the fifteenth century when the Spaniards invaded the Caribbean region, they found the Ciboneys, the first inhabitants of these islands, living on the western coast of Cuba and in the remote areas of Haiti. They lived in caves and fed on fish, oysters and other types of seafood.[3]

The Tainos, a branch of the great Arawak population, inhabited the centre and east of Cuba, Jamaica, Haiti and Puerto Rico. They lived in huts called *bohíos* or *caneyes*, which were circular structures around a central pole with wooden beams, thatched with reed brambles, palm leaves and straw. They practised agriculture with very simple tools and techniques on the most arable land, but also hunted and fished. At sea they used canoes measuring up to 30 metres long. Their social stratification consisted of nobles, freed men and servants (*naborias*) and their leader was a *cacique*. When Columbus arrived, La Española was divided into five principal domains or *cacicazcos*: the Marién, located in the northwest, was ruled by the cacique Goacanagari (or Accangari); in the northeast cacique Guarionex ruled Magua; in the southeast, Higuey was controlled by the cacique Cayacoa (or Cutubanama); in the centre, Maguana was under the rule of the cacique Caonabo; and in the southwest, the cacique Behechio controlled Xaragua. Similar domains existed in Cuba and Puerto Rico.[4]

The Caribs lived in the east and south of Puerto Rico, in the Lesser Antilles. Expert navigators, they were belligerent and were feared by the Tainos because of their many assaults.[5] This bad reputation quickly spread among the Spanish conquerors, as the chronicler Peter Martyr accused them of being cannibals.[6]

Towards the end of 1493, Columbus landed for a second time, in La Española, this time with 17 ships and approximately 1,500 people. Among them was Revd Bernardo Boyl, appointed apostolic vicar of the newly discovered regions, who made the journey with twelve other members of the clergy.[7] The majority of these first missionaries returned to Europe between 1494 and 1495. Only the lay brothers Juan Deledeule, Juan Tisin and Ramón Pané remained longer in the island and were witnesses to the transformation of a peaceful colonial undertaking into a violent invasion. Thousands of Tainos were enslaved and forced to work by men who had belonged principally to the lower classes in Spain. Bartolomé Columbus, brother of Christopher Columbus, who had been appointed governor by the latter, soon lost control of the situation. The three lay brothers who remained in the island watched, powerless, as this conquest unfolded.[8]

At Christopher Columbus' request, Ramón Pané, one of these three brothers, wrote an account of his experience with the Tainos in 1498, in which he also related his missionary exploits.[9] Pané, who called himself *pobre ermitaño* (poor hermit), spent one year learning one of the three languages spoken, the one in La Española in the Macorís region. From there he went to the cacique Guarionex, accompanied by Guatícaba, an Indian baptized by him, whom he renamed Juan Mateo.

He remained with Guarionex until 1496, but did not succeed in his missionary attempts, even witnessing the death of his companion.[10] After that experience, Pané attempted to convert cacique Mabiatué and in 1498, related this last endeavour: "*el cual hace ya tres años que continúa con buena voluntad, diciendo que quiere ser cristiano, y que no quiere tener más que una mujer, aunque suelen tener dos o tres, y los principales diez, quince y veinte*".[11]

The religious instruction given by Pané was very rudimentary: he taught the people the Ave Maria and the Pater Noster and explained to them in simple words that God was the Creator of heaven and earth. The use of religious paintings for this purpose led to a major misunderstanding. The Tainos buried these religious images, since they associated this act with a fertility ritual. Instead of interpreting the act as a first attempt at inculcating the Christian faith into the world of the Tainos, the Spaniards saw it as an act of desecration and Bartolomé Columbus ordered them to be punished severely. Pané, however, had acquired valuable knowledge about the Tainos' religion and therefore became known as the first American anthropologist.[12] Thanks to him, we know that the Tainos worshipped a supreme being, Yocohuguama, and believed in lesser divine beings, the Zemen, who manifested themselves as forces of the sun, wind and rain with power over life on earth. The Zemen were represented by stone, wooden and clay images and were worshipped through music and dance by the Shamanes. The Tainos spread their myths among them regarding the cosmos and the origin of man through musical plays known as *areytos*. They also practised ancestral worship and totemic customs.[13]

Ramón Pané's companions, Juan Deledeule and Juan Tisin, left for Spain in 1499 to ask the primate for more missionaries. Upon their return to the West Indies one year later, as members of Francisco de Bobadilla's group (appointed by the king as governor and judge for Columbus' government), they were joined by three Franciscans: Juan de Robles, Juan de Trasierra and Francisco Ruiz. In less than two years, Nicolás de Ovando (future governor) arrived in La Española with 2,500 men, among them sixteen Franciscans (twelve priests and four lay brothers) with their superior, Alonso de Espinal.[14] Bartolomé de Las Casas, who also travelled to the Americas with Ovando's team, later wrote that these friars undoubtedly lived an honest religious life, but did not carry out any missionary activity, except to educate a few of the caciques' sons.[15]

Queen Isabel had, more than once, ordered the return of the Indians whom Columbus had taken as slaves to Spain to their lands. She had also criticized the ill treatment of the Indians, because she saw them as free low vassals of the Castillian Crown. According to the queen, the Indians were to pay low taxes (a tax similar to that paid by servants in Spain) and receive protection from the authorities.[16] Thus, on 20 March 1503, Governor Ovando received an order to treat the Indians well and to let them live in their own communities, ruled by a state governor who was to defend their rights and give them protection. Each community was also to receive a church with a priest to educate the inhabitants in the Catholic faith and allegiance to the Castillian Crown. Moreover, a school was to be built next to the church, where the children would assemble twice daily so that the priest could teach them reading and writing and basic Christian prayers.[17]

Soon Governor Ovando understood that the queen's idea was totally contrary to the colonists' interest, and that the lucrative Spanish domination over the island was based on land distribution among the colonists as well as on Indian enslavement.[18] Later he insisted that the queen legalize the existing distribution system which he had organized perfectly. The royal decree of 20 December 1503 accomplished his objective of giving the taxes paid by the Indians to the colonists instead of to the Crown. In return, it forced the colonists to give protection to the Indians and educate them in the Catholic faith with the help of priests.[19] This was the beginning of the encomienda system (under which land and inhabitants were granted to colonists). Legally this did not include the distribution of land, but in reality the Spaniards used the system to obtain land and to enrich themselves through excessive exploitation of the Indians. The colonists or *encomenderos* totally reneged on their responsibility to Christianize the Indians.[20]

In this way the Crown achieved high economic growth but at a high cost: forced labour resulted in the suicide of thousands of Indians who drank cassava juice; many women aborted or killed their offspring while others were victims of hunger[21] or of the newly acquired diseases introduced by the Europeans against which they had no defence.[22] A survey of 1508 indicated that in that year, there were only 60,000 Indians on the island.[23] It is estimated that in 1492 the population had been five or six times greater.[24]

To remedy the critical shortage of labourers, King Fernando agreed through three decrees (issued on 15 June 1510, 3 June 1511 and 23 February 1512) to the capture of Indians in the Lesser Antilles, with the exception of Trinidad and the Caribbean coast of the South American continent.[25] Thus, between 1508 and 1513, approximately 40,000 persons were deported to La Española.[26] On 14 August 1509, Diego Columbus, who was appointed successor to Governor Ovando in 1508, was also authorized to carry out a new *repartimiento de Indios*.[27]

In La Española a legal difference was established between the *indios encomendados*, considered free low vassals of the Crown, and the Indian slaves brought from other regions. This, however, made no difference to the everyday life of the Indians.[28] Nevertheless, a royal decree of 13 May 1509 addressed to Columbus, insisted on fulfilment of the obligations of converting the Indians to Christians, stating that even the priests, *encomenderos*, had not been respecting this religious obligation.[29]

In the years after 1508, the neighbouring islands of Puerto Rico, Jamaica and Cuba were conquered, and the encomienda system was established in these countries. King Fernando, in a letter written on 6 June 1511, expressed his desire to give priority to Catholic education in the process of conquest[30] and admitted that, in this respect, there were shortcomings in the La Española system, and insisted that this should not be repeated in Jamaica.[31] He issued a similar warning when referring to the conquest of Cuba by Diego Velázquez.[32]

Ecclesiastic protests against the conquest and the first attempts to save the Indians

The small group of Dominican friars that had just arrived in Santo Domingo, revealed the total uselessness of the encomienda system for the conversion of the Indians to Christianity and protested against overexploitation and genocide. Preaching from the gospel during Advent (John 1:23: "I am the voice of one crying in the wilderness"), Father Antonio Montesino, in the presence of Diego Columbus and the distinguished citizens of the city, spoke out against the atrocities committed by the Spaniards on the island and accused his countrymen of mortal sin because they kept the Indians in such a state of cruel and horrible servitude, violating every right and law, oppressing and exploiting them without feeding them or treating their illnesses, caused by excessive and forced labour, leaving them to die or killing them in order to maintain the daily intake of gold. Montesino exclaimed: "*¿éstos no son hombres? ¿no tienen ánimas racionales? ¿no sois obligados a amarlos como a vosotros mismos?*"[33] Montesino's sermon angered Columbus, the Crown's officers and the colonists but they did not succeed in dividing the Dominicans or in changing their opinion. On the contrary, the following Sunday, this time starting with the biblical text "For truly my words shall not be false" (Job 36:1, 6), Montesino went even further and announced in the name of his Dominican brothers that he would deny sacramental absolution to all those who persisted in accumulating wealth by exploiting and enslaving the Indians.[34] With these sermons, the Dominicans destroyed the image of the conquerors as the bearers of the cross and opened a debate that lasted for decades over the Spaniard's land rights in the Americas.[35]

At the beginning of 1512, Diego Columbus informed King Fernando of the incidents in Santo Domingo and proposed an immediate expulsion of the Dominicans from the island. He even got Alonso de Espinal, the Franciscan superior, involved, since he knew that this order had not questioned the system of domination over La Española.[36] The court reacted to this information in a strange manner and the king's response was that the judges and theologians had decreed that forced labour of the Indians was *conforme a derecho humano y devyno.*[37] Alonso de Loaysa, the Dominican's provincial in Spain who was consulted by the king, was astounded and prohibited such scandal provoking sermons, threatening immediate return to Spain if this order was disobeyed.[38]

During this period Antonio Montesino left for Spain to defend his position, arriving there at the end of March or the beginning of April. After obtaining the provincial's comment, the prior of Santo Domingo's community, Pedro de Córdoba, followed him. Notwithstanding the resistance of the court, Montesino and Córdoba managed to have an audience with the king and presented to him their opinion on the condition of the Indians, without sacrificing their principles.[39] This resulted in the creation of a mixed commission which included lawyers and theologians headed by the bishop of Palencia, Juan Rodríguez de Fonseca, to investigate this issue. This commission drafted the new *Leyes de Burgos* (Burgos Laws) of 27 December 1512. Once again the legal status of the natives of America was redefined as "free vassals of the Spanish Crown", free people with the right to their own homeland and their own economy. But as vassals, they were also obliged to serve the Crown with their labour provided that this included regular time off and payment in kind of clothes and furniture. At the same time, these laws reconfirmed the conditions imposed by the Pope to convert the Indians to the Christian faith. These laws also perpetuated a false impression of an interrelated community life between the newcomers and the natives, including the encomienda system, by assuming that the Europeans would, by example, promote a fraternal reorientation of the Indians to Christian life. It was evident that the *Leyes de Burgos* did not take into account the proven selfishness of the colonists and their desire for power and riches which was contrary to the Christian faith.[40]

The Dominicans were not happy with these laws and achieved, through tough negotiations, certain modifications which were approved in Valladolid on 28 June 1513. Under the terms of these negotiations, forced labour was prohibited for married women. Indians were to work for only nine months in the encomiendas, to give them enough time to cultivate their own land.[41]

Similarly in the year 1513, the Crown had the attorney Palacios Rubios draft the *requerimiento* (notification), an *evangelio muy raro*.[42] This text was to be read to the Indians before force was used against them, informing them that there was only one God, who had placed the Pope as a supreme authority on earth. This document stipulated that the lands be given to the Catholic kings and that the Christian faith had to be taught there. The inhabitants of these lands were expected to accept Christianity as had the inhabitants of other islands. If they resisted, they were threatened with war and slavery. Naturally, no one succumbed voluntarily, so the *requerimiento* became a true war declaration, which had the effect of putting the conscience of the colonists to rest. The Dominicans heavily criticized the *requerimiento*.[43]

Pedro de Córdoba was not happy with what had been achieved on behalf of the Indians and was convinced that his principles were correct and realistic. His aim was to preach the gospel in a remote part of the colony, far from the negative influences of the bad example and atrocities of the colonists and to create Indian Christian communities through a devoted apostolate, under the absolute supremacy of the king, and guidance from the members of the Orders according to Christian teachings. So, supported by the rest of his Dominican brothers, he proposed to King Fernando to christianize the Indians on the Venezuelan coast and the Gulf of Paria, provided that the Spaniards stayed away from that region.[44] This project was welcomed by the king who liked Pedro de Córdoba so much that he was able to gather a group of twenty missionaries. He ordered Diego Columbus (12 May

1513) to provide the Dominicans with a ship, food and a translator, and on 28 May he requested Jerónimo de Vich, his representative at the Holy See, to seek permission from the Pope for the missionaries "*para poder confirmar en ausencia de obispos, poder usar el óleo viejo y crisma, donde no hubiere obispos, . . . bendecir aras y cálices*".[45] In the winter of 1513–14, Pedro de Córdoba and Antonio Montesino, together with eighteen members of the Order and two postulants, returned to Santo Domingo from Spain in three groups.[46] In the second half of 1514, Antonio Montesino, Francisco de Córdoba and the layman Juan Garcés left for Venezuela. Montesino had to stay behind in Puerto Rico for health reasons, while the other two continued and landed on the continent close to Píritu, 130 kilometres to the west of Cumaná. They died there in 1515 as martyrs, because a Spanish ship, violating the agreement, appeared on the coast and captured natives in order to enslave them.[47]

Meanwhile the Crown had, in 1511, limited the authority of Diego Columbus as governor by instituting an *audiencia* (high court) in Santo Domingo. King Fernando also limited Columbus' right to distribute Indians and asked Rodrigo de Albuquerque to draft a new and final *requerimiento* in La Española. Upon its completion in 1514, the island had only 25,503 Indians.[48] Of these, 14,000 were distributed among 86 encomenderos who later formed the élite of the colonial society. For the Indians, this was not an improvement of their situation.[49]

In the spring of 1513, King Fernando authorized Diego Velázquez, conquistador of Cuba, to carry out a *repartimiento* of the natives of this island.[50] Consequently, Velázquez assigned his soldiers to encomiendas during that year and the next. Among those who received an encomienda was the thirty-year-old Bartolomé de Las Casas, then the army's chaplain to Pánfilo Narváez, Velázquez's companion. He got Indians as labourers from Canarreo, in the Arimao River valley. Las Casas had arrived with Governor Ovando in La Española in 1502, where he had already received an encomienda in the Cibao region. However, before leaving for Cuba he felt guilty when a Dominican priest refused to absolve him of his sins, because he did not agree to free his Indians. For his conversion, however, the biblical phrases from the Ecclesiasticus (34:21–27) were decisive when he was preparing himself to celebrate mass. With that text, for Las Casas it became clear that the conquest was contrary to God's will because "*sacrificios de bienes injustos robados a los pobres son impuros*".[51] Also, many biblical texts that he continued to study gave him additional reason since they spoke out against looting, evil and injustice and spoke of rights for the peoples of the West Indies.[52] So Las Casas decided to give up his encomienda and to remain free to commit himself to the struggle to save the Indians, which was initiated by the Dominicans.

Las Casas had known Pedro de Córdoba since 1510. He familiarized himself with his points of view and also met four other Dominicans (Gutierre de Ampudia, Bernardo de Santo Domingo, Pedro de San Martín and Diego de Alberca) who were sent to that island immediately after the conquest of Cuba. Aware that the Indian situation would worsen in Cuba as had happened in La Española, Gutierre de Ampudia and Las Casas decided to travel to Santo Domingo to inform the community there.[53] In July 1515, Las Casas met Pedro de Córdoba and their mutual objectives led to a close friendship. Las Casas promised de Córdoba, who was two years older than he was, that he would do his utmost to continue what had been started. With God's help, and even if the goal was not achieved, at least he could say at the end of his life that he had fulfilled his Christian duties.[54]

After their discussion in Santo Domingo, Las Casas went to Spain, accompanied by Antonio Montesino. Through the intervention of the Archbishop of Sevilla, King Fernando authorized the creation of a commission to study the "Indian question". When the king died in January 1516, they had not come to any conclusions. Within a month, Las Casas, Montesino and Pedro de Córdoba (who had also arrived in Spain) managed to convince the interim regent, Francisco Cardinal Jiménez de Cisneros, of the need for a radical change in the system prevailing in the West Indies.[55] Cisneros asked Las Casas to work out a *"plan para la reformación de las Indias"* and he appointed the latter, in September 1516, as *"procurador o protector universal de todos los indios"*.[56] He entrusted the government of those regions to three Hieronymite monks: Luis de Figueroa, Alonso de Santo Domingo and Bernardino Manzanedo. By decree of September 1516, they were advised, upon their arrival in Santo Domingo, to organize a meeting of the most distinguished colonists and leaders of the caciques to determine if the following measures were possible: the settlement of Indians in communities with churches, schools and hospitals; the introduction of livestock into the communities; the governing of communities by caciques; the employment of one-third of the men between the ages of twenty and fifty years in the area of mining and the participation of the Indian communities in the profits of the mining industry. Failing implementation of this government programme, the *Leyes de Burgos* and of Valladolid (1512–13) had to prevail, with the strict prohibition of forced labour of women and children.[57] The Hieronymites left Spain on 11 November 1516 and arrived in Santo Domingo on 20 December 1516. Las Casas and Pedro de Córdoba returned to America at the same time.

Faced with hostility on the part of the colonists, the Hieronymites proceeded with caution: they began by collecting statistics on the entire Indian population in La Española, which had been reduced to 11,000 persons,[58] but they delayed in promoting concrete measures.[59] This attitude worried the Dominicans and Las Casas since they felt that the well-needed modifications were not being carried out. As far as the Dominicans were concerned, it was imperative to free the Indians who faced death. Thus, the priority should have been to save their lives, even without their being baptized, since this would have been better than to leave them in the encomiendas, where they probably would have been baptized but would have died quickly. The encomienda system should therefore have been abolished and the capture of Indians as slaves prohibited in the Bahamas, the Lesser Antilles and on the Venezuelan coast. After these measures, the Indians had the option of regenerating themselves and later on they were to be evangelized by the Dominicans.[60] Pedro de Córdoba was very optimistic, believing that, through this, they could establish a church for the Indians, inspired by the gospel: "*gentes tan mansas, tan obedientes y tan buenas que si entre ellos entraran predicadores solos sin las fuerzas e violencias destos mal aventurados cristianos, pienso que se podiera en ellos fundar quasi tan excelente iglesia, como fue la primitiva*".[61]

Disappointed by the weak Hieronymite policy,[62] Las Casas went to the court in mid 1517, to outline the Dominicans' plans and to gain support from the Spanish Dominicans. At the convent of San Esteban, a theological dispute developed, initiated by Reginaldo, Antonio Montesino's brother, with the participation of thirteen scholars from various convents. This group declared itself in favour of a reform of the laws of the colonies and supported the alternatives presented by Las Casas and Pedro de Córdoba: to take the Indians without reverting to slavery, to establish a regular work schedule, and for priests and lay-brothers to introduce them to the Christian faith. The possibility of a rebirth of the church in America according to the ideals of the first Christians awakened great enthusiasm among them.[63]

After the assassination of Francisco de Córdoba and Juan Garcés, and before his voyage to Spain accompanied by Las Casas and Antonio Montesino, Pedro de Córdoba led a group of missionaries to La Costa de las Perlas in the autumn of 1515, with the participation of Dominicans and Franciscans (some of the persons called together by Alonso de Espinal in the years 1512–13 in the convents of Spain). The Franciscans of this group founded a convent in Cumaná, while the Dominicans settled in the Chiribichí region located more in the interior.[64] In Spain, Pedro de Córdoba gained official support from Cardinal Cisneros, who on 3 September 1516 allocated the region of Cariaco to Cuquibacoa for this project.[65] Notwithstanding these guarantees, this missionary experience evolved slowly, especially because of the very complex ethnic situation of the region. Additionally, it had a negative influence on the fact that Spanish ships, under the pretext of trading, continued to invade the region to capture Indians for slavery.[66]

Meanwhile, in accordance with the decree authorizing them to govern the island (1516), the Hieronymites at La Española also started to prepare twenty-five communities for approximately 400 to 500 Indians each.[67] Preparations continued throughout 1518. Accommodation was already available for 7,000 persons, goods provided for one year, including ecclesiastical vestments, and ornaments for these new communities, when disaster struck: "*lo que ahora ha acontecido, que ya que estaban para salir de las minas en el mes de diciembre del año pasado é ir a sus pueblos, ha placido a Nuestro Señor de dar una pestilencia de viruelas en los dichos indios que no cesa.*"[68] Two-thirds of the Indians died and in 1519, only 3,000 were still alive. The Hieronymites found themselves in a state of disaster, their Indian policy was a failure and the colonists, who were only interested in keeping their slaves, were harassing them. In August 1518, their political powers, which had been authorized by Cardinal Cisneros, who himself died 8 November 1517, were also suspended when the successor to the Crown, Charles, had arrived in Spain. They were notified to remain in office until the arrival of their successors.[69]

In December 1518, Rodrigo de Figueroa was appointed the new "*juez supremo de las Indias*".[70] He assumed office the following year and carried out a survey on the situation in the Costa de las Perlas. Pedro de Córdoba had to admit that up to then (4 October 1519), the missions had not been successful and that the task of learning native languages had been an obstacle.[71] In the end, after concluding his investigation on 5 November 1519, Figueroa authorized the enslavement of Carib tribes in the region and in December, gave concessions to slave traders to include the Arawak tribes.[72] Consequently, during the course of 1520, Spanish slave trade ships carried out numerous cruel and violent acts against the Indians in Venezuela. The latter finally organized a great rebellion in September 1520, in which the convents of Cumaná and Chiribichí were set on fire and two Dominicans lost their lives.[73]

Las Casas was not aware of these incidents that Governor Figueroa had been allowing, when on 19 May 1520, King Charles, in appreciation of his many years of service, granted him the right to carry out his plan for peaceful coexistence between Christians and Indians in a region of Venezuela with a 800-kilometre coastline.[74] This concession far exceeded those obtained by Pedro de Córdoba from King Fernando and Cardinal Cisneros. This attempt at evangelization through preaching, testimony and the absence of swords, would have achieved new dimensions; but it could not be accomplished. In the beginning Las Casas encountered problems in finding labourers and artisans as civil collaborators, but finally he succeeded in November 1520 by gathering seventy persons. When the group arrived in Puerto Rico, he became aware of the events that had taken place. They met Captain Gonzalo de Ocampo who had been sent by the governor of Santo Domingo on an expedition of revenge and punishment in Cumaná; but Las Casas did not succeed in discouraging him from this act of violence.[75] He then went to Santo Domingo to protest, and then to Cumaná where he met some Franciscans who had returned to rebuild their burnt-out missions. He was welcomed with open arms, with the hope of once again being able to carry out this missionary experience.[76]

Thereafter, Las Casas left for Puerto Rico to collect the people brought from Spain to reinforce the project; in the meantime, many had gone their separate ways. While Las Casas was experiencing this frustration, the Indians once again launched a surprise attack on Cumaná killing five persons. The other Europeans fled. It was obvious that the events had destroyed the Indians' confidence. Once again, the Spaniards organized, with the help of Jácome de Castellón, an expedition of revenge and finally put an end to the peaceful missionary experience.[77]

Amidst these tragic happenings, on 4 May 1521 in the convent of Santo Domingo, Pedro de Córdoba died of tuberculosis at the age of 39.[78] But the deep Christian and friendly conviction he had shown to the Indians remained alive among the Dominicans of the West Indies. His vision was published through a collection of sermons that Córdoba had preached since 1510 concerning the evangelization of the Indians.[79] Through Domingo de Betanzos (since 1513, a member of the convent in Santo Domingo and later founder of the Mexican province of the Order), this text reached the hands of Bishop Juan de Zumárraga, who ordered it printed in 1544 as *Doctrina cristiana para instrucción y información de los indios* at the Cromberger printery in Mexico City.[80] In 1548, another edition was published by the Mexican Dominicans in the Spanish and Nahuatl languages.[81] In the first part of this text (sermons 1–17), the Christian creed was explained, beginning with the creation through the incarnation, death and resurrection of Jesus Christ and ending with the final judgement. The second part dealt with moral instruction through an explanation of the Ten Commandments, the seven sacraments and charity work. The final part consisted of sermons about the cross, Our Father, the Hail Mary and a "*sermón para después de bautizados*", obviously a catechism within the general act of administration of baptism.[82] The basic teaching of this "book of faith" was respect for the dignity of the indigenous peoples as individuals created in God's image and destined to be their friends. The wide use of the holy word calls to attention the desire to simplify the catechism through examples and concrete illustrations. This very profound, Christian and peaceful way of teaching the faith used by Pedro de Córdoba met with little success during his lifetime, but it had a permanent effect on Bishop Zumárraga and on the fathers of the first Mexican provincial council in 1555 and, through them, on the evangelization of Mexico.[83]

The struggle for legal reform

At the end of the Hieronymite government, the majority of the Indian communities established in La Española had disappeared. By 1520, those who had not been killed by disease, had fled to the mountains to escape the encomenderos who remained in need of slaves, not so much for work in the mines but for their booming plantations.[84] Despite formal declarations in favour of the freedom of the native population, the official position of the Crown was very contradictory in the 1520s and 1530s. The government and the colonists who had been on the island for many years, were in conflict with the cacique Enriquillo, the last Indian *guerrillero* on the island, who had reclaimed the mountain range of Bahoruco in the south, and had declared it an autonomous region.[85] They did not succeed in suppressing his rebellion by military means. Finally, in August 1533, Bartolomé de Las Casas went personally to meet Enriquillo, stayed with him for a few weeks and managed to reconcile the interests of the colonists in Azua with those of the cacique, who on 6 June 1534 accepted by writing his submission to the emperor.[86]

Upon the suggestion of Domingo de Betanzos, Las Casas was formally initiated into the Order of the Dominicans, after the death of his friend Pedro de Córdoba, and took his vows in December 1523.[87] Out of public view, he dedicated those years primarily to the study of history and theology at first, while in a cell in the convent of Santo Domingo and later on in the convent which he himself founded in 1526 in Puerto de Plata on the northern coast of La Española. During this time he worked at improving his critical skills and proposing new arguments for the political struggle.[88] He relaunched this struggle by criticizing, in a letter written on 20 January 1531, the dramatic situation existing in America. No one had imagined the cruelty suffered by the natives of this continent, with entire nations dying without being converted to the Christian faith, the only right and obligation the Spaniards could use as justification for keeping the Indians. On the contrary, the conquistadores were only interested in enriching themselves at the expense of the Indians who were forced to work. This uncontrollable drive for money led to the inevitable death of the Indians who were used and abused as mere tools.

Las Casas argued that Christ did not come to the world to die for gold, but to save humanity through suffering. For this reason he proposed to remove all the colonists from this continent, with the exception of the members of religious orders who could serve as bishops and representatives of the government, to eliminate these horrible abuses and truly save the Indians who were peaceful by nature, and so extend the gospel in America.[89] Criticized by many for his radical criticism of the form of Spanish dominion in America, Las Casas defended himself in a letter dated 30 April 1534, addressed to the *Consejo de Indias* (Council of the Indies). In it, he expressed his intention not to destroy the royal sovereignty, but to promote a more just system than the prevailing one: "*la evangelica via y que Cristo, nuestro Dios vino a enseñarnos*".[90] Accompanied by Tomás de Berlanga (his superior and Bishop of Panamá), Las Casas departed a few months later from La Española to continue the defence of the Indians on the American continent,[91] since the battle front could no longer be the Caribbean, where few of the original population had survived.

During a visit to one of these remaining communities *"de los indios libres"* (free Indians) in 1531, the *provisor* (administrator) of the Santo Domingo diocese, Francisco de Mendoza, had to acknowledge the precarious situation and the high mortality rate among the eighteen men and fifteen women survivors, despite an adequate supply of cattle, corn and water.[92] In 1535, Bishop Tomás de Toro OP of Cartagena calculated that only 200 Indians lived in La Española. A decade later, the last two communities had also disappeared: cacique Enriquillos' community on the slope of Bahoruco and the other close to La Vega.[93] The original population of the island was practically extinct.[94]

A similar process took place in the islands of the Greater Antilles:

- Of the original 80,000 inhabitants of Puerto Rico,[95] only 473 Indians had survived (despite preventive methods implemented here by the Hieronymites) up to 1530,[96] when Francisco Manuel de Lando carried out his census.[97] Additionally, there were 675 Indian slaves originally from the Lesser Antilles and from La Costa de las Perlas who had been deported by the traders.[98] Up to the 1530s, the original population of Puerto Rico was practically extinct, leaving very few natives in the smaller islands of Mona, Monito and Vieques facing Puerto Rico.[99]

- It seems that the original population of Jamaica consisted of 60,000 persons.[100] The *repartimiento*, executed in 1515 by Francisco de Garay and Pedro de Mazuelo, registered 14,636 Indians.[101] The population decrease was so uncontrollable that at the end of the following decade, the Indians were almost completely extinct.[102]

- Cuba, with a population of hundreds of thousands of inhabitants prior to the conquest,[103] in 1532 consisted (according to the records of Juan de Vadillo) of only 4,500 to 5,000 Indians,[104] who on several occasions unsuccessfully opposed this mortal process.[105]

The Dominican, Bernardino de Minaya, requested that Pope Paul III express his opinion concerning "the Indian question", and subsequently the pope's declaration became an important document in the struggle for survival and the human rights of the Indians. Minaya had handed the pope a letter from Bishop Julián Garcés of Tlaxcala in Mexico, requesting that His Holiness change the negative view of the Indians held by Europeans and the conquistadores.[106] On 2 June 1537, the pope declared in his bull *Sublimis Deus*, that the Indians, like all human beings, were rational and had the capacity to convert to the Christian faith. For this reason it was forbidden to deny them their freedom and their goods, and that as future nations, they should receive the Christian faith only through preaching and good example and in no way through violent deeds.[107] The pope also instructed Archbishop Juan Cardinal de Tavera in a brief *Pastorale officium* (dated 29 May 1537) to supervise the implementation of the rules stated in the *Sublimis Deus*, excommunicating those who persisted in enslaving the Indians.[108] In another document, the *Altitudo Divini Consilii*, dated 1 June 1537, Paul III granted permission to simplify the baptism rite for Indians, emphasizing the importance of Christian education.[109] These documents arrived in America without the approval of the Crown and the Council of the West Indies, who considered this as an offence to their *patronato* rights and forced the pope to withdraw them. This was done on 19 June 1538. However, this did not halt the distribution of the documents which, later, were constantly quoted by Las Casas and others, in solidarity with the Indians.[110]

A few years later, on 20 November 1542, Charles V approved the *Leyes Nuevas* (New Laws), in which he accepted the criticisms expressed for many years before by the Dominicans. These laws banned the running of *encomiendas* by civil and religious officials, stipulating that upon the death of their current owners, they were to be abolished; donations in money and in kind to the *encomenderos* by the Indians, were to be maintained but moderated and supervised by the *Audiencias*. The Indians were declared free: "*por ninguna causa de guerra ni otra alguna . . . no se pueda hacer esclavo indio alguno; y queremos que sean tratados como vasallos nuestros de la corona de Castilla, pues lo son*".[111] The few remaining Indian populations in the Caribbean gladly welcomed these new laws. This is confirmed by Bishop Rodrigo de Bastidas in a letter addressed to the emperor dated 20 March 1544: "*para que sean bien doctrinados y tratados los naturales . . .; entre chicos y grandes no ay en toda esta ysla sessenta yndios que sean naturales, y esos pocos recebieron con alegre cara la merced y no les falta capacidad para conocer el bien que se les hace*".[112] Nevertheless, by 1545 the Crown had to revoke several key reforms of the *Leyes Nuevas* renouncing their implementation, due to resistance from the colonists who carried out an armed rebellion in Peru.[113] However, the humanitarian aspects of these laws impacted positively on certain reforms, such as the special separation of the two races and the fact that donations paid by the Indians were also converted to rent.[114] But the original owners of America never truly recovered their freedom.[115] The dean of the Cathedral of Santo Domingo, Montoño, to whom the Crown had assigned the protection of the few living Indians, wrote with resignation in a report on 15 January 1547: "*estando los indios de la*

17

condición de servidumbre que han estado siempre . . . y esto es lo que pasa, porque Vra. Alteza sepa que yo he hecho lo que en mi es y el defecto no es a mi cargo."[116]

Evangelization efforts for the remaining Indians

About a half-century after the conquest of Indian lands by the Spaniards, the Indian nations of the Caribbean were practically extinct. Attempts to bring about change by political means were largely unsuccessful. However, according to isolated reports, some members of the Indian population were still alive in the second half of the sixteenth century. These reaffirmed that the church had sometimes acted responsibly toward the Indians, who, in the meantime, were a minority group living on their own land. On 31 July 1556, the Audiencia of Santo Domingo reported that on the northeast of La Española, between Puerto de Plata and the peninsula of Samaná, and on the extreme northwest facing Cuba, a total of four Indian communities had been discovered.[117] The *relación* (report) of the *oidor* (judge) Juan de Echagoian (1568), mentions that some Indians were still living in the surroundings of La Vega and La Yaguana.[118] Statistics given by Juan López de Velasco (1570) record two communities in La Española with a total of fifty Indians paying donations.[119] In 1571, Archbishop Andrés de Carvajal noted that in the Indian community of Boyá, located eight *leguas* (leagues) from Santo Domingo, an Augustine friar had succeeded in persuading the natives of the surrounding mountains to settle there.

Due to the decreasing numbers of the inhabitants of the island, Carvajal proposed, in 1572, to transfer Indians from other regions to his diocese where they would be allowed to cultivate the land and at the same time be converted into good Christians.[120] These measures were never accomplished.

In the meanwhile, the number of Indians continued to decrease in La Española. Yet in 1577, it was confirmed that some of them were still alive, working as cattle rangers for an inhabitant of La Yaguana, in the vicinity of Puerto de Yáquimo.[121] At the beginning of the seventeenth century, the extinction of the original population of the island was final. Based on his knowledge of other regions of Spanish America, Archbishop Domingo de Valderrama y Centeno responded to a questionnaire from Spain, aimed at improving pastoral work among Indians. In referring to his diocese, he explains: "*ninguna dellas (pre-*

guntas) *corre en esta ysla por no haber en toda ella doctrinas de Yndios ni haber quedado memoria de ellos de mas de un millon y seiscientas mill familias que havia, cuando los Españoles entraron en ella"*.[122]

The same happened in Puerto Rico. On 11 March 1549, Bishop Bastidas wrote that there were less than 50 native Indians and that he was paying special attention to them and to those who had been brought to Puerto Rico from other countries, but that also *"cada día se van disminuiendo y en nada augmentando"*.[123] Twenty years later, López de Velasco knew that only the community of Cibuco, close to San Germán, was inhabited by Indians of other regions and that additionally, some of these lived in the Puerto de Arecibo.[124] Bishop Diego de Salamanca, second successor of Bastidas, wrote in 1581 at the request of the Council of the West Indies, that in Puerto Rico there were neither Indian nor native communities *"por averse acabado"*.[125] He wrote also that approximately 20 Indians who were scattered on the island were descendants of people *"venidos de tierra firme; no saben otra lengua sino la nuestra"*.[126] This was also confirmed by Governor Juan de Melgarejo, in a letter dated 1 January 1582 addressed to the king.[127]

An exceptional case was observed on the island of Mona where the Indians lived without the presence of a white population. In 1548, after visiting the island, Bishop Bastidas was moved by the pious and honest way of life of the Indians. He proposed that some of the Indians who had arrived in Puerto Rico from other regions be sent to the island of Mona, to increase its population.[128] But here, also, reality had a negative impact: Echagoian estimated in 1568 a population of about 50 natives;[129] ten years later, only 10 to 12 natives remained. At this time, Bishop Diego de Salamanca wrote to the king, informing him that he could not guarantee regular pastoral work in Mona and requested permission to transfer the Indian population to Puerto Rico so he could give them his personal protection. And in the event that it was not resolved as stated, he asked for the king's forgiveness in not fulfilling his pastoral obligation at Mona.[130]

Contrary to data provided by *Geografía y descripción universal de las Indias* (*Location and Comprehensive Description of the Indies*) written by Juan López de Velasco, which stated that in 1570, the extinction of the original population of Jamaica was already evident,[131] according to Governor Melgarejo some Indians were still alive and had been hired by Spanish colonists as shepherds and wood cutters or hunters by the end of the sixteenth century. This latter had the intention of establishing a new Indian community and succeeded also in obtaining their consent, with the exception of three individuals. In the end, his proposal failed due to opposition from the colonists who believed that this plan signalled the end of their agriculture based on Indian labour. The plan therefore did not receive the support of the Council of the West Indies.[132] Some years later (1601–2), Melgarejo sent an expedition to Sierra de Bastida in the interior of Jamaica to investigate whether the original inhabitants still existed.[133] Bernardo de Balbuena, the educated abbot of Jamaica, on 14 July 1611 informed the authorities in Spain of the size of the population. According to him, of the 1,510 inhabitants of the island, only 74 were Indians.[134]

In Cuba the Indian situation was more favourable, due, among other reasons, to the existence of the *naborias*, a pre-Hispanic form of social stratification. The *naborias* formed part of the servant class, but were free, not slaves. Once the Council of the Indies became aware of the fact that the colonists in Cuba treated the Indians as slaves, selling and exchanging them, an order was sent on 5 November 1540 stating that the *naborias* were free to choose their masters and that any objection to the order carried a penalty of 100 golden pesos.[135] Bishop Diego de Sarmiento, himself a beneficiary of this Indian labour force and opposer of the *Leyes Nuevas*,[136] gave, in the report of his pastoral visit (25 July 1544), statistical data of the number of *indios naborias* in some of the cities in Cuba: 400 in Bayamo, 235 in Puerto del Príncipe, 80 in La Zavana (El Cayo), 58 in Sancti Spiritus and 126 in Havana.[137] This document contains no information on Santiago de Cuba and Baracoa.[138] There were also indigenous slaves from Yucatán in some cities.

Governors Juanés Dávila (1543–46) and Antonio Chávez (1546–49), in their attempts to liberate the remaining Indians in Cuba, were faced with strong opposition from the colonists and had therefore to make concessions.[139] Finally, Gonzalo Pérez de Angulo, who had been governor since 1549, was able to implement the *Leyes Nuevas*. In 1554, Guanabacoa (located half a mile from Havana) was declared an Indian community with approximately 100 inhabitants by 1555. Governor Mazariegos, successor to Angulo, estimated the total number of Indians in Cuba in 1556 to be 2,000, among them 200 originally from other regions.[140] Approximately fifteen years later, Juan López de Velasco spoke of 270 Indian families in Cuba: 17 in Baracoa, 80 in Bayamo, 40 in Puerto del Príncipe, 15 in Sancti Spiritus, 10 in El Cayo, 50 in Trinidad and 60 in Guanabacoa. He also stated that about one and a half leagues from Santiago de Cuba there was "*un pueblo de indios, que llaman los Caneyes, en que habrá veinte casas*".[141]

Despite the protection laws in effect from the middle of the century, the Indians in Cuba did not have the same status as the white population but were constantly watched like children.[142] On 31 December 1582, Bishop Juan del Castillo informed the king of the many abuses inflicted on the Indians, even by their civilian protectorates, and requested of the king *"que se les quiten los protectores y que las justicias tengan mucha cuenta con ellos, porque dalles un protector es dalles un encomendero, siendo ellos pobrissimos, que toda la tierra, onde puede aver granjerias, les tienen tomados los Españoles, y ellos están allí como estraños y parece convenir que se descarguen de todas molestias"*.[143] Castillo also proposed that the Indians of Guanabacoa, whose spiritual needs had been met until then by a Franciscan friar sent by the parish priest from Havana, receive a *"cura particular, que asista a los indios"*, since *"reciben muchos agravios de los Españoles"* due to the proximity of this community to Havana.[144]

Bishop Juan de las Cabezas Altamirano recorded the precise situation prevailing in Cuba at the beginning of the seventeenth century. According to this document, there were, around 1608, a little more than 1,000 Indians in Cuba distributed as follows: 300 in Guanabacoa and 100 in Baracoa (two Indian communities),[145] 250 in Bayamo, 150 in Puerto del Príncipe, 100 in Sancti Spiritus, 77 in Santiago de Cuba[146] and 50 in Trinidad. To summarize, the Indians still represented 6.5 percent of the population.[147] However, only a minority descended from the original Cuban population since many had arrived from Nueva España and were classified by Cabezas as *ya como españolizados* due to their level of integration.[148] They were exempted from taxes, lived very poorly, cultivated small plots (if these had not been taken by the whites many years before) or worked as labourers on the farms.

Governor Bitrian de Biamonte complained in 1631 that the inhabitants of Havana behaved like *encomenderos* toward the Indians, ordering them to cultivate cane for their refineries on lands belonging to the Indians, violating the judiciary system and thereafter expelling them.[149] A typical and badly paid job was *las velas*, which involved the monitoring and protection of the coastal areas by the Indians. Bishop Cabezas Altamirano had requested a professional coast guard for the coast of Santiago de Cuba. He reported that no Spaniard settler wanted to accept that serious responsibility. Furthermore, he did not understand why this responsibility was to be given to the Indians, since he himself (for spiritual reasons) had recommended that some of them leave this job, return to their wives and lead a normal family life.[150]

In the meanwhile, in the Greater Antilles, the Ciboney and Taino populations had become victims of the Spanish conquest. In the Lesser Antilles, which had not yet been colonized by the Spaniards, the Carib Indians survived throughout the sixteenth century. The latter were known as warriors and were feared because of their surprise attacks from their *piraguas* (canoes), especially during the months of September and October when the sea winds had subsided.[151] Unlike the Archbishop of Santo Domingo, Andrés de Carvajal, who in 1572 proposed the transfer of the Indians of other regions to La Española and who still showed a certain benevolence towards the Caribs ("*los traxesen a esta isla, o libres o captivos, . . . y lo mejor sería libres, aunque fuesen Caribes*"),[152] Bishop Diego de Salamanca of Puerto Rico was a passionate adversary of this community. For him, the Indians from Dominica, Guadeloupe and Martinique were the enemies of the Christians and of everything to which the natural law obliged them, as he wrote on 3 January 1578 to Spain. In this letter he expressed indignation at the daring assaults by the Caribs and their incursions into Puerto Rico, the most recent one occurring in the city of San Germán. The bishop supported the enslavement, not only of men fourteen years and older, but also that of women and children.[153] Nine years later, Salamanca was in favour of pacification of the island of Dominica through a declaration in which information was provided by accounts of prisoners who had escaped from the Caribs: according to a black woman named Luisa who was in Dominica for four years as a prisoner held by the Caribs, this island consisted of eight communities with fifty houses; they had few warriors at that time due to losses suffered in fights against Indians of other islands, and to disease. Salamanca saw an additional justification for the conquest of the island based on the abundance of its fruit, gold and precious stones, but especially for the liberation of thirty supposedly Spanish prisoners, among them one who had renounced the Christian faith out of desperation.[154] In truth, an attack on Dominica by Captain Pedro Gómez de Rojas, was considered possible in 1587, but this never occurred. When the English, Dutch and French in the seventeenth century occupied the Lesser Antilles and exterminated the native population, Dominica, St Vincent and the Grenadines were the only refuge for the Caribs.[155] By the Treaty of Paris in 1763, the islands were finally declared English colonies.

From the beginning of the Spanish conquest, the islands near the Venezuelan coast were under a different system because of the pearl banks. Cubagua was the centre of pearl exportation in the 1520s and

1530s and several Indians from these islands and Venezuela lost their lives in this undertaking. In the 1540s when these banks were depleted, Nueva Cádiz, the city of the Spanish colonists, also declined in importance. With all this, the native population also became extinct.[156] The boom of Margarita, the biggest neighbouring island, started following improvement to legislation in favour of the Indians. Several bishops from Puerto Rico intervened in favour of the native population of Margarita, the *Guaiqueríes*, who were fishermen and hunters.[157] Thus, Rodrigo de Bastidas during a visit in 1560 observed with concern, the unfavourable treatment of the Indians by the Spanish colonists[158] and obtained two royal decrees in favour of Indian rights that were handed over by the Dominicans, Francisco Montesinos and Alvaro de Castro. During the presentation of these decrees, the white inhabitants of Margarita maintained that they had always respected the liberty and dignity of the Indians as well as their Catholic education.[159] Bishop Bastidas maintained his criticism but showed a greater understanding of the situation of the settlers and involved Bartolomé de Las Casas in the matter:

Es pobre gente, los vezinos y estantes en aquella ysla; todos se mantienen de unos ganadillos y sementera de mahiz que tienen y de sudor de yndios, assi de los naturales y mas detraydos de tierra firme, que no acertaré a dezir, que diferencia puede aver entre ellos y esclavos, y a escondidas los saltean o rescatan en la tierra firme y traen y venden y contractan; provey en esto lo que pude; los que goviernan tienen la mano en ello. Tengo que dezir lo que passa, que es esto, y tambien digo, que sin esto alli no pueden vivir ni sustentarse; los naturales son mollestados con los que goviernan, y con otros con trabajos, a cuya causa andan los mas en los montes, tienen nescesidad de ser favorecidos. Al obispo de Chiapa lo scrivo para que lo solicite en ese Real consejo, y con esto descargo.[160]

Twenty years later, Bishop Diego de Salamanca reported that the native population of Margarita consisted of 224 Indians who lived in four small communities. Furthermore, the Spaniards kept many Indians in their service, many who had been kidnapped from among the Arawaks of the Gulf of Cumaná and from the island of Trinidad. He also explained that the teaching of the Indians was so bad, that during his visit, he had decided to remain there for two or three years *"para dar horden en la salvacion de tanta gente como ay perdida en aquella ysla y a los alrededores"* and that many things still needed to be improved. He felt that many Indians would be easily converted if someone took charge of this mission.[161]

After a brief visit to Margarita on his trip to Puerto Rico his successor, Nicolás de Ramos, had a different opinion of this issue: *"los yndios son tan mal ynclinados a poner cuydado en las cosas de su salvacion que creo, que muchos dellos no les a de servir el ser bautizados más de para mayor pena y tormento, especialmente los que llaman Guayquerìesque siempre andan por los montes y despoblados"*.[162] Bishop Ramos therefore did not promote any evangelization effort in favour of the Indians of that island. But at least his succesor, Antonio Calderón founded a church for the Indians in Pueblo del Mar.[163] Special interest was demonstrated by Bishop Martín Vázquez de Arce to overcome *ygnorancia de lo del evangelio* on the part of the Guayqueríes. Arce initially estimated that there were 200 of them, wanting to *"reduzirlos a poblado, poniendoles un sacerdote que los doctrine y administre los sacramentos"* in order to overcome their religious ignorance.[164] He ordered that no one should, in future, abuse and exploit the Indians by engaging them in pearl diving.[165] In order to build a solid foundation for Christian work among the Indians in Margarita, the bishop finally got the priest of Asunción, Diego Núñez Brito, and three other religious friars to pay a visit to the entire interior of the island. They carried out a thorough *enpadronamiento* (census) on 30 April 1604 where they recorded fourteen different communities with a total of 499 Indians.[166] They also investigated the religious knowledge of the *Guayqueríes* who, in many instances, did not even know the sign of the cross nor the important Christian prayers. The visitors urged the Indians to abide by the ecclesiastical laws and to participate as much as possible in the religious services. For Bishop Vázquez, the results of this visit served as the basis for the *Constituciones* (Constitutions) of 26 July 1624. Through them he reorganized the spiritual work for Margarita before his departure to Puerto Rico. In this way the Indians would receive spiritual attention from three *doctrinas* (doctrines) in their own language for as long as possible,[167] initiating clear and obvious improvement for the upcoming decades.[168]

The missionary challenges for the bishops of Puerto Rico were even bigger in Cumaná, Guayana and on the island of Trinidad which were the most distant *anejos* (annexes) of the Puerto Rican diocese. For many decades the ecclesiastical work was limited to the attention of Spanish colonists in Cumaná (re-established in 1562 as Nueva Córdoba), Santo Tomé de Guayana and San José de Oruña in Trinidad (founded in 1590). Only the Provincial Council of Santo Domingo

(1622–23) gave effective impetus to the evangelization of the Indians in those regions. In Cumaná, a parish was established to promote Christian work among the *Guayqueríes* of that region.[169] After Governor Juan de Lezama's plan had been abandoned, one in which he requested a separate apostolic vicariate for Trinidad and Guayana,[170] the bishop of Puerto Rico, Juan López Agurto de la Mata, paid an extensive visit to this region in 1633–34.[171] Nevertheless, only the Capuchin friars who had arrived in 1654 in Píritu, in 1657 in Cumaná and in 1686 in Guayana, began a systematic mission[172] and were able to follow the legislations of the Provincial Council of Santo Domingo that had been approved during the sixth public session on 28 December 1622.

Pastoral work among the Indians in the Provincial Council of Santo Domingo, 1622–1623

In this ecclesiastical meeting, Gonzalo de Angulo, bishop of Coro, showed great interest in the Indian question. Thanks to his initiative, the meeting discussed a variety of questions from an integrated point of view with Bishop Angulo presiding over the sixth session dedicated to Christian work among the Indians.[173] The following regulations were approved:

• Adult candidates could only receive the sacrament of baptism if they knew the Our Father, Hail Mary, the Creed and the Ten Commandments; if they believed in the effectiveness of baptism and if they tried to live a life free of sin. The baptism of children was to be administered by the common rite in the parish church, but exceptions were permitted if the birth place was more than two miles from the church. In each parish, elderly men and women were to be appointed as godparents. The parish priest was to keep a record of baptisms and to register the names of those baptized, their parents and godparents, the date of baptism and the encomienda to which they belonged.[174]

• Similar regulations were implemented for confirmation. Special mention was made of the obligation of the *encomenderos* to take the Indians to a place where the bishop would officiate at the confirmation ceremony and provide free candles and white clothing for the poorest among them.[175]

• Like all church members, the Indians were also obliged to receive the sacraments of confession and the Holy Eucharist once a year and the parish priest was to instruct them in these sacraments. They were also to administer Holy Communion to the sick and the Last Sacrament in certain circumstances.[176]

- With regard to the marriage of baptized Indians, the regulation of the Council of Trent was to be observed. However the parish priest was obliged to familiarize himself with traditional marriages among the nonbaptized Indians, who used certain symbols as gifts, or verbal expressions, because their marriages were also monogamous and indissoluble by divine right. At the same time, the Provincial Council made reference to the Pauline Privilege (a wife converted to Christianity could divorce her non-Christian husband if her faith was threatened by the marriage). All divorce cases were to be handled by the episcopal official.[177]

The Provincial Council was very demanding of the Christians who worked in the Indian pastorate:

- They had to master the natives' language.
- They were to leave their parish only for important reasons and were to visit the villages that had no chapel at least once a month.
- They were not entitled to work either in agriculture or in commerce, nor to receive a stipend for the administration of sacraments from the Indians since the *encomenderos* were responsible for their subsistence.
- They were to be kind and patient when dealing with the Indians, without resorting to indiscriminate punishment.
- In addition to their religious duties, they also had educational and cultural ones: through the use of Christian doctrine, they were to teach the children to read and write in Spanish and instruct adults to organize their daily lives and festivities in a civilized manner.[178]

As in other Spanish-American synods,[179] the Provincial Council of Santo Domingo was also in favour of setting up Indian communities, since it was thought that this measure meant more favourable conditions for Christian civilization.[180] The transfer of this population was to be organized once the future location had been urbanized and a food supply guaranteed.[181]

The Provincial Council strictly prohibited the *encomenderos* to use forced labour on children under the age of twelve; men and women over sixty were only to work in the master's house and the plantation house.[182] No one was to be forced to work on Sundays and holidays.[183] The violent and unjust expeditions to loot regions where Indians lived were severely condemned.[184] The Council even declared that the physical and spiritual welfare of the Indians was the main purpose of the meeting.[185]

Through these regulations, the Council reconfirmed the rights of the Indians which Christian opposition against the encomienda system had achieved in the sixteenth century.[186]

However, the moderate resolutions of the ecclesiastical assembly also indicated that the enthusiastic optimism with which the Orders preached the Christian faith, which extended to America during the sixteenth century, had disappeared over the course of time. Repeatedly, the Council passed rules against the Indians, doubting their religious capacity[187] or charging them with all types of vices.[188] Church efforts in favour of the Indians also continued during the seventeenth century, but the church did not condemn the horrible injustices that the native population of America had suffered. Rather, they accepted the sociopolitical reality of the Indians as natural within this framework. Nevertheless, the church continued to defend the human dignity of the Indian nations and worked in favour of their integration within the Christian community.[189] However, the Caribbean remained on the fringe of this process.

The Whites

The Spaniards in the Caribbean

Contrary to the situation in Portugal, where imperialism depended on public companies with paid workers, Spain pursued a system of territorial expansionism. From 1495, Catholic kings allowed Spaniards to settle in the West Indies and granted them certain privileges.[190] After 1503, the *casa de contratación* (trading house) of Sevilla coordinated migration to America. To achieve control, they did not oppose racial intermarriages, as proven by a 1503 decree, that "*algunos cristianos se casen con algunas mujeres indias y las mujeres cristianas con algunos indios, por que los unos y otros se comuniquen y enseñen, para ser doctrinados en las cosas de nuestra santa fe católica*".[191] This, in fact, was never carried out.

Colonial politics was limited in relation to the settlement of foreigners in America. The *casa de contratación* was obliged to reject foreigners. This prohibition was also valid from 1530 for members of religious orders who wanted to establish missions among the Indians.[192] Exceptions to this law were allowed in settlements with small populations, since settlement in the American mainland had become more attractive to the majority of the foreigners. Nevertheless, the complaint about the small white population continued. Archbishop Andrés de Carvajal said in a letter to the king dated 20 April 1572: *"que viniesen labradores para cultivar la tierra, señaladamente portugueses, que son grandes cultivadores"*.[193] In effect, in the second half of the sixteenth century and at the beginning of the seventeenth, a significant number of Portuguese, Flemish and Genoese persons arrived in the West Indies.[194]

With respect to the origins of the Spanish settlers, it can be said that the majority were from Andalucía; many also came from Castilla, Extremadura and León, as well as a few from other regions.[195] Until approximately 1600, between 250,000 and 300,000 Spaniards had migrated to America.[196] Around 1570, there were 8,800 whites living in the *ciudades y villas* (cities and towns) in the Caribbean, of which a half lived in La Española, representing 7 percent of the total white population in the Spanish Americas.[197] Towards the middle of the seventeenth century, the number of *ciudades y villas* increased, especially in the *anejos* of the diocese of Puerto Rico. During that time, 23,400 whites lived in the Caribbean – 40 percent of whom lived in Cuba, mostly in Havana – representing only 3.5 percent of whites living in the Spanish Americas.[198] Population instability and increased migration to the continent were the norm in the Caribbean, as written by the Cathedral chapter of Santo Domingo on 5 June 1533: *"las personas, que en estas partes residen, por la mayor parte se van y mudan de cada día a otras nuevas poblaciones"*.[199]

Spiritual life of the laity

Throughout the Americas, the Spanish colonists looked for ways in which they could make their environment resemble their European homeland. If they constructed a church in the square of their cities, this usually indicated that their religion was the centre of their social life. Sunday mass was generally a social event. It not only served for spiritual upliftment but also for the enforcement of their citizenship and as well for the strengthening of their social life. At the end of the mass, news and messages of general interest were circulated. The people would then gather in the shops and nearby bars which were not allowed to be opened before the end of the mass.[200]

For the honourable citizens, attendance at church was also an opportunity to make themselves known.[201] The desire for ostentation led to absence from religious ceremonies, particularly in the case of the women who, in times of economic crisis, had no elegant clothing or were too proud to take those that were donated.[202] The poor attendance at church of the women of Santo Domingo had been noticed already by Archbishop Pedro de Solier y Vargas.[203]

His successor Pedro de Oviedo wrote in detail to the king that upon his arrival in the city, he observed a rare custom of celebrating mass after midnight, almost two hours before dawn, "*como si cada dia de fiesta lo fuera de navidad*",[204] a custom that was opposed to canon law and which had the negative effect of creating absenteeism from solemn mass and from preaching in the church, "*porque dezian habian ydo por la mañana*".[205] Oviedo banned the early morning masses, but had to acknowledge that the people ceased to attend mass altogether, "*como si fueran gentiles, y particularmente las mas culpadas eran las mugeres*";[206] the archbishop preached, warned and threatened but to no avail. The women justified their action by saying that "*no tenian mantos, y algunos hombres que no tenian vestido*".[207] Oviedo also declared that he had waited a long time and they were not yet properly attained; he believed that more than a half of the population did not go to mass "*y de mugeres no son veinte de las principales las que oyen sermon, y la causa es su mucha vanidad porque si no es mucha seda y ostentacion, no quiere nadie venir a la iglesia, aunque sean mugeres de oficiales*".[208] On realizing that ecclesiastic prohibitions were not successful, he placed his hopes on the fines that the king would impose through the *Audiencia*. In the event of continued resistance, excommunication would follow; only with such strict measures could these circumstances of blasphemy be overcome.[209] The violation of the Sunday obligation, and even a "*libertad rebelde con que viven casi sin reconocer a Dios ni Rey*", was also widespread in rural areas among the inhabitants of farms and ranches.[210]

On the other hand, evidence was not lacking, so that the bishops and the parish priests, as well as the representatives of the bourgeoisie, continuously made efforts to provide the best conditions for the celebration of religious services. From the beginning they tried to build churches of concrete to keep the consecrated hosts;[211] new constructions and restoration of temples were commonly motivated by the sentiment that the Most Sacred was kept "*con mucha indecencia*".[212] They also ensured that a lighted candle was permanently placed at the tabernacle; for this they needed olive oil from Spain, which was very expensive and for which the parishioners regularly made donations.[213] Candles and wines also had to be imported for the celebration of mass and the poor churches often requested financial support from the Council of the Indies.[214] In the parish churches of Havana and Bayamo in Cuba, a lot of importance was placed on Christian music. Bishop Castillo expressed his opinion about the sacristan Jerónimo Martínez in Havana: "*Canta canto llano rrazonablemente y con rrazonable voz y cumple muy bien su officio.*"[215] This sacristan was succeeded by Blas López in Bayamo, a recognized organist and choir leader; they celebrated the masses and the vespers in Bayamo "*con mucha solemnidad*"[216]

After the Council of Trent the use of ecclesiastical books was introduced in the Caribbean for recording baptisms, marriages and deaths. This renewal was the work of the Council, but the need for registration corresponded to its significant importance in social life.[217] Baptism was the sacrament which linked the newborn to the church; normally the sacrament of baptism was administered within the first fifteen days of birth by the parish priest in the parish church, but it could also be carried out in other churches or chapels if this could be justified by distance, or by a midwife also in the event of an emergency.[218] There were very strict regulations laid down by the Council of Trent for the sacrament of marriage but they could not all be implemented, especially in rural areas.[219] There were many unmarried couples.[220] Other problems arose if the husbands were separated for a long time from their wives, as in the case of soldiers.[221] Finally, the colonial situation led to conflicts with the stipulations of the Council concerning the wedding obstacles.[222]

While the Church faced many difficulties in reconciling its differences regarding the sacrament of marriage with the social reality, it fulfilled its obligations with respect to dying and the dead. A priest would be absent only in cases where circumstances, such as long distances to the interior, would prevent his attendance. The Last Sacrament was usually administered to the dying, including confession, absolution and communion. All who were present had to kneel and pray in silence as an expression of their devotion to the Blessed Sacrament and appreciation of the dying.[223] It was customary for the dead to leave donations for the church in their will.[224] The burial took place in the corresponding parish or in the church's cemetery. Very often, the social differences among the living were also visible in the appearance of the tombs.[225]

Despite adverse conditions, the church made efforts to maintain a certain level of religious knowledge and moral principles among the white population of the Caribbean. This was not an easy task due to difficult living conditions, especially in the outskirts of large cities.[226] A document from the dean of the Concepción de la Vega Cathedral, dated 2 October 1550, stated *"que los mas de los españoles del obispado ygnoraban las oraciones de la yglesia"*. Henceforth, the dean made it a practice that during Sunday mass, after confession, basic prayers would be said in three-week terms (Our Father, Hail Mary, the Creed and the Salve Regina).[227] Religious negligence, especially in the region of La Española, *"los ynormes pecados"* (many sins) and the *"vicios pesimos"* (terrible vices) of the colonists in the north of La Española, half a century later, were considered justification for the deportations ordered by Governor Osorio.[228]

There were also many breaches of the regulations relating to the practices of fasting and abstinence. While Archbishop Andrés de Carvajal defended the custom in many sectors of society to consume meat during periods of fasting and on Saturdays with papal dispensation *"con cargo de cierta limosna"*,[229] Bishop Diego de Salamanca in Puerto Rico had a stricter approach – days of fasting could be observed without too many regulations, if the citizens were interested in fishing as before.[230] The most important measure used to inculcate church regulations in the people's conscience was the sacrament of confession. Each believer was obliged to confess to the parish priest during Lent. Compliance was ensured through registration of the confessed. Those who did not abide by this were punished; in the worst cases they were excommunicated. Absolution for sins such as stealing, murder and abortion had to be carried out by the bishop.[231] The church was successful in ensuring that moral laws were respected, especially when these were welcomed by the civil authorities.[232]

The *Cofradías* (Fraternities)

According to canon law, ecclesiastical life included taking sacraments and obeying the rules; it was controlled by the clergy and the lay people were bound by its guidelines. An element developed in Spanish-American Catholicism, which represented a certain counterbalance and made it possible for lay people to participate actively in religious ceremonies. This element was the *cofradía*. Nearly every citizen, especially in the city, was a member of a *cofradía*. The *cofradía* represented lay associations, in which different social and professional groups participated. They had a spiritual and charitable aim and encompassed a specific and intense communitarian attitude. The organizations were autonomous, electing their own leaders and administering their own finances. They usually had their own place of worship, either an *ermita* or a chapel close to a bigger temple, or their parish church. Their religious guidance and care were in the hands of a priest of their own choice, nearly always a member of an order, who would preach, celebrate mass, organize the services and accompany them in processions.

The *cofradías* were responsible for prayers and charity. Motivated by charity work, as written in the gospel, they nearly always chose a specific task in a specific place, which could include service to the sick, the poor or the most needy, accommodation for strangers, and help to orphans and homeless children. The *cofradías* often became the owners of hospitals and orphanages and accumulated considerable material wealth which increased over time due to inheritances left by members in their wills. This capital was not only invested in charity and construction work, but was also used for granting loans that directly impacted on economic and commercial activity.[233]

The oldest *cofradía* of Santo Domingo was the *Cofradía de la pura y limpia Concepción de Nuestra Señora*.[234] It was founded in 1503 by Governor Nicolás de Ovando and was responsible for collecting donations for the construction and maintenance of the San Nicolás hospital, which according to oral tradition, was the charitable initiative of a black woman. Its beginnings were precarious, but in 1519, it was constructed with concrete. The chapel of the *cofradía* can be traced to this second phase of construction, and to date, remains in the same place. Over the following decades, considerable funds were allocated to the *cofradía* which facilitated the construction of an impressive building.[235] The peculiar behaviour of the *cofrades* (members of the *cofradías*) sometimes bothered the bishops. In 1619, Pedro de Solier y Vargas criticized them with these words: "*siempre anda la rueda entre dies o doce ricos y poderosos*".[236]

The *Cofradía de Nuestra Señora de los Remedios del Carmen y Jesús Nazareno* was just as prestigious, although it was constructed later. It was founded on 2 July 1592 and was linked to San Andrés, the other hospital in the city, on whose territory and with its own resources a chapel was constructed in 1615.[237] On 24 July 1636, Archbishop Facundo de la Torre gave this *cofradía* permission to carry a cross with the image of Jesus of Nazareth from the chapel every year at 9:00 pm on Wednesday during Holy Week, "*por ser acto de penitencia y devoción*".[238] The *cofradía* also organized a procession, the feast of the "Virgen del Carmen" on 16 July.[239] The *cofradía*, which was called Nuestra Señora del Rosario, had a chapel next to the Church of the Dominicans, whose order promoted devotion to the rosary. The Feast of the Rosary, held in October, lasted eight days, and included a procession with the image of the "Virgen del Rosario" through the entire city.[240] This *cofradía* was so rich, that in the mid seventeenth century, its chapel was almost completely restored and the ceiling painted with cosmotheological designs, unique to Spanish America.[241]

The *cofradías* of Santísimo Sacramento del Altar and Benditas Almas had their place in the cathedral; the aim of the former was the promotion of devotion to the Eucharist, organizing the solemn mass of Corpus Christi and the octave of preparation, every third Sunday of the month. They also accompanied the priest to take communion to the sick; the latter was dedicated to the organization of a solemn mass in the cathedral with a procession for the deceased held every Monday and they prayed in groups for the souls in purgatory.[242] In Santo Domingo, there were other *cofradías* which influenced the religious life of the city, and were particularly famous for their Holy Week and Corpus Christi processions.[243] This was also true for the communities of the Third Order of the Franciscans and Dominicans, which both had chapels in these convents.[244]

A situation similar to that of Santo Domingo was that of San Juan, Puerto Rico. In describing the city, Canon Diego de Torres Vargas in 1647 mentioned the existence of twelve *cofradías* in the cathedral: Santísimo Sacramento del Altar, Benditas Almas, Virgen del Carmen, Nuestra Señora de Altagracia, San Antonio, San Pedro, Nuestro Señor Jesús, San Miguel; in the hospital, the *cofradías* of Rosario, Nuestra Señora de la Soledad, de la Vera Cruz, and finally in the convent of the Franciscans, the *cofradía* of Santiago. He also mentioned the rich *cofradía* which was always linked to the hospital, known as Nuestra Señora de la Concepción.[245] The Santísimo Sacramento del Altar and the Benditas Almas *cofradías* had the same objectives as the homonymous *cofradías* in Santo Domingo. As was the case there, the *cofradía* of the Inmaculada Concepción de María was very wealthy, as reflected in its impressive buildings.[246] The Portuguese living in San Juan had gathered in the *cofradía* of San Antonio named after the saint from Lisbon and this helped in the social unity of the Portuguese.[247] In addition to those in the episcopal city, many *cofradías* existed in the diocese of Puerto Rico.[248]

The biggest *cofradía* in Cuba was the Cofradía de la soledad de la Madre de Dios y del entierro de Cristo in Havana. It was located at the San Juan de Dios hospital and its members were drawn from among the military personnel who frequently visited the hospital.[249] The *cofradía* of La Misericordia, which was associated with the parish church, was responsible for organizing the burial of Christians who died without receiving spiritual help and who lived near Havana. The *cofradía* of Nuestra Señora de la Candelaria and its organization of the feast of *La Candelaria* were very popular.[250] Additionally, the Rosario and Santísimo Sacramento del Altar *cofradías* of San Telmo to which many sailors and a few other persons belonged were located in Havana.[251]

Cuba had an excellent bishop in the person of Juan de las Cabezas Altamirano, who promoted the institution of *cofradía*. In Trinidad many *cofradías* were already in existence. During the bishop's visit in 1603–4, he proposed "*haser una ermita de la cofradía de la Sancta Vera Cruz por no la aver*".[252] In the Santiago de Cuba Cathedral, he founded a *cofradía* in 1604, known as *de las benditas ánimas del Purgatorio*, to which he gave a significant donation upon his departure from the diocese in 1610.[253] The Minas del Prado church, based in a mining area to the west of Santiago, had the *cofradías* of Santa Bárbara, the miners' patron, and El Rosario.[254]

At La Vega in Jamaica, a *cofradía*, Nuestra Señora de la Concepción, was established at the Franciscans' church, which in 1625, received a new statue of their patron saint from Spain.[255] *Cofradías* were established in all the Caribbean communities in this way. Within them, the citizens found structures independent of the clergy, in which creatively they were able to develop their religious beliefs.

Religious feasts

Similar to the architecture of cities, the social life of Spanish America also followed a seasonal model, determined mainly by religion. The order of the day was organized around the three prayers of the "Angelus": morning, midday and evening prayer. The week was organized in a similar fashion, for example with regard to the rules of fasting, and of course, the year followed the ecclesiastic year which followed a sacred religious pattern.[256] The Holy Year was also celebrated every twenty-five years in America.[257]

In the ecclesiastical province of Santo Domingo, according to the decisions of the Provincial Council (1622–23), the following festive days, in addition to having no work on Sundays, were to be observed: Easter, Ascension, Pentecost, Corpus Christi, the feasts in honour of Jesus, Christmas, Holy Family, Epiphany, Crucifixion and the death of Jesus, the feasts in honour of Mary, Candlemass, Annunciation, Assumption, the Immaculate Conception and Birth, the feasts in honour of Saint Joseph, and the birth of John the Baptist, the feast of Holy Ann, the feast of the Innocent Children, the feasts of all the apostles and evangelists, the feast of the Holy Magdalene, the feast of the Archangel St Michael, the feast of St Barnabas, the feasts of the deacons St Stephen and St Lauren and the feast of All Saints. Additionally, each city was to solemnly celebrate the feast of its respective patron and in some instances, other feasts.[258] The Council advised the governors, the officials and the court members in particular, to set the example by attending mass on Sundays and on festive days, and the most important feasts of the ecclesiastical year.[259]

Over time, the official liturgical calendar was filled with several local and regional feasts wherein peoples' devotion was particularly manifest. Mention must first be made of the feasts of patron saints of the great sanctuaries in honour of Mary celebrated in the dioceses of the Caribbean. In Higuey, La Española, "*la imagen de Nra. Señora de Altagracia, que es de grande debocion y esta allí desde que se fundo la villa, y Nra. Sra. a ynbocacion suya ha hecho y haze muchos milagros y cada dia ba creciendo la debución*" was found.[260] The patron feast of Higuey was celebrated on 21 January. National influence gave rise to the feast of Nuestra Señora de las Mercedes, which was celebrated on 24 September at the Santo Cerro close to Concepción de la Vega and also in Santo Domingo.[261] In the seventeenth century, the devotion to Nuestra Señora de Aguas Santas at the church of Boyá enjoyed tremendous success.[262] Alcocer states that God performed many miracles through the icon that the people carried in the pilgrimage "*y así es frequentada de romeria y como está ocho o dies leguas de Santo Domingo, acuden mas a esta santa casa y ymagen; es de vulto de una quarta de alto pero muy perfectissima y que causa devocion*".[263] According to the same source the most important feast in honour of Mary in the city of Santo Domingo was the feast of the Virgen de Rosario held on the first Sunday of October.[264] In Arecibo, Puerto Rico, this date was celebrated with special solemnity, while in the city of San Juan the Virgen del Carmen was very popular and was celebrated on 16 July.[265] Many people came to Hormigueros from the interior to see the image of Nuestra Señora de Monserrat.[266] The image of "Nuestra Señora del Valle" was considered miraculous on the island of Margarita.[267] Finally, mention must be made of Nuestra Señora de la Caridad del Cobre at Minas del Prado in Cuba, whose feast on 8 September, attracted many believers from all over the country to the mining community.[268] In Havana, la Virgen de Candelaria was very popular.[269]

In La Española there was great devotion to the Cruz del Santo Cerro (Cross of the Holy Hill) which, according to oral tradition, was erected by Christopher Columbus. A visit by Archbishop Alonso López de Avila to La Vega in 1583 resulted in the restoration of the cross.[270] After the formal closure of the diocese Concepción de la Vega, the cross was taken to the Santo Domingo Cathedral; there, a procession was organized as part of the feast in honour of the Veneration of the Cross. This started at the cathedral with people carrying the cross and ended at the church of the Dominicans.[271] In the parish of Cumaná, a miraculous cross was also revered. The cross was linked to an unexpected liberation of the city from an imminent pirate attack.[272] Under the declaration of "Ecce Homo" in Santiago de Cuba, an image that represented Christ's suffering, painted by Francisco Antonio, was venerated. This image had arrived in Cuba from Cartagena de Indias in 1619. In three different years, the *cantor* (singer), Juan de Lizano, observed that on every last Wednesday of August while mass was being celebrated, perspiration poured from the image. On his initiative in 1652, the "Ecce Homo" was declared the patron of the city of Santiago de Cuba. The festive day in its honour was the last Wednesday in August. It was said that the image helped in many ways during starvation, diseases, wars and all kinds of disasters.[273]

Some of the feasts in honour of saints which were celebrated solemnly at dioceses across the Caribbean were of special importance. In San Juan, the capital of Puerto Rico, the patron feast of John the Baptist was celebrated for five days. Governor Íñigo de la Mota Sarmiento (1635–41) was a fervent devotee to this saint.[274] St James, national patron saint of Spain, was well-liked by the military, and Governor Gabriel de Roxas (1608–14) even gave his name to the fort of Boquerón in Puerto Rico.[275] In Jamaica, they were especially devoted to this saint, in gratitude for Governor Fernando Melgarejo's victory over the pirates who attacked the island, "*le hizo voto la villa y le tiene por patron y su día se hace fiesta en ella y alarde general en memoria de esta victoria y merced, que Dios les hizo por intercesión del santo*".[276]

In 1649, Governor Felipe de Rivera inaugurated a procession on St Michael's Day[277] in Santiago de Cuba, after the *cantor*, Juan de Lizano, had in the previous year requested the organization of a feast in honour of "Santa Ursula" on 21 October.[278] In both cases, personal motives played a role. If the Bishop Rodrigo de Bastidas consecrated the new diocese of Coro to St Ann as its patroness, and also gave her name to the chapel close to the Santo Domingo cathedral and to his family's biggest plantation at La Española, this was certainly explained by the fact that the parish of Triana in which he was baptized was also consecrated to St Ann.[279] It was believed that the saints effectively met certain needs. Accordingly, in Havana, they prayed to the apostle Simon for protection from a plague of ants,[280] and in Puerto Rico, St Patrick was venerated through vows, which had been effective during a famine caused by a plague that had attacked the cassava plants.[281] The belief in miracles sometimes took absurd forms. For example it was believed that the dust from the famous Cruz de la Vega could alleviate a fever if taken with a liquid.[282]

While the period from Ash Wednesday to the "Quasimodo" was being observed as something special, the other annual feasts could also have been joyous if they were in keeping with the nature of feasts. There were dances, games, bullfighting, horse racing, parades and fireworks.[283] In fact, carnival was a feast *sui generis*. When there was excessive celebration, the authorities took measures against such activities. When Archbishop Alonso López de Avila wanted to impose a papal *motu propio* in Santo Domingo prohibiting bullfighting on Sundays in keeping with the sacred tendencies proposed by the Council of Trent, this caused a lot of protest.[284]

The feast of Corpus Christi had a unique religious character. On this day, and later during other feasts, at the end of the procession and the liturgical celebration, the *autos sacramentales* (eucharistic plays) determined the form these feasts should take, referring to the religious theatre performances presented in the open on makeshift stages. Originating from the *misterios* (mysteries) of the Middle Ages, the Spanish theatre with works by Lope de Vega, Calderón de la Barca and Tirso de Molina, were performed in the cities of *Las Indias*. In the most adverse situations in the Caribbean, theatre also contributed to the spiritual enlightenment and upliftment of the people of that region.[285]

Afro-Americans

Black slavery in the Spanish Caribbean

Black slavery was present in the Mediterranean countries, both Christian and Islamic, even before European expansion. But with the Portuguese expedition to the coast of West Africa, black slavery increased significantly and became more visible in the societies of southern Europe. The navigator Antão Gonçalvez discovered blacks for the first time in 1441–42 in the region of Cabo Blanco; he captured some of them and took them to Lisbon. This marked the beginning of the black slave trade by Portugal, which was interested in finding cheap labour.[286] The trade was not so difficult due to the fact that in the black kingdoms of Benin, Oyo and Asante the institution of domestic slavery already existed.[287] At the beginning of the sixteenth century, the Portuguese brought approximately 2,000 slaves per year and sold them on the Iberian markets.[288] They became a well-known group of the population of the cities of southern Europe. Sevilla, for example, including Triana, had in 1565 a total of 85,538 inhabitants of which 6,327 or 7.4 percent were slaves.[289]

Domestic slaves arrived in Las Indias almost at the onset of the conquest. The instructions given to Governor Nicolás de Ovando in 1502, allowed blacks born "*en poder de cristianos*", and therefore baptized, to be shipped to America.[290] Nevertheless, besides domestic slaves, others were brought in, even at this early stage for specific tasks: for example, in 1505 seventeen slaves from Spain were shipped for work in the mines of La Española;[291] another group was used for the construction of the Santo Domingo fort.[292]

The accelerated genocide of the Indians of La Española led to a significant decrease in the labour force. From the point of view of the colonists, the government of the Hieronymites complicated the situation because of their policy in favour of the Indians. Under pressure from the colonists, the friars proposed to substitute the Indians with black slaves. More specifically, they were not using *ladinos* (domestic slaves) baptized and accustomed to life in Spain, but *negros bozales francos de derecho* (free blacks) imported directly from Africa.[293] This started the intercontinental triangular slave trade involving Africa, America and Europe.[294]

The Spanish Crown did not participate in the trade itself, but provided export licences for interested businessmen. For example, in 1518 this licence was granted to the governor of Bresse, Laurent de Gorrevod. His licence was limited to 4,000 slaves whose selling price was not determined.[295] Another licence, in 1523, provided for 4,000 slaves, of whom 1,400 went to La Española, 700 to Cuba, 600 to Mexico, 500 each to Puerto Rico and Castilla de Oro (Penamé) and 300 to Jamaica.[296] The smuggling of slaves even at this advanced stage existed. By the year 1526, the Audiencia of Santo Domingo had about six hundred slaves imported through smuggling.[297] In 1528, Welsers', a German company, entered the business, monopolizing it for ten years.[298] Thus, by 1546, only fifty-four years after the "discovery" and conquest of the island, there were 12,000 black Africans, the majority of whom worked in the thirty-five sugar factories.[299]

In the neighbouring islands, a situation similar to that in La Española was developing. According to the survey done by Governor Francisco Manuel de Lando in Puerto Rico in 1530, there were 1,168 male and 335 female slaves.[300] In Cuba, the report on Bishop Diego de Sarmiento's visit in 1544, speaks of 200 blacks in Bayamo, 120 in Zavana (El Layo), 14 in Sancti Spiritus, 160 "*negros e indios de Yucatán esclavos*" in Puerto del Príncipe, and 200 Indian and black slaves in Havana. This report does not provide concrete figures for Santiago de Cuba.[301]

By then, Cardinal Cisneros had already thought that the importation of slaves could possibly provoke rebellions in the Caribbean. He wrote that a greater number of slaves "*adversus Hispanorum imperium servile bellum aliquando concitarent*" (would frequently incite slave wars against the Spanish empire).[302] This fear was not without foundation, since in 1522, slave rebellions had already occurred at the Diego Columbus and Melchor de Castro sugar factories. Some of the rebels took refuge in the Sierra de Bahoruco, where they received protection from the cacique Enriquillo.[303] Other rebellions took place in Puerto Rico in 1523, Cuba in 1533 and 1538, among others.[304] In 1540, between 2,000 and 3,000 *cimarrones* (runaway slaves) lived in the mountains of La Española. The governors had many problems with the maroon uprisings. Finally, in September 1548, the slaves lost their remaining operating bases in Higuey; the decapitated head of their leader, known as Lemba, was publicly exhibited in the main square in Santo Domingo.[305]

Over the following decades, the number of slaves continued to grow. A report by the *oidor* Juan de Echagoian mentions the existence of 20,000 black slaves on the island in 1568.[306] Our estimation is that there were 56,000 blacks throughout the Caribbean around this time.[307] This increase is explained by the continuous growth of the sugar economy. However, a small decline was experienced in the years after the 1570s. Several colonists then left the Antilles in search of a better life in other parts of the Americas and took their slaves with them. Eventually, fewer slave ships arrived, and the black population which remained in the island grew older.

The economy of La Española suffered greatly due to the English invasion led by Captain Drake in 1586. Agriculture and livestock gradually became the island's economy. In 1588, for example, the colonists in Jamaica were unable to pay for the 150 slaves when they finally arrived in Jamaica. They were then forced to pay for the borrowed slaves with agricultural products for the following years.[308] Livestock and the production of leather needed vast expanses of land, but relatively few labourers. Consequently, the number of slaves in the island decreased. Additionally, due to the livestock situation, the slaves had to carry knives and cutlasses, which led to increasing possibilities of slave rebellions. At the end of the sixteenth century, several uprisings by Maroon slaves took place. The government did not gain control until the western and northern portions of the island were completely depopulated.[309]

As a result of this, there were only 9,648 slaves in October 1606, half of the estimated amount in 1568. Approximately 800 worked in the sugar factories; the remainder were engaged in agriculture and in domestic work.[310] This regressive tendency was maintained during the decades that followed. The Carmelite Antonio Vázquez de Espinosa writes in 1628 in his work: "*hay en la isla para las crias del ganado y beneficio de las demás haciendas mas de 4,000 esclavos de los vecinos de Santo Domingo y muchos mulatos libres*".[311] Canon Luis Jerónimo Alcocer also comments in his writing on the inadequate number of black slaves in the island in 1650, "*porque mueren muchos y en estos tiempos no vienen mas de Etiopia*".[312] The total figure, according to Alcocer was 4,000 slaves: half of whom were in the capital, the other half in the interior, in addition to 1,000 free blacks and mulattoes.[313]

A bishop gave the exact number of the black slaves in Cuba. It was none other than the well-known Juan de las Cabezas, who frequently travelled and visited his diocese.[314] According to his data, in 1608 there were 7,000 Africans living in Cuba, 3,000 in Havana, 600 in Puerto Príncipe, 1,000 in Bayamo and 1,500 in the *hatos y corrales del interior*.[315] The blacks represented 44.5 percent of the total Cuban population. This number increased, although slowly, during the following decades, particularly because of the need for a labour force for the copper mines located near Santiago de Cuba and for the construction of the fort in Havana. However, in Cuba as in the other Spanish islands, slavery was more patriarchal. Over time, the number of free blacks or *negros horros* increased, quite contrary to the emerging plantation economies in the English and French islands.[316]

Information on Puerto Rico and the Lesser Antilles can be found in the book written by Antonio Vásquez de Espinosa. There were 2,000 blacks and mulattoes in Puerto Rico.[317] In Margarita, black slaves replaced the Indians in pearl mining.[318] The Caribs from Grenada had 500 blacks under their control as a result of the shipwreck of a Portuguese slaver.[319] Jamaica had, in the middle of the seventeenth century, 1,500 blacks; the Spaniards gave them their freedom when faced with the threat of an English occupation. Following the traditions of the runaway slaves,[320] it was the Afro-Jamaicans who for five years resisted control of the island.

By 1612, the Dutch put an end to the Portuguese monopoly of the international slave trade. During the Dutch occupation of northeast Brazil, they were mainly responsible for the shipping of slaves to America.[321] After the war between Holland and England in 1654, the English also entered into this activity. The plantation economy of the Dutch, English and French islands of the Caribbean implied a continuous interest in the transportation of slaves.[322] Thus, throughout the seventeenth century, three million slaves were taken to the Americas.[323]

The number of slaves shipped to Spanish islands during this period, including the entire Spanish America, was very low. In fact, estimates reveal a total of 200,000 slaves in the entire Spanish America in the sixteenth century and 270,000 in the first half of the seventeenth century.[324] In 1645, about 300,000 blacks lived in Spanish America, but of these, only 18,000 lived in the Antilles where there was a tendency to grant them their freedom, for example, in the masters' wills. Thus, the historic role of the mulattoes became important.[325] This explains the fact that in 1789 the French colony that occupied only one-third of La Española, had 450,000 slaves, especially on the sugar plantations, while the Spanish colony, with two-thirds of the island, had 125,000 inhabitants, including many free blacks and mulattoes and approximately 15,000 slaves who worked in agriculture.[326]

The church and black slavery

The church and its representatives generally did not question the slavery system that had been established during the sixteenth century in the Caribbean islands and in the rest of Spanish America. In fact, the church benefited from slavery. The slaves were employed as domestics in the residences of the clergy, they worked in the construction of cathedrals and convents and cultivated the land of the property of the convents. Under these conditions, no one in the clergy imagined other social and economic structures without the existence of African slaves in the Spanish colonies of the "Indias". The case of Bartolomé de Las Casas is well known: under the government of the Hieronymites (1516–19), he recommended, in a letter to the Crown, that a certain number of slaves be put at the colonists' disposal, with the object of preserving the remaining Indians of La Española.[327] Las Casas at this time did not consider the cruelty of the transatlantic slave trade.[328] Nearly all the representatives of the church thought and acted in like manner at this time. In 1521, Alonso Manso, the first bishop of Puerto Rico, requested twenty black slaves as compensation for the Indians assigned to him.[329] Ten years later, the bishop of Santo Domingo, Sebastián Ramírez de Fuenleal, spoke in favour of free slave importation (*sin licencia*) and demanded an end to Welser's monopoly. He believed that colonization and stability in La Española would depend on the presence of these blacks "*para sacar oro y beneficiar las otras grangerías*";[330] the blacks would guarantee the growth of the island and would increase the extraction of gold, while the money that the colonists paid to the slave traders "*se convertirá en provecho de la tierra*".[331] Bishop Rodrigo de Bastidas, who had paid a lot of attention to the well-being of the Indians (and during the visit by the officials from Puerto Rico in April 1532 had passed an order whereby the administrator of the cathedral was to ensure the "*mantenimiento e vestuario*" of the blacks who worked there),[332] also naturally resorted to the employment of slaves[333] and valued their labour force as a vital element for the prosperity of the colony.[334]

Bastidas's successor, Manuel de Mercado, informed the king on 1 March 1573 that the blacks of the San Juan cathedral were so old that they cost more than they contributed and argued that "*en esta isla como en las demas destas partes es todo el caudal y servicio de negros*". For this reason, he stated, the king should authorize the provision of new slaves to the church.[335] Later on, Mercado thanked the Crown for the sixteen slaves he received from Cuba.[336] On 28 June 1577, the dean and chapter of Santo Domingo wrote to the king requesting slaves for work in the cathedral, using the same reasons that the church in Puerto Rico had used to obtain slaves.[337] On 20 April 1572, Archbishop Andrés de Carvajal granted the request of those who had demanded a numerous supply of slaves, resulting in a boom in sugar production, a resumption of gold mining and an increase in agricultural production.[338] Diego de Salamanca, bishop of San Juan, agreed, claiming that the island needed 1,000 slaves *frescos* (new) to once again promote the reputation of the island of Puerto Rico, to promote gold mining, and to cultivate and refine sugar.[339] The bishop also added that the royal treasury would benefit from this economic growth and mentioned in this context the Brazilian experience: "*Dizen me que la provincia del Brazil solía ser de muy poco provecho y que teniendo su Rey este aviso de los de la tierra les hizo gracia de gran cantidad de negros con lo qual se a poblado y quedado tan provechosa a su Rey que saca della aora mas en un año que solía en tres*", adding that the Portuguese ambassador in the Spanish Court could offer more details about this successful and exemplary policy.[340] Similar but more modest measures were proposed by the Abbot Francisco Márquez de Villalobos to boost the economy of Jamaica.[341]

However, after the attack on Santo Domingo by Francis Drake in 1586, the economic situation worsened in the following years, especially in La Española. Archbishop Dávila y Padilla described in letters to the king dated 8 October 1600 and 20 November 1601, the poverty that existed on the island. No slaver had arrived in eleven years and despite the discovery of deposits of silver, the situation had not changed, because the riches could not be exploited. Only eleven factories were operating and consequently, 1,000 blacks were urgently needed, 500 for mining and 500 for the factories, but more would be needed in the future. The archbishop argued that economic growth in the island would also end the poverty of the clergy and the friars.[342]

All of the previously mentioned groups acccepted the social system in which blacks had the lowest rank and in which they were treated as objects or instruments but not human beings.[343] However, mention must be made of some persons who considered the slavery of blacks as an injustice and argued for their human dignity but were unable to promote a similar movement such as the one organized for the protection of Indians. Las Casas, who in 1544 (after he was ordained bishop) arrived in Chiapas with four slaves for his personal use, changed his attitude in 1547 or a little later and became convinced that the rights of the blacks were equal to those of the Indians. He prepared a passionate treatise in favour of the blacks, assuring them that he would never have supported the African labour trade to the Americas, if he had had knowledge of the unjust capture of human beings by the Portuguese.[344] In Mexico, Archbishop Alonso de Montúfar, in a letter addressed to the king on 30 June 1560, expressed doubt about the justification of black slavery, and moreover because they did not oppose Christianity.[345] Some years earlier in Brazil, Father Fernando Oliveira, in his manual *Arte da guerra do mar*, had demanded the abolition of the transatlantic trade of human beings and had accused the Portuguese of initiating this horrible activity for purely economic reasons and not for the purpose of converting the slaves to Christianity.[346]

The work of Alonso de Sandoval, rector of the Jesuit college in Cartagena de Indias, entitled *De instauranda Aethiopum salute*, was published in 1627. This work integrated the anthropological-ethnological interest of the Africans who arrived in America, with a thorough critique of slavery practices. Moved by the misery of the slaves, Sandoval elaborated concepts for his pastoral work in the ports of arrival and departure, with a call to the Society of Jesus to assume this mission.[347] In continuation of this spiritual initiative, his younger companion, Pedro Claver, while in Cartagena, dedicated his life to the service of the slaves. But Claver's example did not result in any fundamental change in the position of the church regarding the legality of slavery.[348] Certainly the Holy See reiterated the condemnation of Indian slavery through the bull *Commissum nobis* of the Pope Urbanus VIII of 22 April 1639 and the apostolic constitution *Immensa pastorum* of Pope Benedict XIV of 22 December 1741, thereby reconfirming the declaration of Pope Paul III. But only later, on 3 December 1839, did Pope Gregory XVI, with his apostolic constitution *In supremo apostolatus fastigio*, join the movement for the abolition of slavery, promoted initially by several evangelical churches, finally condemning black slavery and considering any form of trade in human beings to be incompatible with the Christian faith.[349]

Pastoral attention to the slaves

While the church showed great interest in Christianizing the American Indians, it was content to ignore the African slaves. It was not by chance that the municipal council of Santo Domingo, on 1 December 1531, accused the bishop of negligence in his religious attention to the blacks.[350] Responding to more than one complaint, the Crown in a *Real cédula* (Royal Letter Patent) of 25 October 1538 ordered the audiencia of Santo Domingo to take measures against religious neglect of the slaves: the masters were obliged to send their slaves to church or to the convent on Sundays and festive days, where they were to receive instruction in the Christian doctrine from a capable priest appointed by the chapter or the convent.[351]

A year later, a diocesan synod, organized by Bishop Alonso de Fuenmayor, took up the challenge of religious instruction for slaves. Its documents were not kept,[352] but the decision was that slaves brought from Africa to La Española should receive religious education for thirty days before being baptized.[353] The second diocesan synod of Santo Domingo held in 1576 explicitly reinforced that commitment. During the discussion, some participants argued "*que los negros boçales que traen de Guinea y de todas aquellas provincias siendo tan boçales y de ningun entendimiento no se avian de bapticar hasta que supiesen la dotrina cristiana y entendiesen que cosa es Dios y que les prestava el baptismo*".[354] Others criticized this position by stating that many other blacks would die before being baptized and consequently face condemnation of their souls to hell, since they were not baptized due to their incapacity and ignorance. They therefore proposed that "*un conocimiento mediano de Dios y de la yglesia para que pudiesen rescevir el baptismo como los niños, pues no tienen mas entendimiento que ellos*" would be acceptable.[355] Archbishop Carvajal finally supported this position. Due to the great number of deaths among the slaves, as well as the risk of condemnation of their souls, the canon of the synod of 1539 reiterated "*que los tengan treinta dias enseñandoles la dotrina y depues los bapticen sin hazer mas diligencia, si saben mucho o poco*".[356]

Some decades later, Archbishop Cristóbal Rodríguez y Suárez was extremely concerned about the baptism of slaves. During this time, it was already customary for slaves to be baptized in Africa before their departure for the Indies. The archbishop ordered that an investigation be carried out among the slave traders in Santo Domingo which revealed doubts regarding the validity of these baptisms in Africa.[357] It seems that Rodríguez also assumed the responsibility of true Christian work among the slaves. This can be concluded from the Third Diocesan Synod of Santo Domingo (30 June 1610) which he organized. During this synod, an appeal was made to the conscience of the plantation and factory owners to teach the slaves the doctrine and prayers of the church daily, either personally or through an employee, before dinner and early morning on Sundays and festive days. It was also decided that attendance at Sunday mass was compulsory, if a church was located less than a mile away; if this was not the case, a mass was to be organized every two weeks with the attendance of 50 percent of the slaves at each. Owners were also required to make the funeral arrangements for their slaves in cases where there was a church within two miles. A fine of 100 *ducados* (ducats) was imposed on owners who breached this law.[358]

Other regulations for the Christian education of the slaves were approved by the provincial council headed by Archbishop Pedro de Oviedo. Once again the problem of baptism arose and detailed research was to be undertaken to prove whether statements made by the slave traders were correct, that is, whether or not the slaves were already baptized when sold. In cases of doubt, they would be baptized again, but not without prior preparation, which would begin immediately upon their arrival in port.[359] With respect to confirmation, the council stated that slave owners should give the slaves an opportunity to receive this sacrament.[360] Similarly, the Africans were urged to attend confession on condition that they know the creed and all that was necessary to receive the sacrament "*quia caeteros omnes ruditate et imperitia vincunt*".[361] Each priest could grant the absolution of sins, an act generally reserved for the bishop.[362]

With respect to Sunday mass, the council did not abide by the regulation of the Diocesan Synod of 1610, because it was satisfied that on Sundays only some of the slaves were allowed to attend mass, the aim being that each one of them would attend mass at least six times a year (to listen to the sermons of the priest on the gospel and to receive instruction on the catechism).[363] Like all other believers, the Africans had the right to receive the Last Sacrament in the event of serious illness or threat of death.[364] With regard to marriage, the council decided that marriage between two baptized Africans or two nonbaptized Africans was valid, but if there was doubt that one or both were not baptized at the time of marriage, the marriage vows were repeated in the presence of the parish priest.[365] The council also opposed having

slaves work on Sundays and holidays.[366] Finally, Africans who cultivated a garden or their own land with their masters' consent were also
obliged to pay tithes.[367]

The regulations of this provincial council provided a temporary
framework and none of the following synods such as that of Puerto
Rico in 1645[368] or Cuba in 1680,[369] could improve the deficiencies of
the Christian education of the slaves. They managed to promote certain improvements while restricting the widespread belief that the
Africans were barbarians and incapable of receiving the gospel.[370] At
the time in Cartagena de Indias, Alonso de Sandoval was in favour of
a more positive perception of the blacks.[371] Thus, the extreme religious
neglect of the slaves, which in the previous decades had been seriously
criticized by the *oidores* Juan de Echagoian,[372] Alonso Cáceres[373] and
others[374] was rectified.

In light of the scant attention paid to the blacks by the church, it
was not surprising that they kept their traditional African religions.
No member of the clergy knew any of the original languages of the
slaves; but the slaves narrated the stories of their broken families in
these languages, they remembered their ancestors, their gods and so
they kept a secret link with their lost homeland.[375] Despite the harsh
forced labour and the cultural repression, the blacks managed to maintain certain free spaces on which they cultivated their heritage. This
gave rise to the origin of Afro-Caribbean cults and of Afro-American
religions in general.

In this process, the numerous feasts in Spanish America that were
held regularly played an important role for the slaves.[376] The customs
of the popular religions of the white colonists, especially those of
Andalucía, were joyous occasions during which there was much celebration, decorations, dances and games. All this appealed to the
blacks.[377] The centre of the feast was generally the veneration of a saint
and the blacks saw their own African gods in the Catholic saint and
asked for his protection through their own expression; a religious syn-
cretism developed in this way.[378]

On the Day of the Three Kings on 6 January a great popular feast
was held in Cuba and, in particular, in Havana. From early morning
they played the drums and slaves arrived from the surrounding areas in
the city to gather with the leaders of their respective tribes. Singing
and dancing, the various groups left for the Plaza de Armas, in the
centre of town, where they mixed with the crowd and impressed their
audience with colourful clothing and the presentation of a short the-

atre performance of Melchor, the black king among the three. This joyful feast lasted until the early morning of the following day.[379] Similarly, they celebrated the Birth of Mary (8 September), Corpus Christi and Holy Week, the latter with large processions in which the blacks participated through the Cofradía del Espíritu Santo.[380]

Cofradías also existed in Santo Domingo. The most important was that of John the Baptist, which had its see in a chapel of the same name behind the high choir of the cathedral. According to Luis Jerónimo Alcocer,[381] "*negros criollos que asi llaman a los negros nacidos en esta ysla*",[382] belonged to that *cofradía*. The feast of St John the Baptist was celebrated with a novena, mass, sermons, solemn processions, dances and bull fights. The *cofradía* was also dedicated to the sick and to the poor members and financed 50 percent of the funeral expenses of those who died as slaves. On 13 July 1606, Pope Paul V endorsed this *cofradía*.[383] Additionally, the Cofradía de Nuestra Señora de la Candelaria had a chapel in the cathedral attended by "*negros biafaras y mandingas*".[384] The Cofradía de los Santos Cósme y Damián consisted of *negros aradaces* and organized annually a great feast in honour of its patrons.[385] The number of *cofradías* increased constantly in the seventeenth and eighteenth centuries and the racial criteria gradually relaxed.

While the blacks in the city were more closely linked to the Catholic faith, the blacks in the factories and on plantations developed a religious subculture that mixed Christian elements, the cult of their ancestors and spirits, with superstition and created their own symbolic world.[386] Frequently, the church reacted against this with violent intolerance. The archbishop of Santo Domingo, Nicolás de Ramos, wrote on 23 July 1594 that as bishop of Puerto Rico (1588–92), he had discovered a large meeting of black men and women who gathered every night to worship Satan "*en figura de cabron*" and to renounce God, the Virgin and the sacraments of the church "*afirmando que no tenian otro dios ni creyan sino en aquel demonio y con siertas sumpciones se ivan a unos campos a hacer estos exercisios*".[387] When Ramos received information about this, he punished the participants; but three women who refused to renounce their satanic beliefs were handed over to the civil authorities and Governor Diego Menéndez de Valdéz had them burnt alive as heretics. Ramos accepted full responsibility for this act.[388] In Puerto Rico, some black women were imprisoned for practising witchcraft and spiritualism under the government of Gabriel de Roxas (1608–14).[389] Archbishop Cristóbal Rodríguez y Suárez reported yet another case.[390] Witchcraft and other types of black magic had been observed and punished since 1610 by the court of Inquisition of Cartagena de Indias.[391]

Despite those persecution measures, the African slaves succeeded in keeping their own religious world. Uprooted from their homeland, they maintained some of their identity and so filled the vacuum to which the church only paid attention in an inadequate way. The church was principally concerned with their baptism, thus this sacrament of salvation of their souls served to integrate them into Christianity. Indirectly, the church recognized the human dignity of the blacks through baptism but this did not inspire the church to fight against slavery, because many of its institutions in the New World were also "*dueños de esclavos en gran escala*"[392] and obtained profits from the material worth of the slave – their labour force.[393]

NOTES

This chapter is a translation of Johannes Meier, *Die Anfänge der Kirche auf den Karibischen Inseln*, Die Geschichte der Bistümer Santo Domingo, Concepción de la Vega, San Juan de Puerto Rico und Santiago de Cuba von ihrer Entstehung (1511/12) bis zur Mitte des 17. Jahrhunderts, Neue Zeitschrift für Missionswissenschaft, Supplementa Vol. 38 (Immensee 1991), 205–89. We wish to express our gratitude to Mrs C. Ken for her invaluable help with the translation.

1. William M. Denevan, *The Native Population of the Americas in 1492* (Madison 1978), 1–12, 289–92. Denevan's opinion gives an idea of the position of Karl Sapper who in 1924 estimated that forty to fifty million natives lived at that time on the American continent: K. Sapper, "Die Zahl und die Volksdichte der indianischen Bevölkerung in Amerika vor der Conquista und in der Gegenwart" in *Proceedings of the Twenty-first International Congress of Americanistas*, held at The Hague, 12–16 August 1924, First Part (Leiden, The Hague 1924), 95–104.

2. Sven Loven, *Über die Wurzeln der tainischen Kultur*. Teil I, "Materielle Kultur" (Göteborg 1924), 1–54; Peter Ashdown, *Caribbean History in Maps* (Kingston and Port of Spain 1979), 5 (map 7); Wolfgang Reinhard, *Geschichte der europäischen Expansion*, II, *Die Neue Welt* (Stuttgart 1985), 9–12; Elisabeth Grewal, "Die Indianer der karibischen Inseln und die Spanier. Vom Untergang der Indianerkulturen", in *Karibik – Wirtschaft, Gesellschaft und Geschichte*, Lateinamerika-Studien 11, edited by Hanns-A. Steger and Jürgen Schneider (München 1982), 65–74.

3. C.O. Sauer, *The Early Spanish Main* (Berkeley and Los Angeles 1966), 48; Frank

Moya Pons, *Manual de historia dominicana*, 8th edition (Santiago de los Caballeros 1984), 2.

4. S. Loven, *Über die Wurzen*, 54–69, 312–424; C.O. Sauer, *The Early Spanish Main*, 51–59; Ricardo E. Alegría, *Descubrimiento, conquista y colonización de Puerto Rico: 1493–1599*, Colección de Estudios Puertorriqueños (San Juan, Puerto Rico 1971), 15–19; Frank Moya Pons, *La sociedad taina*, Cuadernos de Historia Dominicana (Santiago de los Caballeros 1973), 4–5, 10, 16–17; Moya Pons *Manual de historia dominicana*, 3–8; Roberto Cassa, *Historia social y económica de la República Dominicana*, I (Santo Domingo 1984), 23.

5. Karl Sapper, *Das Aussterben der Naturvölker*, Rektoratsrede (Würzburg 1929), 28–29; Germán Arciniegas, *Karibische Rhapsodie. Biographie eines Meeres* (München 1960), 17; Paulino Castañeda Delgado, "La política española con los Caribes durante el siglo XVI", *Revista de Indias* 30 (1970): 73–130; Grewal, "Die Indianer", 66–67.

6. Peter Martyr von Anghiera, *Acht Dekaden über die Neue Welt*, Bd. I–II (Darmstadt 1972–75) 29, 104–5, 197–98.

7. The names of eight of them are known: the Franciscans – Revd Rodrigo Pérez, Juan Deledeule, Juan Tisin and Juan Pérez (lay brothers); the Mercedarians – Juan de los Infantes and Juan de Solórzano; Friar Jorge (Caballeros de Santiago) and the Hieronymite brother Ramón Pané; Benno M. Biermann, *Die ersten Missionen Amerikas*, Festschrift 50 Jahre Katholische Missionswissenschaft in Münster (Münster 1961), 120–22; Leandro Tormo, "Historia de la iglesia en América Latina. I, La evangelización de la América Latina", *Estudios Socio-Religiosos Latinoamericanos* 8 (1962): 66–68.

8. The estimate given by Frank Moya Pons and Antonio Lluberes is more realistic: 300,000 inhabitants in La Española at the time of Christopher Columbus' arrival (see note 24).

9. Ramón Pané, "Relación acerca de las antigüedades de los indios" (Report on the history of the Indians), the first treatise written in America. New version with notes, map and appendices edited by José J. Arrom, in *Colección América Nuestra* 5 (México 1984), 21–56. It was first published in Venice in 1571, as part of the biography of Christopher Columbus by his son Ferdinand. Peter Martyr was already acquainted with this work by Pané (*Acht Dekaden über die Neue Welt*, 114–22).

10. R. Pané, "Relación", 111–19. According to Pané, Juan Mateo was the first Christian martyr (he wrote that he died on 21 September 1496, crying out: "soy siervo de Dios" – I am a servant of God). For Las Casas, faith was not the reason for their deaths, the tribes considered the first baptized Indians to be traitors. B. de Las Casas, *Apologética Historia*, Works chosen from Fray Bartolomé de Las Casas (Madrid 1958), BAE 105, 416–19, BAE 106, 121–25.

11. "who for the last three years has continued to show good will, indicating his desire to become a Christian and to have no more than one wife, although the custom is to have two or three, with elders having ten, fifteen or even twenty". R. Pané, "Relación", 56.

12. Robert Streit, "Fr. Roman Pané O.S. Hier., der erste Ethnograph Amerikas", *Zeitschrift für Missionswissenschaft* 10 (1920), 192–93; Constantino Bayle, *El clero secular y la evangelización de América*, Biblioteca Missionalia Hispanica, vol. VI (Madrid 1950), 42, 197; Hugo E. Polanco Brito, "Fray Ramón Pané, primer maestro, catequizador y antropólogo del nuevo mundo", in *Para una historia de la evangelización en América Latina*, edited by Carlos E. Deive (Barcelona 1977), 127–40; Carlos E. Deive, "Fray Ramón Pané y el nacimiento de la etnología americana", in *El indio, el negro y la vida tradicional dominicana* (Santo Domingo 1978), 13–42; José J. Arrom, "Fray Ramón Pané o el rescate de un mundo mítico", *La Revista del Centro de Estudios Avanzados de Puerto Rico y el Caribe* 3 (1986): 2–8; Juan G. Durán (ed.), *Monumenta Catechetica Hispanoamericana* (Siglos XVI–XVIII), vol. I, siglo XVI (Buenos Aires 1984), 84–87.

13. In the first twenty-four chapters Pané explains the relationships, myths and religious practices of the Tainos ("Relación", 22–47). With the assistance of Cardinal Cisneros, Las Casas defended the "areytos". Only the devil's masks were prohibited. The "areytos" continues to the present day; see Silvio Zavala, *Aspectos religiosos de la historia colonial americana*, Estudios históricos (Guadalajara, México 1959), 11–12; Fernando Ortíz, *La africanía de la música folklórica de Cuba* (Havana 1965), 73–74. With respect to the natives' religion in La Española see W. Krickeberg et al., *Die Religionen des alten Amerika* (Stuttgart 1961), 293, 350, 352–53, 376; Leandro Tormo, "Historia de la iglesia", 59–60; F. Moya Pons, *La sociedad taina*, 18–20; Moya Pons, *Manual*, 9–10; Cassa, *Historia social*, 25–26.

14. Antonine Tibesar, "The Franciscan Province of the Holy Cross of Española, 1505–1559", *Americas* 13 (1956–57): 377–89; José L. Saez, *Testigos de la esperanza, Historia de la vida religiosa en Santo Domingo* (Santo Domingo 1979), 30–31.

15. B. de Las Casas, *Historia de las Indias*, II, 13 (Madrid 1961) BAE 96, 37: "*Sólo esto vi que hicieron, conviene a saber: que pedieron licencia para tener en sus casas algunos muchachos, hijos de algunos caciques, pero pocos, dos o tres o cuatro, y así, a los cuales enseñaron a leer y escrebir, pero no sé qué más con ellos de la doctrina cristiana y buenas costumbres aprendieron, más de dalles muy buen ejemplo, porque eran buenos y vivían bien*" (I only saw what they did, that is, that they requested permission to keep children in their homes, children of some caciques, only a few, two, three or four, whom they taught to read and write, but I do not know what they taught them about Christianity and good customs, other than setting a good example for them because they were good people and they lived well). Regarding this missionary method of the Franciscans, cf. Pedro Borges Morán, *Métodos misionales en la cristianización de América*, Siglo XVI, Biblioteca Missionalia Hispanica, vol. XII (Madrid 1960), 394–95.

16. CDIA – Colección de documentos inéditos relativos al descubrimiento, conquista y organización [colonización] de las antiguas posesiones españolas de América y Oceanía (Collection of unpublished documents on the discovery, conquest and organization [colonization] of the former Spanish possessions in the Americas and Oceania), taken from the Archives of the Kingdom, and in

particular, from the Archives of the Indies, 1–42 (Madrid 1864–84), 38, 439–40; Paulino Castañeda Delgado, "Un problema ciudadano: La tributación urbana", *Revista de Indias* 33–34 (1973–74): 493–550; Antonio Lluberes, "La iglesia ante el indio 1492–1533", *Amigo del hogar* 43 (1984): 394–95.

17. CDIA 31, 156–74.

18. Mario Bonetti, *Staat und Geselschafft im karibischen Raum im 16 Jahrhundert*, Beiträge zur Soziologie und Sozialkunde Lateinamerikas, Bd. 25 (München 1984), 53–57; Hartmut Heine, *Geschichte Spaniens in der frühen Neuzeit 1400–1800* (München 1984), 82–83; F. Moya Pons, *Manual de historia dominicana*, 22–25.

19. CDIA 31, 210–11: "*compelays e apremieys a los dichos yndios, que traten e conversen con los cristhianos de la dicha isla, e trabaxen en sus edeficios e coxer e sacar oro e otros metales . . . e fagays pagar a cada uno el dia que trabaxare el xornal e manenymiento que sygund la calidad de la tierra e de la persona e del oficio, vos paresciere . . lo qual fagan e complan como personas libres, como lo son, e non como siervos; e faced que sean bien tratados los dichos yndios*" (subdue and compel said Indians to work in their buildings, to extract and bring out gold and other metals . . . and make sure that each one when he works is paid such wages and maintenance as you deem appropriate in accordance with the condition of the land, the person and the job in question . . ., all of this they shall do and perform as free persons, as they are, and not as servants; and make sure that said Indians are treated well). José M. Chacón y Calvo, Cedulario Cubano, "Los orígines de la colonización I (1493–1512)", *Colección de documentos inéditos para la historia de Hispano-América*, VI (Madrid 1929), 86.

20. "Encomienda" – land and slaves granted to a colonist. "Encomenderos" – holder of an encomienda. See Johann Specker, "Kirchliche und staatliche Siedlungspolitik in Spanisch-Amerika im 16. Jahrhundert mit besonderer Berücksichtigung der Konzilien und Synoden", in *Missionswissenschaftliche Studien, Festgabe Johannes Dindlinger* edited by J. Rommerskirchen and N. Kowalsky (Aachen 1951), 426–38; Manfred Tietz, "Der Indio als Christ und Priester: Zu den Grenzen der Akkulturation", in *Literatur und Kolonialismus I*, Die Verarbeitung der kolonialen Expansion in der europäischen Literatur edited by W. Bader and
J. Riesz, Bayreuther Beiträge zur Literaturwissenschaft, Bd. 4 (Frankfurt and Bern 1983), 93–116; Horst Pietschmann, "Die Kirche in Hispanoamerika", in *Die Konzilien in Lateinamerika*, I Mexico 1555–1897 edited by Willi Henkel (Paderborn 1984), 1–48, 15.

21. Peter Martyr stated that in 1494, 50,000 persons died from starvation, instigated by the Indians in the Cibao and Cibango regions. The Indians ceased to cultivate crops in a bid to get rid of the Spaniards. P. Martyr, *Acht Dekaden über die Neue Welt*, 65.

22. K. Sapper, *Das Aussterben*, 33–34, 36, 42; Germán Arciniegas, *Karibische Rhap-*

sodie, 67; Magnus Mörner, "Evolución demográfica de Hispanoamérica durante el período colonial" (draft of a chapter prepared for the *Historia General de América* [General History of America], Institute of Latin American Studies, Research Paper Series 14 [Stockholm 1979], 7); E. Grewal, *Die Indianer*, 68–69.

23. Frank Moya Pons, *La Española en el siglo XVI, 1493–1520, Trabajo, sociedad y política en la economía del oro*, Colección Estudios 10 2d editon (Santiago de los Caballeros 1973), 6–67; Moya Pons, *Manual de historia dominicana*, 26.

24. Frank Moya Pons, "Datos para el estudio de la demografía aborigen en Santo Domingo", in *Jahrbuch für Geschichte von Staat, Wirtschaft und Gesellschaft Lateinamerikas* 16 (1979): 1–11, estimates that in 1494 there were 377,559 Indians. Antonio Lluberes ("La iglesia ante el indio 1492–1533", 394) and Eric Williams (*From Columbus to Castro: The History of the Caribbean 1492–1969* [London 1970], 33) estimate that there were about 300,000 Indians or, rather, between 200,000 and 300,000.

25. Juan Friede, *Los Welser en la conquista de Venezuela*, Commemorative edition of the fourth centenary of the death of Bartolomé Welser, head of the German company in Augsburg (Caracas and Madrid 1961), 541–42, 619–20; Enrique Otte, "Los jerónimos y el tráfico humano en el Caribe: una rectificación", *Anuario de Estudios Americanos* 32 (1975): 187–204.

26. F. Moya Pons, "Datos", 4; Moya Pons, *Manual de historia dominicana*, 26.

27. "Distribution of the Indians"; CDIA 31, 449–52.

28. CDIA 31, 436–39, 470–76; León Lopetegui and Felix Zubillaga, *Historia de la iglesia en la América española desde el descubrimiento hasta comienzos del siglo XIX*, México, América Central, Antillas, Biblioteca de Autores Cristianos 248 (Madrid 1965), 255–56.

29. CDIA 31, 391; Fidel Fita, "Primeros años del episcopado en América", *Boletín de la Real Academia de la Historia* 20 (1892): 261–300, 283–84: "*los Indios se conviertan a Nuestra Santa Fe Católica, para que sus ánimas no se pierdan; para lo qual es menester que sean ynformados de las cosas de Nuestra Fe Católica; terneis muy gran cuidado como sin les hacer fuerza alguna ansí las personas religiosas como aquellos á quienes los diesen en Nuestro Nombre que encomiende, los ynstruyan é ynformen . . . con mucho amor*" (the Indians shall be converted to Our Holy Catholic faith, so that their souls may be saved; it is therefore necessary that they be informed about Our Catholic Faith; religious persons as well as persons to whose care you have entrusted the Indians in Our Name must be very careful not to force them in any way but shall instruct and inform them with a lot of love).

30. CDIU – Colección de documentos inéditos relativos al descubrimiento, conquista y organización de las antiguas posesiones españolas de ultramar (Collection of unpublished documents on the discovery, conquest and organization of former Spanish overseas possessions). Second series, published by the Real Academia de la Historia, 1–25 (Madrid 1885–1932) 5, 323–24: "*Mucho placer ove en ver la carta que Juan de Esquivel escribió á vos el almirante por ver los muchos yndios que allí se han convertido á nuestra santa feé catolica; en aquello se debe continuar*"

hasta que todos los desla ysla esten bautizados y pues la ysla no es muy grande y los yndios della ynclinados en alguna manera á nuestra feé y muy mansos agora á los principios, se debe tener mucho cuydado en ordenar las cosas de manera que sean mejor dotrinados los yndios de aquella isla que lo han sydo los desa en las cosas de nuestra santa feé católica y pues esto es el camino principal sobre que mandamos la conquista destas partes, visto es lo que principalmente se debe proveer" (I was very pleased to see the letter that J. de Esquivel wrote to you, Admiral, how many Indians there had converted to our holy Catholic faith; this effort should be continued until all of them on this island are baptized and since this island is not very large and the Indians seem to be in some way attracted to our faith and very accepting of the principles, care must be taken to organize things in such a way that the Indians of that island will be better taught than the Indians on this island have been about our holy Catholic faith for as much as this is the principal reason for which we have ordered the conquest of these territories, this is what needs to be done).

31. CDIU 1, 1–14, here 11: *"que los indios sean cristianos, así de obras como de nombre, y que no sean como en esa isla Española, que no tienen más de cristianos sino el nombre"* (that the Indians are Christians, in practice and in name, and that they are not like those in La Española, who are only Christian in name).

32. Letter dated 20 March 1512 to Diego Colón, CDIA 32, 372–79, here 374. Velázquez was accompanied by four friars, one of them was Juan Tisin, who arrived in 1493 in La Española: Ismael Testé, *Historia eclesiástica de Cuba*, I–V (Burgos and Barcelona 1965–75), IV, 31 and 41; Levi Marrero, *Cuba: economía y sociedad*, II, siglo XVI, "La economía" (Barcelona 1974), 380.

33. "Are these not men? Are they not rational beings? Should you not be obligated to love them as you love yourselves?" B. de Las Casas, *Historia de las Indias*, III, 4, BAE 96, 176.

34. B. de Las Casas, *Historia de las Indias*, III, 5, BAE 96, 178–81.

35. Richard Konetzke, "Forschungsprobleme zur Geschichte der Religion und ihrer Bedeutung in den Kolonisationen Amerikas", *Saeculum* 10 (1959): 82–101; Lewis Hanke, *The Spanish Struggle for Justice in the Conquest of America*, 7th edition (Boston 1965), 17–22; Joseph Höffner, *Kolonialismus und Evangelium, Spanische Kolonialethik im Goldenen Zeitalter*, 3rd edition (Trier 1972), 189–96; E. Otte, "Los jerónimos", 193–94; M.A. Medina, *Una comunidad al servicio del indio: La obra de Fr. Pedro de Córdoba O.P. 1482–1521* (Madrid 1983), 121–38; Paulo Suess, "Glaubensfreiheit und Zwangsarbeit. Spanische Missionare, Theologen und Juristen des 16. Jahrhunderts zur Rechtslage der Indios", *Zeitschrift für Missionswissenschaft und Religionswissenschaft* 71 (1987): 292–315.

36. L. Lopetegui and F. Zubillaga, *Historia de la iglesia en la América española*, 257; Enrique Dussel, *Historia general de la iglesia en América Latina*, I/1, *Introducción general a la historia de la iglesia en América Latina* (Salamanca 1983), 304–5.

37. "In accordance with human and divine rights", in letter written to Diego Colón dated 20 March 1512; CDIA 32, 375–76.

38. Manuel Serrano y Sanz, *Orígenes de la dominación española en América*, I (Estudios históricos), Nueva Biblioteca de Autores Españoles 25 (Madrid 1918), 349–50; J.M. Chacón y Calvo, *Cedulario Cubano*, 425–26, 443–44 and 445–47; M.A. Medina, *Una comunidad*, 63, 130–34; P. Suess, "Glaubensfreiheit und Zwangsarbeit. Spanische Missionare", 296–97.

39. B. de Las Casas, *Historia de las Indias*, III, 6, BAE 96, 181–83; M.A. Medina, *Una comunidad*, 128–30, 137–38.

40. B. de Las Casas, *Historia de las Indias*, III, 7–16, BAE 96, 183–211; Robert Streit, "Die erste Junta von Burgos im Jahre 1512", *Zeitschrift für Missionswissenschaft* 13 (1923): 65–78; L. Tormo, "Historia de la iglesia", 183–84; J. Höffner, *Kolonialismus und Evangelium*, 194; F. Moya Pons, *La Española en el siglo XVI, 1493–1520, Trabajo, sociedad y política en la economía del oro*, Colección Estudios 10, 2nd edition (Santiago de los Caballeros 1973), 132–35; M.A. Medina, *Una comunidad*, 138–39, 144–46.

41. B. de Las Casas, *Historia de las Indias*, III, 17–18, BAE 96, 211–16; Benno M. Biermann, "Die ersten Dominikaner in Amerika", *Zeitschrift für Missionswissenschaft und Religionswissenschaft* 32 (1947–48): 57–64, 107–21; M.A. Medina, *Una comunidad*, 41, 147–50.

42. "Notification"; "an extremely rare gospel". See J. Höffner, *Kolonialismus und Evangelium*, 156.

43. CDIU 20, 311–14; B. de Las Casas, *Historia de las Indias*, III, 57–58, BAE 96, 308–12; K. Sapper, *Das Aussterben*, 49–51; B. Biermann, "Das Requerimiento in der spanischen Conquista", *Neue Zeitschrift für Missionswissenschaft* 6 (1950): 94–114; also Biermann, *Las Casas und seine Sendung, Das Evangelium und die Rechte des Menschen*, Walberberger Studien, Theologische Reihe 5 (Mainz 1968), 55; Mario Góngora, *Studies in the Colonial History of Spanish America*, Cambridge Latin American Studies 20 (Cambridge 1975), 41–43; H. Pietschmann, *Staat und staatliche Entwicklung am Beginn der spanischen Kolonisation Amerikas*, Spanische Forschungen der Görresgesellschaft, Zweite Reihe, Bd. 19 (Münster 1980), 65–68; Wolfgang Reinhard, *Geschichte der europäischen Expansion*, 58–59; Tzvetan Todorov, *Die Eroberung Amerikas, Das Problem des Anderen* (Frankfurt 1985), 177–80.

44. B. de Las Casas, *Historia de las Indias*, III, 19, BAE 96, 216–19; R. Konetzke, *Süd-und Mittelamerika I, Die Indianerkulturen Altamerikas und die spanisch-portugiesische Kolonialherrschaft*, Fischer Weltgeschichte Bd. 22, 6th edition (Frankfurt 1977), 262; E. Otte, "Los jerónimos", 194.

45. ". . . to have the power to carry out confirmation in the absence of a bishop, to be able to use old holy oil for baptisms . . . and to bless altars and chalices". J. Castro Seoane, "Aviamiento y catálogo de las misiones que en el siglo XVI pasaron de Espanä a Indias y Filipinas segun los libros de Contratación, I, Franciscanos y dominicos a la Española 1503–1525", *Missionalia Hispanica* 13 (1956): 83–140, 128–33; M.A. Medina, *Una comunidad*, 101–3.

46. M.A. Medina, *Una comunidad* , 64–66.

47. B. de Las Casas, *Historia de las Indias*, III, 33–34, BAE 96, 253–57; Rodolfo R.

de Roux (ed.), *Historia general de la iglesia en América Latina,* VII, Colombia, Venezuela (Salamanca 1981), 217–18; M.A. Medina, *Una comunidad,* 104–10; Demetrio Ramos Pérez, "El P. Córdoba y Las Casas en el plan de conquista pacífica de tierra firme", in *Boletín Americanista* III (Barcelona 1950), 175–210.

48. F. Moya Pons, "Datos", 3; Moya Pons, *Manual,* 27–28.

49. CDIA 1, 50–236; Emilio Rodríguez Demorizi, *Los dominicos y las encomiendas de indios dela isla Española,* Academia Dominicana de la Historia 30 (Santo Domingo 1971), 73–248; cf. F. Moya Pons, *La Española en el siglo XVI,* 295–337. Sixty of the encomenderos were married to caciques' daughters. As a consequence, a social structure developed similar to that which later developed on the American continent.

50. CDIU 6, 2–3; L. Marrero, *Cuba: economía y sociedad,* I, 169.

51. "Sacrifice made up of goods unjustly stolen from the poor is not sacred."

52. B. de Las Casas, *Historia de las Indias,* III, 79, BAE 96, 356–58; B. Biermann, *Las Casas und seine Sendung,* 7–8; I. Pérez Fernández, *Fray Bartolomé de Las Casas, Brevísima relación de su vida, Diseño de su personalidad, Síntesis de su doctrina* (Synopsis of his life, his personality, summary of his doctrine) (Caleruega 1984), 23–25.

53. B. de Las Casas, *Historia de las Indias,* III, 81–2, BAE 96, 360–65.

54. Ibid., 366.

55. L. Lopetegui and F. Zubillaga, *Historia de la iglesia,* 258–59; D. Ramos Pérez, "El P. Córdoba y Las Casas", 191–94.

56. ". . . plan for the reform of the West Indies"; ". . . solicitor and overall protector of all the Indians". B. de Las Casas, *Historia de las Indias,* III, 90, BAE 96, 387–89; Constantino Bayle, *El protector de indios,* Publicaciones de la Escuela de Estudios Hispanoamericanos 10 (Sevilla 1945), 16.

57. CDIA 23, 310–31; CDIU 9, 53–74; J. Höffner, *Kolonialismus und Evangelium,* 198–200; M.A. Medina, *Una comunidad,* 153–59.

58. F. Moya Pons, *Manual de historia dominicana,* 29.

59. Letter d.d. 20 January 1517, CDIA 1, 264–81; Letter d.d. 22 June 1517, CDIA 1, 281–89; Manuel Giménez Fernández, *Bartolomé de Las Casas,* I, *Delegado de Cisneros para la reformación de las Indias 1516–1517,* 2nd edition (Madrid 1984), 295–339. The complicated consultation process of the Hieronymites is documented in E. Rodríguez Demorizi, *Los dominicos y las encomiendas,* 273–354.

60. The letter from the Dominicans at the end of April and the beginning of May 1517 and the two documents written by the Dominicans and the Franciscans (27 May and 4 June 1517) were edited by M.A. Medina, *Una comunidad,* 248–51, 252–57 and 269–87.

61 ". . . people who were so meek, so obedient and so good that if preachers were to enter into their ranks, as individuals who were not as powerful and as violent as these unfortunate Christians, I believe that they would be able to establish a church that would be almost as efficient as the original one". Letter from Pedro de Córdoba to the king dated 28 May 1517: M.A. Medina, *Una comunidad,* 264.

62. B. de Las Casas, *Historia de las Indias*, III, 93, BAE 96, 395. He wrote also that the priest of the mining region Arroyos had explained to the Hieronymites that the encomenderos were ill-treating the Indians, but that they did not take any initiative to protest against those abuses. Then the priest exclaimed: "*¿sabéis, padres reverendos, qué voy viendo? Pues no habéis de hacer a estos tristes indios más bien que los otros gobernadores, o no habéis de ser más que los otros gobernadores*" (Do you know Reverend Fathers, what I am beginning to realize? That you do not have to do more for these poor Indians than the other governors did, nor do you have to be more to them than the other governors were). In a letter dated 26 September 1517 from Pedro de Córdoba to Antonio Montesino, he explains that the Hieronymites hired a ship to transfer 155 Indians (young men and women) from the Costa de Perlas to La Española, where they were enslaved. M.A. Medina, *Una comunidad*, 115, 288–91.

63. The idea of a true, poor and pure church arose constantly in the Mendicant Orders; in those times, this spirituality was especially promoted by Erasmus (*Enchiridion militis christiani*, 1502) and Thomas More (*Utopia*, 1516). C.R. Boxer, *The Church Militant and the Iberian Expansion 1440–1770* (Baltimore and London 1978), 113–14 and M.A. Medina, *Una comunidad*, 181.

64. B. de Las Casas, *Historia de las Indias*, III, 83, BAE 96, 365–67; B. Biermann, *Die erste Dominikanermission*, 408–25; E. Otte, "Los jerónimos", 196.

65. Manuel Serrano y Sanz, *Orígenes de la dominación española en América*, I, 372–77; M.A. Medina, *Una comunidad*, 110–11; D. Ramos Pérez, "El P. Córdoba y Las Casas", 192–93.

66. Pedro de Córdoba sent information about those events to Las Casas in Spain through Friar Pedro de San Martín, who went to Spain in July 1518: B. de Las Casas, *Historia de las Indias*, III, 104, BAE 96, 422–25; M.A. Medina, *Una comunidad*, 115–16, 292.

67. Report (18 January 1518), CDIA 1, 298–304; G. Arciniegas, *Karibische Rhapsodie*, 72–73.

68. ". . . what has happened now is that since they were preparing to leave the mines in December last year to return to their villages, it pleased Our Lord to inflict an endless smallpox plague on the Indians". Report (10 January 1519), CDIA 1, 366–68; C.O. Sauer, *The Early Spanish Main*, 205.

69. Erwin W. Palm, *Los monumentos arquitectónicos de la Española*, I (Ciudad Trujillo 1955), 40, 93–95; L. Lopetegui and F. Zubillaga, *Historia de la iglesia*, 258–61; A. Lluberes, "La iglesia ante el indio", 395.

70. ". . . chief judge of the West Indies" (CDIA 23, 332–53).

71. M. Giménez Fernández, *Bartolomé de Las Casas* II, Capellán de S.M. Carlos I, polador de Cumaná 1511–1523, 2nd edition (Madrid 1984), 1033, note 3503; E. Otte, *Las perlas del Caribe* (Caracas 1977), 162–64. M.A. Medina, *Una comunidad*, 115.

72. Figueroa did not side with either the settlers (with their economic interests) or with the clergy (with their humanitarian vision); therefore he was criticized by

both sides. He wrote (CDIA 1, 418, 421): "*Aquí tenemos infinitos enojos e perjuicios a la jurisdicción Real por las descommuniones muchas e muy injustas, que los oficiales de las iglesias catedrales ponen a las justicias*"; "*Yo estoy martir e mal quisto por hacer penar a los, que los (indios) maltratan*" (Here we have many troubles and harm done to the royal jurisdiction by the excessive and unjust violation of the justices by officers of cathedrals; I am a martyr and am unpopular because I have made both sides suffer for having mistreated the Indians). E. Otte, *Las perlas del Caribe*, 166–68; Otte, "Los jerónimos", 204.

73. B. de Las Casas, *Historia de las Indias*, III, 156, BAE 96, 550–53; E. Otte, *Las perlas del Caribe*, 168–90; M.A. Medina, *Una comunidad*, 98–99, 115–16; D. Ramos Pérez, "El P. Córdoba y Las Casas", 202–7.

74. Frantisek Gel, *Las Casas, Leben und Werk* (Leipzig 1958), 36; B. Biermann, *Las Casas und seine Sendung*, 11.

75. F. Gel, *Las Casas*, 37; E. Otte, "La expedición de Gonzalo de Ocampo en Cumaná en 1521 en las cuentas de tesorería de Santo Domingo", *Revista de Indias* 16 (1956): 51–82.

76. L. Gómez Cañedo, "Primeros intentos de evangelización franciscana en tierra firme (1508–1553)", *Archivum Franciscanum Historicum* 50 (1957): 99–118; M. de Castro, "Misiones franciscanas en Cumaná", *Boletín de la Academia Nacional de la Historia* 45 (1962): 73–104.

77. B. de Las Casas, *Historia de las Indias*, III, 158–59, BAE 96, 557–64; E. Otte, *Las perlas del Caribe*, 190–93; Felix Becker, "Indianermission und Entwicklungsgedanke unter spanischer Kolonialherrschaft", in *Entwicklungsstrategien in Lateinamerika in Vergangenheit und Gegenwart*, edited by I. Buisson and M. Mols (Paderborn 1983), 45–66.

78. Concerning the circumstances and date of his death see M.A. Medina, *Una comunidad*, 46–50.

79. Pedro de Córdoba preached for the first time to the Tainos in Concepción de la Vega in 1510; B. de Las Casas, *Historia de las Indias*, II, 54, BAE 96, 134: "*él, asentado en un banco y en la mano un crucifijo y con algunas lenguas o intérpretes, comenzóles a predicar desde la creación del mundo, discurriendo hasta que Cristo, Hijo de Dios, se puso en la cruz. Fué sermón dignísimo . . ., de gran provecho*" (He was seated on a bench and had a crucifix in his hand and through different interpreters he began to preach to them about the creation of the world, right up to the time when Christ, the son of God, was nailed to the cross. It was a very commendable sermon . . . of great benefit).

80. ". . . Christian doctrine for the religious instruction of the Indians". Probably Betanzos and Zumárraga made some modifications to this text, applying it to the reality of Mexico: M.A. Medina, *Una comunidad*, 183–207; J.G. Durán (ed.), *Monumenta Catechetica Hispanoamericana*, I, 198–204, 209–13, and 227–83 (critical edition); Pedro de Córdoba, *Doctrina cristiana para instrucción e información de los indios, por manera de historia*, Publicaciones de la Universidad de Santo Domingo 38 (Ciudad Trujillo 1945), 1–61.

81. This bilingual edition does not mention Pedro de Córdoba as the author, but says it was *"hecha por los religiosos de la Orden de Santo Domingo"* (done by friars of the order of Santo Domingo); with respect to the edition of 1544 it contains some changes and appendices; in 1550 there were two new editions: J.G. Durán, *Monumenta Catechetica Hispanoamericana*, 205–6.

82. ". . . post-baptismal sermon immediately following the baptism". See E. Dussel, *Historia general de la iglesia*, I, 620–26. M.A. Medina, *Una comunidad*, 224–39.

83. J. Specker, "Die Einschätzung der Hl. Schrift in den spanisch-amerikanischen Missionen", in *Die Heilige Schrift in den katholischen Missionen*, edited by J. Beckmann, Neue Zeitschrift für Missionswissenschaft, Supplementa 14 (Schöneck-Beckenried 1966), 37–71; J.L. Saez, *Testigos de la esperanza*, 36; M.A. Medina, *Una comunidad*, 207–24, 244–45.

84. J. Specker, *Die Missionsmethode in Spanisch-Amerika im 16. Jahrhundert mit besonderer Berücksichtigung der Konzilien und Synoden*, Neue Zeitschrft für Missionswissenschaft, Supplementa 4 (Schöneck-Beckenried 1953), 110–13; M. Bataillon, *Erasmo y España, Estudios sobre la historia espiritual del siglo XVI*, 2nd edition (México and Buenos Aires 1966), 540–41, 821–27; W. Henkel, *Die Konzilien in Lateinamerika, I, Mexiko 1555–1897* (Paderborn 1984), 67–68.

85. G. Arciniegas, *Karibische Rhapsodie*, 73–74; F. Moya Pons, *Historia colonial de Santo Domingo* (Santiago de los Caballeros 1974), 71–73; Moya Pons, *Manual de historia dominicana*, 29.

86. P. Suess, "Glaubensfreiheit und Zwangsarbeit. Spanische Missionare", 300. The four contradictory decrees about the Indians' enslavement (dated 4 August 1525, 19 September 1528, 2 August 1530 and 20 February 1534) are documented in J. Friede, *Los Welser*, 620 n. 37, 621 n. 74, 623 n. 123, 625 n. 197. Julián Garcés, bishop of Tlaxcala (Mexico), was the first to receive the title of "protector de indios" (according to Las Casas, n. 56). E. Dussel, *El episcopado hispanoamericano, Institución misionera en defensa del indio (1504–1620)* (Cuernavaca 1969–70), III, 44–45.

87. B. de Las Casas, *Historia de las Indias*, III, 125–27. BAE, 476–84; B. Biermann, *Las Casas und seine Sendung*, 14–17; M.A. Peña Battle, *La rebelión del Bahoruco*, Colección Pensamiento Dominicano 45 (Santo Domingo 1970), 133–48; M. Bonetti, *Staat und Gesellschaft im karibischen Raum im 16. Jahrhundert*, 135–46; A. Lluberes, "La iglesia antel el indio", 395.

88. B. de Las Casas, *Historia de las Indias*, I, 110, BAE 95, 300 and *Historia de las Indias*, III, 160. BAE 96, 564–67; R. Hernández, "El misionero dominico fray Tomás de Berlanga", *Archivo Dominicano* 6 (1985): 57–93; H. Rand Parish, "Bartolomé de Las Casas, una saga para nuestro tiempo", in *Bartolomé de Las Casas – Liberación para los oprimidos*, edited by Marie Zobelein (Mission San José, California 1985), 4–17.

89. Archivo General de Indias (AGI), Santo Domingo 95, no. 8; B. de Las Casas, *Opúsculos, cartas y memoriales*, BAE 110 (Madrid 1958), 43–55; Gustavo Gutiérrez, "En busca de los pobres de Jesucristo. Evangelización y teología en el siglo XVI", in *Materiales para una historia de la teología en América Latina*, edited

by Pablo Richard (San José 1981), 137–63.

90. ". . . the path to righteousness and that Christ, our God came to show it to us". AGI, Santo Domingo 95, no. 11; B. de Las Casas, *Opúsculos, cartas y memoriales*, BAE 110, 58. He wrote this letter in Santo Domingo and the one quoted in Puerto de Plata.

91. B. Biermann, *Las Casas und seine Sendung*, 17; R. Hernández, "El misionero dominico fray Tomás de Berlanga", 78–79. H. Rand Parish, "Bartolomé de Las Casas, una saga para nuestro tiempo", 9–10.

92. AGI, Santo Domingo 95, no. 7. Before his departure for Mexico, Bishop Sebastián Ramírez de Fuenleal wrote to the emperor that in the Caribbean the cruelties committed by the traders against the black people continued and he criticized in particular the settlers of Santa Marta. AGI, Santo Domingo 93, no. 2.

93. E.W. Palm, *Los monumentos arquitectónicos*, I, 95–96 n. 291.

94. The statement made by Gonzalo Fernández de Oviedo in 1548 did not completely reflect reality: *"que hay al presente . . . quinientas personas entre chicos e grandes, que sean naturales e de la progenie o estirpe de aquellos primeros"* (there are currently . . . 500 people, including children and adults, natives and offspring of the first generation), he himself accepted: *"lo más, que ahora hay, son traídos por los cristianos de otras islas o de la tierra firme para se servir dellos"* (the others who are now there were brought by Christians from other islands or from the mainland to serve them). *Historia general y natural de las Indias*, BAE 117 (Madrid 1959), 66–67.

95. There are significant differences in population estimates. Eugenio Fernández Méndez (*Proceso histórico de la conquista de Puerto Rico, 1508–1640* [San Juan de Puerto Rico 1970], 24) estimates that there were 60,000 to 85,000 natives; according to Angel Rosenblat (*La población indígena y el mestizaje en América, 1492–1950*, I, *La población indígena* [Buenos Aires 1954], 102, 301–2), there were 50,000; nowadays his estimates are considered to be too low.

96. Antonio de la Gama was appointed "protector de indios". The bishop of Santo Domingo, Sebastián Ramírez de Fuenleal remained in San Juan in 1528 and he wrote: *"En lo tocante a los indios, entiendo en saber cuantos hay y como son tratados; los que en esta ciudad están encomendados, van los domingos desde septiembre al monasterio de Santo Domingo a las dos de la tarde, y los viernes van solas las mujeres y no los indios; los que están fuera de la ciudad no pueden ser así doctrinados y es gran dificultad proveer el cómo se conservarlán"* (I know how many Indians there are and how they are treated; those who are in the city under the encomienda system and go on Sundays, beginning in September, to the Santo Domingo monastery at 2 p.m., and on Fridays the women go alone without the Indian men. Those who are outside of the city are not taught in this manner and it is difficult to determine how they should be treated). L. Lopetegui and F. Zubillaga, *Historia de la iglesia*, 482–83.

97. A. Rosenblat, *La población indígena* I, 302; Juan Bosch, *De Cristóbal Colón a Fidel Castro, El Caribe, frontera imperial* (Madrid and Barcelona 1970), 88; E. Fernán-

dez Méndez, *Proceso histórico de la conquista de Puerto Rico*, 59.

98. J. Friede, *Los Welser*, 147–49, 541–46 and 586 n. 63.

99. A. Rosenblat, *La población indígena* I, 119 n. 1.

100. Cf. G. Sandner and H.-A. Steger, *Lateinamerika, Fischer-Länderkunde*, Bd. 7 (Frankfurt 1973), 192; N.L. Erskine, *Decolonizing theology: A Caribbean perspective* (Maryknoll 1981), 16.

101. F. Morales Padrón, *Jamaica española*, Publicaciones de la Escuela de Estudios Hispanoamericanos 67 (Sevilla 1952), 260–61, n. 3, 7, 8; A. Rosenblat, *La población indígena* I, 303.

102. B. de Las Casas, *Historia de las Indias*, III, 94, BAE 96, 397; F. Morales Padrón, *Jamaica española*, 264–66.

103. E. Dussel estimates that there were about 500,000 (*Historia General de la iglesia*, I/1, 225). Scholars agree that Cuba was less populated than La Española although Cuba (110.922 km^2) is one and a half times as big as La Española (76.484 km^2). W. Denevan, *The Native Population of the Americans in 1492*, 37–38.

104. CDIU 4, 252.

105. J. Castellanos, *Crónica de la rebeldía de los indios cubanos 1520–1550* (Havana 1959), 17–39; L. Marrero, *Cuba: economía y sociedad*, I, 184–88.

106. B. Biermann, "Zur Auseinandersetzung um die Menschenrechte der Indianer, Fray Bernardino de Minaya O.P. und sein Werk", *Neue Zeitschrift für Missionswissenschaft* 24 (1968): 179–89.

107. AGI, Patronato 1-1-1, no. 38 (43); Bulas y Breves, 23; B. de Tobar, *Compendio Bulario Indico*, I, Publicaciones de la Escuela de Estudios Hispanoamericanos 82 (Sevilla 1954), 216–17; F.J. Hernaez, *Colección de bulas, breves y otros documentos relativos a la iglesia de América y Filipinas*, I (Brussels 1879), 102–3; B. Biermann, "Die Anfänge der Dominikanertätigkeit in Neu-Spanien und Peru", *Archivum Fratrum Praedicatorum* 13 (1943): 5–58, 44–46; H. Pietschmann, "Die Kirche in Hispanoamerika", 19.

108. AGI, Patronato 1-1-1, no. 37 (42); Bulas y Breves, 22; B. de Tobar, *Compendio Bulario Indico*, I, 209; F.J. Hernaez, *Colección de bulas*, I, 101–2.

109. B. de Tobar, *Compendio Bulario Indico*, I, 210–16. F.J. Hernaez, *Colección de bulas*, I, 65–67; E. Dussel, *El episcopado hispanoamericano*, IX, 162–66; Dussel, *Historia General de la iglesia*, I/1, 614.

110. B. Biermann, "Die Anfänge der Dominikanertätigkeit in Neu–Spanien und Peru", *Archivum fratum Praedicatorum* 13 (1943): 5–58; Biermann, "Zur Auseinandersetzung um die Menschenrechte der Indianer", 183–84.

111. "Not for war nor for any reason whatsoever shall an Indian be made a slave; and we wish for them to be treated as vassals of the Castillian kingdom, which they are." J. Höffner, *Kolonialismus und Evangelium*, 203–4; B. Biermann, *Las Casas und seine Sendung*, 56 n. 27; G. Kahle, "Bartolomé de Las Casas" (Köln-Opladen 1968), 17–18; P. Castañeda Delgado, "Un problema ciudadano: La tributación urbana", 509.

112. ". . . in order that the natives be well instructed and well treated . . .; there are not even sixty Indians among the adults and children on this island who are natives and this small number happily received the blessing and they are quite capable of recognizing that they are being well-treated". AGI, Santo Domingo 172, no. 11. Bastidas also explains that the plan to unite the Indians of Puerto Rico in one community was cancelled, because they considered this a "pesadumbre" (affliction).

113. In his letter from Santo Domingo (15 September 1544) to Prince Phillip, Las Casas dealt with the first negative reactions to the "Nuevas Leyes" and insisted that in no way should they be abolished: B. de Las Casas, *Opúsculos, cartas y memoriales*, BAE 110, 213–15.

114. J. Specker, "Kirchliche und staatliche Siedlungspolitik", 434–38; Silvio Zavala, *Aspectos religiosos de la historia colonial americana*, Estudios históricos (Guadalajara, México 1959), 23, 27–28; H. Schottelius, "Die spanische Conquista", *Saeculum* 3 (1952): 161–74; B. Biermann, Las Casas und seine Sendung, 30–31; G. Kahle, "Bartolomé de Las Casas", 25; E. Grewal, "Die Indianer", 71; E. Dussel, *Historia General de la iglesia* I/1: 390; H. Pietschmann, "Die Kirche in Hispanoamerika", 24–25.

115. In 1680 the legislation still required that Indians "sean castigados como justamente merecieren" (be punished as they deserve to be). *Recopilación de Leyes de los Reynos de las Indias*, edited by Ramón Menéndez Piotal and Juan Manzano Manzano, Book III, Title IV, Art. 9 (Madrid 1973), II, f. 25r. In the same way, the Crown continued to consider the enslavement of the Caribs legal in the Lesser Antilles. See J. Friede, *Los Welser*, 543–65.

116. "As the Indians are in a state of servitude in which they have always been held . . . and this is what happens because Your Highness knows that I have done all that I can and I am not responsible for the shortcoming." AGI, Santo Domingo 94, no. 14.

117. CDIU 18, 10.

118. E. Rodríguez Demorizi, *Relaciones históricas de Santo Domingo*, I (Ciudad Trujillo 1942), 136–37.

119. J. López de Velasco, *Geografía y descripción universal de las Indias*, BAE 248 (Madrid 1971), 52; B. Biermann, "Die 'Geografía y descripción universal de las Indias' des Juan López de Velasco als Quelle fur die Missionsgeschichte", *Neue Zeitschrift für Missionswissenschaft* 17 (1961): 291–302.

120. Letter to the King (21 July 1571), C. de Utrera, *Dilucidaciones históricas*, I (Santo Domingo 1927), 303; Letter to the King (20 April 1572), AGI, Santo Domingo 93, no. 17.

121. In the "Relación sobre cosas de la Isla Española" of Jerónimo de Torres: E. Rodríguez Demorizi, *Relaciones históricas de Santo Domingo*, II (Ciudad Trujillo 1945), 131.

122. "None of the questions was relevant to the island because there are no doctrines for the Indians nor were there any records on them and on the more than

1,600,000 families in the island when the Spaniards arrived." Letter dated 5 January 1608, AGI, Santo Domingo 93, no. 63.

In the community of Boya, the Indians survived until the seventeenth century; around 1650, Luis Jerónimo Alcocer wrote: "*los indios se an acabado: solo resta de ellos un pueblo, que llaman Boya, que oy no tiene seis vecinos*" (the Indians have been exterminated: there are only a few of them in a town called Boya which today does not have six inhabitants). E. Rodríguez Demorizi, *Relaciones históricas de Santo Domingo*, I, 209.

123. "Each day the numbers continued to fall and they increased in no way." AGI, Santo Domingo 172, no. 16; E. Fernández Méndez, *Proceso histórico de la conquista de Puerto Rico*, 82.

124. J. López de Velasco, *Geografía y descripción universal*, 67–68; B. Biermann, "Die 'Geografía'", 293–94.

125. ". . . as they had been exterminated".

126. ". . . who had come from the mainland, they do not know any other language but ours". AGI, Santo Domingo 174, no. 26, f. 1r.

127. Melgarejo estimates that there were 12 to 15 Indians: E. Williams (ed.), *Documents of West Indian History I (1492–1655): From the Spanish Discovery to the British Conquest of Jamaica* (Port of Spain 1963), 85.

128. AGI, Santo Domingo 172, no. 15. Bastidas made the following comment about the inhabitants of Mona: "*Son de razón y venden su miseria a navios que alli llegan, y son capaces de contratarla*" (They are well ordered, they sell their trifles to the ships that go there and they are adept at peddling).

129. E. Rodríguez Demorizi, *Relaciones históricas de Santo Domingo*, I, 136.

130. Letter dated 3 January 1578, AGI, Santo Domingo 172, no. 49.

131. See J. López de Velasco, *Geografía y descripción universal*, 62; B. Biermann, "Die 'Geografía'", 293–94.

132. F. Morales Padrón, *Jamaica española*, 264 n. 15, 266 n. 23 and n. 24.

133. Ibid., *Jamaica española*, 266–67 n. 25.

134. AGI, Santo Domingo 177, no. 78.

135. R. Konetzke, *Colección de documentos para la historia de la formación social de Hispanoamérica, 1493–1810*, I (Madrid 1953), 197–98.

136. Sarmiento insisted that the Indians should be put to work during the three or four months that the "Leyes de Burgos y Valladolid" (1512–13) granted them free: "*como los yndios no tengan que hazer, no se ocuparán sino en areitos y en otros vicios . . . y en los quatro meses que les dan de huelga no se ocupan sino en esto y en andarse pescando por los ríos . . . que más servicio de Dios sería que les hiziesen travajar los quatro meses que huelgan . . .*" (as the Indians do not have any work, they will have time to get involved in parties and other vices . . . and during the four months resting period, they spend their time doing only this and going fishing in the river . . . it would be better service to God to make them work during these four months). Letter of 15 June 1543, CDIU 6, 184; T.G. Werner, "Das Kupferhüttenwerk des Hans Tetzel aus Nürnberg auf Kuba

(1545–1571) und seine Beziehungen zu europäischem Finanzkapital", *Viertel-jahrschrift für Sozial und Wirtschaftsgeschichte* 48 (1961): 289–328, 444–502; L. Marrero, *Cuba: economía y sociedad*, I, 189.

137. CDIU 6, 221–232. A. Rosenblat, *La población indígena*, I, 299–300, 301; I. Testé, *Historia eclesiástica de Cuba*, I, 77–83; J.A. Carreras, *Terratenientes e iglesia en Cuba colonial* (Havana 1972), 147–57.

138. In 1533 there were 212 Indians in Baracao. E. Bacardi y Moreau (ed.), *Crónicas de Santiago de Cuba*, I re-edited by Amalia Bacardi Cape (Madrid 1972), 94.

139. Protest letters of settlers and city councillors (22 and 31 March 1544), CDIU 6, 210–12 and 213–18. Report (30 June 1546) of Governor Chávez, with a critical evaluation of the evangelization process of the Indians: they had "*poca boluntad . . . a las cosas de la fe . . . no guardan la horden de la yglesia*" (little will . . . to be converted to the faith . . . they do not respect the order of the church); used as an argument critical of the liberation of the Indians, that "*la livertad de los cuerpos no les cause mayor cativerio en sus animas*" (freedom of the body may not lead to greater enslavement of their souls). CDIU 6, 271.

140. A. Rosenblat, *La población indígena*, I, 300; J. Castellanos, *Crónica de la rebeldía de los indios cubanos*, 53; I. Testé, *Historia eclesiástica de Cuba*, II, 319–20 and V, 31–32. Bishop Uranga proposed (20 April 1556) the introduction in Cuba of Indian women from Florida. AGI, Santo Domingo 115, f. 179r–181v; CDIA 5, 553–55.

141. " . . . a Caneyes Indian town in which there were twenty houses". J. López de Velasco, *Geografía y descripción universal*, 57–59. Something similar appears in the report of Bishop Castillo's visit (1569–70). See I. Testé, *Historia eclesiástica de Cuba*, I, 90.

142. They could not participate in the elections for councillors nor could they be registered in the same ecclesiastical books as the settlers; see: L. Lopetegui and F. Zubillaga, *Historia de la iglesia*, 471.

143. " . . . that he remove and ensure that they be given justice, because giving them a protector was the same as giving them an 'encomendero'. They were all very poor as all farmlands had been taken by the Spaniards; they are like strangers there and it seems only fair that they should be rid of all inconveniences." AGI, Santo Domingo 150, no. 17. Castillo made reference to the following event: "*Yo vi, cuando me venia de camino que acabava de visitar a los yndios de La Çavana, el teniente Carillo, vezino que es del Puerto de Principe, y les avia llevado a quatro reales a cada yndio, y yo sé, que su visita no fue de ningun provecho a los yndios, más de dexar catorze yndios en poder de Juan de Yllanes, alcalde y protector, que traya a montear para vender carne para un barco de la Florida que allí estava, e hiziera mejor visita el teniente, si pusiera los yndios en su libertad para que hizieran la carne y la vendieran por su cuenta, pues cierto que no avia otros tantos en el pueblo*" (When I was on my way after having just visited the Indians in La Cavana, I saw Lieutenant Carillo, resident of Puerto de Principe [= Camagüey], who had given each Indian 1 peseta and I know that his visit was of no benefit to the

Indians, except to leave fourteen Indians in the power of Juan de Yllanes, mayor and protector, who took them hunting in order to sell meat to a ship from Florida that was there, and the lieutenant's visit would be of more benefit, if he were to free the Indians so that they could get the meat and sell it themselves, as it is certain that there weren't others like them in the town).

144. " . . . special priest who would attend to the Indians since they were unjustly treated by the Spaniards". AGI, Santo Domingo 150, no. 17.

145. The one hundred inhabitants were distributed in twenty houses; according to the bishop's description (dated 20 September 1608) it was like a *"pueblo de yndios aunque españolados"*. *"Tiene correspondencia con Cartagena y Florida y este puerto (La Habana); tiene palo de hebano y algunas monterias de ganado mayor y corrales de ganado menor"* (. . . a town of Indians although they were Hispanicized. They are in contact with Cartagena and Florida and this port [Havana]; it has ebony trees and some big game hunting grounds and small cattle farms for goats and pigs). AGI, Santo Domingo 150, no. 48. He wrote in his "Visita a Cuba y Florida" (24 June 1606): "Baracoa es un pueblo, que está en el extremo de la isla y de los menores de toda ella, donde los más son indios" (Baracao is a town located on the end of the island; it is among the smallest one on the island where the majority are Indians). AGI, Santo Domingo 150, no. 34, f. 4r.

146. "Minuta y padrón de la gente y casas de la ciudad de Santiago de Cuba fecho ano de 1604", AGI, Santo Domingo 150, no. 33. Of the 77 Indians, 41 were men and 36 women, 6 lived as slaves in the houses of the white inhabitants and 71 were *"naturales, que residen en esta ciudad de Cuba"* (natives who live in this city of Cuba), living in the Indian community of El Caney or Los Caneyes.

147. I. Macias, *Cuba en la primera mitad del siglo XVII*, Publicaciones de la Escuela de Estudios Hispanoamericanos 251 (Sevilla 1978), 21–25.

148. " . . . having already been Hispanicized". AGI, Santo Domingo 150, no. 48; I.A. Wright, *Historia documentada de San Cristóbal de la Habana en la primera mitad del siglo XVII* (Havana 1930), 25 n. 4.

149. I. Macias, *Cuba en la primera mitad del siglo XVII*, 32–34.

150. "Visita de Cuba y Florida" (24 June 1606), AGI, Santo Domingo 150, no. 34, f. 3v–4r.

151. Letter written by Bishop Ramírez de Fuenleal from Santo Domingo (dated 11 August 1531), AGI, Santo Domingo 93, no. 2.

152. ". . . who were brought to this island whether as free men or slaves, . . . and better yet free, although they were Caribs". AGI, Santo Domingo 93, no. 17.

153. AGI, Santo Domingo 172, no. 49.

154. AGI, Santo Domingo 172, no. 62.

155. In 1628, Vázquez de Espinosa estimated that there were 18,000 natives in the Lesser Antilles. He was in favour of the control of the Caribs by Spain and had a very negative opinion of the inhabitants of Grenada: A. Vázquez de Espinosa, *Compendio y descripción de las Indias occidentales*, II/XVIII, 198–200, BAE 231 (Madrid 1969), 56. With regard to the other events: P. Castañeda Delgado, "La

política española con los Caribes durante el siglo XVI", *Revista de Indias* 30 (1970): 73–130; P. Ashdown, *Caribbean History in Maps,* 12 (16) and 21 (32).

156. R. Konetzke, *Süd-und Mittelamerika* I, 302–3; J. Friede, *Los Welser,* 146–50.

157. About this tribe: M. Acosta Saignes, *Estudios de etnología antigua de Venezuela,* Ediciones de la Biblioteca de la Universidad Central de Venezuela III, Colección Ciencias Sociales 2, 2nd edition (Caracas 1961), 169–87.

158. AGI, Santo Domingo 172, nos. 28 and 29.

159. Declaration of 8 July 1561, AGI, Santo Domingo 172, no. 31.

160. "The inhabitants of that island are all poor; they are all sustained by a limited supply of livestock and cornfields that they own and maintain by the sweat of the Indians, the natives and others brought from the mainland, and I will be untruthful if I say that there is a difference between them and the slaves and that secretly they are kidnapped and sold; they are brought to the island, sold and contracted to work. I have done all that I can where this matter is concerned, it is now in the hands of those who govern. I have to recount what is happening and also that without this situation they cannot survive. The natives are ill-treated by those who govern them and by those with whom they work which forces them into the mountains; they need to be protected. I am writing the Bishop of Chiapa to request that he demand this of the Royal Council and in so doing relieve myself of that responsibility". Letter dated 9 July 1561, AGI, Santo Domingo 172, no. 32; F.A. Maldonado, *Analectas de historia eclesiástica venezolana, Seis primeros obispos de la iglesia venezolana en la época hispánica, 1532–1600,* Biblioteca de la Academia Nacional de la Historia, Fuentes para la historia colonial de Venezuela 117 (Caracas 1973), 66.

161. " . . . to arrange for the salvation of so many lost people in that island as well as neighbouring ones". AGI, Santo Domingo 174, no. 26, f. 5r.

162. "The Indians unfortunately are not concerned with their salvation, and I believe that for many of them baptism only signifies more pain and suffering, especially the Guayqueríes Indians who are always wandering throughout the mountains and wilderness." Letter dated 19 January 1589, AGI, Santo Domingo 172, no. 65. E. Dussel, *El episcopado hispanoamericano* IV, 83–84.

163. Letter dated 17 June 1594: AGI, Santo Domingo 172, no. 71.

164. " . . . ignorance of the gospel"; " . . . settle them in a village, providing them with a priest who will instruct them and administer the sacraments". Letter dated 2 October 1602, AGI, Santo Domingo 172, no. 73; E. Dussel, *El episcopado hispanoamericano,* IV, 86: "*y porque entienda V.M. a quanto extremo llega esto que no lo puedo referir a V.M. sin gran dolor, sentimiento de mi alma, saliendo el otro dia el sanctíssimo sacramento para darse a un enfermo . . . yendo yo acompañarlos, y con decirles que se hincasen como lo hacian los demás fieles cristianos, no hicieron movimiento, sino que se estuvieron sentados y comiendo, es negocio este en que V.M. a de mandar poner remedio*" (and so that your Majesty may understand the extremes to which this has gone, I relate to your Majesty with great sorrow and a heavy heart that the other day I was with them and on taking out the holy sacrament

to administer it to a sick man I asked them to kneel as other faithful Christians did and they did not budge but remained seated and eating. Your Majesty must command that an end be put to this state of affairs).

165. In response to those accusations, Bishop Vázquez argued with Governor Fadrique Cáncer. AGI, Santo Domingo 172, no. 74, 74 A and B. Similar accusations appeared in a letter dated 26 July 1604, AGI, Santo Domingo 172, no. 75; C. Campo Lacasa, *Historia de la iglesia en Puerto Rico 1511-1802* (San Juan, Puerto Rico 1977), 50: "*Los gobernadores les obligan a que les sustenten sus casas de leña, pescado, sal, conejos venados y otras cosas sin darles un maravedí. No sé que ley divina ni humana manda hacer esto. . . . Otra de las vejaciones mayores es que les obligan por fuerza a pescar perlas de los que se quejan los indios. Igual que este gobernador hacia el anterior*" (The governors oblige them to keep firewood, fish, salt, rabbits, deer and other things in their house without giving them a penny. I do not know which divine or human law decrees this . . . another irksome matter is that they are obliged to fish for pearls about which the Indians complain. This governor does the same as his predecessor).

166. "Census", AGI, Santo Domingo 172, no. 75, f. 65r–69r; E. Dussel, *El episcopado hispanoamericano*, VIII, 12–34.

167. E. Dussel, *El episcopado hispanoamericano*, IV, 87 n. 122; R. de Roux (ed.), *Historia general de la iglesia*, VII, 176.

168. A. Vázquez de Espinosa, *Compendio y descripción de las Indias occidentales*, 39, described in 1628 the "Guaiqueríes" as "*caballeros y nobles por merced que Su Majestad les ha hecho, por lo bien, que le han servido con fidelidad y lealtad en todas las occasiones, que se han ofrecido*" (made gentlemen and nobles by Her Majesty because they have served faithfully and loyally on all occasions).

169. This parish was first mentioned in a document d.d. 9 February 1632. AGI, Santo Domingo 192, no. 9.

170. AGI, Santo Domingo 179, nos. 50 and 50A.

171. A. Caulín, *Historia de la Nueva Andalucía*, Biblioteca de la Academia Nacional de la Historia, Fuentes para la historia colonial de Venezuela 81–82 (Caracas 1966), I, 323–24 n. 12; C. Campo Lacasa, *Historia de la iglesia en Puerto Rico*, 71; J.T. Harricharan, *The Catholic Church in Trinidad 1498–1852* (Port of Spain 1981), 18.

172. R. de Roux, *Historia general de la iglesia*, VII, 66–70.

173. C. de Armellada (ed.), "Concilio Provincial de Santo Domingo, 1622–1623", *Missionalia Hispanica* 27 (1970): 129–252; J. Meier, "Das Provinzialkonzil von Santo Domingo (1622–1623). Seine Aussagen über kirchliche Rechte und Pflichten der Indianer und Afrikaner in den karibischen Ländern", *Annuarium Historiae Conciliorum* 12 (1980): 441–51, 446; Bishop Angulos' interest was due to the fact that large groups of Indians were to be found only in his diocese (with the exception of Florida and the "Anejos" of the diocese of Puerto Rico).

174. Sessio VI, ch. I, n. 1–3: C. de Armellada, "Concilio Provincial de Santo Domingo, 1622–1623", 218–19. These regulations were similar to those of the great provincial councils of Mexico and Lima of the second half of the six-

teenth century. J. Specker, *Die Missionsmethode in Spanisch-Amerika*, 100–104; A. M. Heinrichs, "La cooperación del poder civil en la evangelización de Hispanoamérica y de las islas Filipinas" (Diss., Univ. Laval, Laval 1971), 183–84.

175. Sessio VI, ch. II, n. 1–2: C. de Armellada, "Concilio Provincial", 219.

176. Sessio VI, ch. III–V: C. de Armellada, "Concilio Provincial", 220–21.

177. Sessio VI, ch. VI, n. 1–4: C. de Armellada, "Concilio Provincial", 222–23.

178. Sessio VI, ch. VII, n. 1–6 and 8–13: C. de Armellada, "Concilio Provincial", 223–31.

179. J. Specker, *Kirchliche und staatliche Siedlungspolitik*, 427–31.

180. Sessio VI, ch. IX, n. 1: C. de Armellada, "Concilio Provincial", 232–33.

181. Sessio VI, ch. IX, n. 3: C. de Armellada, "Concilio Provincial", 234.

182. Sessio VI, ch. IX, n. 5: C. de Armellada, "Concilio Provincial", 235.

183. Sessio VI, ch. VII, n. 15 and 16: C. de Armellada, "Concilio Provincial", 230–31.

184. Sessio VI, ch. IX, n. 6: C. de Armellada, "Concilio Provincial", 236–37. This prohibition was in accordance with the "Ordenanzas sobre descubrimientos" of Phillip II (1573). CDIA 8, 484–537 and 16, 141–87; C.R. Boxer, *The Church Militant and the Iberian Expansion*, 71–72.

185. Sessio VI, ch. IX, n. 7: C. de Armellada, "Concilio Provincia", 237.

186. J. Meier, "Das Provinzialkonzil von Santo Domingo", 446 and 449–50.

187. With reference to the preparation for the first communion: "*Indorum ineptitudo . . . efficit, ut plures cognitione et necessaria dispositione ad sanctissimum Eucharistiae sacramentum suscipiendum careant.*" Sessio VI, ch. IV, n. 1: C. de Armellada, "Concilio Provincia", 220–21. But the council was not happy with this situation and insisted that the priest provide the Indians with a proper Christian education and give the Holy Communion to the "*rite pro captu dispositis*".

188. They constantly made reference to the "ruditas" (primitive ways) of the Indians. The Council unequivocally justified the exclusion of the Indians from the priestly ordination: "*ex natura sua ad ebrietatem, libidinem, et idololatriam ita sunt proni, ut facile ad gentilitatem redeant . . . Insuper ipsi propter nativam barbariam et abreptam vitae normam ita in his partibus apud omnes vilescunt, ut in eorum conspectu servi ethiopes tanquam superiores compareant.*" Sessio II, ch. III, n. 2: C. de Armellada, "Concilio Provincial", 150–51.

189. H. Pietschmann, "Die Kirche in Hispanoamerika", 36–37.

190. R. Konetzke, "Christentum und Conquista im spanischen Amerika", *Saeculum* 23 (1973): 59–73.

191. "Some Christian men may marry Indian women and Christian women may marry some Indians; so they may communicate with and teach each other in order that they may learn about our holy Catholic faith." Konetzke, *Colección de documentos* I, 12; M.T. Villafañe Casal, "La mujer española en la conquista y colonización de América", *Cuadernos Hispanoamericanos* 175/176 (1964): 125–42; M. Mörner, "La corona española y los foráneos en los pueblos de indios

de América", in *Skrifter utgivna av Latinamerika-institutet i Stockholm*, Series A, Monografier 1 (Stockholm 1970), 22.

192. R. Konetzke, *Süd-und Mittelamerika*, I, 65–66.

193. ". . . that labourers were coming to cultivate the land, especially from Portugal who are great farmers". AGI, Santo Domingo 93, no. 17. The bishop of Puerto Rico, Diego de Salamanca, was also in favour of the Portuguese settlers and wrote (dated 3 January 1578, AGI, Santo Domingo 172, no. 49): "*y no paresce ser ynconveniente, que estos pobladores o parte dellos fuesen portugueses porque para este efecto apruevan por aca tambien o mejor que los castellanos*" (It does not seem inappropriate that these colonists or some of them were Portuguese because they proved themselves as good or better than the Spaniards).

194. The ban against Portuguese settlers was strictly applied even at the beginning of the sixties; the lack of white settlers, however, led to a change: M. Bataillon, "Santo Domingo era Portugal", in *Historia y sociedad en el mundo de habla española, Homenaje a José Miranda* (Mexico 1970), 113–20.

195. R. Konetzke, *Süd-und Mittelamerika*, I, 70–71; Konetzke, "Christentum und Conquista im spanischen Amerika", 62; B. Boyd-Bowman, "Patterns of Spanish Emigration to the Indies until 1600", *Hispanic American Historical Review* 56 (1976): 580–604.

196. M. Mörner, "Evolución demográfica de Hispanoamérica", 8–9 and 65.

197. The most important source is *Geografía y descripción de las Indias* by Juan López de Velasco. Cf. M. Mörner, "Evolución demográfica de Hispanoamérica", 10.

198. R. Konetzke, *Süd-und Mittelamerika*, I, 103. The Caribbean became a marginal region of "Las Indias" around the mid seventeenth century: B. Slicher von Bath, "Economic diversification in Spanish America around 1600: Centres, intermediate zones and peripheries", *Jahrbuch für Geschichte von Staat, Wirtschaft und Gesellschaft Lateinamerikas* 16 (1979): 53–95; Slicher von Bath, *Spaans Amerika omstreeks 1600* (Utrecht and Antwerp 1979), 76–85, 98–99.

199. "For the most part, people who live in these areas leave each day to go and live in other new town." AGI, Santo Domingo 94, no. 6; E. Williams, *Documents of West Indian History*, I, 39–40.

200. I. Wright, *Historia documentada de San Cristóbal de La Habana*, 26–27; L. Marrero, *Cuba: economía y sociedad*, II, 381–82.

201. With respect to these citizens from San Juan de Puerto Rico, Bernardo de Balbuena said on 22 November 1623: "*Los ciudadanos del estado de los caballeros que en esta ciudad hay muchos de calidad conocida aunque pobres por no ser la tierra de mas sustancias, se tratan sino con superflua pompa con buen lustre y autoridad de sus personas; acuden bien a sus obligaciones y en las del culto divino se extreman notablemente y no dudan de empeñarse por este fin mas que por ninguna otra causa profana*" (Citizens of the status of gentlemen there are many in this city of great recognized quality although they are poor and because the land is not fertile they do not treat each other with unnecessary pomp, but with honour and authority; they fulfil their obligations and in matters relating to the divine faith show

themselves to be noble and they spare no effort to this end more so than for profane matters). AGI, Santo Domingo 172, no. 99.

202. Quotation from Bishop Damián López de Haro (dated 27 September 1644) by C. Campo Lacasa, *Historia de la iglesia en Puerto Rico*, 75.

203. Document dated 18 September 1619, AGI, Santo Domingo 93, no. 73 bis.

204. ". . . as if each holiday was Christmas".

205. ". . . because they said that they have already attended mass in the morning".

206. ". . . as if they were pagans and women primarily were absent".

207. ". . . did not have dresses and that some men did not have clothes".

208. "Not more than twenty women hear the sermon, because they are too vain; if they did not have silk and other fancy clothing to wear, they did not want to come to church, even though they were wives of officials."

209. Document dated 12 February 1625, AGI, Santo Domingo 93, no. 85. On 26 March 1626, the archbishop complained again about the same problem. See AGI, Santo Domingo 93, no. 88.

210. ". . . rebel freedom that they enjoyed, almost oblivious of God and the King". C. Campo Lacasa, *Historia de la iglesia en Puerto Rico*, 73. The quotation is from a letter written by Bishop Diego de Salamanca of Puerto Rico (dated 3 January 1578). AGI, Santo Domingo 172, no. 49.

211. Cf. the "Real cédula" (Royal Document) to Governor Ovando on 30 April 1508, CDIU 5, 126–27.

212. ". . . in a very indecent manner". See for example the documents dated 12 April 1609 and 13 and 21 April 1612, AGI, Santo Domingo 150, no. 64, A–C.

213. A. Cuesta Mendoza, *Historia eclesiástica del Puerto Rico Colonial*. Vol. I: *1508–1700* (Ciudad Trujillo: 1948), 242.

214. Bishop Manuel de Mercado wrote on 1 March 1573 about the lack of oil, candles and wine in Puerto Rico. AGI, Santo Domingo 172, no. 39. His successor, Diego de Salamanca, complained on 4 April 1579 about the lack of altar ornaments, liturgical clothing and prayerbooks. AGI, Santo Domingo 172, no. 51.

215. "He sings reasonably simple songs in a beautiful voice and very ably fulfils his duties." Document dated 31 December 1582, AGI, Santo Domingo 150, no. 17.

216. Document of the sacristan (dated 10 October 1594), AGI, Santo Domingo 153, no. 57. Silvestre de Balboa dedicated the last strophe of his poem "Espejo de paciencia" to the sacristan, "*a quien todo el Bayamo estima y aprecia*". P.A. Morell de Santa Cruz, *Historia de la isla y catedral de Cuba* (Havana 1929), 175–76; A. Carpentier, *La música en Cuba* (Havana 1961), 34.

217. The oldest registration in Cuba was the baptism of Beatriz Carrión y Osorio in Havana in 1582. I. Testé, *Historia eclesiástica de Cuba*, V, 121.
There are old church registers from Trinidad (from 1585), Guanabacoa and Sancti Spiritus (from 1608), and from Santiago de Cuba (from 1662). Cf. the observations of Francisco Morales Padrón in his preface to I. Macias, *Cuba en la primera mitad del siglo XVII*, XVI. The Abbott Francisco Márquez de Villalobos from Jamaica wrote on 8 November 1582: "*Esta ysla nunca a sido visitada por*

ningun abad ni an tenido orden ni pulicia en inguna cossa; solo halle un libro de baup-tismo desojado ya pocos años que no avia ninguno; porque mas cuydado tenian los abades de adquirir alguna hazienda que de acudir a lo que eran obligados" (This island has never been visited by any abbot nor had any kind of order or management of any kind. I only found a ragged baptismal book where a few years ago there was none. All because the abbots were more intent on acquiring a sugar planta-tion than in performing their duties). AGI, Santo Domingo 177, no. 67. In Santo Domingo there are baptismal matriculations from 1590 in the archives of the cathedral. R. Bello Peguero (ed.), *Cofradía de Nuestra Señora del Carmen y Jesús Nazareno 1592–1872*, Documentos eclesiásticos de Santo Domingo I (Santo Domingo 1974), VII.

218. A. Cuesta Mendoza, *Historia eclesiástica*, 232–33; M.A. Rodríguez León, "Sínodo de San Juan de Puerto Rico de 1645, Introducción", *Sínodos Americanos*, 4, edited by H. Santiago-Otero and A. García y García (Madrid and Salamanca 1986), xxxi–xxxiii.

219. A. Cuesta Mendoza, *Historia eclesiástica*, 239; M.A. Rodríguez León, "Sínodo de San Juan", xxi–xxxv.

220. Cf. AGI, Santo Domingo 172, nos. 79 and 80.

221. AGI, Santo Domingo 150, no. 34, f. 7r: *"Suplico a V.Magd., se sirva de que se de orden, como no vivan apartados de sus mugeres por la mejor traza, que a V.Magd. le pareciera, pues es servicio de Dios, nro. señor"* (I entreat Your Majesty to order them not to live separated from their wives for such greater good as is deemed by Your Majesty for it is all in the service of our Lord God), Bishop Juan de las Cabezas Altamirano.

222. AGI, Santo Domingo 177, no. 78: *"hallo cundido este pecado con tan graves raices y circunstancias que me tiene atajado y suspenso sin saber por donde caminar porque si no es despoblando la tierra y lastimando muchas onrras no se puede apagar fuego tan grande porque las censuras y otros medios eclesiasticos mas sirven aquí de lacos que no de remedio"* (I have found this sin to be rife and has such serious roots and cir-cumstances that I am ashamed and overcome by confusion and know not which way to turn because if the land is not wasted and many honours besmirched a fire of this magnitude cannot be put out because censure and other ecclesiastical measures serve more as palliatives than as a remedy). Abbot Bernardo de Bal-buena on 14 July 1611.

223. A. Cuesta Mendoza, *Historia eclesiástica*, 237–38, 246; M.A. Rodríguez León, "Sínodo de San Juan", xixxx f.

224. Recopilación, Book I, Title XVIII, Art. 4 (I, f. 89v–90r): *"Encargamos a los Provinciales, Prelados y otros Religiosos y Clérigos, que tengan mucho cuidado en los sermones, consejos y confessiones de dar á entender á los vezinos como deven principal-mente tener atencion en las buenas obras que hizieren y mandaren en sus ultimas vol-untades á aquella tierra, Iglesias y lugares pios, y personas pobres"* (We charge the superiors of the provinces, prelates and other religious persons and clergymen to take care in sermons, advice and confessions to make residents understand how

they should primarily pay attention to good works and that they should bequeath their estate to the churches, pious places and poor persons).

225. L. Marrero, *Cuba: economía y sociedad*, II, 381–82.

226. L. Lopetegui and F. Zubillaga, *Historia de la iglesia*, 472–73.

227. ". . . that most of the Spaniards who belonged to the bishopric did not recite the prayers of the church". AGI, Santo Domingo 94, no. 20.

228. The quotation is taken from a letter written by Friar Luis de Quero (dated 24 August 1608), who defended Osorio's politics. AGI, Santo Domingo 97, no. 27.

229. ". . . by condition of a donation". Document dated 20 April 1576, AGI, Santo Domingo 93, no. 20.

230. Documents dated 3 January 1578 and 4 April 1579, AGI, Santo Domingo 172, nos. 49 and 51.

231. A. Cuesta Mendoza, *Historia eclesiástica*, 234–36; M.A. Rodríguez León, "Sínodo de San Juan", xxxvi–xxxvii.

232. The Dominicans of San Juan expressed themselves positively on this issue concerning Governor Sancho Ochoa de Castro of Puerto Rico. Document dated 20 February 1604, AGI, Santo Domingo no. 71.

233. E. Dussel, *Historia General de la iglesia* I/1, 598–601; H. Pietschmann, "Die Kirche in Hispanoamerika", 37–38; M.A. Rodríguez León, "Sínodo de San Juan", liii–liv.

234. "Fraternity of our Lady of the Immaculate Conception".

235. C. de Utrera, *La Inmaculada Concepción*, Documentos y noticias para la historia de la arquidiócesis de Sto. Domingo, primada de América (Ciudad Trujillo 1946), 22–27; A. Lugo, *Edad media de la isla Española, Historia de Santo Domingo desde el 1556 hasta 1608* (Ciudad Trujillo 1952), 291–92 and 326–27; E.W. Palm, *Los monumentos arquitectónicos de la Española*, II (Ciudad Trujillo 1955), 25, 61–62; M.I. Paredes Vera, "San Nicolás de Bari en la Española, primer hospital de América", *Anuario de Estudios Americanos* 33 (1976): 933–48.

236. "Fortune only befalls ten to twelve rich and powerful people." AGI, Santo Domingo 93, no. 73 bis.

237. "Fraternity of the Miracles of our Lady of Carmen and of Jesus of Nazareth." C. de Utrera, *Santo Domingo, Dilucidaciones históricas*, I (Santo Domingo 1927), 282–86; E.W. Palm, *Los monumentos arquitectónicos de la Española*, II, 123; R. Bello Peguero, *Cofradía de Nuestra Señora del Carmen y Jesús Nazareno 1592–1872*, 76–78 (doc. 49–51). This *cofradía* still exists.

238. ". . . as an act of penitence and devotion". C. de Utrera, *Santo Domingo*, I, 306–9; R. Bello Peguero, *Cofradía de Nuestra Señora del Carmen y Jesús Nazareno 1592–1872*, 80–83 (doc. 54).

239. "Virgin of Carmen". C. de Utrera, *Santo Domingo*, I, 305.

240. "Virgin of the Rosary". Luis Jerónimo Alcocer, *Relación sumaria del estado presente de la Isla Española*, quoted by E. Rodríguez Demorizi, *Relaciones históricas de Santo Domingo*, I, 244.

241. E.W. Palm, *Los monumentos arquitectónicos de la Española*, I, 133 and II, 142–54.

242. E. Rodríguez Demorizi, *Relaciones históricas de Santo Domingo*, I, 229.

243. C. de Utrera, *Santo Domingo*, I, 328–35.

244. Ibid., 198.

245. "Most Blessed Sacrament of the Altar"; "All Souls"; "The Virgin of Carmen", "Our Lady of Altagracia"; "Our Lord Jesus"; "Our Lady of Sorrow"; "The Holy Cross"; "Our Lady of Conception". A. Tapia y Rivera (ed.), *Biblioteca histórica de Puerto Rico*, with documents from the fifteenth to the eighteenth centuries, 2nd edition (San Juan, Puerto Rico 1945), 499–500.

246. "Immaculate Conception of Mary". A. Cuesta Mendoza, *Historia eclesiástica*, 251–52.

247. Ibid., 156–57.

248. One example is San José de Oruña, the most important place in Trinidad: in 1644, a Most Blessed Sacrament of the Altar *cofradía* was founded here and some years later the *cofradía* of the Apostle Paul; the latter was committed to the conversion and evangelization of the Indians. J.T. Harricharan, *The Catholic Church in Trinidad, 1498–1852*, 19.

249. "Fraternity of our Lady of Sorrows and the Burial of Jesus". I. Wright, *Historia documentada de San Cristóbal*, 27.

250. "Fraternities of Mercy and Our Lady of Candlemass".

251. I. Macias, *Cuba en la primera mitad del siglo XVI*, 40–41; L. Marrero (*Cuba: economía y sociedad*, II, 389) mentions also: "Nuestra Señora del Carmen", "Nuestra Señora de la Consolación" (Our Lady of Consolation) and the "Cofradía de la Vera Cruz".

252. ". . . that a shrine be built to the Fraternity of Sancta Vera Cruz since there was none". E. Dussel, *El episcopado hispanoamericano*, VIII, 7–8.

253. ". . . blessed souls in purgatory". P.A. Morell de Santa Cruz, *Historia de la isla*, 196–97.

254. Was mentioned when the mine was handed over on 30 January 1620 to Juan de Eguiluz by Francisco Sánchez de Moya. I. Wright, "Our Lady of Charity, Nuestra Señora de la Caridad de Cobre (Santiago de Cuba) – Nuestra Señora de la Caridad de Illescas (Castilla, Spain)", *Hispanic American Historical Review* 5 (1922): 709–17.

255. F. Morales Padrón, *Jamaica española*, 206.

256. L. Pfandl, *Spanische Kultur und Sitte des 16. und 17. Jahrhunderts*, Eine Einführung in die Blütezeit der spanischen Literatur und Kunst (München 1924), 90–91; E. Dussel, *Historia General de la iglesia*, I/1: 574–78.

257. Document from Bishop Rodrigo de Bastidas (dated 29 March 1552), AGI, Santo Domingo 172, no. 20.

258. Sessio III, ch. I, n. 7: C. de Armellada, "Concilio Provincial", 168–71.

259. Sessio III, ch. I, n. 8: C. de Armellada, "Concilio Provincial", 171.

260. ". . . the statue of Our Lady of Altagracia which has been devoutly worshipped since the city was erected and through our Lady many miracles have been performed and are performed, with devotion growing each day". Quotation from a

document written by a citizen of Higuey to the "Council of the Indies" (dated 16 September 1600), AGI, Santo Domingo 1, no. 30.

261. "Our Lady of Mercy". The feast was introduced by the Order of the Mercedarians: see C. Nouel, *Historia eclesiástica de la arquidiócesis de Santo Domingo, primada de América* (Santo Domingo 1979), I, 139–41, 170–92, 309–12; C. de Utrera, *Nuestra Señora de las Mercedes, Patrona de la República Dominicana*, Historia documentada de su Santuario en la Ciudad de Santo Domingo y de su culto (Santo Domingo 1932), 39–45; R. Vargas Ugarte, *Historia del culto de María en Iberoamérica y sus imágenes y santuarios más celebrados*, I (Madrid 1956), 325–28.

262. "Our Lady of Holy Water". E.W. Palm, *Los monumentos arquitectónicos de la Española*, I, 133; R. Vargas Ugarte, *Historia del culto de María en Iberoamérica*, I, 331.

263. ". . . and so there are many pilgrimages there and since it is about 8 or 10 leagues from Santo Domingo, more people came to this holy place and to this statue". E. Rodríguez Demorizi, *Relaciones históricas de Santo Domingo*, I, 215.

264. Ibid., 244.

265. A. Cuesta Mendoza, *Historia eclesiástica*, 256–57.

266. A. Tapia y Rivera, *Biblioteca histórica de Puerto Rico*, 466; R. Vargas Ugarte, *Historia del culto de María en Iberoamérica*, I, 332–33; A. Mendoza, "La iglesia en Puerto Rico", *Informes de Pro Mundi Vita, América Latina* 40 (1985): 4.

267. "Our Lady of the Valley", document written by the church warden Saint Diego García (dated 21 May 1608), AGI, Santo Domingo 186, no. 20.

268. "Our Lady of Charity", J.M. Leiseca, *Apuntes para la historia eclesiástica de Cuba* (Havana 1938), 51–55; R. Vargas Ugarte, *Historia del culto de María en Iberoamérica*, I, 315–21; R. Gómez Treto, "Las advocaciones cubanas de la Santísima Virgen Maria", CEHILA–Cuba, Boletín especial I (1987), 20–38.

269. I. Wright, *Historia documentada de San Cristóbal de la Habana*, 27; R. Gómez Treto, "Las advocaciones cubanas", 14–15.

270. "Cross of the Holy Hill", document prepared by the archbishop (dated 24 February 1583): "*Hallé dos trocos del palo de la cruz antigua que aquí se tiene en mucha beneración por el milagro que Nro. Señor en ella obró cuando se ganó esta isla como es notorio; y por aparecer que estando esta sancta reliquia assi sin forma se pudiera presto acabar porque iban tomando della, se hizo una cruz lo que mejor que se pudo y se puso en guardia y custodia con tres llaves, de suerte que no se pueda tomar della ni perderse esta memoria*" (I found two pieces of the post of the ancient cross which is held in great veneration here because of the miracle our Lord worked through them, when the island was won, as it is well known. As it appeared that this formless holy relic could rapidly disappear because parts of it were being taken, a cross was made as best it could be and it was put under guard and custody, under lock and key so that no piece of it could be taken and so result in the loss of this memory), AGI, Santo Domingo 93, no. 26. About the legend, see J. López de Velasco, *Geografía y descripción universal*, 54.

271. Undated document of Archbishop Cristóbal Rodríguez y Suárez, AGI, Santo Domingo 1, no. 108A. He complained that the judges of the high court did not participate in the procession and that they did not arrive at the mass before the "Kyrie".

272. Document prepared by Diego de Torres Vargas. See A. Tapia y Rivera, *Biblioteca histórica de Puerto Rico*, 492.

273. P.A. Morrel de Santa Cruz, *Historia de la isla*, 258–60 , 268–70; E. Bacardi y Moreau, *Crónicas de Santiago de Cuba*, I, 43–44.

274. A. Cuesta Mendoza, *Historia eclesiástica*, 152, 282; E. Vila Vilar, *Historia de Puerto Rico (1600–1650)*, Publicaciones de la Escuela de Estudios Hispanoamericanos 239 (Sevilla 1977), 38–39; M.A. Rodríguez León, "Sínodo de San Juan", liv.

275. A. Cuesta Mendoza, *Historia eclesiástica*, 274.

276. "The town made a vow to him, he became their patron saint and on this day there is a celebration and general parade in honour of this victory and reward that God has bestowed on them through his saint." A. Vázquez de Espinosa, *Compendio y descripción de las Indias occidentales*, 82–83.

At the end of January 1600, Governor Melgarejo had defeated the English General Christopher Newport who had arrived with sixteen ships and 1,500 soldiers to conquer La Vega. F. Morales Padrón, *Jamaica española*, 248–49.

277. E. Bacardi y Moreau, *Crónicas de Santiago de Cuba*, I, 105.

278. Ibid., 44.

279. C. de Utrera, "Don Rodrigo de Bastidas", Colección de artículos en el semanario dominical "Dios y Patria" (Santo Domingo 1930), 249–60.

280. L. Marrero, *Cuba: economía y sociedad*, II, 384–85.

281. A. Cuesta Mendoza, *Historia eclesiástica*, 272–74.

282. So it was documented by Echagoian in his "Relación de la Isla Española". E. Rodríguez Demorizi, *Relaciones históricas de Santo Domingo*, I, 141.

283. E.W. Palm, *Los monumentos arquitectónicos de la Española*, I, 134; L. Marrero, *Cuba: economía y sociedad*, II, 383–84; I. Macias, *Cuba en la primera mitad del siglo XVI*, 44–45.

284. Documents dated 30 October and 1 December 1583: AGI, Santo Domingo 93, nos. 29 and 30. A. Lugo, *Edad media de la isla Española*, 328.

285. L. Pfandl, *Spanische Kultur und Sitte des 16. und 17. Jahrhunderts*, 91–93; P. Henríquez Ureña, *La cultura y las letras coloniales en Santo Domingo* (Buenos Aires 1936), 93–95, 100, 153–57; A. Cuesta Mendoza, *Historia eclesiástica*, 245; F. Mateos, "Ensayo sobre espiritualidad en América del Sur (1510–1810)", *Missionalia Hispanica* 15 (1958): 85–118; M.A. Rodríguez León, "Sínodo de San Juan", lvi.

286. F. Salentiny, *Aufstieg und Fall des portugiesischen Imperiums* (Wien-Köln-Graz 1977), 45–44; C. Verlinden, "Die transatlantische Zwangsmigration afrikanischer Neger", in *Europäisierung der Erde?* edited by G. Klingenstein et al. (München 1980), 73–94; H. Loth, *Sklaverei, Die Geschichte des Sklavenhandels zwischen Afrika und Amerika* (Wuppertal 1981), 23–24, 46.

287. P. Ashdown, *Caribbean History in Maps*, 14 (19).

288. F. Salentiny, *Aufstieg und Fall des portugiesischen Imperiums*, 222, 258–59.

289. R. Konetzke, "La esclavitud de los indios como elemento en la estructuración social de Hispanoamérica", in *Latinamerika, Entdeckung, Eroberung, Kolonisation*, edited by G. Kahle and H. Pietschmann (Köln-Wien 1983), 257–93.

290. ". . . in ownership of Christians". A. de Herrera y Tordesillas, *Historia general de los hechos de los Castellanos en las islas y tierra firme del mar océano*, I–IV (Madrid 1726–29). I, 118; C.E. Deive, *La esclavitud del negro en Santo Domingo 1492–1844* (Santo Domingo 1980), II, 379.

291. C. Larrázabal Blanco, *Los negros y la esclavitud en Santo Domingo*, Colección Pensamiento Dominicano 35 (Santo Domingo 1967), 13.

292. E.W. Palm, *Los monumentos arquitectónicos de la Española*, I, 101, n. 327.

293. Reports of 22 June 1517, CDIA 1, 281–89, and of 10 January 1519, CDIA 1, 366–68.

294. W. Reinhard, *Geschichte der europäischen Expansion*, II, 142.

295. J. Friede, *Los Welser*, 121–23.

296. A. de Herrera y Tordesillas, *Historia general de los hechos de los Castellanos*, III/V, 6 (164).

297. J. Friede, *Los Welser*, 124.

298. Ibid., 124–27; C.E. Deive, *La esclavitud del negro*, I, 78–80.

299. F. Moya Pons, *Manual de historia dominicana*, 34; A. Lluberes, "La iglesia ante el negro, 1492–1822", *Amigo del hogar* 43 (1984): 431–32.

300. E. Fernández Méndez, *Proceso histórico de la conquista de Puerto Rico 1508–1640*, 59.

301. ". . . black and Yucatan Indian slaves". I. Testé, *Historia eclesiástica de Cuba*, V, 41.

302. A. Gómez, *De rebus gestis a Francisco Ximenio Cisnerio*, lib. VI (Frankfurt 1581), 185.

303. C. de Utrera, *Santo Domingo*, I, 226; M. Bonetti, "Sklavenrebellionen auf Santo Domingo im 16.Jahrhundert", in *Karibik. Wirtschaft, Gesellschaft und Geschichte*, edited by H.-A. Steger and J. Schneider, Lateinamerika-Studien 11 (München 1982), 75–99, 97 n. 4.

304. P. Ashdown, *Caribbean History in Maps*, 19 (30).

305. C. Larrázabal Blanco, *Los negros y la esclavitud*, 147–48.

306. E. Rodríguez Demorizi, *Relaciones históricas de Santo Domingo*, I, 131.

307. M. Mörner, "Evolución demográfica de Hispanoamérica", 14, 67.

308. F. Morales Padrón, *Jamaica española*, 272–73, nos. 39 and 41.

309. C. Larrázabal Blanco, *Los negros y la esclavitud*, 149–50; M. Bonetti, "Sklavenrebellionen", 89–99; Bonetti, *Staat und Geselschafft*, 230–32.

310. E. Rodríguez Demorizi, *Relaciones históricas de Santo Domingo*, II, 443.

311. "On the island there are more than 4,000 slaves and many more free mulattoes in the areas surrounding Santo Domingo for the purpose of cattle rearing and the general benefit of the remaining farms." A. Vázquez de Espinosa, *Compendio y descripción de las Indias occidentales*, 34–35.

312. ". . . because many of them were dying and no more were currently coming from Ethiopia".

313. E. Rodríguez Demorizi, *Relaciones históricas de Santo Domingo*, I, 209, 217.

314. AGI, Santo Domingo 150, no. 48.

315. ". . . cattle ranches and farms of the inlands". I. Macias, *Cuba en la primera mitad del siglo XVI*, 20–22.

316. Ibid., 34–37.

317. A. Vázquez de Espinosa, *Compendio y descripción de las Indias occidentales*, 38.

318. Ibid., 40–41.

319. Ibid., 56.

320. Ibid., 82 and 83; F. Morales Padrón, *Jamaica española*, 274–75. N.L. Erskine, *Decolonizing theology*, 18.

321. H. Loth, *Sklaverei*, 85–86.

322. Ibid., 11, 93–94.

323. K. Sapper, *Das Aussterben der Naturvölker*, 36; P. Ashdown, *Caribbean History in Maps*, 17 (26 and 26).

324. E. Vila Vilar, *Hispanoamérica y el comercio de esclavos*, Publicaciones de la Escuela de Estudios Hispanoamericanos 239 (Sevilla 1977), V, 194–95, 209; E.L. Sanz, *Comercio de España con América en la época de Felipe II*, vol. I, *Los mercaderes y el tráfico indiano* (Valladolid 1979), 541–42.

325. E. Vila Vilar, *Hispanoamérica y el comercio de esclavos*, 226–28; M. Mörner, "Evolución demográfica de Hispanoamérica", 13; M. Bonetti, *Staat und Geselschafft*, 123–31.

326. A. Gisler, *L'esclavage aux Antilles françaises (XVIIe–XIXe siècle), Contribution au problème de l'esclavage* (Fribourg 1965), 34; H. Loth, *Sklaverei*, 181.

327. B. de Las Casas, *Historia de las Indias*, III, 102, BAE 96, 417: "Y porque algunos de los españoles desta isla dijeron al clérigo Casas, viendo lo que pretendía y que los religiosos de Sancto Domingo no querían absolver a los que tenian indios, si no los dejaban, que si les traia licencia del rey para que pudiesen traer de Castilla una docena de negros esclavos que abrirían mano de los indios, acordándose desto el clérigo, dijo en sus memoriales que se hiciese merced a los españoles vecinos dellas de darles licencia para traer de España una docena, más o menos, de esclavos negros . . ." (Some of the Spaniards on this island said to the priest Casas, in light of what he was claiming and the fact that the Dominicans did not wish to absolve those who had Indians, but forsook them, that if he obtained permission from the king for them to bring a dozen Negro slaves from Castilla this would stimulate the hand of the Indians. The priest agreed and begged in his petition for pity to be taken on the Spanish residents of the island so that they be given permission to take a dozen or so black slaves from Spain). From the "Memorial de remedios para las Indias" of 1516 we can conclude that Las Casas at this time was not only thinking of black slaves but also of white slaves. Cf. B. de Las Casas, *Opúsculos, cartas y memoriales*, BAE 110, 17: "*dandoles su Alteza licencia para ello y haciendoles merced de que puedan tener esclavos negros y blancos*" (Your Highness granting

them permission to do this and granting them the favour of having black and white slaves).

328. I. Pérez Fernández, *Fray Bartolomé de Las Casas*, 44–45.

329. Bishop Manso received fourteen slaves on 4 February 1528, and according to Governor Lando's survey (1530), he was the owner of forty-three black slaves: E. Fernández Méndez, *Proceso histórico de la conquista de Puerto Rico*, 53–54; J. Sued-Badillo, "Igreja e escravidão em Porto Rico do século XVI", in CEHILA, *Escravidão negra e História da Igreja na América Latina e no Caribe* (Petrópolis 1987), 67–83.

330. ". . . to mine gold and benefit from other profit making activities".

331. ". . . will be converted into profits from the land". Letter dated 11 August 1531: AGI, Santo Domingo 93, no. 2.

332. ". . . maintenance and clothing". AGI, Santo Domingo 172, no. 3, f. 47r.

333. Letter dated 20 June 1559, AGI, Santo Domingo 172, no. 26: "*Ya V. Magd. Real sabe como en estas yslas no ay indios de servicio y aunque los uviera yo no pretendo dellos ser servido. Y los salarios de Españoles son muy grandes, que no los sufre la renta y possibilidad. Supplico a V. Magd. se me de licencia para poder traer de Cabo Verde o de otra parte seis negros de que tengo nescessidad para mi servicio*" (Your Royal Highness already knows that there are no Indian servants in these islands and even if there were I do not aspire to be served by them. And the salaries of the Spaniards are very high and services have to be paid for from it. I entreat Your Majesty to grant me permission to bring from Cape Verde or elsewhere six Negroes whom I need to help me).

334. On 9 July 1561 he expressed remorse at the decrease in the number of black slaves in Puerto Rico "*y estos acabados de salir no ay isla . . . y presto se acabaron los yngenios*" (and for those who have just left there is no island and soon all sugar mills come to a halt). AGI, Santo Domingo 172, no. 32.

335. AGI, Santo Domingo 172, no. 39.

336. Letter dated 3 September 1573, AGI, Santo Domingo 172, no. 40, and 15 January 1574, AGI, Santo Domingo 172, no. 41.

337. AGI, Santo Domingo 94, no. 34; J.M. de la Casa Rivas, "Los diezmos como fuente de la iglesia dominicana (1492–1577)", *Casas Reales*, Organo del Museo de Las Casas Reales, 12 (1980): 43–73, 58 n. 24.

338. AGI, Santo Domingo 93, no. 17.

338. Letter dated 6 April 1579, AGI, Santo Domingo 172, no. 51; E. Williams, *Documents of West Indian History*, I, 144; J. Sued-Badillo, "Igreja e escravidão em Porto Rico do século XVI", 77.

339. Letter dated 3 January 1578, AGI, Santo Domingo 172, no. 49.

340. "They tell me that the province of Brazil used to be rather unprofitable and that their king, upon hearing this, provided them with a large number of blacks who populated their province. This proved very beneficial to the king as he was able to earn more in one year than he did in three."

341. In his letter dated 8 November 1582, the abbot recommended the importation

of "cinquenta piezas de esclavos negros para hazer labor" (fifty additional Negro slaves to work). AGI, Santo Domingo 177, no. 67, f. 4r; F. Morales Padrón, *Jamaica española*, 270 n. 34 and 272 n. 38.

342. AGI, Santo Domingo 93, nos. 48 and 49.

343. As in the case of the Indians, separate ecclesiastical books were kept for the black slaves in order to register their baptisms, marriages and deaths, see L. Lopetegui and F. Zubillaga, *Historia de la iglesia*, 471; R. Konetzke, *Süd-und Mittel-amerika* I, 101. In many churches, for example in the Minas del Prado Church in Cuba, there was a rail "para que detras della oygan misa los negros, separados de los blancos" (so that the Negroes can attend to mass behind them separated from the whites), 1620. I. Wright, "Our Lady of Charity", 716.

344. B. de Las Casas, *Historia de las Indias*, III, 129, BAE 96, 487: "*Deste aviso que dió el clérigo, no poco después se halló arrepiso, juzgándose culpado por inadvertente, porque como después vido y averiguó según parecerá, ser tan injusto el captiverio de los negros como el de los indios, no fué discreto remedio el que aconsejó que se trujesen negros para que se libertasen los indios . . .*" (A short time after giving this advice the priest was repentant judging himself to be guilty through inadvertence because as will be seen, he came to realize and be recognized that enslaving Negroes was as unjust as enslaving Indians and that the remedy he had recommended for Negroes to be brought in exchange for freeing the Indians was not a wise one). B. de Las Casas, *Historia de las Indias*, III, 102, BAE 96, 417: "*porque la misma razón es dellos [= de los esclavos negros] que de los indios*" (because the same reasoning applies in their case [that of the enslaved Negroes] as in the case of the Indians); I. Pérez Fernández, *Fray Bartolomé de Las Casas*, 45.

345. F. del Paso y Troncoso (ed.), *Epistolario de Nueva España 1508–1818*, IX (1560–1563), Biblioteca Histórica Mexicana de obras inéditas, Second series, 9 (México 1940), 53–54: "*en esta tierra Vuestra Majestad ha proveído . . . que los indios eran captivos fuesen puestos en libertad y ansi lo están . . . y muy contrario a tan justa y católica provisión pasa en estas partes con los negros y es que vienen a bar-cadas de todas partes de Guinea y de las conquistas de Portugal y se tiene por contrat-ación comprar negros allá para traerlos a vender acá, que no es la menor granjería de estas partes; no sabemos qué causa haya para que los negros sean captivos más que los indios, pues ellos según dicen de buena voluntad resciben el Santo Evangelio y no hacen guerra a los cristianos*" (In this territory Your Majesty has proclaimed that the Indians who were captives should be freed and so they are . . . and in contrast to such a just and enlightened provision Negroes are brought in by shiploads from all parts of Guinea and the conquered territories of Portugal and are brought under contract to be sold here and in no way do they constitute the least earnings in these parts; we know of no reason why Negroes should be enslaved more than Indians because, as persons of good will pay, they receive the Holy Gospel and do not wage war on Christians); C.R. Boxer, *The Church Militant*, 32.

346. C.R. Boxer, *The Portuguese Seaborne Empire 1415–1825* (London 1969), 263–64; also Boxer, *The Church Militant*, 32–34. Here Boxer makes reference to two

books written by the Dominicans Tomás de Mercado (*Suma de tratos y contratos* [Sevilla 1569]) and Bartolomé de Albornoz (*Arte de los contractos* [Valencia 1573]), who criticized slavery.

347. J. Baumgartner, "P. Alonso de Sandoval SJ und die Negersklaverei, Die Missions-pastoral 'De instauranda Aethiopum salute' von 1627", in *Vermittlung zwi-schenkirchlicher Gemeinschaft*, edited by Baumgartner, Neue Zeitschrift für Missionswissenschaft, Suppplementa 17 (Schöneck-Beckenried 1971), 409–48; H. Klein, "Anglicanism, Catholicism and the Negro Slave", in *Slavery in the New World: a Reader in Comparative History*, edited by L. Foner and E.D. Genovese (Englewood Cliffs 1969), 138–66, 142 n. 14; H. Triana y Antorveza, *Evangelización y sociedades negras en América Latina*, Pro Mundi Vita Reports, América Latina 47 (Brussels 1987), 21–22.

348. The Carmelite Antonio Vázquez de Espinosa (*Compendio y descripción de las Indias occidentales*, BAE 231, 40) made a mild criticism of the ill treatment of those black slaves, who were used in the mining of pearls in the eastern part of Venezuela: "*para los que no han sacado a gusto del amo o son traviesos, tienen en sus dormitorios o cárceles, grillos y prisiones, y los castigan, azotan y brean cruel e inhumanamente; acción bien ajena de la profesión cristiana, si bien para lo que toca a aquel oficio todo es menester, porque de otra suerte no harian cosa*" (for those who were not liked by their master, were kept in their rooms or in prisons, in shackles and in dungeons, and punished, whipped and ill treated in an inhumane fashion; this is hardly Christian behaviour, although it is necessary because otherwise they would do nothing).

The provincial of the Jesuits in Peru, Diego de Avendaño, stated (in his work "Thesaurus Indicus" of 1668) that the slave trade was an "*injusticia malvada*" (a wicked injustice), because the capture of slaves as a result of a war was rare:

K. Schatz, "Einsatz für Gerechtigkeit und Abfinden mit den Verhältnissen, Jesuiten und Sklaverei im 16. und 17. Jahrhundert", *Stimmen der Zeit* 197 (1979): 99–113, 110; A. Losada, "Diego de Avendaño SJ, moralista y jurista, defensor de la dignidad humana de indios y negros en América", *Missionalia Hispanica* 39 (1982): 1–18.

The case of two Capuchins, Francisco José de Yaca and Epifanio de Moirans, who worked in Venezuela (and Jaca in Cuba as well) was of great importance. While fighting for the liberation of the blacks, they demanded reparations for the injustices that they had suffered. A serious conflict began in 1681 with the ecclesiastical and civil bureaucracy and they were finally expelled from Spanish America. Propaganda Fide, whom they asked to intervene while in prison in Spain, agreed that they were right, but they did not succeed in returning to their mission, they came out of jail and went back to their original convents: J.T. López García, *Dos defensores de los esclavos negros en el siglo XVII, Francisco José de Jaca y Epifanio de Moirans*, Biblioteca Corpozulia 3 (Maracaibo, Caracas 1981), 29–108.

349. F.J. Hernaez, *Colección* I, 109–10, 112–14, 114–16; J.F. Maxwell, *Slavery and*

the Catholic Church: The History of Catholic Teaching Concerning the Moral Legitimacy of the Institution of Slavery (London 1975), 68–74; C.R. Boxer, *The Church Militant*, 35–38, 126 n. 45; K. Schatz, "Einsatz für Gerechtigkeit", 100–101, 107; E. Heiniger, *Ideologie des Rassismus, Problemsicht und ethische Verurteilung in der kirchlichen Sozialverkündigung*, Neue Zeitschrift für Missionswissenschaft, Supplementa 28 (Immensee 1980), 54–56, 70–71, 84–85.

350. C.E. Deive, *La esclavitud del negro* II, 382.

351. K.S. Latourette, *Three Centuries of Advance* A.D. *1500–A.D. 1800: A History of the Expansion of Christianity*, III (New York and London 1939), 108; C. Larrázabal Blanco, *Los negros y la esclavitud*, 129–30; C.E. Deive, *La esclavitud del negro*, II, 382.

352. At this synod, Archbishop Andrés de Carvajal made reference to the second diocesan synod of Santo Domingo in his report of 17 July 1576 (AGI, Santo Domingo 93, no. 22). This catechism was also mentioned in Hernando Gorjón's testament (dated 14 June 1540); in this document the establishment of a foundation was also mentioned in order to facilitate the payment of the salary of a priest for the sugar factory in Azua. C.E. Deive, *La eslavitud del negro*, II, 385.

353. A. Lugo, *Edad media de la isla Española*, 286–87; C. de Utrera, "Episcopologio dominicopolitano", *Boletín del Archivo General de la Nación*, Ciudad Trujillo 18 (1955): 228–49, 243, 324–49; E. Dussel, *El episcopado hispanoamericano*, III, 171 and IV, 47.

354. ". . . that pure blacks who were brought from Guinea and all other provinces with pure blacks were not to be baptized until they knew the Christian doctrine and understood who God was and that it was he who gave them the sacrament of baptism".

355. ". . . an average understanding of God and church so that they can be baptized like children, since they have just as much knowledge as children".

356. Letter dated 17 July 1576, AGI, Santo Domingo 93, no. 22. The Council of the Indies approved this decision, but without mentioning the lapse of thirty days; letter dated 8 May 1577, AGI, Santo Domingo 868, G3, f. 61r/v: "*ha parescido que deveis hordenar que los dichos negros bocales se cathecizen como por Nra. Santa Madre Yglesia esta hordenado sin hazer novedad y cuando paresciere estar dispuestos para ello los baptizen, proveereis se haga así*" (it looks as if you should order that said Negro representatives be quietly given instruction as our Holy Mother of the Church orders and when they appear to be ready they should be baptized, make provisions for this to be done).

357. Letter dated 18 September 1610, AGI, Santo Domingo 93, no. 68. Other friars expressed similar doubts in Spanish America; this led to the instruction of the archbishop of Sevilla, Pedro Castro y Quiñones, in 1614, who ordered the priests to evangelize the slaves at the ports of embarkation and upon their arrival, he demanded an examination to see if all the passengers had received baptism "rite et valide". He threatened the slave traders, who tried to put up obstacles to this measure, with drastic ecclesiastical punishments: J. Baumgart-

ner, "P. Alonso de Sandoval SJ und die Negersklaverei", 430–32; H. Triana y Antorveza, *Evangelización y sociedades negras*, 20–21.

358. Diocesan Synod of 1610, tit. 4, can. LXXII–LXXIV: E. Dussel, *El episcopado hispanoamericano*, VIII, 71–72. It is interesting to note that the synod at an other moment emphasized that the priests should not give preference to the whites while confessing, in order not to provoke discontent among the blacks: tit.3, can. LXI; E. Dussel, *El episcopado hispanoamericano*, VII, 69.

359. Sessio II, ch. I, n. 7–10: C. de Armellada, "Concilio Provincial", 146–48; H. Klein, "Anglicanism, Catholicism and the Negro Slave", 143–44.

360. Sessio II, ch. II, n. 3: C. de Armellada, "Concilio Provincial", 149.

361. Sessio II, ch. V, n. 1: C. de Armellada, "Concilio Provincial", 158–59.

362. Sessio II, ch. V, n. 6: C. de Armellada, "Concilio Provincial", 161.

363. Sessio III, ch. I, n. 4 and Sessio IV, cap.VII, n. 2: C. de Armellada, "Concilio Provincial", 167–68, 189.

364. Sessio II, ch. VII, n. 4: C. de Armellada, "Concilio Provincial", 164.

365. Sessio II, ch. IV, n. 7–9: C. de Armellada, "Concilio Provincial", 157–58. The church was unable to harmonize its marriage doctrine with the African family vision of the slaves. Cf. a letter dated 5 October 1574 from the abbott of Jamaica, AGI, Santo Domingo 177, no. 65: "*tambien halle que ay muchos esclavos amancebados . . . de mucho tiempo morando juntos en un buhio en las estancias de sus amos criando sus hijuelos y gallinillas y otras cosas como si fuesen maridos y mugeres. Y para remediar lo hice informacion y voy llamando a los que de ella resulta estarlo y ellos lo confiesan llanamente. Adviertoles el mal estado que tienen y mandoles salgan de el. Algunos se les hace muy dificil apartarse y concuerdanse en casarse y en estos proveo se hagan las moniciones en forma . . .*" (I also found that there were many slaves living together . . . cohabiting for a long time as husband and wife in a hut on their masters' estates raising their children and chickens and other things. To remedy the situation I made enquiries and I went calling on all those in this situation and they openly confessed to it. I warned them of the wrong they are committing and ordered them to cease cohabiting. Some of them found it difficult to stay apart and agreed to marry and in such cases I made proper arrangements for the formalities to be performed).

366. Sessio III, ch. I, n. 5: C. de Armellada, "Concilio Provincial", 168.

367. Sessio III, ch. V, n. 2: C. de Armellada, "Concilio Provincial", 176.

368. J. Margraf, *Kirche und Sklaverei seit der Entdeckung Amerika's* (Tübingen 1865), 167 n. 1; E. Williams, *Documents of West Indian History*, I, 157; C. Campo Lacasa, *Historia de la iglesia en Puerto Rico*, 302; M.A. Rodríguez León, "Sínodo de San Juan", xxxi–xxxiii.

369. This synod regulated a period of two to twelve months of preparation of the black slaves before their baptism. K.S. Latourette, *Three Centuries of Advance*, 108; H. Klein, "Anglicanism, Catholicism and the Negro Slave", 144–45.

370. A very discriminatory opinion was expressed by Archbishop Cristóbal Rodríguez y Suárez (who made a positive contribution to the pastoral work among blacks by having organized the diocesan synod of 1610) in his report that one specific

priest was not useful "ni aun para confesar negros" (not even to give confession to Negroes): AGI, Santo Domingo 1, no. 108 A.

371. A. de Sandoval, *De instauranda Aethiopum salute, El mundo de la esclavitud negra en América* (Bogotá 1956), III, 3 (345–46): *"estos negros no son bestias como he oído decir a algunos que por aquí los quieren hacer incapaces del cristianismo, ni se deben refutar por infantes o amantes, porque no son sino hombres adultos, y como a tales se ha de dar el bautismo; . . se experimenta en ellos capacidad grande y un piadoso afecto a las cosas de la fe"* (These Negroes are not beasts as I have heard it said by persons here who make them out to be incapable of Christianity, nor should Christianity be withheld from infants nor from lovers for they are but adult men and as such they should be baptized . . . They have great inner strength and a pious attachment to the Christian faith); J. Baumgartner, "P. Alonso de Sandoval SJ", 447–48.

372. Report of 1568 (E. Rodríguez Demorizi, *Relaciones históricas de Santo Domingo*, I, 137): *"en los más de estos ingenios y estancias grandes no hay sacerdote que administre los Santísimos Sacramentos y les enseñe la doctrina cristiana; y muchos de ellos mueren sin confesión, y aun sin recibir el agua del bautismo; y no solamente son muy maltratados en el cuerpo, como es con el mucho trabajo que tienen que no duermen de noche, y asimismo no comen, y en muchos ingenios no les dan casabi, si no es vaca y algunos plátanos, y andan en cuero los mas"* (On most of these sugar mills and large estates there are no priests to administer the Holy Sacraments nor to teach them the Christian doctrine; many die without confession and even without receiving baptismal waters; not only are they ill treated physically because with the great amount of work they have to do they do not sleep at night, likewise they do not eat and on many sugar mills they are not given cassava but meat and some plantains and most times they go about naked).

373. Statement of 1570, CDIA 11, 69–70: *"tiene cada ingenio cient negros. . . y algunos ay de ciento y cincuenta y doscientos y más negros, y estos viven barbaramente, así en lo temporal como en lo espiritual; porque los menos dellos saben las oraciones de la iglesia, ni aun la ley en que viven; y éstos, como no son visitados de los prelados, . . . no tienen orden . . . y se mueren muchos sin confesión ni otros sacramentos"* (Each sugar mill has 100 Negroes and some have 150 and 200 and more Negroes and they live in barbaric conditions both temporally and spiritually; only a minority of them know the prayers of the church and not even the law under which they live and as they are not visited by prelates . . . have no order and many die without confession or other sacraments).

374. Two Italian priests, Alessandro Ferrari and Geronimo Maricelli, who arrived at the interior of Puerto Rico (during a voyage to San Germán in 1597), wrote about and criticized the complete religious ignorance of the blacks at the sugar factories; there was no catechism and there was no administering of the sacraments: J. Sued-Badillo, "Igreja e escravidão em Porto Rico do século XVI", 79.

375. A. Lluberes, "La iglesia ante el negro", 432.

376. Similar regulations originated in the time of Governor Ovando: A. de Herrera y Tordesillas, *Historia general de los hechos de los Castellanos*, 174; C.E. Deive, *La esclavitud del negro* II, 390.
377. H. Triana y Antorveza, *Evangelización y sociedades negras*, 18.
378. C.E. Deive, *La esclavitud del negro* II, 394–95.
379. F. Ortíz, *La antigua fiesta afrocubana del 'Día de Reyes'* (Havana 1960), 9–33; H. Klein, "Anglicanism, Catholicism and the Negro Slave", 149–50.
380. I. Wright, "Historia documentada de San Cristobal de la Habana", 27 n. 3. F. Ortíz, *La antigua fiesta*, 28. The *cofradía* of the blacks of Cotuí in La Española also carried the name of "Espíritu Santo": E.W. Palm, *Los monumentos arquitectónicos de la Española*, II, 96 n. 493.
381. E. Rodríguez Demorizi, *Relaciones históricas de Santo Domingo*, I, 225.
382. ". . . they called blacks who were born on this island creole blacks".
383. C. Larrázabal Blanco, *Los negros y la esclavitud*, 136–38; C.E. Deive, *La esclavitud del negro*, II, 396.
384. E. Rodríguez Demorizi, *Relaciones históricas de Santo Domingo* I, 226; E.W. Palm, *Los monumentos arquitectónicos de la Española*, II, 37 n. 112; A. Lluberes, "La iglesia ante el negro", 432.
385. E. Rodríguez Demorizi, *Relaciones históricas de Santo Domingo*, I, 227. The "culto de los gemelos" (homage to the twins), as it was known in West Africa, was incarnated in this feast. C.E. Deive, *La esclavitud del negro*, II, 397.
386. C. Larrázabal Blanco, *Los negros y la esclavitud*, 133–34; M. Bonetti, "Sklavenrebellionen auf Santo Domingo", 78, 99.
387. ". . . represented by a goat"; ". . . affirming that they have no other god and that they believe only in that demon and based on certain assumptions they were going away to other areas to worship it".
388. AGI, Santo Domingo 93, no. 43. J. Sued-Badillo,"Igreja e escravidão em Porto Rico. do século XVI", 81–82.
389. E. Fernández Méndez (*Proceso histórico de la conquista de Puerto Rico.*, 89–90) quotes from the chronicles of Torres Vargas (1647): *"Llevóse a la iglesia la dicha negra y exercisose, y dijo el espiritu llamarse Pedro Lorenzo, y cuanto le preguntaban decía de las cosas ausentes y ocultas . . . y mandó el comisario de la inquisición no se hablase con pena de excomunión, y luego se descubrió otro segundo y de otros que despues han salido no se hace mucho caso. Dicen las negras que le tienen, que en su tierra se les entra en el vientre en forma visible de animalejo, y que le heredan de unas a otras como mayorazgo"* (The said black woman was taken to the church and exorcized; the spirit gave his name as Pedro Lorenzo and when questioned he spoke of absent and occult things and the commissioner of the Inquisition ordered him not to speak on pain of excommunication and then a second one was discovered and others who later came out were paid scant attention. Black women say that the spirits possess them, that they enter their bellies in the visible form of an ugly-looking creature and they are inherited from one generation to the next through the first-born).

390. Cf. an undated report (AGI, Santo Domingo 1, no. 108 A; Consejo de Indias, 5 May 1612): "*Una negra inducida de un su amigo presso busco con cuydado las palabras de la consagracion, segun depussieron della cinco testigos a quien se pidieron y por aver aquí algunas hechiceras y sortilegas, andamos mi provisor y yo con cuidado para remediar este daño; . . . mando mi provisor ponerla en la carcel pidiendo el auxilio del braço seglar*" (A black woman, seduced by her arrested male friend, was looking carefully for the words of consecration, according to five witnesses, and because there are witches and sorcery in this region, my administrator and I are treading carefully in order to remedy this wrong. I have asked my administrator to put her in jail with the help of the secular arm).

391. J.T. Medina, *La inquisición en Cartagena de Indias* (Bogotá 1978), 62 n. 1.

392. K. Schatz, "Einsatz für Gerechtigkeit", 107.

393. C.E. Deive, *La esclavitud del negro*, II, 377–78.

KEITH HUNTE

Protestantism and Slavery in the British Caribbean

Foundation

The English established colonies in the Eastern Caribbean between 1623 and 1635, and in Jamaica in 1655. Ministers of the Church of England were at work among their coreligionists from the early days of settlement. At first, provision for the recruitment and employment of clergy in each of the colonies was tentative and unsystematic. It was only as the colonial society felt relatively secure and was able to provide for civil administration that systematic provision was made for the maintenance of the church.

The process developed most smoothly in Barbados. There, the absence of indigenous people allowed the English colonists to clear the land and establish homesteads without having first to conduct a war for occupation. As early as 1629, therefore, the governor was able to lay the foundation for civil administration when he divided the island into six parishes. Between 1629 and 1645 further subdivisions were made and by the latter date, there were eleven parishes altogether.[1]

In St Kitts, "the first priority was defence; against the Caribs on the island, and against the Spanish threats from the sea". A military operation was established with seven divisions, three to the windward side and four to the leeward side.[2] Once the combined resources of English and French colonists in St Kitts had succeeded in averting the danger of extermination at the hands of the Caribs, and once the Spanish naval squadron, which had expelled the colonists in 1679, had left quickly to halt the Dutch invasion of the South American mainland, civil authorities in the English part of the colony were able to establish parishes.[3] By 1655 there were five parishes. The French captured the English district in 1666. When the territory was restored to the

English in accordance with the Treaty of Breda in 1671, no less than three of the parish churches had been destroyed. The job of reconstruction was undertaken by Sir Charles Wheler who assumed office that year as governor of the Leeward Islands.

In Nevis and in Montserrat, parishes had also been established and some churches were built before 1666. The two churches in Montserrat had suffered damage as a result of the French invasion, and there were no ministers in four parishes in Nevis when Wheler assumed responsibility for the government of the Leeward Islands.[4]

In Jamaica, following the establishment of civil jurisdiction after 1661, the state also undertook "to discourage vice and debauchery and to encourage ministers, that Christianity and the Protestant religion, according to the Church of England, might have due reverence and exercise".[5] The parochial system developed in Jamaica thereafter. The legislature in 1681 divided the island into fifteen parishes and spelled out the duties and obligations of parochial officers.[6]

It is evident, therefore, that in each colony, "the small and highly organized parish . . . became the centre both of ecclesiastical life and of civil administration".[7] In the Leeward Islands, Antigua was the last to fall into line. There, for a number of reasons, colonial settlement expanded more slowly than in other English territories. Consequently, until 1681, the military division (there were ten such divisions) remained the basic unit for purposes of administration. In that year five parishes were created by act of the local legislature and a number of civil responsibilities were transferred from the military division to the parish.[8]

The parish became the basic unit of ecclesiastical and civil administration in the West Indies. Each parish had a vestry (or governing body) elected annually by the freeholders of property within the boundaries of the parish.[9] The vestry was required by law to make provision for the maintenance of the church. This included the responsibility of providing a church building as well as a salary and suitable accommodation for the incumbent minister. The rector of the parish was a member (ex officio) of the vestry. The ability of the vestry to discharge these obligations depended on the size and economic circumstances of the parochial community of freeholders. In defining parish boundaries, due regard had to be paid to demography and to the projected pattern of the economy. In all the colonies, parish boundaries had to be adjusted from time to time in keeping with demographic and economic factors. In Jamaica, the existence of large plantations and the long distances between plantations made for the application of the parochial model in the administration of ecclesiastical affairs particularly difficult. Writing in 1664, Governor Modyford illustrated that point as follows:

Five parishes only have churches; the rest are coming on as fast as their small means will permit them; but alas, my lords, these five do not preach to one-third of the island. The plantations are at such distance each from the other that it is impossible to make up convenient congregations or find fitting places for the rest to meet in; but they agree among themselves to meet alternatively at each other's houses, as the primitive Christians did, and there to pray, read a chapter, sing a Psalm and home again . . .[10]

The issue of distance between residential areas continued to be a problem which affected church organization in Jamaica throughout the colonial period, particularly the choice of a site for the church building or mission station.[11]

The function of the parish as the basic unit of civil administration and especially as the basic unit of local government took precedence over its function as an ecclesiastical district. In placing parishioners under an obligation to provide, through taxation, support for the work of the established church, the colonial legislature was evidently seeking to re-establish a relationship between the church and the state, somewhat akin to that which had been established in England.[12] Certain key factors and conditions, however, were conspicuously absent in the colonies. Among the most important of these was the fact that in England the ecclesiastical authority had the capacity to act independently of the civil authority. In the early days of settlement, several parishes had not been provided with any real resources. For several years many parishes went without the services of a minister of religion. Sir Charles Wheler was quick to notice those deficiencies, and to propose a remedy.[13] Through observation of the large number of vacant cures in the Leeward Islands, and the behaviour of some of the clergy in the parishes, Wheler traced the problems to its source. "The trouble," he wrote, "arose because bishops had no power to send out young ministers."[14] He urged that a system should be established for the selection and recruitment of clergy required to serve in the colonies. He felt that the exercise of episcopal jurisdiction through the office of a resident bishop in the Leeward Islands was necessary. Wheler even gave the name of his candidate for the office of bishop. He appointed Dr Turner, master of St John's College, Cambridge. The governor also urged that special incentives should be offered to young graduates from the universities in order to induce them to serve in the colonial mission field for a while. His proposal did not immediately impress the Lords Committee of Trade and Plantations. In fact, recurrent submissions in a similar vein from interested persons in the colonies in the seventeenth and eighteenth centuries met with a similar fate so that resident bishops did not make their appearance in the West Indies until 1824. Until that time, recruitment of the clergy was conducted through the initiatives of the local vestry and the colonial governor. The bishop of London was responsible for issuing a licence to clergy intending to hold ecclesiastical office in the colonies. Upon arrival in the colonies, the clergy was subject to the supervision of the civil authorities.[15]

By 1681, the parish had become first and foremost a part of the civil administrative system. A series of acts in the legislature of several territories had resulted in the emergence of a system of local government centred around the parish. The vestry was empowered to fix the rates and taxes payable by freeholders for the building and maintenance of highways, poor relief, maintenance of church buildings and salaries of ministers. The society that had developed in the West Indies by 1681 was a far cry from that which had emerged in the early days of settlement. In the earlier phase, the intention of the colonial authorities, when they made the first efforts to build churches and to recruit clergy, had been to establish centres of public worship for a predominantly English and white population. The emergence of sugar plantations and the demographic changes that accompanied this transformation had altered all that. The colonial ruling class perceived two distinct societies in each colony: these could be defined as the society of free persons, and that of the slaves. In time, the distinction was essentially between whites and blacks. At any point, the question as to whom the church should serve was critical.

The need to encourage colonists to settle in the islands in order to ensure the military and economic security of the colonies led to the application of a higher level of religious tolerance than that of seventeenth century England. Barbados therefore received an influx of political exiles at the height of the English Civil War, while feeble and unavailing efforts were made in the period prior to 1660, to enforce some form of orthodoxy. In the Leeward Islands, in particular, manpower considerations led to the adoption of a more relaxed official attitude toward nonconformists, and other religious dissenters.

Montserrat had attracted a sizeable Irish, Roman Catholic community. Under the administration of Sir William Stapleton, Wheler's successor, the Roman Catholic community in Montserrat was assured of religious freedom.[16] Their position was further protected under the administration of Sir Nathaniel Johnson, who formally gave Roman Catholics the right to public worship and exempted them from the payment of church rates in support of the established Church of England.[17]

The juxtaposition of English and French communities in St Kitts gave rise to increased religious tension in the second half of the seventeenth century. There, "a large number of French nationals remained as planters within the English quarters" after the Treaty of Breda (1671), "until a series of vexatious regulations drove them away".[18]

In addition to that, the Revocation of the Edict of Nantes in France apparently resulted in an increase in the number of French Huguenot residents in the English district. That community petitioned Wheler for permission to recruit a minister of their own faith.[19] The presence on the island of Roman Catholic clergy, as well as French and Dutch colonists prompted Stapleton to support the request of the Island Council that every effort should be made to recruit Anglican clergymen of high calibre. The council did not conceal its poor opinion of the quality of the ministers then serving in St Kitts and asked the authorities in England to send men "of riper years and better read in divinity than those young graduates that came hither, for fear of being foyled in argument, if any dispute should happen between them and the clergy men of the Church of Rome".[20]

Colonial governors in the West Indies after 1660 were under instruction to apply very cautiously, the policy of religious conformity which was in force in England.[21] Wheler's instructions urged him to "dispense with the taking the path of allegiance and supremacy to those that bear any part in the government (except Members and officers of the Council . . .), finding out some other way of securing yourself to their allegiance to us and our government here".[22] In other words, what the governor was required to do was to ignore the Test Act and to ensure that colonists under his jurisdiction remained loyal to the Crown. In Jamaica, a similar policy was in effect. The governor was under instruction to encourage "persons of different judgement and opinions in matters of religion, to transport them with their effects to Jamaica".[23] Despite these instructions to colonial governors, nonconformists were barred from holding high office within the colony, and in a number of ways the road to preferment depended on one's membership of the Church of England. The one body of religious dissenters among the white community that was frequently in conflict with the civil establishment in the colonies was the Quakers, or Brethren of the Inner Light. Their commitment to pacifism earned them the antipathy of colonial officials and the rank and file colonists alike. Higham ascribed the degree of persecution suffered by Quakers "to the inherent impossibility of a conscientious pacifist like the Quaker fitting into the life of a frontier state, the basis of whose organization was essentially military".[24]

The only other significant body of religious dissenters in the West Indies was the Jews. They were mainly engaged in commerce and resided for the most part in the towns. Exempt from the obligation to attend Christian centres of worship, and permitted to erect their own synagogues, members of the Jewish community were quite often obliged to pay parish rates, a substantial part of which went towards the maintenance of the established church.[25]

As far as the colonial legislators were concerned, the established church was to serve the needs of a white society. Early attempts to extend the church's mission toward the blacks met with widespread resistance in the West Indies. Planters in the West Indies resisted attempts to extend the mission of the church to their African slaves because they were determined to emphasize the fact that slavery was a permanent condition. The Barbadian planter with whom the English visitor Francis Ligon spoke at mid century, had expressed the opinion that according to the laws of England a Christian could not be enslaved.[26] That view, though it may have been held in certain quarters, was without foundation. In any case, the Lords Committee on Trade and Plantations, when it chose to address the issue, urged Governor Willoughby, who was at that time in charge of Barbados and the Leeward Islands, to take appropiate action to spread the Christian faith to all slaves and servants within his jurisdiction. Willoughby's instructions were as follows:

And for the propagation, and Encrease of ye Christians faith and Religion, you shall make it your special care, that all Negro Slaves, and servants remaining in the said colonies be instructed in the Principle of the same Religion (Church of England).

And that such who shall arrive at a competent knowledge therein, be admitted to the Sacrament of Baptism. *And that it be declared by Law in the respective Colonies that such Baptism shall not at all be extended to their Enfranchisement or Manumissions.*[27]

In the text of the governor's instructions, we find a suggested solution to the problem identified by Ligon's planter: that colonial legislatures should make it clear that baptism did not lead to manumission. But the source of the resistance to the conversion of blacks was not as superficial as Ligon's planter had suggested. Some years after Willoughby had received his instruction, another governor in Barbados attempted to persuade the legislature to improve the living conditions of Christian servants and to promote the conversion of Negroes. The reply of the Legislative Assembly determined the position of that body beyond a doubt. The members of the assembly stated that "they are ready to do anything for the encouragement and good usage of Christian servants, but for making the negroes Christians their savage brutishness renders them wholly incapable".[28]

In this instance, ascribed racial character was being used to justify the enslavement of the African and his debarment from membership of the church. The convenience of this myth in support of the position of the church society was that it could be applied not only to the African slaves but to the free coloureds and free blacks as well. It is clear that the English government was not prepared to press the issue any further. The colonial legislatures were able to define the scope of the church's mission as they saw fit. In Barbados, legislation was enacted to prevent the Quakers from admitting slaves to their meetings.[29] In Jamaica, in spite of the pious injunction inserted in the slave code of 1696 requesting "All masters, mistresses, owners, and employers"[30] to make provision for the religious instruction and conversion of their slaves, little action was taken to give effect to it. The real intention of the Jamaican legislators in this regard seemed to have been more accurately expressed in the text of the law[31] in which that legislature fixed the fee for administering the sacrament of Holy Baptism to a slave at £1 3s. 9d. "a sum large enough to be prohibitory".[32] Whether by legislation or by conversion, the extent of the church's mission to the slaves was discouraged in all territories, a fact which prompted the church historian, Caldecott, to complete part of a chapter in which he examined "The church in the slavery period" with this cryptic comment: "We cannot deny that for one hundred and fifty years the vast majority of our fellow-subjects in the West Indies continued to live as heathens in the so-called 'parishes' of Jamaica, Barbados, and the Leeward Islands."[33]

Character and Influence of the Established Church in the Eighteenth Century

By the end of the seventeenth century a fairly uniform pattern of church government had been established throughout the English colonies of the Caribbean. Parishes existed everywhere.[34] Vestries, dominated by planters, were firmly in control of public policy at central and local government levels. In theory, the bishop of London enjoyed full ecclesiastical jurisdiction in the colonies, "except only the receiving of Benefices, granting Licences for Marriage and Probate of Wills. Authority to act with respect to these matters lay with the colonial governors".[35] In fact, it did not prove "convenient" for the bishop of London to exercise much of that jurisdiction over his spiritual charges in several colonies. One reason for this was that the source of the bishop's authority was not clearly defined. It is clear that from about 1660, the bishop of London was authorized to issue licences to clergy leaving for the colonies. Colonial governors often wrote to the bishop requesting him to send them suitable candidates for vacant cures within their territories. But there were times when governors and other officials were obliged to challenge the scope and extent of the bishop's authority.[36] In 1727 Bishop Gibson faced such a challenge. When he discovered that there did not appear to be any legal instrument defining his powers in that regard, he applied for and obtained a royal patent, which was renewed in 1728, assuring him of his jurisdiction.[37] Bishop Gibson's successors, however, did not seek such assurances. Consequently, they continued to function as diocesan until 1824 by virtue of custom and convention.

The source of resistance to the extension of ecclesiastical jurisdiction to the colonies, however, was the desire of the colonists to control local institutions including the church, or at any rate, to prevent the establishment of a local authority that would not be answerable to them in the legislature, nor in the vestry. Accordingly, they resisted every attempt that was made to give muscle to the exercise of episcopal authority in the colonies. It was Bishop Compton who first sought to provide a system for local supervision of the work of the clergy by creating the office of the commissary in each territory.[38] The office of the commissary was entrusted to a senior clergyman residing in the colony and his main function was to act as episcopal delegate, keep his diocesan informed of the state of the church and in particular the behaviour of the local clergy and other related matters. The first commissaries were appointed in about 1690. Their appointment took place at a time when several colonial legislatures were taking steps to define the responsibilities of vestries with regard to the maintenance of the church. The Jamaican legislature took such action in 1681. It not only divided the island into fifteen parishes, but also authorized parochial officers to raise taxes for the maintenance of ministers and for the erection of new, or the repair of old, churches. The legislature also determined the salaries of the rectors of the various parishes.[39] Around the same time, similar action was taken to standardize the salaries of rectors in the Leeward Islands, or at any rate to assure every incumbent a certain basic salary. The coinciding of such constructive action taken in the colonies and the action taken by the bishops to give effect to their ecclesiastical authority, encouraged some clergymen and not least, those who were appointed commissaries, to seek to carve out an area for independent action by the church which they represented. The story of the experience of William Gordon who was the third clergyman to hold the office of commissary in Barbados is enlightening.

Gordon, in observing that the church was having little impact on the lives and morals of the local population, drew the attention of his diocesan to the high incidence of incest, adultery, sharp practice, swearing and other acts which he claimed were punishable by law in England, but which went unpunished in Barbados. Gordon recommended the establishment of an ecclesiastical court in Barbados as a solution to these problems. "For want of this Power . . ." Gordon urged, ". . . Church wardens neglected their duty and committed many abuses of office; Bastardy and adultery go unpunished; the provision made for the poor is misapplied; ministers are often assaulted and their rights invaded; and, all crimes of Ecclesiastical cognizance are committed with Impunity."[40] When Governor Lowther became aware of the content of Gordon's submission to his diocesan, the bishop of London, and that the latter had appointed Gordon as his commissary in Barbados, he immediately demanded to know the source of the episcopal authority under which Gordon was claiming to act. In the end, the legislature supported the governor in rejecting the proposal to set up an ecclesiastical court that would have jurisdiction over the laity. The legislature formally recognized the authority of the bishop with respect to the discipline of the clergy, but ruled that the punishment of "spiritual crimes committed by laymen" was fully within the jurisdiction of the civil courts.[41] The Jamaican legislature went even further and declared that "no ecclesiastical law, or jurisdiction, shall have the power to enforce, confirm or establish any penal mulet or punishment in any case whatsoever".[42] What this meant was that even the right of the bishop of London to discipline members of the clergy for offences committed in Jamaica was being challenged.

In practice, therefore, the role of the bishop of London in relation to the exercise of church discipline in the West Indies was merely a formality. Once the minister had received a licence from the bishop and had arrived in the West Indies, he was under the direct influence of the civil authorities. It was the governor who had the power to appoint rectors to parishes (the power of receiving benefice). As such he performed the duties of ordinary in place of the clergy of the established church. When ministers assumed office in the parish they came under the direct influence and control of the planter dominated vestry. There, while incumbents enjoyed a certain security of tenure in that, once appointed, they could not easily be removed from office,[43] they could easily be influenced by a variety of forces which tended to make them more or less willing pawns of the local oligarchy. In the first place, even though their basic salary was in a sense guaranteed by law, church wardens were not always strict about collecting the rates and taxes out of which that salary would be taken. At times, the church wardens had to be reminded, and even coerced, to do their job. Second, in addition to their basic salary, ministers were likely to receive an annual bonus, or "presents", from a vestry that was well disposed towards them. Third, the speed with which the vestry moved to provide facilities, church buildings, rectories and globes depended in large measure on the rapport that had been established between the rector and leading parishioners. But perhaps the most significant point of all was that the vast majority of persons who served as ministers in the colonies were men intent on gain. Very few could be said to have been drawn to the colonies out of a sense of duty. For the majority of them, the salary, the other perquisites and the opportunity for upward social mobility were significant considerations. Apart from a few exceptions, the clergy of the established church serving in the West Indies did not distinguish itself either by scholarship or piety. It is not surprising, therefore, that there is little evidence of clergymen taking an independent view of the basic issues affecting the local society.[44]

Influenced by the work of the regular clergy of the Roman Catholic Church in the French West Indies, Christopher Codrington,[45] governor of the Leeward Islands and owner of several plantations there and in Barbados, believed that it was unlikely that the secular clergy of the Church of England would extend the church's mission to the slaves, even if a change in public policy made it possible for them to do so. Codrington's view on the subject is illuminating:

Indeed work of this nature (converting the slaves) is only fit for a regular clergy who are under vows of poverty and obedience. The secular clergy who will be sure of their wine before they set about their talk do not think the home of reward in another world sufficient encouragement to turn missionaries. I would humbly propose this might be recommended to the consideration of the Archbishop and Bishop of London. If they can find such a number of apostolic men who are able to take much pains for little reward my protection and countenance shall not be wanting.[46]

Codrington, anxious as he was to appoint those whose training and discipline would qualify them for missionary work among the slaves, was unable to recruit anyone. In his will, he sought to remove the deficiency. He bequeathed his estates in Barbados to the recently formed Society for the Propagation of the Gospel (SPG) into foreign parts for the purpose of establishing a college in Barbados to train ministers for missionary work in the colonies. He directed that the estates should be kept intact, and that the slave population should be maintained and provided with the means for conversion. The Codrington bequest was a challenge to local planters and clergy alike. The planters were concerned that a bad example for slaves on neighbouring plantations was about to be set on the Codrington estates, in that the admission of slaves to membership in the church would lead to their entertaining notions of equality which would disturb the social order.[47]

The local clergy, who offered many reasons why missionary work among the slaves could not, or should not, be undertaken, could not help but be challenged by the Codrington experiment. Such a combination of local forces might well have resulted in the abandonment of the experiment, but it was saved largely because Codrington had chosen as trustees a newly formed body which was anxious to make some impact on the colonial mission field, and whose membership included influential persons such as the archbishop of Canterbury and the bishop of London.

Although the SPG was able to keep the project alive,[48] there were times during the course of the eighteenth century when it was struggling to remain alive. Much depended on efficient local management of the estates. Failure in that area meant that for many years the project was deprived of the material resources it needed. However, an attempt was made. The SPG appointed catechists who were employed to instruct slaves in the rudiments of the Christian faith. In 1740 the catechist, Sampson Smirk, reported that out of a slave population of 207, some 64 had been baptized.[49] Smirk's progress report was not supported by any other evidence. For example, he did not advise the SPG that, unlike his predecessor Wilkie, he had given in to the local pressure and had abandoned any attempt to teach his charges to read and write.[50] The local attorneys, who certainly were very sceptical of the social experiment, were highly critical of the result that had been achieved up to this point and even indicated that they were in favour of abandoning it altogether.[51]

The matter of founding a college to train missionaries in theology and medicine met with strong resistance in Barbados. The local magnates were in favour of using the funds to establish grammar schools. In any event, it would have been difficult for the Anglican missionary body, the SPG, to give expression to Codrington's ideal of a monastic institution. Duly impressed with the difficulties facing the immediate implementation of the bequest, the trustees agreed to the establishment of a grammar school which opened its doors in 1745.[52] The college was only established in 1830 when the estate's financial situation had improved and the first bishop of Barbados was in a position to resurrect the idea.

Meanwhile, local management of estates went from bad to worse. By 1783 the estates were so burdened with debt that the SPG was happy to lease them to a local planter, Brathwaite, who sought to liquidate the debts. Brathwaite was true to his word, and ten years later, he returned the estates to the trustees in a viable state.

In every respect, however, the Codrington experiment had been kept within such limits as were acceptable to the local planter class. There is no evidence that the local clergy was encouraged to give material assistance to the missionary outreach.[53] In 1746 the rector of the parish of St John, within whose boundaries the Codrington estates lay, far from giving encouragement to the principal and catechist at the college, sought to prevent free persons living on or near the estates from attending services in the college chapel on Sundays, insisting that they should make the long trek to the parish church.[54]

The striking feature of this period, however, is not the failure of the established church to launch a mission for the slaves, but its failure to make any impact on the lives of the free and white members of the colonial society. Caldecott fittingly draws attention to the paucity of the number of clergy resident in the West Indies at any time prior to 1800.[55] Given that fewer than fifty clergymen had settled throughout the region, the drop-out rate due to prolonged periods of leave, absence, resignation and death was alarmingly high.[56] Some governors tried their best to reduce the incidence of absenteeism. Those who remained at their station were married to the ruling class which controlled them through patronage. Initial appointment depended on the grace and favour of the governor. Any local aspirant for a clerical office would go to London armed with a testimonial from the governor and from other local residents who had good connections in England, and there was every likelihood of his being ordained and licensed by the Bishop of London. While the majority of the clergy were from England there was a growing number of persons who were born in the West Indies or who, having first tried their hand at a less rewarding occupation in the West Indies, joined the church without any formal theological training. Some of the incumbents held university degrees and seemed, on paper, to be eligible for appointment in England, given the right connections. For the more qualified individuals, as well as for those who were less qualified for their jobs, the road to preferment and promotion in the colonial milieu lay through their ability to win favour with the civil authorities. The clergy in the respective colonies seldom met as a body. On the few occasions on which those in Barbados met, it was either to draft a petition expressing their allegiance to the new monarch or to devise a strategy to persuade the local legislature to authorize an increase in their basic salary.[57]

Other factors may be seen as contributing to the weak impression made by the church on society. Reporting on the situation from Jamaica, Edward Long, highlighted the dull and unappealing character of the ritual followed by the Church of England in the eighteenth century.[58]

Church buildings in the plantation colonies did not become community centres to any significant extent. Contemporaries report that Sunday services (when they were held) were poorly attended.[59] Christenings and weddings sponsored by members of the upper class were normally held in private homes; the minister would travel there to do the honours. One has the distinct impression from some of these accounts that the poorer members of the white community in many cases, were scarcely better served by the church than were the free coloureds.[60] In some instances the poorer members of the white community tried to avoid the expense contingent on hosting christening parties by postponing the baptism of their children until a more opportune moment, or by neglecting to have them baptized at all.[61] The free coloureds and blacks only benefited from the ministrations of the clergy if and when the former took the initiative. As the latter was mainly resident in the towns, it is possible to follow the story of their limited involvement in the activities of the Anglican Church by examining the parish records for the principal towns.

For all persons attending public worship, the seating arrangements in the churches emphasized the distinctions based on class and race which the local magnates considered necessary for the preservation of a slave society. There was limited seating accommodation in most church buildings. In fact, few buildings provided seating accommodation for a congregation of more than 150. In addition, the system of renting pews, which was managed by the vestry, operated in such a way as to ensure that the correct social order was observed in church as the number of coloureds and blacks attending church services increased towards the end of the eighteenth century. They were forced to take their places at the back of the church and in the gallery.[62]

Many poor whites who were finding it difficult to make ends meet were particularly hard pressed to fulfil their social obligations, including attendance at church services, having their children christened and other similar acts. Invariably, the coloureds and blacks who went to church were properly attired. This contrasted sharply with the 'down-at-the-heels' appearance of those poor whites who, by strict order of racial precedence, sat in front of them.

In light of these factors, it is clear that a fundamental change in the structure and orientation of the established church was necessary before it could begin to exert a positive influence on society. It is significant that, in facing the challenge posed by the nonconformist missionaries who came to the West Indies in the second half of the eighteenth century, the clergy and the civil establishment stood together. These two groups were drawn together by mutual self-interest. Over the years, colonial legislature had made relatively generous provisions for the maintenance of the clergy of the Church of England. In 1748, the Jamaican legislature resolved that the provision made for the clergy was "too scanty for proper and suitable maintenance".[63] It decided to increase salaries and to pay the clergy out of the colonial treasury, instead of the parochial treasury. By so doing, it removed what had become a source of considerable inconvenience to the clergy.

Expansion of the Church's Mission

In the fifty years following the Treaty of Paris (1763), the imperial world, within which the planter class in the older West Indian colonies had been able to exercise tight control over social policy and institutions, was transformed by a series of events which took place within and outside of the Caribbean region. Within the Caribbean, the recurrent social disturbances in the slave societies reached a climax in the Haitian Revolution. As a result of the fortunes of war or diplomacy, the British acquired the following additional territories in the West Indies: Grenada, St Vincent, St Lucia, Dominica, Tobago, Trinidad, and the South American coast, the former Dutch colonies of Demerara, Berbice and Essequibo, which were later called British Guiana. Moravian, Methodist and Baptist missionaries established themselves in the older and the more recently acquired British colonies. Outside of the region, the American and French Revolutions, as well as the evangelical movement in Britain, together with the industrial revolution, had a positive influence on colonial societies in the Caribbean. At the end of the day, the nature of the relationship between church and society, and between church and state, had undergone significant changes.

In a real sense, the coming of the nonconformist missionaries to the West Indies acted as a catalyst in the transformation of West Indian slave societies. In the first place, the newcomers directed their religious message mainly towards the slaves, the free coloureds and the blacks whom the Church of England's clergy had neglected. Second, they strove to preserve for themselves a certain degree of independence from the local ruling classes. Third, they committed themselves to the task of demonstrating that preaching the gospel to the slaves was far from subversive to the social order. Fourth, when the local authorities wished to remove them from the local society, they used their status as British subjects and insisted on their right to remain in the West Indies and to spread the faith. Finally, the evangelical and missionary movement to which they belonged embraced sectors within the Church of England and the Church of Scotland leading to the launching of the missionary agencies sponsored by these two denominations.[64]

The patron of the Moravians, Count Zinzendorf, placed a great deal of emphasis on the need to train prospective missionaries and the need to enforce discipline among those in the field.[65] Zinzendorf, who had a keen interest in the work of Frederick IV's Missionary College in Copenhagen, not only emphasized the training of the missionaries, but recognized the importance of preparing manuals for the guidance of missionaries and their assistants.[66] As early as 1734, the Moravian Brethren published *Instructions for the Colony in Georgia*. This was followed in 1737 by another publication entitled *Instructions for Missionaries to the East* and by two other manuals in 1738 and 1740 entitled *Instructions for all Missionaries* and *The Right Way to Convert the Heathen*, respectively.[67] From the start, the Moravian missions were intended to be self-sufficient. In Antigua and Jamaica, they acquired small estates worked by slaves exactly as they had done in the Danish West Indies. But they were soon embarrassed by the many problems inherent in plantation management and reverted to dependence on financial support from their headquarters. As was the case with all visitors to the plantations, the Moravians depended on the initial cooperation of individual planters to gain access to the slaves.

The Moravians stressed the importance of an outward manifestation of the effects of conversion to Christianity in the life of an individual convert. In the words of the historian, Hutton, they "introduced, where possible, the strict system of moral discipline which already existed at Herrnhut".[68] The missionaries established a system for monitoring the behaviour of prospective and new converts. Many laypersons assisted with the teaching and the enforcement of discipline. These persons, known as "helpers", enabled the missionaries to extend their influence to a much wider congregation than their small number would otherwise have allowed. Helpers were expected to visit members of the congregation at regular intervals and to hold private interviews with them in order to determine the quality of their religious and moral life. Care was taken to guard against the abuse of this encounter by insisting on a separation of the sexes. Male helpers were required to visit and speak with the men while female helpers spoke with the women.[69]

The Methodists first arrived in the Caribbean in Antigua in 1754 and established a chain of missionary centres in other territories between 1786 and 1814. The first effort was the direct result of a meeting in England between Gilbert, the speaker of the Legislative Assembly of that island, and John Wesley, the founder of Methodism.[70] Upon Gilbert's return to Antigua, he held regular meetings at his home, which became the centre of Methodist activity on the island.

The later arrival in Antigua of John Baxter just about bridged the gap in time between the death of Gilbert in 1774 and arrival of Dr Thomas Coke in Antigua in 1786. Coke had left England with the intention of going to North America but had landed in Antigua after his ship was blown off course. Between 1786 and 1789, Coke placed Methodist missionaries in several colonies within the Caribbean.[71]

As the Methodists attempted to move out of the towns and extend their influence to the plantations, they met with greater resistance from the planter class than did the Moravians initially. What early success they had had, they owed to their ability to cash in on the hospitality extended to them by local persons of some substance who had been moved to assist them either due to the high regard in which they held Dr Coke, to the impact of letters of introduction from the right people, or to the influence of their own personalities. They made an important breakthrough even when they succeeded in bringing together small groups of whites, free coloureds and slaves in Christian fellowship. The Methodists managed to attract a high proportion of the free coloureds and a few whites who resided in the towns. By the time Dr Coke started establishing missionary centres around the Caribbean, it had become fairly common knowledge among the planters that the founder of Methodism, John Wesley, had taken a stand against slavery.[72] This knowledge probably contributed to the degree of hostility directed by several planters in the West Indies towards the Methodists.

The third nonconformist missionary presence that was felt came from neither the Moravians nor the Methodists. The first Baptist missionary to introduce the teachings of that denomination to the West Indies was George Liele, "a black man, and a native of Virginia".[73] Liele, who was born a slave in the British colony of Virginia, came to Jamaica as an indentured labourer to a Loyalist refugee from the American Revolution, Colonel Kirkland. A practising Baptist, he sought to keep his religion alive by conducting religious services in a small private home. From these modest beginnings, Liele's congregation expanded so that by 1795, he was being assisted by four deacons.

When the owner of the Adelphi plantation in the parish of St James purchased some slaves in Kingston, they included some who had been members of Liele's congregations.[74] To enable them to maintain their connection with their church, the planter permitted Moses Baker, a deacon, to establish a congregation in the vicinity of Crooked Spring. The spread of Baptist missions from these centres largely followed the movement of Baptist converts to various parts of the country. The rapid growth of these Baptist congregations prompted the leaders to invite the Baptist Missionary Society in London to send missionaries to assist with the work. The first to arrive was John Rowe, who went to Falmouth in 1814.

At the turn of the century, the evangelical movement in England was at its peak. No less than three missionary societies were established with headquarters in London, all during the decade 1790–1800. The Baptist Missionary Society was founded in 1792, the London Missionary Society in 1795 and the Church Missionary Society in 1799.[75] The London Missionary Society seemed quite anxious to learn from the experience of the Moravian missionaries. They asked specific questions of the Brethren Society, ranging from the methods employed to recruit missionaries and the kind of training given to prospective missionaries and the modus operandi for establishing a mission station, to the most effective way of ensuring the conversion of heathens. The secretary of the society, La Trobe, provided detailed answers to their questions. The first batch of missionaries sent out by the London Missionary Society received instructions and guidelines that were largely based on the experience of the Moravians.[76] Other missionary societies copied the Moravians by instructing their missionaries to refrain from disturbing the existing social and political order in the West Indies. The Baptists were instructed to "have nothing whatsoever to do with [Jamaica's] civil and political affairs".[77] They were reminded that Christ's gospel, "far from producing or countenancing a spirit of rebellion or insubordination, has a directly opposite tendency".[78] Citing the occasion in Antigua in the 1790s, when more than a thousand blacks came forward to defend the island which faced the threat of invasion by the French, the distinguished leader of the Methodists, Dr Coke, considered that event to be a manifestation of "the power of divine grace"[79] working through the church's missions. Referring to the role of the missionaries in the Leeward Islands at the end of the eighteenth century, Goveia argues persuasively that "by preaching submission to the slaves, the missionaries were making a highly significant contribution to the maintenance of the slave system and the slave society".[80]

Yet, in spite of those intentions, the response of the civil authorities and of leading members of the Anglican clergy alternated between passive and active resistance to the presence and work of the missionaries in the West Indies. To understand the reasons for the reaction of the local authorities, it should be noted that the rapid increase in missionary activities in the West Indies following Dr Coke's chance visit to Antigua in 1786 roughly coincided with the launching of the campaign in England to improve the condition of the slaves. For many years, West Indian planters, with the support of the clergy of the established church, had successfully discouraged efforts to convert the slaves. Now Moravians, Methodists and, in Jamaica, Baptists, albeit with the concurrence of a small number of slave masters, were preaching to the slaves, and admitting them into full membership of their congregations even as abolitionists in English, several of whom were active members of the growing number of missionary societies, were calling for substantial amelioration of the spiritual and physical conditions under which slaves in the West Indies lived. The outbreak of the Haitian Revolution merely served to heighten the concern of planters in the British West Indies who feared that subversive activities within their societies would go undetected and unchecked.

Faced with the prospect of increased activity by nonconformist missionaries and with pressure from London to improve the living conditions of the slaves, West Indian legislators moved to give the established church a vote of confidence even as they sought to curb the growing influence of these nonconformist missions. Some of the legislative measures amounted to little more than window dressing, implemented to conceal the true state of the slave society in the West Indies from an increasingly curious English public. But members of the Anglican hierarchy in England, especially Bishop Porteus, were themselves interested in involving the church in missionary outreach programmes.[81] Therefore, in 1800, the Jamaican legislature reversed its earlier position on the establishment in Jamaica of the Commissary Court comprising five rectors to be appointed by the Bishop of London, and having certain powers of discipline over the clergy, although these were subject to the concurrence of the governor.[82] Paradoxically, the same legislature sought to prevent nonconformists from preaching to the slaves. The bill to that effect was enacted in 1800 and was used by the vestries to harass nonconformist preachers who did not have the necessary licence authorizing them to conduct religious services or to engage in teaching.[83] Ultimately, the law was disallowed by the Crown, following representation made by the Methodist Missionary Society. In 1807, the Jamaicans again tried to use legislative power to prevent nonconformists from instructing the slaves. This measure was also struck down by the Crown and the opportunity seized to instruct governors in the West Indies to refer all laws dealing with religious matters to Britain for royal scrutiny and assent.[84]

The response of Barbadian planters to the missionaries' activities was quite similar to that of the Jamaicans. In 1807, they voted to increase the salaries of the Anglican clergy.[85] At the same time, they kept a watchful eye on the activities of the missionaries and, in particular, on those being carried out by the Methodists who were based in Bridgetown. In 1823, a gang of thugs, secure in the knowledge that they would not have to account for their actions, destroyed the Methodist chapel in Bridgetown and forced the missionary, William Shrewsbury, to flee the island. As expected, none of the perpetrators of this crime was brought before the courts.

By fair means or foul, the majority of the West Indian planters had succeeded by 1823 in keeping the activities of nonconformist missionaries within acceptable limits, except for the few isolated cases where some planters who were sympathetic towards the missionaries had invited or allowed them to establish missionary centres on or near their estates. The Moravians, Methodists and Baptist missionaries were obliged to concentrate their activities in the urban areas. Even there, the long arm of the law and the strong-arm tactics of hirelings were effectively used to restrict missionary activity even further.

The turning point came when, yielding to pressure from the abolitionists, the British government placed before Parliament a number of resolutions in which it committed itself to a policy of reform that would lead to "a progressive improvement in the character of the slave population, which would give the access to the civil rights and privileges enjoyed by other classes of Her Majesty's subjects".[86] In other words, the government was committed to emancipation by degrees.

As the authority of the imperial government to legislate on domestic matters had not yet been reduced in the newly acquired colonies of Trinidad, St Lucia, Demerara and Berbice, steps were taken to have resolutions implemented in those territories; legislators in other colonies were urged to take similar action in accordance with the spirit of the resolutions. In Demerara, speculation among the slaves regarding the content of the resolutions, a copy of which had been received by the governor, provided the encouragement for an uprising which was quickly quashed by the authorities with characteristic severity. After dealing with the rebels, the authorities ordered the arrest of the Congregationalist minister, John Smith, charged him as the instigator of the revolt, convicted him and kept him in gaol where he died before the Crown's decision to set aside his conviction was communicated to Demerara. Smith's fate provided Buxton and his fellow abolitionists with the material they needed to press even harder, for the intervention of the British government. At the height of the controversy, the British government announced its decision to strengthen the Church of England in the West Indies by creating two dioceses and appointing the first resident bishops.[87]

Preparing the Society for Freedom?

The decision of the British government to establish two Anglican dioceses in the West Indies, to pay the salaries of the bishops as well as the salaries of a certain number of additional clergymen was considered a means of putting into effect part of its policy of reform.

The slaves were to be prepared for freedom, even though no timetable for the transition had yet been drawn up. Religious instruction was seen as the key to the fundamental problem that emancipation posed for the decision makers in England and the West Indies. If slavery were to be abolished, what would motivate the ex-slaves and their descendants to work industriously on the sugar plantations? In 1824, the answer of the imperial government clearly was that, given enough time, religious instruction could be the most powerful motivating force among the labouring classes.

To arrive at this conclusion, the government would have had to be well acquainted with the results of the first efforts of nonconformist missionaries as well as with those of the more remote experiment carried out on the Codrington Estates in Barbados. Despite the harassment of the colonial officials, the response of the slaves, of manumitted persons and of free coloureds to the missionaries and their teaching, gave reason to hope that a more systematic attempt to Christianize the slave community would be successful in every respect. The decision, however, to entrust that task primarily to the established church and to provide a substantial subsidy from the treasury for that purpose, clearly indicated that the British government, rather like the governments of the older West Indian colonies over the years, felt that it could more safely rely on the loyalty and support of the Church of England, since it had been established by law, than it could on the nonconformist churches.[89] Perhaps an even more compelling consideration was the government's knowledge that in terms of resources already available in the older colonies, and also in light of the partiality shown by local planters, it was political to assign the task to the Church of England.

The dioceses of Barbados and Jamaica were created. The diocese of Barbados included the territories of Barbados, St Vincent, Grenada, Trinidad, Tobago and British Guiana. The Jamaican diocese included that territory, the Bahamas and British Honduras. The first incumbents were William Hart Coleridge and Christopher Lipscomb, respectively. The success of the mission assigned to them by the Colonial Office in London depended on their perception of the role as bishops, on the response of the clergy to their leadership and on the cooperation which they received from the local authorities. Some writers have claimed that the mission of both bishops was eminently successful and have produced, in support of that claim, statistical evidence showing significant increases in the number of clergy employed in the colonies, in the number of church buildings and schools, in the improvement of the system to enforce church discipline especially among the clergy, in the lay membership of the church and in related areas.[90] It is clear that both Coleridge and Lipscomb showed remarkable strength in taking control of their dioceses. It is not entirely clear from the evidence provided that either bishop was particularly imaginative or innovative in his approach to the business of the religious instruction of the slaves.[91] Consequently, when the timetable of events was radically adjusted in England and the British Parliament decided on emancipation, following a period of apprenticeship of four and six years respectively,[92] there was no evidence to support the claim that the business of preparing the apprentices for freedom could be left exclusively in the hands of the Church of England. Accordingly, different arrangements were made for the administration of the Negro Education Grant.[93]

It would be unfair to even suggest that the only, or main reason, for the revision of the British government's evaluation of the capacity of the Anglican Church in this regard, was the shortcomings of its episcopal leaders. One important contributing factor was the hidebound attitude of several of the older clergymen who found it extremely difficult to adjust to a rapidly changing situation.[94] It is not evident that there were many ministers who believed that the objectives of the policy of reform were attainable. Those who showed some willingness to adjust to the new situation found that events were occurring more rapidly than they had anticipated. Up to 1829, the abolitionists in

England were able to embarrass the SPG by publicly revealing the fact that some of the main proposals for reform, such as the banning of the use of the whip in the field, had not been implemented on the Codrington estates in Barbados.[95]

While it cannot be said that the new bishops and their clergy closed "the gap between the upper and lower classes through the bond of Christian fellowship" (Caldecott),[96] their administration of their dioceses did effect significant changes in the character and outreach of that denomination. While social and racial distinctions continued to be observed in the seating arrangements in churches, Anglicans, through Sunday schools, day schools on the plantations and other such means, sought to prepare the slaves for membership in the church. This period saw the extensive use of the services of laymen in the church's outreach. They were used as cathechists, lay readers and teachers.

This development did, however, give rise to tension. The rector of St Lucy was convicted and fined for refusing to allow an appropriate period of time to pass between offering the sacrament of communion to the white members of his congregation and to the blacks. Not surprisingly, Coleridge supported the rector, and on appeal, the conviction was set aside.[97]

It was in Jamaica, however, that tension was at its highest. There, following the outbreak of the slave revolt of 1831, it was widely believed that the Baptists were implicated. The meeting houses and chapels of nonconformist missionaries were attacked, and some of them were burnt to the ground. At the height of this tension, a delegation of Baptist missionaries left for England in order to give a first-hand account of the situation they were facing in Jamaica. While in England, Parliament voted to end slavery after a period of apprenticeship. Slavery was to end and the apprenticeship system take effect from 1 August 1834.

In 1835, Parliament voted a sum of £30,000 a year to promote the education of ex-slaves. It decided that the grant would be made in five successive years after which it would be reduced annually until it ended altogether in 1845.[98] Both the Church of England and other missionary societies working in the West Indies were eligible to receive monies from the fund in accordance with certain clearly defined criteria. In adopting such a policy, the government was now prepared to recognize officially the presence of the several Christian denominations in the West Indies. Such recognition came at the end of a ten-year period, during which the nonconformist churches in the West Indies had experienced significant growth in spite of local pressures to which they had been subjected. The Baptists adhered to their principle of declining state assistance and drew on their own resources in Jamaica and abroad. The Anglican Church Missionary Society doubled its efforts to promote the growth of schools. The Methodists, Presbyterians and Moravians also increased their efforts. As a result of these efforts, the foundation for a public elementary school system was laid in the West Indies. Naturally, the syllabuses and curricula reflected the desire of the educators to "pacify" the masses and to make them an industrious and God-fearing labour force.[99]

Accounts given by missionaries and other contemporary observers paint a vivid picture of churches packed to capacity on Emancipation Day, as the former slaves went to do their religious duty as their first formal act as free persons. Omitted from these accounts were the many sermons, "speakings" and conversations prior to that big occasion when they and their helpers impressed on their captive audience the moral and Christian obligation. It is not possible, therefore, to determine the level of spontaneous reaction of the large congregations on that day. The churchmen of the various denominations were responsible for the psychological and spiritual preparation of the society for freedom. Church leaders were quick to claim victory and proclaim it because they were well aware of the gloomy predictions made by those in England and the West Indies who had opposed emancipation, and because they themselves were somewhat uncertain as to how the emancipated people would behave.

But as the holiday passed and the emancipated people began to exploit fully their freedom of choice, statistics for church attendance, baptisms, marriages and related ceremonies fluctuated, puzzling the church leaders. The same was true of statistics with regard to attendance at day schools. In the years immediately following emancipation, there was a significant increase in school attendance. However, this was followed by a sharp decline in the latter part of the century. Internal migration took place in those territories where land was available for peasant holdings. In Jamaica, where this type of movement occurred, churches steadily lost contact with members of their congregations who had moved away from the traditional areas of settlement while some missionaries followed the trend, and by actively participating in land settlement schemes, sought to maintain contact with the new communiities. In the eastern and southern Caribbean, including Guiana, the movement was not only within territories, but also between territories. For example, Trinidad and Guyana received migrants from Barbados and the Leeward Islands.[100] Indeed, the process had significant antecedents. The settlement in Trinidad of a group of Negro soldiers who were born in America and who had fought on the side of the British in the Anglo-American War of 1812, and had been offered land in Trinidad, brought to that country its first congregation of Baptists.

In Trinidad, they provided religious leadership from their own ranks, developing their own style of worship and self-expression. In other instances also, the movement from one area to another of a number of members of one denomination led to the eventual extension of missionary activity in the new area.

In the mid nineteenth century, the Anglican Church attempted to consolidate its position within the older colonies and to win converts and increase its influence in the more recently acquired colonies.[101] Though it was the established church in Grenada, it had not succeeded in claiming more than a few adherents there. The majority of the population were Roman Catholics. In St Vincent and Tobago, where the size of the English-speaking groups was relatively larger than in other Windward Islands, Anglicans and Methodists made some headway. The colonies of St Lucia and Dominica were in a somewhat different situation. There, the Church of England was not established but the Roman Catholic Church was officially recognized. In British Guiana, the Dutch Reformed, the Presbyterian and the Anglican Churches had been jointly established and endowed in 1824. In the case of Trinidad, the Church of England was the established church, but it had few adherents; the Roman Catholic Church enjoyed the support of the majority of the population. In all these territories, religious tolerance had been promised to the colonists in the Articles of Capitulation.

Given the limited sphere of influence of the Church of England in these colonies, state sponsored schemes for the extension of religious instruction and other forms of education, the implementation of which depended on the involvement of the Anglican and nonconformist churches, were not particularly relevant to them. It was necessary for the colonial governments in these colonies to work out schemes that were more appropriate to their particular circumstances. This was done in the second half of the nineteenth century.

Ten years after emancipation, the nonconformist churches were claiming substantial increases in the size of their congregations and in the scope of their education and other social activities.[102] Like the

Anglicans, they too continued to benefit from regular allocations of financial grants and personnel sent from their parent societies. In most colonies, the tension of the last days of slavery had given way to mutual tolerance and cooperation among denominations. The one significant exception was the altercation between Presbyterians and Baptists in Jamaica over what seemed to be points of theology, but which were in fact partly cultural elements. At that time, the Baptists were reporting more dramatic increases in the size of their congregations than any other denomination. The basis of the complaint by the Presbyterians was that the Baptist missionaries had allowed their congregations to grow beyond their capacity to supervise them effectively. The task of supervision was once again the responsibility of the uneducated and relatively untrained "leaders" drawn from among the people. Consequently, a number of unorthodox and heathenish practices became evident in the various forms of worship and the people were being falsely instructed about matters such as the efficacy of baptism in the sea and the value of membership tickets.[103]

The challenge, which in this instance came from the Presbyterians, could well have come from either the Moravians, the Methodists, the Anglicans or even the British Baptist missionaries. It is interesting to note the comments of the secretary of the British Baptist Society on the occasion of his visit to Trinidad. He wrote:

A short time before my arrival, there had however been a withdrawal of many from the missionary's charge. An American negro introduced the wild and fanatical notions and practices so frequent in the camp-meetings of the Southern States . . . Jumpings were mingled with prayers, and the songs of the sanctuary degenerated into discordant shouts . . . These follies did not, however, reach Montserrat (a district in Trinidad); under the watchful care of the native pastor, Mr Webb, the church abode in peace.[104]

Church leaders were fearful that without their watchful supervision and the exercise of strict discipline, their charges of African descent were likely to taint Christian rituals and beliefs with pagan practices and superstitions. The Anglicans, for example, while they made effective and extensive use of laypersons as catechists, teachers and lay readers, held a tight reign on these assistants. These first bishops of the diocese of Barbados drew up a certificate which that category of persons was required to sign. The first part of the document read as follows:

Declarations made and subscribed to by each Person Previous to his being licensed as a Catechist by the Bishop

I . . . will not preach nor interpret, nor minister the Sacraments, or other public rites of the Church but only teach and read on the plantations or other places committed to my care, that which the minister shall direct for the instruction of the young and ignorant in the principles of the Christian religion.[105]

In light of what we know of the church organization of the Moravians, Presbyterians and Methodists, it is clear that they were able to prevent, or at any rate restrict, the emergence of syncretization. The strong heritage of the native Baptists in Jamaica coupled with the inability of the churches to bring the entire community under its influence were two factors which distinguished the Jamaican experience from that of Barbados where Anglicans, Moravians and Methodists were the only denominations.[106]

As the scope of their work increased, churches in the West Indies became increasingly conscious of the need to train local clergy. This need was most keenly felt in the second half of the century when the influx of subsidies and personnel was systematically reduced by the missionary societies, which were anxious to direct their resources to new mission fields. The Anglicans were the first to take action in this area. Two factors in particular explain this. First, the extensive nature of the church's commitment in the area made it unlikely that the two dioceses would be able to recruit all the clergy they needed from Britain. Secondly, resources were available to Coleridge in Barbados. The terms of the Codrington request had included provision for the establishment of a theological college. Coleridge urged the SPG to act. As a result, Codrington College opened as a theological college in 1830 with J.H. Pinder as its first principal.[107] Beginning with a small intake of students, the college produced its first graduates in 1834 and continued to produce a growing number of clergymen for the West Indian dioceses. Over time, the college became more than a training school for the clergy. In 1875, Bishop Mitchinson negotiated an arrangement whereby it became affiliated with the University of Durham, after which it attracted a steady stream of students who earned degrees in the arts and theology.

The Baptists in Jamaica also felt the need to establish a training centre.[108] Calabar College was opened in 1843. It was originally located at Rio Bueno, but was finally transferred to Kingston in 1869. In 1842 the Baptists in Jamaica became self-supporting. Their decision to depend on local financial resources was evidently linked to their decision to establish a college for the training of local recruits. Within twenty years of its establishment, the team of ministers at work in Jamaica primarily comprised graduates of Calabar.

The Presbyterians opened their Academy in Montego Bay in 1845.[109] The institution offered a good secondary education to those who were likely candidates for the ministry and to students who wanted and could afford to pay for it. Theological training was organized by the Presbytery as an additional component of the academic programme.

It is significant to note that all three theological training centres, in addition to training candidates for the local ministry, also trained local candidates wishing to serve as missionaries in Africa.[110] The Baptists in Jamaica, actively encouraged by William Knibb, participated in the mission to Fernando Poo and East Cameroon, which had been organized and directed by the Baptist Missionary Society of London. The Jamaicans became involved as early as 1842. Similarly, the Presbyterian mission to Calabar was a project directed by the Scottish Missionary Society. Jamaican ministers led by Hope Waddell became involved in the project from about 1846. In contrast, the Anglican mission to the Rio Pongas was actively supported by the Anglican dioceses in the West Indies. The project got underway in 1855. The first missionaries were a white Barbadian clergyman and a black student of the college. According to Caldecott, "since 1864, the Missionaries have all been men of colour".[111] The promoters of these missionary efforts considered it important to recruit local blacks, though not exclusively. The promoters, who were themselves leaders of church missions in the West Indies, saw it as evidence of the state of maturity of the local churches that they were able to provide men for service overseas. However, they did not think that the time was right for giving local candidates a greater share of the responsibility for the administration of the churches in the West Indies.

While the attention of churches in the West Indies was steadily being drawn to the mission field in Africa, certain churches sought to do something about missionary opportunities at home. Since 1842, the Anglicans had broken up the overextended diocese of Barbados into three separate dioceses: Antigua, which encompassed the Leeward Islands; Barbados, which now extended only to the Windward Islands and to Trinidad (the latter becoming a separate diocese in 1872) and

Guiana. The missionary challenge was greatest in the diocese of Guiana[112] because of the emancipated population in the plantation areas and in the growing peasant village. The Amerindian peoples who were spread over a vast and forbidding hinterland, would have absorbed all the energies of neighbouring Caribbean churches for missionary endeavour, had they been so directed. Characteristically, the Anglicans, one of the three established churches in the colony, adopted the parochial system of church administration. The colony was divided into eighteen parishes in the same year that the new diocese was established. These were distributed as follows: Anglicans were in charge of ten while the remaining eight went to the Church of Scotland. Great efforts made by Christian churches in Guiana at this time were directed towards the expanding population of Europeans and persons of African descent who had settled near the coast. The Anglican Church, which received a lot of assistance from the Society for the Propagation of the Gospel, to the extent that it became involved in missionary activity among the Amerindians, did not establish any particular organization for that purpose. All the work was carried out at the parish level.

A second opportunity for Christian missionary outreach in the Caribbean was made possible by the immigration of over 500,000 Indians into the British West Indies between 1840 and 1871. The Indians, together with a much smaller number of Africans and Chinese, came as indentured servants to supplement the labour force on those sugar plantations which seemed to be unable to recruit an adequate number of labourers from within the West Indies. Some 300,000 went to Guiana, Trinidad received approximately 144,000, Jamaica received 36,000 and 10,000 migrated to the Windward Islands of Grenada, St Vincent and St Lucia. The Anglicans and Methodists in Guiana undertook some missionary work among the Indians in the colony, but this was done on a modest scale. In Trinidad, the Anglicans did not attempt anything of the sort until the latter years of the century when some assistance from the SPG was given to the few mission schools which had been established.[113]

The Presbyterians who worked in the Indian community in Trinidad after 1864 had a more impressive record of achievement. The project was initiated by John Morton, a Presbyterian minister from Nova Scotia.[114] Recognizing that education and other social services were not being provided for the growing number of Indians coming to Trinidad, Morton organized support for his project in Canada and personally took charge of the activity in Trinidad. His main thrust was in the area of schooling. Beginning with one school on an estate in 1871, he succeeded in developing a network of similar institutions by the end of the century. From Trinidad, the influence of the mission extended to Guiana, Grenada and Jamaica, to which Morton travelled in a manner somewhat reminiscent of the Methodist missionary organizer, Thomas Coke, assisting the more feeble local efforts that had been started. Having established contact with Indians on the estates, the mission followed those who opted to settle on Crown lands at the end of their period of indenture. The significance of the Presbyterian mission to the Indians lay not in the extent of its appeal and influence (because the missionaries were faced with quite strong cultural and religious barriers), but rather in the fact that it represented the first and the major effort to integrate Indians into the mainstream of the English-speaking and Christian societies of the West Indies. Not surprisingly, their education outreach extended far beyond their religious appeal.

Disestablishment and Movement Towards Autonomy

A number of events in the period after emancipation forced colonial governments in the West Indies, with the active encouragement of the British government, to redefine the relationship between the church and the state within their respective territories. The fact that the Church of England was the established church in several territories was proving increasingly inconvenient for those governments and increasingly distressing to the large number of people who belonged to other denominations. By the middle of the nineteenth century, the Anglican Church in Jamaica was claiming a nominal membership of 48,824 and an active membership of 36,300 persons, or just about a quarter of the population whose religious affiliation could be identified.[115] The Methodists and Baptists ranked second and third respectively with each claiming nominal membership of approximately 41,775 and 31,640, respectively. By virtue of its status as the established church, the Church of England in Jamaica received more than £40,000 a year from the treasury. In the Leeward Islands, the Church of England was also in a minority, though privileged, position in relation to the total number of persons belonging to other religious denominations. In Trinidad, the anomaly of its position was even more glaring, for the Church of England was in a distinctly minority position, as indeed it was in Grenada.

Appropriate adjustments had already been made in some territories. In Guiana, for example, the precedent of joint establishment and concurrent endowment had been set in 1824 and no decision had been taken to establish the Church of England in St Lucia and Dominica. In Trinidad, the Roman Catholic Church received grants from the treasury.

In Britain, the decision was taken in 1868 to terminate the imperial grant of £20,000 which had been voted annually since 1824 to support the Anglican dioceses in the West Indies. This was done to urge their legislatures to proceed with the disestablishment of the church. With the exception of Barbados, the old representative governments had been replaced by Crown Colony governments in the older colonies. Faced with the problems of declining revenue and escalating costs in social services and public works, Crown Colony governments were constrained to be very cost-conscious. In that context, the privileged position of the Anglican Church in most colonies appeared to be unacceptable. However, while most governments agreed on disestablishment, some agreed to grant subsidies to denominations on a more equitable basis. In Jamaica, the governor advised the Church of England that the Clergy Act of 1858 would enable clergymen to draw their salaries from the treasury. In the Leeward Islands, no consensus was arrived at by the constituent territories served by the Anglican diocese of Antigua. In Antigua, for example, the legislature also agreed on disestablishment in much the same way as did Jamaica. But the decision was taken in Montserrat to apply the principle of equity and adopt the policy of concurrent endowment. No change was introduced in the arrangements that were in effect in Guiana.[116]

The one exception to this general trend in favour of disestablishment was Barbados. There, the position of the Anglican Church was quite straightforward; that denomination claimed a membership that was seven times bigger than the total membership of other denominations.[117] Moreover, the Barbadian planters had succeeded in holding on to their Legislative Assembly and they carefully deliberated on the matter. It would seem that their decision to reject the proposal for disestablishment was based not only on sentiment, but on a keen sense of self-interest as well as on some regard for economy. Over the years, they had succeeded in restricting the spread of the influence of nonconformist churches. Through their vestries and through kinship ties with the clergy, they continued to exercise great influence and control over the policy of the established church, in spite of the best efforts of the more energetic bishops. In addition, as Caldecott reminds us, the advantage of not disturbing the current arrangements, as a result of which absentee proprietors were obliged to contribute to the upkeep of the church establishment, did not escape their notice. Accordingly, the legislature re-established the Anglican Church in 1872, and agreed to give small grants to the Methodists and the Moravians, and a further grant of £50 a year to the Roman Catholic chaplain for the British troops stationed in Barbados.[118]

In the British West Indies, disestablishment marked the end of a special relationship between church and state and the start of a new kind of relationship which has persisted well into the present century. It is not quite accurate to describe that relationship as one that is based strictly on the principle of the separation of church and state. In the light of disestablishment, the practice of concurrent endowment of Christian denominations was generally adopted. Such denominations continued to receive subsidies and grants to enable them to carry out what was perceived as a form of public service in education[119] and even in ecclesiastical (or strictly church) work. What was new then was that, increasingly, the state accepted the principle that the level of financial assistance should be linked in some way to the relative size of church membership. The new policy was of no obvious benefit to non-Christian religious groups in the West Indies, nor to the growing number of native and local churches, which increased significantly in the early years of the century.

Where governments were forced to terminate or drastically reduce the size of grants to particular denominations, that trend represented a move towards the voluntarist position long favoured by the Baptists, the principle that the congregation should be materially self-sufficient. For the other nonconformist denominations, including the Roman Catholic Church, a move towards the application of the principle of equality or non-partisanship was a welcome change. It signalled the end of their struggle for the right to exist and to function freely in the society.

For the Anglican Church, this new position made it imperative for it to reorganize itself. It already had a resident episcopate. New dioceses had been created out of the original two in 1842 (Antigua and Guiana) and 1861 (Nassau). The diocese of Trinidad was created in 1872, while one was established in British Honduras in 1883. But it was Jamaica that took the lead in the reorganization of church government. The need to make the diocese financially self-sufficient clearly influenced the form which reorganization took. The bishop retained his authority as head of the church in the diocese, but the synod, comprising the clergy and a representative number of the laity meeting under the chairmanship of the bishop, shared responsibility for the management of the church. Under this new dispensation, the old concept that, once inducted in his cure, the priest would enjoy a sort of freehold tenure, was no longer viable.

Following two informal meetings of some of the Anglican bishops of the West Indies in 1873 and again in 1878 on the occasion of the Lambeth Conference, the decision was taken to constitute a regional body for the members of the Anglican communion.[120] On the advice of the Lambeth Conference, they decided to create a provincial synod. The first meeting of that body took place in Jamaica in 1883. The Anglican province of the West Indies formally came into being in 1893 when Enos Nuttall, at that time bishop of Jamaica, became the first archbishop. Membership in the provincial synod was restricted to the diocesan bishops. It was Nuttall who recognized that it would be economical and more convenient for that body to meet at regular intervals[121] if membership were to be restricted to bishops. The decision was considered reasonable in light of the fact that, in the Anglican church, effective management was in the hands of the diocesan authorities.

When the Methodists turned their attention to the reorganization of the church government, they were beset by more difficult problems than the Anglicans. The Methodists did not suffer the threat of disestablishment, or any similar shock that might otherwise have forced them to close ranks and proceed with the business of reorganization. It would seem that the parent body, the Missionary Society of London, had raised the question several years before the local church convened the first conference in 1884. However anxious the parent society was to encourage the West Indian branch to be autonomous, it is apparent that the strongest resistance to the idea came from English ministers serving in the West Indies.

The debate within the church centred around such questions as the wisdom of cutting ties with the parent society, the implications of that step for the recruitment of staff, and the capacity of the local bodies to manage the church efficiently. Two levels of regional government emerged. One was the General Council, which would meet once every three years, and which would have jurisdiction throughout the region as well as final authority in all matters referred to it. More routine matters would be handled by two annual conferences, one of which had jurisdiction in Jamaica and Haiti, the other having jurisdiction over territories in the Southern Caribbean, including Guiana. These bodies were superimposed on a structure that already provided for some decision making to be done at the level of the circuit and the district. The structure was ambitious in that it placed great strain on the slender resources of a church whose adherents were widely dispersed throughout an extensive region. It required regular movement of large numbers of persons and the frequent referral of matters which were clearly of local import for decisions by higher authorities. Given the circumstances and the unresolved tensions among the ranks of the membership itself, it is not surprising that the experiment in regional organization and management failed and that the Methodist Church in the West Indies once again assumed the status of a district in 1903.

The experience of the Moravians with respect to this same matter was no better. Oliver Maynard, in his *History of the Moravian Church: Eastern West Indies Province*, points out that, prior to 1861, there was little evidence of lay representation in the management of the local congregations. Mission headquarters required ministers to constitute local committees to assist the ministers in fundraising and other important areas. In this case, as in that of the Methodists, the parent societies had taken the initiative because they were anxious to be rid of the burden of local churches, given the size of their congregations and the length of time that had elapsed since they were first introduced into the area. The decision was taken in 1879 to phase in the transition from the status of mission to that of an autonomous province. To that end, executive authority was given to the newly constituted Provincial Elders Conference, a small group that would meet regularly. The main goal of the executive, from the time of its election in 1880, was to steer the church in the Eastern Caribbean towards autonomy. But the painfully slow progress made in this regard forced several postponements of the transfer of authority from the mission board to a locally constituted synod. When the first provincial synod was convened in 1899, one of the first resolutions it adopted was that of informing the General Synod "that the Province was not ready for full self-government as the Mission Board desired". And so the process was further prolonged. The main obstacles to the process were a lack of funds and the absence of a native clergy. Those problems persisted well into the course of the twentieth century.

Moravians, Baptists, Methodists and Anglicans had therefore been forced, mainly by external pressures, to assume greater responsibility for the management of their affairs. In addition to their dependence on parent bodies and affiliated associations outside the region for injections of money and personnel, the local church leaders were anxious to avoid what they perceived as the dangers of isolation. This point may be illustrated by reference to the Anglicans.

The provincial synod of that church was easily persuaded by Enos Nuttall, the first primate of the Anglican Church in the West Indies, to adopt a procedure that would provide for certain matters, especially those relating to doctrine, to be referred to a committee in England comprising the archbishop and a bishop. Nuttall described that decision as a wise one insofar as it guarded against the danger of losing "that conservative influence which is imposed by the connection of the Mother Church".

In addition to money, local denominations needed other resources in order to effect the transition from a foreign directed mission to that of a local church. Those who agonized over the decisions that had to be taken on these matters at the turn of the century became aware of the additional developmental work that had to be done before the church could sever its main ties. There was the need to increase the number, and expand the scope of existing theological schools so that the imbalance between foreign and native clergy would be corrected. Many of the white church leaders entertained doubts about the capacity for leadership of their black coreligionists. Caldecott, writing at the turn of the century, saw the situation in this light:

No coloured man, much less a Negro, has yet become a British West Indian bishop; but the majority of the bishops have come from England, and so long as men of the same stamp can be secured there is likely to be a preference for them, as there is for President of the Wesleyan Conferences or pastors of the chief Congregationalist Churches or Principals of Calabar College.

Those prejudices contributed to the slow pace of change towards self-government. The congregations themselves had been accustomed to perceiving their minister as a white man. They had to be taught to look amongst themselves for their own leaders.

These congregations sided with other sections of the West Indian society in that, as colonials, they looked outwards for leadership. A serious approach to resolving that problem had to await developments in the wider society. The awakening of political consciousness and independence was a process which enabled congregations to develop keener perspectives with regard to the question of leadership in the church.

It is clear, however, that the first positive step taken following those first efforts towards some degree of autonomy, was to expand opportunities for the training of a native ministry. The Anglican diocese of Jamaica opened St Peter's College in Kingston in 1893. The Presbyterian church in 1898 began training East Indian catechists in Trinidad. That programme was later expanded and became St Andrew's Theological College located in San Fernando. The Methodists improved on the work being done at Calabar College, by establishing Caenwood College in Jamaica in 1928.

Over time, the factor of limited resources and the high cost of training prompted some churches to establish joint training programmes. The first of these got underway in Jamaica in 1937. The Presbyterians, who had opened St Colmes College in Kingston, joined with the Methodists, Moravians, and the Disciples of Christ to implement a common programme.

NOTES

1. N. Darnell Davis, "History of the church in Barbados", in manuscript, in Davis Papers.
2. C.S.S. Higham, "The early days of the church in the West Indies", in *The Church Quarterly Reviews* 92 (1921): 104.
3. Ibid.
4. Ibid., 109.
5. Quoted in J.B. Ellis, *A Short Sketch of the History of the Church of England in Jamaica* (Kingston 1891), 17.
6. Ellis, *A Short Sketch of the History of the Church of England*, 19.
7. Higham, "Early days", 107.
8. Ibid., 118–19.
9. William W. Manross, *A History of the American Episcopal Church* (New York 1959), 15.
10. Ellis, *A Short Sketch of the History of the Church of England*, 18.
11. J.B. Ellis, *The Diocese of Jamaica: A Short Account of its History, Growth and Organization* (London 1913), 94.

12. Manross, *History of the American Episcopal Church*, 15.
13. Higham, "Early days", 110. Wheler was at the time governor of the Leewards.
14. Ibid. It is apparent from the full context of the passage quoted that Wheler did not mean to say that bishops lacked the "authority" to send out clergy, but rather that they lacked the resources. These resources were identified as men willing to serve in the colonies, and money with which to pay their passages and their expenses.
15. For a discussion of this matter as it affected Barbados, see K.D. Hunte, "Church and society in Barbados in the eighteenth century" (paper presented at Sixth Conference of Caribbean Historians in Puerto Rico, 1974).
16. Higham, "Early days", 122.
17. Ibid., 119.
18. Ibid., 122.
19. Ibid.
20. Ibid., 123.
21. A. Caldecott, *The Church in the West Indies*, (1898; reprint, London 1970), 45.
22. Higham, "Early days", 120.
23. Caldecott, *The Church in the West Indies*, 45.
24. Higham, "Early days", 124.
25. C.O. 31/1 ends 211 and 508.
26. Richard Ligon, *A True and Exact History of the Island of Barbados* (1657; reprint, London 1970), 50.
27. C.O. 29/1. end 35.
28. C.O. 31/1. end 500.
29. C.O. 28/1. end 41.
30. Cited in Caldecott, *The Church in the West Indies*, 64.
31. Ellis, *A Short Sketch of the History of the Church of England*, 32.
32. The comment is made by Ellis.
33. Caldecott, *The Church in the West Indies*, 70.
34. In 1713 when the French finally withdrew from St Kitts and the English assumed control over the entire island, three new parishes were added.
35. Fulham, MSS, Vol. XV, no. 127.
36. Manross, *History of the American Episcopal Church*, 46.
37. Hans Cnattingius, *Bishops and Societies: A Study of Anglican Colonial and Missionary Expansion 1698–1850* (London 1952), 24.
38. Fulham MSS, Vol. XV, no. 134.
39. Ellis, *A Short Sketch*, 19.
40. Fulham MSS, Vol. XV, no. 139.
41. Ibid., 157–58.
42. Ellis, *A Short Sketch*, 20
43. Fulham MSS, Vol. XVI, no. 85.
44. These impressions have been gleaned from a study by the author of such documents as are available on the subject. It is interesting that over two centuries

later the comments of Edward Long may not seriously be challenged. Edward Long, *History of Jamaica*, Vol. 2 (London 1774), 238.

45. See T. Bennett, *Bondsmen and Bishops: Slavery and Apprenticeship on the Codrington Plantations of Barbados, 1710–1838* (Berkeley 1958).

46. Cited by J.C. Wippell in *Barbados Diocesan History*, edited by J.E. Reece and C.G. Clark-Hunt (London 1925), 65.

47. SPG, Vol. 26, no. 381; see letter from Johnson to Secretary, Bridgetown, 14 January 1736.

48. A useful source is C.F. Pascoe, *Two Hundred Years of the SPG* (London 1901).

49. SPG, Box 8, no. 36.

50. Bennett, *Bondsmen and Bishops*, 79 ff.

51. SPG Box 8, no. 39.

52. The Lodge School.

53. From time to time the rector of St John and other ministers did visit the estates, examine the work of the catechist and baptize them.

54. Fulham MSS, Vol. XV, no. 216.

55. Caldecott, *The Church in the West Indies*, 57. Caldecott gives the following picture of the establishment in the colonies identified between 1800 and 1812.

Colony	Number of clergy
In 1800 Jamaica	20
In 1812 Barbados	14
In 1812 Antigua	6
In 1812 St Kitts	5
In 1812 Nevis	3
	48

56. The picture for the region changes somewhat in the second half of the eighteenth century. Additional clergy, though very few in number, were licensed for service in the Windward Islands during this period. Gerald Fothergill, *A List of Emigrant Ministers to America 1690–1811* (London 1904).

57. C.O. 28/86 and 87 give examples of the clergy in Barbados meeting for the purposes indicated. In Jamaica a commissary explained that the sheer distance between parishes and the poor state of communications made a meeting of the clergy impossible.

58. Long's observations are discussed by Caldecott, *The Church in the West Indies*, 70.

59. Replies of clergy and commissaries to questionnaire in 1723 in Fulham MSS.

60. William Dickson, *Letters on Slavery* (Westport, Connecticut 1970), 22.

61. Ibid., 26.

62. Useful sources are E.V. Goveia, *Slave Society in the British Leeward Islands at the end of the Eighteenth Century* (New Haven 1965); E. Brathwaite, *The Development of Creole Society in Jamaica, 1770–1820* (London 1971); J. Handler, *The Unappropriated People: Freedmen in the Slave Society of Barbados* (Baltimore 1974).

63. Ellis, *A Short Sketch*, 32.

64. Cnattingius, *Bishops and Societies*.

65. G.O. Maynard, A History of the Moravian Church: Eastern West Indies Province (Port of Spain 1968), 5.
66. J.E. Hutton. A History of the Moravian Church (London 1909), 248.
67. Ibid.
68. Ibid.
69. Ibid.
70. Caldecott, The Church in the West Indies, 73.
71. T. Coke, History of the West Indies 3 vols. (reprint, London 1970). Missions were started in Tobago, St Kitts, St Vincent, Barbados, Nevis, Dominica, Jamaica, the Virgin Islands, Canada and Montserrat.
72. Note that his adherents in the West Indies, however, did not propagate that view. Led by Coke, they urged that the spread of Christianity among the slaves was not incompatible with the maintenance of the slave requirements. As Underhill points out (see note 73), Coke, unlike the Moravians, openly commented on the inadequacies of the Anglican clergy in the West Indies.
73. E.B. Underhill, The West Indies: Their Social and Religious Condition (London 1862), 195.
74. F J. Osborne and G. Johnston, "Coastlands and islands: first thoughts on Caribbean church history" (Manuscript presented to the United Theological College, University of the West Indies, Mona, Jamaica 1972)
75. Cnattingius, Bishops and Societies, 57–58.
76. Hutton, A History of the Moravian Church, 252.
77. Osborne and Johnston, "Coastlands and islands". They refer to E.A. Payne, The Baptists in Jamaica, as the source.
78. Ibid.
79. Goveia, Slave Society, 253.
80. Ibid., 306.
81. Cnattingius, Bishops and Societies, 58 ff.
82. Caldecott, The Church in the West Indies, 81–82.
83. Ibid.
84. Ibid., 83.
85. Ibid.
86. Osborne and Johnson, "Coastlands and islands", source identified as T. Rain, Life of John Wray, 180.
87. Caldecott, The Church in the West Indies, 88 ff.
88. Cnattingius, Bishops and Societies, 148.
89. Mary Turner, "The bishop of Jamaica and slave instruction", Journal of Ecclesiastical History 26, no. 4 (1975): 2.
90. See works by Caldecott, Ellis, and Reece and Clark-Hunt, titles of which are given above.
91. For an illuminating discussion and Lipscomb's approach to his task see Mary Turner, "The bishop of Jamaica", 10 ff.
92. According to the original terms of the act abolishing slavery with effect from

August 1834, the period of apprenticeship should have ended in 1838 for non-praedials and in 1840 for praedials. The decision was taken to end apprenticeship for all in 1838.

93. S.C. Gordon, *A Century of West Indian Education* (London 1963), 20–23.

94. Caldecott, *The Church in the West Indies*, 97.

95 Osborne and Johnston, "Coastlands and islands", 97.

96. Caldecott, *The Church in the West Indies*, 96.

97. Ibid., 93.

98. Gordon, *A Century of West Indian Education*, 23–26.

99. Ibid.

100. D.G. Hall, *Five of the Leewards 1834–1870* (London 1971), see table 5.

101. Caldecott, *The Church in the West Indies*, 99, 132–33.

102. Osborne and Johnston, "Coastlands and islands", 121 ff.

103. Ibid., 137–41.

104. Underhill, *The West Indies*, 47–48.

105. Sadler Phillip (ed.), *The Early English Colonies: A Summary of the Lecture by the Lord Bishop of London* (London 1908), 161.

106. P.D. Curtin, *Two Jamaicas: The Role of Ideas in a Tropical Colony* (London 1955), 25–32.

107. T.C. Wippell "Codrington College", in Reece and Clark-Hunt, *Barbados Diocesan History*, 65 ff.

108. Osborne and Johnston, "Coastlands and islands", 153.

109. Ibid., 154.

110. Ibid., 170 ff.

111. Caldecott, *The Church in the West Indies*, 221.

112. T. Farrar, *Notes on the History of the Church in Guiana* (Guiana 1892).

113. Caldecott, *The Church in the West Indies*, 207.

114. S.E. Morton (ed.), *John Morton of Trinidad* (Toronto 1916).

115. Ellis, *The Diocese of Jamaica*, 104.

116. Caldecott, *The Church in the West Indies*, 140.

117. Reece and Clark-Hunt, *Barbados Diocesan History*, 63.

118. Ibid., 33 ff.

119. See S.C. Gordon, *A Century of West Indian Education*.

120. Reece and Clark-Hunt, *Barbados Diocesan History*, 49.

121. Osborne and Johnston, "Coastlands and islands", 198.

ARMANDO LAMPE

Christianity and Slavery in the Dutch Caribbean

The Slave Society

The inhumane trade

The Dutch invaded Curaçao in 1634[1] and the dramatic history of Africans on this island began. In 1637, Holland conquered the fort at Elmina, on the coast of Guinea, which remained under Dutch control until 1729. The West Indies Company transformed it from a "war machine" into a slave trade enterprise. The Dutch colony of Curaçao became the most important slave trade centre in the Dutch West Indies particularly after the loss of Brazil in 1654.[2] The West Indies Company supplied the Caribbean market from Curaçao.

The Dutch slave trade was a triangular commercial activity. The ships sailed to Africa with products from the metropolis. There they exchanged those products for slaves, who were transported to the West Indies and sold to plantation owners there. Finally, they shipped colonial products from America to the republic. The foreigners could only trade with the Spanish colonies illegally. Curaçao, which had an excellent natural harbour and a splendid geographical position, became an important smuggling centre.

In the seventeenth and the eighteenth centuries, the Dutch shipped about half a million slaves from Africa to America. The slave trade from West Africa to the Caribbean was inhumane and Curaçao became an important commercial centre. The last ship with slaves may have arrived in Curaçao in 1778[3] and a slave community was established there. Soon there were many freemen, either slaves who had gained their freedom or blacks who were born free. Both groups lived in conditions of extreme poverty. The social stratification also had a racial character as the blacks were poor.

The local élite consisted of the plantation owners, the business-men and the bureaucrats who settled with their families on the island. Generally, the whites were Protestants. The Jews also belonged to this local élite. In 1659, twelve Jewish families arrived from Holland to establish an agricultural community in Curaçao[4] while others arrived from Brazil, Suriname, Portugal and Italy. Soon they were involved in commercial activities, although one sector remained linked with the plantation system. The symbol of this élite was the possession of a plantation with a "landhuis", the master's castle which was surrounded by the slave huts.

The plantation system of Curaçao was very different from that of the rest of the Caribbean.[5] There were no farming crops or products for export. The owners were not foreigners but local residents and there was no foreign investment nor any efficient system of organiza-tion. Not many slaves could be found on the plantations and prestige was very important to the master. Consequently, Curaçao did not have a so-called plantation economy like other Caribbean islands. The slav-ery system in Curaçao was, therefore, different from the other Caribbean slave societies.[6] However, the slave labour force was com-mon to both Curaçao and those societies. In this peculiar institution the slave was considered another person's private property, available to be sold like any other product.

Between 1816 and 1900, there were forty-four unsuccessful har-vests and only twenty-one good harvests due primarily to very low levels of rainfall. Low productivity standards were caused not only by the climate, but also by the trade crisis, as well as the lack of knowl-edge and of creativity in introducing new methods. During those times of crisis, the master was then forced to buy food for his slaves and would sell slaves in order to earn cash. Between 1816 and 1848, 4,000 slaves from the community of Curaçao were sold and transported by ship. This was a very high number for the small community of Curaçao, consequently it must have been disastrous for the family and social bonds of the slave community.

The slave was extremely valuable to the master. Therefore, the so-called "good treatment" of the slave in Curaçao was a consequence of the need to protect the owner's most valuable merchandise. Curaçao was one of the few places where the annual birth rate was higher than the mortality rate in the slave community. The selling of slaves was financially safer than taking out a loan, therefore the slave's life was important to the master. Generally, the plantation system in Curaçao was unprofitable, as it produced only that which was necessary for the maintenance of the "great family". The slave had to do various types of jobs within that structure; in this sense too, he was indispensable to the plantation owner.

If the plantation system in Curaçao was unprofitable for the owner, why did it survive for so many years? It went on because it was more than an enterprise: it produced a peculiar civilization based on the aristocratic lifestyle of the local élite to which the blacks were indispensable. The whites expected to be served by the blacks and the plantation owners were already satisfied with the survival of the plantation system. Therefore, the members of the élite defended the plantation system, although it was economically unprofitable, because it was a symbol of their social status. They could not conceive of their society without slavery.

Domination of the slaves

Slavery cannot only be interpreted in legal terms as it refers primarily to a social system of domination. The master had absolute power to dominate the slave, while the slave was considered a being without dignity. The slave had been alienated from his past and did not have a life of his own. The Jamaican scholar Orlando Patterson refers to the social death of the slave.[7] Consequently, the slave society was based on violence and fear. The élite knew that the slave would sooner or later resist this humiliation. Therefore the legislation contained many repressive measures. Even in the nineteenth century regulations which, among other things, prohibited slave gatherings, were published in Curaçao. The first seven articles of the publication of 1824 dealt with the problem of the slaves' escape while the next ten articles stipulated an improvement in the treatment of slaves. After the slave revolution in 1795, the aim of those reforms was to humanize slavery, without challenging the system, and thus prevent another revolution. The protection of the slave's life also corresponded with a new historical fact: the importation of slaves was prohibited and consequently, the slave community of Curaçao had to be preserved.

Although the slave in Curaçao was treated as if he were not human, the slave society was characterized as docile.[8] However, this myth of the good master is not acceptable, because there is no evidence that slaves were better treated in one place than in another. All of the owners were convinced that their slaves were the happiest. But, all slaves, regardless of where they were, hated slavery. With respect to the material living conditions of the slaves in Curaçao, oral history, based on testimonies of ex-slaves, has shown that the slaves lived in conditions of extreme poverty, and that old slaves and children had to work. With respect to social living conditions, the slaves could not marry or go to school and their cultural customs were repressed. We have already mentioned that due to the selling of local slaves, families were separated. Only nonproductive slaves could gain freedom. In light of widespread poverty on the island, it was very difficult for the slaves to buy their freedom.

The only valid conclusion is that the institution of slavery in Curaçao was severe. In order to be able to justify slavery, the élite wrote that slavery in Curaçao was humane and that the slaves were well treated.[9] However, according to oral history, the slaves were ill treated. One of the constant themes was the suffering of the slaves as a consequence of violent physical punishments. One of the popular stories states that when a pregnant slave woman was punished, her belly was placed in a hole in order to protect the future slave (*pa jui no haya sla*, as the Papiamento proverb says), the most valuable good of the owner.

Resistance by the slaves

To treat a human being as though he were not human is to provoke his resistance. In 1750, the first great slave rebellion in Curaçao was organized. It was not a mere coincidence that the slaves attacked the Hato plantation, the property of the West Indies Company and one of the residences of the director, the highest authority of the colony. It was not just a spontaneous action to obtain food or ensure better treatment, but an organized movement to gain freedom. It was repressed by the colonial authorities, but the revolution resurged in 1795.

An impressive army of revolutionary slaves was organized by their leader, Tula. After one month of resistance, this revolution was unsuccessful also. The leaders were brutally tortured and cruelly executed in public. The aim of this revolution was not only to put an end to slavery but also to colonialism. That was the greatest fear of the élite. After the creation of Haiti, the first black republic of the Americas, the élite of Curaçao used ideological methods to perpetuate the domination of the slaves.

In the nineteenth century, there were no slave rebellions in Curaçao, but the slaves' resistance to this injustice continued. Their most common method was to flee, either individually or in groups, particularly to the Venezuelan coast. After formal emancipation in Venezuela in 1854, more slaves fled there, because the treaty signed in 1842 by Venezuela and Holland regarding the return of captured slaves was declared null and void. Several Maroon societies existed outside Curaçao. Communities of ex-slaves from Curaçao were established in Coro.

The slaves' resistance was manifested through culture. They created their own culture which was linked to African tradition and adapted to the Caribbean reality. The Afro-Antillian "slave culture" was an important weapon of self-defence, which sought to nourish their human dignity in a society that did not consider them as human beings.

The Catholic Church and Slavery

Catholics and slaves

The Spaniards arrived in Curaçao in 1499.[10] They called it the island of giants due to the height of the Indian people. Those Indians belonged to the Arawak tribe, which was linked to that of the peninsula of Coro. The Spaniards believed that Aruba, Bonaire and Curaçao (the ABC islands) were unprofitable, because they did not find gold there. The bishops of the Coro diocese, which was founded in 1531, presented themselves also as the bishops of Aruba, Bonaire and Curaçao. In 1638, the diocese of Caracas was created and since that time these islands became a part of this diocese. The Spanish evangelization method used laypersons for certain pastoral tasks when there were no priests available. This pastoral worker was responsible for teaching catechism, the rosary and administering the sacrament of baptism. Despite the very irregular presence of priests, Catholicism survived in the ABC islands with the assistance of those laypersons and the Indian community which allowed Catholicism to be integrated into the popular traditions of these islands.

The Dutch invaded Curaçao in 1634. As a Dutch colony, it was rather surprising that priests and Catholics had more religious freedom, although the official laws were more restrictive.[11] Curaçao had become an important commercial centre, so the religious issue could not be an obstacle to any commercial transaction; the colonial authorities were therefore more tolerant. Spanish and French priests arrived in Curaçao on their way to other destinations. In 1677, the bishop of Caracas stipulated that all resident priests in Curaçao should be, *ipso facto*, instructed in religious education. Furthermore, he sent two priests to Curaçao where they found an indigenous community in which all adult members were already baptized, and a slave community in which many members had received the sacrament of baptism. Some slaves requested the additional ceremonies, because they had been quickly baptized. It is possible that those slaves were baptized by the "fiscales" of the Indian community. Had the oppressed been evangelized by the oppressed?

Since the beginning of the eighteenth century almost all of the slaves had been converted to Catholicism, which was not the case in Suriname, another Dutch colony. In Curaçao a peculiar situation arose as the social differentiation was not only racial but religious as well. M.A. Schabel, a Jesuit priest who worked in Curaçao from 1704 to 1713, wrote in his diary that the oppressed had a common religious system which was different from that of the oppressors. Slaves and free men who comprised the majority of the population were Catholics, while the members of the élite were either Protestant or Jewish. Since 1767, the three islands constituted an apostolic prefecture. The apostolic prefect was appointed by Propaganda Fide in Rome. Between 1776 and 1820, the Dutch Franciscans were in charge of this prefecture.[12]

In 1842, this prefecture became an apostolic vicariate. Martinus J. Niewindt, a secular priest from Holland, was appointed the first apostolic vicar. Niewindt arrived in Curaçao in 1824 and remained until his death in 1860.[13] Between 1824 and 1860, Niewindt established a powerful Catholic regime in these islands. He founded numerous new parishes and brought more priests from Holland. The first religious sisters came to Curaçao from Holland. Catechism and the administration of sacraments were better organized. Schools were founded in each parish and other social Catholic organizations were promoted. In order to establish a standard body for the local clergy, Niewindt even started a local seminary that trained young men from Holland. But it did not last long. Niewindt was ordained bishop in 1843 and this strengthened the church's power in these islands.

The élite and Catholicism

In 1635, the Dutch colonists established a Protestant community in Curaçao. The only church with privileged status was the Reformed

Church.[14] The church was built within Fort Amsterdam, a clear sign of the close collaboration between the colonial state and the Protestant community. The West Indies Company stated that its director on the island was, *qualitate qua*, president of the Council of the Reformed Church. One of the important duties of the director was the defence of the Reformed Church. According to an official document of the West Indies Company the Protestant pastors had to evangelize the Negroes, but there is no evidence that slaves were converted to Protestantism in any organized or systematic manner.

In 1741, Pastor W. Rasvelt received a letter from his superiors in Amsterdam, in which they criticized Rasvelt for not succeeding in converting even a single Negro, while the Catholic priest was very successful in the evangelization of Negroes and mulattoes. They urged him to convert the Negroes to the Reformed Church through educational programmes and his lifestyle. Rasvelt responded, stating that he had accepted mulattoes, who were born free, as members of the Reformed Church. He therefore excluded slaves and mulattoes born as slaves and who later gained their freedom. He justified this by using an historical argument, which declared that Protestant pastors had never accepted slaves, blacks or mulattoes, as members of the Reformed Church. His other argument was that the white masters did not allow the pastor to evangelize the slaves, because they had to work and could not lose time receiving religious instruction. He wrote: "It is well-known that mulattoes and Negroes, *ex nativitate et quasi ex natura*, are Catholics or were inclined to Catholicism."[15]

In 1821, another official committee proposed that Protestant pastors should evangelize the slaves. But once again this process was not carried out, because in the context of the Curaçao slave society, the social and racial differentiation was also a religious one. This was also evident in the attitude of the Jewish community, the other half of the dominant élite of Curaçao.[16] In 1735, a third of the richest families belonged to the Jewish community. They constituted a separate segment within the slave society and were important slaveowners. A Jewish author wrote this about the Jewish community of Curaçao: "The slaves of the Jews were not circumcised . . . The Jews of Curaçao baptised their slaves in the Catholic Church, the majority of the Protestants did the same".[17]

The slave society of Curaçao was a segmented one which existed from the arrival of the Dutch and lasted until the first half of the twentieth century. The two dominant segments consisted of

Protestants and Jews, who at the same time were whites. The dominated or subordinated segment consisted of blacks, who were also Catholics. It is clear that a total differentiation between the segments did not exist in reality. Neither the élite nor the oppressed was homogeneous. The élite used Roman Catholicism to strengthen the established system. In 1708, Father Schabel wrote in his diary: "The Governor ordered me to preach to the slaves about the virtues of obedience and loyalty to their masters."[18] The aristocratic ideology, a product of the Curaçao slave society, demanded a social differentiation (master–slave), a racial differentiation (white–black) and a religious differentiation (Catholic–non-Catholic).

The racial discrimination of blacks already existed in Western Europe before the colonial institution of slavery, but once this form of slavery was a fact, European ethnocentrism and racial prejudice were transformed into racism. In Curaçao, this racist ideology was reinforced by a peculiar element: the Protestants from Holland brought the tradition of discrimination against Catholics. Ironically, the slaves in Curaçao were also Catholics. Until 1796, when religious freedom was instituted in Holland, the Reformed Church was the dominant and privileged church, while the Catholic Church led a secret life from the beginning of the sixteenth century. In light of this, Dutch Protestantism was more sensitive to the notion of superiority and Protestants created a negative view of Catholics, who were considered "stupid" and "superstitious". This prejudice against Catholics strengthened the discrimination against slaves and free blacks in Curaçao. Catholicism became an important element in the aristocratic and racist ideology: being a black Catholic slave meant being inferior to the master.

The slave system was based on the belief that slaves were not human beings and therefore all kinds of differentiations had to be created between the oppressed and the oppressors. The black was considered inferior, ugly, backward, and so on. In 1855, a member of the local élite accepted the fact that the majority of the slaves were Catholics and wrote that this was primarily the fault of his ancestors, who, motivated by prejudice, did not want to accept slaves in their church.[19] In 1770 a governor's decision, based on the opinions of the leaders of the Protestant community, expressed a similar discriminatory attitude: "Catholics cannot be buried in the Protestant cemetery, unless they are white." Being white meant that they were neither slaves nor ex-slaves.[20] Even after death, a distinction continued to be made between the oppressed and the oppressors.

Catholicism and the historical strength of the oppressed

In 1828 the district chief, M.E. van der Dijs, wrote the following letter to the governor of Curaçao:

> A few weeks ago Father Niewindt started to work . . . at the plantation Kabrietenberg (also known as Barber) and from there he paid a visit to the Catholics living on other plantations, a worthy initiative . . . A great barn on that plantation . . . was transformed into a Church . . . An action . . . that will unite 500 to 600 slaves in an area so far from the city, that they will have the opportunity to discover their strength . . . and this can have disastrous consequences for peace and order . . . in the colony. Niewindt's apostolic zeal makes him blind and he is not aware of the fact that he is in a mixed colony with slaves, who will erroneously interpret the most sincere and the best intentions.[21]

This representative of the élite expressed clearly the existing link between Catholicism and the social issue in the slave society of Curaçao. A Catholic meeting was at the same time a meeting of the oppressed and despite Niewindt's religious intentions, the slaves could have their own "dangerous" interpretation of the act. A church in Barber, a region where the majority were slaves, could become a meeting place for the oppressed.

Niewindt replied,[22] making the following points:

1. There was no need for the slaves to go to a church in Barber in order to discover their strength, because they were well aware of their situation.

2. Until then, Curaçao had only one Catholic church, which was located in the capital, and visited by all the slaves of the island. This was much more dangerous.

3. It was more in the interest of the plantation owners if the slaves received religious education close to their plantation, because this would mean that less time would be lost and the slaves would become more docile due to the religious influence.

4. The priest was responsible for teaching the slaves to be obedient to their masters and for using his authority to prevent any rebellion.

In the slave society, slave meetings were prohibited, because the authorities knew that such meetings could strengthen their unity. Van der Dijs was well aware that a collective meeting of the slaves, even in a church, was dangerous to the system. Niewindt did not refute this logic: he accepted that an increased number of slaves in one church was much more dangerous to the system. Both accepted the existing link between the religious meeting and the historical force of the oppressed. According to Niewindt, the aim of the Catholic mission was to teach the slaves to be obedient and submissive. As evidence, he sent letters of thanks written to him by several plantation owners. Niewindt was so well aware of the link between the Catholic and the social issue that he gave a political objective to the Catholic mission: to oppose any slave rebellion.

The Conflict of Slave Marriages

The Catholic Church and secret marriages

The marriage laws of Holland were also valid in Curaçao. A civil ceremony had to precede a religious one. But in Curaçao, Catholics who could not abide by those laws, either because they were poor and could not pay the legal fees, or because they were slaves, could be married in the presence of a priest and two witnesses.[23] The apostolic prefect of Curaçao, A. De Bruyn, who arrived in 1773, wrote to Rome that he was granted permission by the civil authorities to bless slave couples. This blessing was considered to be a valid church marriage. He also asked Rome to declare valid marriages between slaves that took place outside of the presence of the two witnesses. He argued that, given the situation in Curaçao, it did not make sense to have witnesses at the religious ceremony. Rome approved these slave marriages, with the ceremonies taking place in the presence of only the priest.

The new apostolic prefect, Th. Brouwers, who arrived in 1776, decided that the poor as well as slaves who wanted to marry could proceed in this way: after confession, in the presence of two witnesses, they could say to each other: "I accept you as my legitimate wife, I accept you as my legitimate husband." But this form of marriage violated the regulations of the Council of Trent, which demanded the presence of a priest. This was not possible in Curaçao after the emergence of the conflict between the civil authorities and Brouwers, who was accused of violating the marriage laws of the colony. Rome therefore approved the form of marriage where a couple could marry without the presence of a priest; the presence of two witnesses was sufficient. However, they had to notify the priest after the religious ceremony. This secret marriage was used by the slaves, who were legally considered as "res" (a thing) and therefore could not marry.

In the oldest register of baptisms in Curaçao, public marriages which included slave marriages and the already mentioned secret slave marriages, had been registered in the presence of a priest and two witnesses. Despite the prohibition of those marriages by the state, the number of slave marriages did not decrease. But a new kind of marriage was introduced. Niewindt wrote in 1828: "so that the secret marriages are valid. Those secret marriages are performed in public so that they may be acceptable."[24] How did this form of secret slave marriage develop in Curaçao?

As a result of Prefect Brouwers' petition in 1785, Rome approved marriages which took place in the presence of only two witnesses. In Curaçao, ceremonies in the presence of only a priest already existed and was approved by Rome thanks to Prefect De Bruyn's petition in 1774. After the approval of the form of marriage without the presence of a priest, a new practice developed: slave marriages without the presence of witnesses or a priest. In 1851, Rome declared all secret marriages valid. The slaves were not considered to be human beings and therefore they could not officially marry, but the Catholic Church respected their human dignity by promoting slave marriages. The slaves had one institution which considered them as human beings: the Catholic marriage, in its different forms.

The state and slave marriages

In 1785, the civil authorities prohibited the apostolic prefect from blessing slave marriages. This led to a conflict between two schools of thought. According to the state, the slave did not have the right to marry, but the church defended this human right of the slave. The official church took sides in favour of slave marriages from a doctrinal point of view, so this did not mean that the church was against the slave system. The civil authorities could not separate the issue of marriage from the social issue. Therefore, after 1785, the state sought to destroy the tradition of slave marriages.

A letter from the governor to the minister of colonial affairs in 1845 states this clearly. The governor received a request to accept secret marriages so that they could be registered as valid civil marriages. The question was whether or not secret marriages had any legal base for the state. The governor answered that he did not have the authority to declare legal an illegal marriage practice. His personal opinion was negative, because those who wanted to marry could proceed without any difficulty (this automatically excluded the slaves). But he categorically opposed any such recognition, because there were slaves among the petitioners. The civil authorities considered the legalization of slave marriages as dangerous to the status quo.

The main reason was economic. In Curaçao they continued to sell slaves. Slave marriages were an obstacle to that trade. The second reason was ideological. In the slave society, marriage was an institution for free persons. If the slave was legally considered as the master's property, it was then a contradiction in terms to speak of slave marriages. The practice of secret slave marriages considered slaves as human beings, while the existing system did not. Thanks to the practice of Catholic slave marriages, the slaves benefited from an institution of the free population. This practice of slave marriages criticized a basic principle of the slave society.

Father Stöppel and slave marriages

In 1817, the Franciscan priest J. Stöppel sent a request to the king of Holland, outlining the three main obstacles to his mission:[25]
(a) that the slaves were not authorized to be instructed in catechism or to let their children be baptized;
(b) that the slaves could not marry, nor could the husband be sold without his wife or vice versa;
(c) that old, sick or dying slaves were not allowed to receive spiritual care.
Father Stöppel proposed several measures to correct this situation, and in particular, defended slave marriages. He argued: "That slaves . . . be allowed to marry legally . . . That the civil and church marriage should be free of charge, because they are really poor . . . That the married slaves cannot be sold without their partner . . ."

The governor wrote that he would have been obliged to suspend Father Stöppel from his duties as a priest if he had lived longer, because his vision was "dangerous" to the peace and order of the colony where slavery was a reality. Stöppel died of cholera in 1818. Stöppel's document was not accepted by the dominant ideology, because it demanded not only a religious ceremony but a civil marriage for the slaves as well. The conflicts between church and state existed because secret church marriages took place without the civil marriage. In fact, the practice of secret marriages meant that civil marriage was not possible for the slaves. Stöppel even requested the possibility of civil marriage for slaves, demanding the abolition of the law which stated that slaves were considered as "res", the basic principle of the slavery system. He also demanded that the secret marriage cease to be secret and become a public event performed in the church.

The official representatives of the élite criticized this point of view put forward by Father Stöppel. They argued that marriage was not possible for slaves, because:

(a) Negroes were, in general, unfaithful to their partner and children, showing a lack of respect for the institution of marriage;

(b) the slave owner could not sell a slave without his or her partner, which signified an economic loss for the master.

They justified their opposition against slave marriages with racist arguments. To accept slave marriages would mean to accept slaves as persons and this was contrary to the economic interests of the élite. The racist ideology justified this situation of oppression: Negroes and mulattoes were inferior and therefore could not marry. The aristocratic ideology did the same: differences were created on all levels between the slave and the master, so the master had the right to marry, but the slave did not. Father Stöppel's request for civil and church marriage of slaves opposed the existing ideology and therefore he was declared *persona non grata*, although he had never criticized slavery.

The slave was considered a being without dignity and therefore sought refuge in the Catholic Church where he found a place that respected his human dignity. By practising secret marriages, the slaves benefited from an institution for free persons. To this effect we can say that the oppressed had their own interpretation of Catholicism, motivated by their search for the recognition of their human dignity. The clergy considered church marriage a means of salvation for the slaves' soul. The slave "played the game", but recognized in the secret marriage the defence of his human dignity. Thus Catholicism became a part of the symbolic nucleus of slave resistance.

The Religion of the Slaves

Black culture

Since the seventeenth century, the slaves of Curaçao were integrated into the Catholic Church, but the official church did not develop a specific method of evangelization for the slaves. Consequently, the slaves developed their own interpretation of Catholicism which reflected their situation of oppression as well as their African beliefs.[26] A form of popular Catholicism *sui generis* developed, in which elements of the Catholic and African religions were combined. Throughout the Caribbean, the Afro-Caribbean culture was a new creation developed by the slave, which involved elements of African and European cultures.

There was, for example, the "ocho dia" (eight days) funeral tradition where Nanzi stories were told.[27] Although several forms did exist, we can note the following characteristics: after the death of a person, all the windows and doors of the house were opened in order to facilitate the flight of the soul. In the house an altar was built, and a lit candle was obligatory. During the nine days after the departure of the deceased or eight days after the burial, which had to occur within twenty-four hours, the community gathered in the house of the deceased to pray the rosary under the guidance of a "rezado", their own religious leader. The last night had a festive character. In addition to chants and prayers, food and drink were available and Nanzi stories were told.

In Curaçao these stories have become an integral part of the oral tradition.[28] At the end of the nineteenth century, the first stories were documented. Those stories on the spider Nanzi were brought by the slaves from Africa to Curaçao. Similar stories exist in Suriname and in the British Caribbean, which also experienced slavery. In Ghana, the Ashanti people knew the Anansesem, the stories about the spider, although they did not always have the spider Ananse as protagonist. The Ashanti people celebrated the Apo ceremony during the eight days prior to their New Year. A carnival atmosphere was created and social differentiations ceased to exist during those days. It was possible to criticize the status quo through the Anansesem.

The "novena" was a popular Spanish custom brought by the Spanish clergy to America. The Spanish priests founded the Catholic Church in Curaçao and the slaves accepted the Catholic religion but imposed their own interpretation of this religion. After nine months of conception a human being is born, so too after nine days the deceased is born again from the "womb" of Mother Earth. Therefore, according to African tradition, the feast was organized on the ninth day, because it meant the rebirth of the deceased in the world of the ancestors. During the eight days after the burial, the slaves in Curaçao would narrate the Nanzi stories. This was similar to the Apo ceremony which lasted for eight days.

Not only did this reflect their own interpretation of the Catholic tradition, but also of the African religious tradition. In the stories from Ghana, Ananse, a mythical figure, was related to the God Nyankopon, the creator, and they had an aetiological function. The slaves preserved the figure of Ananse, but gave new meaning to his image. The Nanzi stories, as part of the oral history of Curaçao, had a common historical basis. They dealt with the master–slave relationship: "Shon Arey" represented the master, while the "Nanzi" represented the slave.[29] As part of the slave culture, the Nanzi stories were apparently entertainment stories, but in essence, they were stories which spoke out against the slaves' situation. Nanzi, the weak, triumphed over Shon Arey, the powerful, and Nanzi's victory was seen as the slave's victory. Thanks to this symbolism, the slave could escape, for a moment, from his or her state of permanent dishonour.

Within the slave society, where every slave meeting was prohibited, the funeral rite with Nanzi stories became a form of protest. Therefore, the civil authorities proclaimed several edicts opposing such gatherings. The rite of the "ocho dia" reinforced the unity of the oppressed. The slaves developed a survival strategy, in order to make daily life more bearable. It was a strategy of resistance against the dehumanization process of the slavery system. They protested in order to survive within the system.

The funeral rite had special meaning for the oppressed. More than a simple rite of passage, it was also an opportunity for "grounding together" (Walter Rodney).[30] Implicit in this religiosity of the oppressed we will find the logic of accommodation within the resistance and resistance within accommodation.[31] The popular religiosity was a way to survive within the oppressive system. Through this, the slaves could express their frustrations, but at the same time it was not an incentive for them to actively protest against the system. In fact, it prevented the spiritual destruction of the oppressed. This popular religiosity was a form of passive resistance against the process of dehumanization.

Christianity and freedom: a contradiction?

A slave's interpretation of Christianity in terms of active resistance against the system is evident in the discussion between Tula and Father Schinck.[32] Tula was the leader of the slave revolution in 1795, while the Franciscan priest, J. Schinck, had been working in Curaçao since 1778 and became the apostolic prefect in 1787. He spoke the slaves' language and was appointed the official mediator between the civil authorities and the revolutionary slaves. Schinck paid a visit to the slaves and presented an official report to the Colonial Council. The slaves welcomed Schinck on 19 August 1795 and he relayed the governor's official message to them. The slaves had to surrender and return to their jobs and there would be a general amnesty for all those who accepted these conditions.

Tula rejected this proposal, and told Schinck: "We have already been ill-treated, we do not want to harm anybody, we only want our freedom. The French blacks have gained their freedom, Holland has been occupied by the French, therefore we too have to be free." Schinck responded to Tula, stating "that our government is in Holland and that we have to obey our government". Tula answered: "If this is true, where are the Dutch ships?" Schinck tried to convince them not to continue with the rebellion, using the argument that Curaçao was too small and could not be compared with St Domingue where it was possible to flee to the mountains. He did not succeed in convincing Tula.

Tula made the following declaration to Father Schinck:

Father, do not all the persons spring from Adam and Eve? Was I wrong in liberating twenty-two of my brothers who were unjustly imprisoned? Father, French liberty was a disaster for us. Each time one of us is punished, we are told: "Are you also looking for your freedom?" One day I was arrested, and I begged mercy for a poor slave, when I was liberated, my mouth was bleeding, I fell on my knees and I cried to God: "O Divine Majesty, O Most Pure Spirit, is it Your will that we are ill-treated? Father, they take better care of an animal".

After this conversation, Schinck was housed for the night. The following morning they brought him coffee and a horse for his return journey. Before leaving, Schinck asked Tula for his final decision. Tula answered: "We want our freedom."[33]

Tula interpreted the Christian message as being compatible with the liberation of the slaves, as is the case with today's black liberation theology. The priests continued to preach obedience, but the slaves would interpret the significance of such a message differently. Tula's interpretation was so independent of that of official Catholicism, that Father Schinck could not understand it. Schinck wrote to the governor: "I have to acknowledge that my expectations were different; the blacks have always obeyed me and have always accepted all my proposals for their salvation. I cannot understand why this did not happen now."

Schinck thought that the slaves would always obey his authority, but the slaves disobeyed him in order to remain faithful to the fight for freedom. For the official church, there was no contradiction between the Christian message and the so-called right of the whites to dominate other human beings; the slaves interpreted the same Christian message in order to justify their right to freedom. This "schism" between official Catholicism and popular Catholicism was surprising to Schinck: "All this made me sad and I have decided to return to my homeland in order to find peace for my soul, which I have lost here in Curaçao." Nevertheless, Schinck stayed in Curaçao and in 1811 he went to Suriname.

Further proof of the schism between the official church and the people was the fact that the revolution of 1795 started with a religious act. Their own religious leader, Mingeel Bulbaaij, prepared a special drink, which was shared by the slaves before the revolution actually began. It is a well known rite which played an important role in several revolutions during different periods and in many countries of Africa. This rite began once the religious leader gave the rebels "medicine" which they had to drink in order to become invincible on the battle field. In other Caribbean countries, it was a well known fact that religious leaders of the slaves inspired resistance movements against slavery, as in the case of the role of the voodoo priest in the Haitian revolution. In an official document, it was stated that Catholic priests paid a visit to several plantations, after the revolution of 1795, in order to liberate the slaves from the curse, due to their participation in that rite. The official church practised a policy of persecution of African religions.

Even before 1795, there were slaves who believed that their baptismal certificate was their freedom paper. In 1773, the apostolic prefect of Curaçao wrote to Rome, implying that many plantation owners were complaining that slaves had been fleeing to Venezuela, on the pretence that in the Spanish colony, they could freely practise their Catholic faith. In 1784, Father Th. Ten Oever was accused of baptizing many adult slaves and of issuing baptismal certificates. In 1785, Father Th. Ten Oever was expelled from the colony by the civil authorities. There were slaves who presented themselves in the Spanish colony with these documents in order to gain their freedom. After 1750, many slaves fled to Venezuela, because the Spanish king ordered that Catholic slaves who sought refuge in a Spanish colony should be considered free persons. Many communities of ex-slaves from Curaçao were established on the outskirts of the city of Coro.

Facing the Challenge of Emancipation

The civil regime and emancipation

Emancipation in the British colonies in 1833 immediately influenced the Dutch government's policy, as British Guiana was close to Suriname. After emancipation in the British colonies, a phase of "apprenticeship" was established in order to keep the ex-slaves within the plantation system and to teach them European values. But in 1838, the British government had already abandoned this project, because there was a great need for a labour force and, consequently, an economic crisis developed in the plantation system. Due to this negative experience, the Dutch government was reluctant to abolish slavery in the Dutch colonies before and after 1840. The Dutch government decided to postpone emancipation to a later date because it did not want to destroy the plantation system in Suriname.

In 1848, emancipation in the French colonies also greatly influenced the Dutch colonies. Slavery was abolished in 1848 in the French colony of St Martin, while the slaves in the Dutch part of St Maarten went on strike until they obtained their freedom.[34] Public protest meetings were held and a group of slaves fled to St Martin. All of the slaves threatened to cross the border and the plantation owners on the Dutch side were obliged to grant them their freedom in order to contract them as labourers. The colonial authorities of St Maarten accepted the free status of the slaves based on the proclamation of 6 June 1848, although formal emancipation did not take effect until 1863. When the slaves of the other Dutch island, St Eustatius, heard of the liberation of the slaves in St Maarten, they organized a rebellion in order to gain their own freedom. There were 1,400 people, 1,100 of whom were slaves, living on the island. On 12 June 1848, the slaves gathered in front of the governor's house. This public manifestation was cruelly repressed by the authorities, and several slaves were killed.

The Dutch government had already been forced to accept the free status of slaves in a Dutch colony in 1848. This unique event obliged the Dutch state to reconsider its plan to grant the immediate emancipation of the slaves, but in 1849, the minister of colonial affairs stressed that the Dutch government was in favour of a period of transition. He based his argument on three facts: the lack of financial means, the negative experience of immediate emancipation in the British, French and Danish colonies and the fear of new rebellions in the Dutch colonies. According to the minister, moral and religious education was an indispensable weapon needed to dominate the slaves and to prevent new outbreaks of violence. In 1847, the Colonial Council of Curaçao arrived at the same conclusion. The local élite also proposed to postpone emancipation, because the slaves were not mature enough to be free and supported the idea that the Catholic clergy should play an important role in this period of transition due to its great influence on the black population.

The Catholic regime and emancipation

While the slaves longed for their immediate freedom, the policy of the official church in the nineteenth century was based on the principle that slaves were not mature enough to be free.[35] Instead of being an emancipator, as the historian C.Ch. Goslinga wrongly described Niewindt, Bishop Niewindt was in favour of the postponement of emancipation. Bishop Niewindt was the owner of one of the largest plantations in Curaçao and until 1859 his plantation, Barber, had twenty-three slaves. In 1853, Niewindt continued the practice of selling slaves. It is not surprising then, that the slaves identified the missionary with the "master".

Before 1848, the official church in Curaçao was not concerned with the project of emancipation. Impressed by the slave rebellions in St Maarten and St Eustatius, Bishop Niewindt wrote, for the first time, on the question of emancipation on 13 July 1848. His message was that the slave should be prepared for freedom, that the colonial order should be preserved and that among the most important issues should be the moral and religious education of the slaves. He wrote that the religious education of the slaves would prevent a revolution such as the Haitian Revolution. He concluded that the status quo should be retained and that it would be best served by Catholic missions among the slaves. According to Niewindt, Jewish and Protestant plantation owners agreed that as a result of the influence of the Catholic priests the slaves would not organize rebellions. Niewindt accepted that emancipation was inevitable, but an immediate and general emancipation would be disastrous for the colony.

In 1849, Niewindt wrote to all the priests, urging the slaves to abide by their religious duties in order to ensure a successful period of transition. He stressed the urgent need to implement measures that would prevent immediate emancipation, fully aware as he was of the growing restlessness among the slaves of Curaçao. In June 1848, Niewindt wrote that "the slaves here speak publicly about freedom. Not only the Governor, but also Protestants and Jews asked me to use all our influence on the population and especially on the slaves in order to prevent a rebellion; we achieved that goal with the full support of the clergy."[36] Here we notice a clear distinction between the people's demand and that of Niewindt. Niewindt was in favour of the postponement of emancipation while the people demanded the immediate abolition of slavery. Niewindt was deeply involved in the system of slavery, as he was still engaged in the selling of slaves in 1853.

Another priest, J.J. Putman, criticized the fact that a bishop could be a slave trader. He also opposed the fact that Niewindt was a slave owner. Niewindt forced him to resign and in 1853 Putman had to leave Curaçao. He returned to Holland, after sixteen years of work with the slaves in Curaçao. In 1855, he opted for the immediate and general emancipation of the slaves, using the following arguments. According to Putman, they were so sufficiently civilized to live with the colonial order, that after emancipation, a black revolution was unlikely. Thanks to the Catholic mission, they were ready to accept colonialism without slavery. Putman compared the situation in Curaçao to that of St Maarten and St Eustatius and concluded that rebellions took place on those islands where Methodism had more influence. Slave rebellions did not occur in Curaçao where Catholicism was influential because of the intensification of pastoral work by Niewindt and a group of priests.

Putman's argument was that the Catholic Church had gained so much power that it was able to convince the slaves not to rebel against the colonial order. The slaves were taught by the Catholic Church to be obedient. The idea of a period of transition was foremost in Putman's thoughts. He opted for immediate emancipation in 1855, because the slaves had been prepared for this change. According to Putman, the slave revolution occurred in Curaçao in 1795, because the Catholic Church did not have as much influence then as it had in the nineteenth century. Both Putman and Niewindt held the paternalistic view that the slaves had to be educated to be free. Both defended the idea of a period of transition, although they both arrived at different conclusions. Neither of them discussed emancipation before the events of 1848 in St Maarten and St Eustatius. In 1849, Niewindt preferred gradual emancipation, while Putman was in favour of immediate freedom. In that same year, the Dutch government praised the achievements of Niewindt and the priests, because, thanks to the religious education of the slaves, they ceased to be rebellious.

Late emancipation

Recent studies on slavery criticized Eric Williams' famous work *Capitalism and Slavery*, which claimed that economics was the sole decisive factor for the abolition of slavery.[37] It is more appropriate to state that there is a complex network of factors that contributed to the abolition of slavery, such as the ideological element and slave rebellions, without excluding the economic factor. In most of the Caribbean cases, the sociopolitical activities in the metropolis, the influence of businessmen and slave owners and the slaves' resistance played an important role in the process of emancipation.

However, this process remained primarily in the hands of the Dutch government and the élite in the Dutch colonies where slavery was abolished at a later date.[38] The emancipation movement in Holland had a secular nature. It was a dispute between politicians and businessmen and until 1863 was deemed necessary for Dutch commercial interests. The slave rebellion in St Maarten forced the Dutch government to consider the possibility of granting immediate emancipation, but the 'peaceful' attitude of the slaves in Curaçao and Suriname encouraged the government to postpone the abolition of slavery.

The Catholic Church was directly responsible for the fact that the slaves did not oppose slavery in 1848. Bishop Niewindt intervened personally, because of the growing unrest in the slave community, to convince the slaves not to rebel against the system. To this effect, the official church was partly responsible for the fact that the emancipation process remained in the hands of Dutch politicians and businessmen and that the abolition of slavery did not take place before 1863. The Catholic mission was one of the elements in the complex network which explains why slavery in the Dutch colonies was not abolished until 1863. The late emancipation in the Dutch colonies was not only a result of economic interests as is generally accepted.

Protestantism and Slavery in Suriname

One hundred years after the "discovery" of America by Columbus, the Spaniard, Domingo de Vera, arrived in Guayana, at the "Costa Brava", and "in the name of God" he took possession of this land. The Spaniards soon abandoned this part of the continent; Guayana – the central part is Suriname – was occupied several times by the imperial European powers. The French, the British, and the Dutch had landed there, but they did not stay to colonize the land. In 1667, Suriname became a Dutch colony, first governed by the States of Zeeland, later by the West Indies Company, which delegated its powers to the Privileged Society of Suriname, and finally by the Kingdom of the Netherlands (1816).[39] In 1975, Suriname obtained its political independence.

Suriname became a plantation colony in which the metropolitan model was imposed, which explains why there was strong unity between church, state and society. It was a clear manifestation of the European Protestant "Christendom", as the church depended completely on the colonial authorities and plantation owners. Liturgical activities were held at the site of the government house. The colonial authorities appointed and dismissed pastors. Decisions of the ecclesiastical councils were only valid after the approval of the civil authorities. Political representatives presided over ecclesiastical meetings.

There was no place for any other church. Only the established church could function in this situation. Nevertheless, the Jewish religion was tolerated, because many planters were Jews and they contributed to the economy of the country. This was also the case of the German migrants, whose Lutheran Church was also respected. The civil authorities practised a policy of intolerance towards the Catholic Church. The inhabitants could profess their Catholic faith, but public gatherings were prohibited.

For many years, the Reformed Church of Suriname maintained the image of being the official church and the church of the traders.[40] The exploitation of the colony was considered a religious task. It was therefore not surprising that the directors of the Society of Suriname provided the colony with pastors, whose duties included the preaching of God's word as well as other liturgical activities. The theme of evangelization of the indigenous population was present in the official documents, but the planters who determined the policy of the local church, boycotted any initiative concerning the indigenous people.

The church could not intervene in the master–slave issue, because black slavery was the foundation of the plantation economy. Those born of unlawful marriages between the master and the slave women enjoyed a privileged status. However, free Indians, Maroons and slaves were not integrated in the official church.

Three Moravian Brothers arrived in Suriname in 1735 and took the initiative to evangelize the Indians and the blacks.[41] This led to a new era with the establishment of the Moravian Church in Suriname, which assumed the challenge of the Christianization of the slaves. However, not everyone was pleased with this plan. In a segmented society with a clear separation between blacks and whites, the Christianization of slaves remained a controversial issue. Their arrival was the result of negotiations between August Gottlieb von Spangenberg, the representative of the Moravian Brothers, and the directors of the Privileged Society of Suriname in Amsterdam. The arrangement with the society stipulated that they had to respect the official church and its pastors, and that they had to preach the virtue of obedience, by telling the slaves that being Christian did not imply that they would gain their freedom.

Spangenberg and the Moravian Brothers accepted those conditions. They believed that slavery was a divine institution and one could not resist God's will, and they kept their promise of obedience to the civil authorities. First, in 1740, they tried unsuccessfully to evangelize the Indians of Berbice and West Suriname. In 1765, thirty years after their arrival, they were authorized by the colonial authorities to baptize the Maroons and the slaves (in 1760 and 1762, peace treaties were signed with the Maroons).

The Moravian Brothers sympathized with the victims of the system, although they were not opposed to it. Their preachings were based on European Christianity. Their missionary work had the blessing of the colonists' church, which prevented blacks and slaves from becoming members of the established church. But it was not until the nineteenth century, while searching for ways to prepare the slaves for freedom, that the élite discovered that the evangelization of slaves was useful to the colonial order. During the eighteenth century, nearly all the plantations remained closed to the missionaries. In 1836, 50 plantations were opened to the missionary work of the Moravians. By 1848, this increased to 130 plantations. Up until 1830, few slaves were baptized in the Moravian Church, and between 1830 and 1836 there was a spectacular growth in this church (from 2,000 to 27,000 members).

This was an important change, as the option for the Christianization of the slaves was something new.[42] Up until 1830, missionary work was considered to be contrary to the interests of the plantation economy. After 1830 they saw missionary work as fundamental to the system. In 1808, the slave trade was prohibited and in 1834, slavery was abolished in England. In this context, missionary work gained a "political" objective: to convince the slaves not to organize any rebellion or to seek refuge in British territories. The hope of the élite was that the missionaries would educate the slaves to be hard working and docile free citizens, who would not question the social structure.

The change in the official policy that supported missionary work was one of the factors that explained the spectacular growth of the Moravian community, but there were also other reasons. Only a slave who was a member of a Christian community could be granted freedom at a certain time, and only members of a religious association could enjoy certain political rights. Between 1832 and 1863, more than 6,000 slaves received their freedom, and those who were liberated were told to become members of the Moravian Church. To be a member of a church signified entering a new world, which could produce the fruits of freedom and social status.

But there was also another reason. In the African religion the antisorcery tradition was fundamental. According to this tradition, the evils of illness, poverty, failure and oppression may be caused by sorcery, and consequently the same religious tradition claims to have the weapons to fight them. Within the African world view, it was possible to use the mystical forces against the well-being of the individual and the society. In Suriname, this belief in the antisocial use of the mystical powers was widely practised during the colonial period. In Surinamese creole it was referred to as "wisi".[43] It is possible that slaves who had been baptized interpreted the Christian religion within their antisorcery tradition; they saw Christianity as a weapon against sorcery. This may explain why the slaves did not oppose the destruction of their religious objects by the Moravian Brothers, a well known practice within their African antisorcery tradition.

When the missionaries in Suriname preached against "idolatry", the slaves interpreted that message as a reference to "sorcery".[44] Similarly in Curaçao, the slaves had their own interpretation of the missionaries' Christian message. The same process was described by Genovese with regard to the case of the southern part of America: that the African principle of believing in stronger gods did not mean to surrender one's own gods. The slaves interpreted Christianity according to their own tradition: "They conquered the religion of those who had conquered them."[45]

The planter's interest in the Christian mission and the slave's interest in the church were based on contradictory motives. The rich planters wanted to keep the slaves on the plantations, by using the Christian mission to preach obedience to the colonial authorities. We should not forget that emancipation in British Guiana had occurred in 1834 and the plantations in Suriname were losing their labour force. For the slaves, the church was a means of liberation of their social misery and of the forces of sorcery.

The abolition of slavery in 1863, however, dealt a serious blow to the plantation economy, as the expectations of the planters were not realized, because the ex-slaves left plantation work en masse. Church and state worked closely together in order to gain the sympathy of the blacks after the abolition of slavery. The colonial authorities had their own interest in supporting the Christian mission: to Christianize the slaves in order to save the colonial system, and to avoid another Haiti, where the slaves not only fought against slavery but also against colonialism.

The Moravian Brothers were happy with the official recognition of their church and expected more support from the state. The state needed the church's support to maintain peace and order in the colony. Due to the official recognition of the Catholic Church, the Moravian Church ceased to be the only church dedicated to the poor of the country. Strong competition developed between Catholic and Moravian missionaries as each church tried to obtain the largest number of baptisms. The majority of the population, namely the blacks, became members of the Moravian and the Catholic Churches. When the Moravian Church threatened to punish couples who were not legally married, many left the Moravian Church and became members of the Catholic Church. This meant, once again, that the slaves did not accept the church's doctrine, instead they had developed their own interpretation of the Christian message.

Differences and similarities can be found when comparing the case of Curaçao with that of Suriname. In Suriname, Christianity was in fact the religion of the whites until the nineteenth century, while in Curaçao, Catholicism had been the religion of the blacks since the seventeenth century.[46] In Suriname, plantation owners feared that the Christian message would promote freedom among the slaves, and thought that the hours dedicated to religious practices could be better used for the production process.[47] The slave society of Curaçao was not similar to that in Suriname, and consequently, the social function of Christianity was different. However, in the nineteenth century, both in Curaçao and in Suriname, the Christianization of slaves gained a political objective, namely to convert slaves to Christianity in order to dominate the oppressed due to the fact that the abolition of slavery was postponed in the Dutch colonies until as late as 1 July 1863.

NOTES

1. C.Ch. Goslinga, A Short History of the Netherlands Antilles and Surinam (The Hague 1979).
2. C.Ch. Goslinga, Los holandeses en el Caribe (Havana 1983).
3. P.C. Emmer, Engeland, Nederland, Afrika en de slavenhandel in de negentiende eeuw (Leiden 1974), 175.
4. I.S. and S.A. Emmanuel, History of the Jews of the Netherlands Antilles, 2 vols. (Cincinnati 1970).
5. W.E. Renkema, Het Curaçaose plantagebedrijf in de negentiende eeuw (Zutphen 1981), 253–57.
6. H. Hoetink, Het patroon van de oude Curaçaose samenleving: een sociologische studie (1st edition 1958; Amsterdam 1987); R.A. Römer, Un pueblo na kaminda: een sociologische historische studie van de Curaçaose samenleving (Leiden 1977), 31–35.
7. O. Patterson, Slavery and Social Death: a Comparative Study (Cambridge, Mass. 1982), 38.
8. H. Hoetink, "Race relations in Curaçao and Suriname", in Slavery in the New World, A Reader in Comparative History, edited by L. Foner and E. Genovese (Englewood Cliffs 1969), 178–88.
9. For the opinion of several planters see "Tot het voorstellen van maatregelen ten aanzien van de slaven in de Nederlandsche Koloniën", Staatscommissie benoemd bij Koninklijk Besluit 66 (29 November 1853), and Tweede Rapport, De Nederlandsche West-Indische eilanden en bezittingen ter kuste van Guinea ('s-Gravenhage 1856).

10. F.C. Cardot, *Curazao hispánico (Antagonismo flamenco-español)* (Caracas 1973).

11. P.A. Eeuwens, "Godsdienstige toestand van Curaçao, in de eerste eeuw (1634–1742) van het hollandsch bestuur", *Historisch Tijdschrift* 9 (1930): 317–37; 10 (1931): 103–25.

12. A. Meersman, "De minderbroeders der Germania Inferior op Curaçao (1776–1820)", in *Collectanea Franciscana Neerlandica*, Deel II ('s-Hertogenbosch 1931), 585–600.

13. C.Ch. Goslinga, *Emancipatie en emancipator, De geschiedenis van de slavernij op de Benedenwindse eilanden en van het werk der bevrijding* (Assen 1956).

14. G.F. de Jong, "The Dutch Reformed Church and negro slavery in colonial America", *Church History* 40 (1971): 423–36.

15. L. Knappert, "Wigbold Rasvelt en zijne gemeente op Curaçao, 1730–1757", *De West-Indische Gids* 21 (1939): 1–11, 33–42.

16. F.P. Karner, *The Sephardics of Curaçao: A Study of Socio-cultural Patterns in Flux* (Assen 1969), 28.

17. JM.L. Maduro, "De Portugeesche Joden in Curaçao", in *Gedenkboek Nederland–Curaçao 1634–1934* (Amsterdam 1934), 69–78.

18. I found a copy of this diary in 1985 at the RC rectory of Pietermaai. In the meanwhile this rectory was closed and nobody knows what really happened with the archives. My most important source for this study has been: G.J.M. Dahlhaus, *Mgr Martinus Joannes Niewindt, Eerste Apostolisch Vicaris van Curaçao, Een levens schets, 27 Aug. 1824–12 Jan.1860* (Baasrode 1924) which includes an impressive collection of Niewindt's letters – a most valuable work taking into account that the archives of the Diocese of Willemstad disappeared in the flames of the May revolution in 1969. All references to Niewindt are taken from this book.

19. H. van der Meulen in *Tweede Rapport*, *De Nederlandsche West-Indische eilanden en bezittingen ter kuste van Guinea*, 260.

20. Quoted by J. Hartog, *Mogen de eilanden zich verheugen, Geschiedenis van het protestantisme op de Nederlandse Antillen* (Curaçao 1969), 50.

21. Algemeen Rijksarchief, *OAC-II 37* (The Hague).

22. P.A. Eeuwens, "Barber, De oudste buitenparochie van Curaçao", *Koloniaal Missie-Tijdschrift* 15 (1932): 122–26; 145–52; 225–34.

23. B.A.J. Gijlswijk, "De huwelijksvorm der burgerlijke wetgeving in de kolonie Curaçao", *Koloniaal Missie-Tijdschrift* 5 (1922): 20–228; Gijlswijk, "De huwelijksvorm van het kerkelijk huwelijk in de kolonie Curaçao", *Koloniaal Missie-Tijdschrift* 6 (1923): 296–308.

24. M.J. Niewindt's letter to the governor of Curaçao dated 1 September 1828, quoted in Dahlaus, *Mgr Martinus Joannes Niewindt*, 99–102.

25. M.F. Abbenhuis, "De requesten van Pater Stöppel en Prefect Wennekers in 1817 en 1819", *De West-Indische Gids* 34 (1953): 38–50.

26. A. Lampe, "O catolicismo negro na sociedade escravista de Curaçao", *Escravidão negra e história da Igreja na América Latina e no Caribe*, edited by J.O. Beozzo (Petrópolis 1987), 169–98.

27. L.F. Triebels, *Ocho dia of novena: een afrikaanse retentie in het Caraibisch Gebied?* (Nijmegen 1980).

28. W.J.H. Baart, "Cuentanan di nanzi, Een onderzoek naar de oorsprong, betekenis en functie van papiamentse spinverhalen" (PhD diss., Oegstgeest 1984).

29. M. Schweitz, "Verborgen protest in Curaçaosche spinvertellingen", *Caraibisch Forum* 1 (1980): 35–65.

30. Walter Rodney, *In gesprek met* (Paramaribo 1982), 17.

31. E.D. Genovese, *Roll, Jordan, Roll: The World the Slaves Made* (New York 1974).

32. L.F. Triebels, *Het Caraibisch Gebied als trefpunt van uitersten* (Nijmegen 1986).

33. A.F. Paula (ed.), *1795. De slavenopstand op Curaçao* (Willemstad 1974). (This is an edition of the primary sources on the slave rebellion in 1795 in Curaçao.)

34. A.F. Paula, "Van slaaf tot quasi-slaaf, Een sociaal-historische studie over de dubbelzinnige slavenemancipatie op Nederlands Sint Maarten, 1816–1863" (PhD diss., Univ. of Utrecht 1992).

35. A. Lampe, "Iglesia y Estado en la sociedad esclavista de Curazao", *Anales del Caribe* 9 (1989): 75–124.

36. M.J. Niewindt's letter to Baron van Wijkerslooth, dated 21 May 1851 (Centraal Historisch Archief nr. 3658, Willemstad).

37. E. Williams, *Capitalism and Slavery* (London 1977).

38. J.M. van Winter, "Public opinion in the Netherlands on the abolition of slavery", in *Dutch Authors on West Indian History, A Historiographical Selection*, edited by M.A.P. Meilink-Roelofsz (The Hague 1982), 100–128.

39. R.A.J. van Lier, *Frontier Society: A Social Analysis of the History of Suriname* (The Hague 1971).

40. A. Helman, *Zaken, zending en bezinning* (Paramaribo 1968); J.W.C. Ort, *Vestiging van de Hervormde Kerk in Suriname (1667–1800)* (Amsterdam 1963).

41. J.M. van der Linde, *Het visioen van Herrnhut en het apostolaat der Moravische Broeders in Suriname 1735–1863* (Paramaribo 1956); K. Zeefuik, "Herrnhutter zending en Haagsche Maatschappij 1828–1867" (PhD diss., Univ. of Utrecht 1973).

42. J. van Raalte, *Secularisatie en zending in Suriname* (Wageningen 1973).

43. H. Zamuel, "Johannes King, Apostel en profeet van het Surinaamse bosland" (PhD diss., Univ. of Utrecht 1994).

44. Harold Jap-A-Joe, "Tussen kruis en kalebas: acculturatie van het christendom onder gedoopte slaven in Suriname" (Theologisch Seminarie der EBGS, Paramaribo 1993).

45. E.D. Genovese, *From Rebellion to Revolution: Afro-American Slave Revolts in the Making of the Modern World* (Baton Rouge 1979), 7–8. This is the leitmotiv of his other work *Roll, Jordan, Roll: The World the Slaves Made*.

46. J. Vernooij, "De Rooms – Katholieke Kerk van Suriname (vanaf 1866)" (PhD diss., Univ. of Nijmegen, Paramaribo 1974).

47. G. Oostindie, "The Enlightenment, Christianity and the Suriname slave", *Journal of Caribbean History* 2 (1992): 147–70.

LAËNNEC HURBON

The Catholic Church and the State in Haiti, 1804–1915

*They surrender themselves to us, asking us
to pacify the souls[1]*

Msgr T. du Cosquer
First archbishop of Port-au-Prince, 1864

The Concordat:
Complicity or Misunderstanding?

The year 1804: Haiti, the first black independent state. The first state of the Third World to challenge the Western empires. In the Caribbean, where slavery continued to exist, there were constant rumours referring to the massacres of white colonists. Dessalines, who continued the fight against Napoleon's troops after the death of Toussaint L'Ouverture, decided that even the memory of France had to be removed. Despite the destruction, a new experience was born. It was not sufficient to cry "Live free or die" or take the oath of an "eternal hatred of France". The boycott measures of the Western countries included the complete isolation of Haiti.

A third institution was involved in this matter: the Catholic Church. What was the role of the church? Was it obliged to play a specific role? Did the church have its own policies, methods or practices? Notwithstanding these questions, the church revealed itself as a powerful institution within the political debate between Haiti and the empires. Could the church be manipulated by a controlling force? That was the beginning of a process which sixty years later would result in the concordat being signed by the Vatican and Haiti, with both powers claiming it as their own victory. The question remains on reading the church's history between 1804 and 1860: do countries come and go without ever showing their true characters? Our purpose is to clarify the mystery of the church in Haiti. Limiting our objectives, we will try to present a new understanding of the different interpretations of that history.

Apparently, the history of the church in Haiti was one of negotiations between the Holy See and the Haitian state with a view to signing the concordat which was considered to be the only means of promoting the evangelization of the Haitian people. For the members of the Catholic hierarchy (superiors of congregations, apostolic prefects and bishops), who were promoting the concordat or who were narrating its history, the concordat was indispensable for the success of any church activity.

The representatives of the Haitian government at the Holy See were also convinced of the absolute necessity of the concordat, in order to promote a clear position of the church. In both cases, they shared the same interpretation of the church: a European power comparable with other great powers, in search of a power beyond its own limits. Consequently, we are dealing with a situation of complicity between church and state, that would become a source of a series of misunderstandings before and after 1860, the year in which the concordat was signed.

The Church: A European Power

The analysis of the ideological problem relating to the interpretation of the church as a Western power is important to an understanding of the period prior to the concordat.

Dessalines: a new beginning

When Haiti became independent, only a few Catholic priests had survived the War of Independence and the massacre of the French by Dessalines' troops. The church tried to unite all the remaining priests on the island, but the problem was how to avoid antipopular feelings, bearing in mind that many priests were slave owners. According to several testimonies, some churches were attacked, the cult objects were destroyed and ceremonies were mocked at amidst the euphoria of victory, in celebrating the defeat of the French colonizers. Dessalines considered the church to be a part of the colonialist system and believed that once the French power was destroyed, the church's power would also be reduced. Articles 50 and 51 of the Imperial Constitution of 1 May 1805, stated: "the law does not allow the existence of a dominant religion . . . freedom of religion is tolerated . . . the state will not finance any religion or pastor".

Consequently, marriage was considered "a civil affair" and divorces were legitimate in certain cases. The aim was to destroy the church's privileges, which were in force during the period of slavery and even during Toussaint L'Ouverture's government, which relied on certain priests, followers of Abbé Grégoire, in order to control the church power. Dessalines, however, wanted to eliminate any memory of the slavery period. But how far could he go? He appointed Father Corneille Brelle as apostolic prefect of Cap and later decided to organize a Te Deum in his honour at the Chapel of the Religious Sisters in Cap. It was clear that he too was in need of the church, but the question was how he would benefit from that institution. Dessalines tried to use all the institutions, even voodoo, the African religion that had been recreated and preserved by the slaves and which played an important role during the anti-slavery struggle. Even the Catholic Church would not have been able to survive if it had not accepted the new independent state, of which Dessalines proclaimed himself "the father".[2]

Dessalines was murdered in 1806. Following his death, two governments were simultaneously created which divided the country into two parts: the first (the west and the south) under the leadership of Pétion, and the other (the north) under the leadership of Christophe. Both did their best to create a powerful church so that Haiti's independence would be recognized by the Western powers. Pétion used elements of the L'Ouverture constitution of 1801 which accepted the Catholic religion as "the religion of all the Haitians" and as the official religion. Christophe searched in vain for priests and especially for an archbishop of his own church. But the anticlerical ideology of the civil constitution, developed amidst the events of 1789, dominated the policies of those two governments with respect to the church. The frictions with Rome were due to the state's tendency to control ecclesiastical internal affairs and the property of the church. These were the controversial issues prior to the drafting of the concordat.

The concordat issue was very important during Boyer's government

(1818–43). Father Cabon, in his "Notes sur l'histoire réligieuse d'Haïti, De la révolution au concordat (1789–1860)",[3] narrates in detail the development of the negotiations. We will focus our attention on the central issues that determined the intentions and the strategies of both parties.

Boyer and the Holy See: two political strategies

Between 1821 and 1842, five of the Pope's representatives arrived in Haiti and had to deal with the same problems: the impossibility of establishing a church discipline and the inability of the proposals of the concordat to guarantee the independence of the church from the state. The first mission, that of Msgr Glory in 1821, did not last more than five months. He was in favour of the royalist system, therefore suspicions rapidly arose about the religious nature of his mission. In order to re-establish the authority of the Holy See, he wanted to prohibit some of the Spanish priests as well as other priests from carrying out their duties. These were not associated with Rome and were strong supporters of Boyer, but Msgr Glory did not succeed in obtaining his objective.

A year later, President Boyer tried to persuade Msgr Valera, archbishop of Santo Domingo, to settle in Port-au-Prince and maintain jurisdiction over the entire island, but he failed in his attempt. This would have meant the loss of the church's independence. Between 1834 and 1837, Rome entrusted three diplomatic missions to Msgr England. The issue was one of drafting a concordat. The Holy See wanted to re-establish the church's discipline and especially to counterbalance the state's intentions, which included the creation of a national church under the control of the Haitian state. Boyer's representatives, Inginac and Ardouin, were nominated to discuss the issue with Msgr England and followed the concordat model, signed in 1802 between Bonaparte and Pius VII, in which the state was committed to give special protection to the Catholic Church. But it was unacceptable to the church's representatives. The Haitian church interpreted the church's resistance as a sign of its alliance with the European powers (especially with France), which were in favour of slavery and colonialism. For the church, this rejection was the condemnation of the civil constitution of the clergy.

Finally, Msgr England was exiled from Haiti, because he refused to appoint the government's candidate as parish priest of Port-au-Prince. The priests elected by Boyer had to be unconditional servants of his cause and that of the nation's independence. In France, there were rumours of the presence of priests and religious personnel who were not tied to Rome. Abbé Grégoire's complete loyalty to the Haitian state led to suspicions regarding the situation of the church in Haiti, after the departure of Msgr England. According to Boyer's government, any concession with respect to the autonomy of the church would mean granting more influence to France and other European powers. Boyer's aim was to establish his own clergy, to establish a seminary in Port-au-Prince, to appoint his own bishop of Port-au-Prince and to have unconditional priests supporting his government, with the approval of Rome. But this was not acceptable to Rome as it would mean betraying the French and international diplomacy.

Between 1841 and 1842, the negotiations concerning the concordat were once again initiated. This time, the Haitian government, troubled by internal political difficulties, accepted all of the conditions imposed by Rome. Ministers Inginac and Ardouin, who in the past had been uncompromising, did not oppose Msgr Rosati, the new representative from Rome. They accepted all of the changes proposed by the Holy See before signing the concordat. At this time, a peasant rebellion was taking place in southern Haiti. They were preparing to invade the capital. A year later, in 1843, Boyer's government was overthrown by a popular revolution. Msgr Rosati had already left for Rome to present the results of the last negotiations to the pope. Upon his arrival, he discovered that there had been a change in power. Between 1844 and 1847, the schemes of the priests increased during the rule of several governments that followed Boyer's fall. Father Tisserant, Msgr Rosati's delegate, lost control of the situation and had to leave the country.

Soulouque and Abbé Cessens

The aim of having a church to serve a Haitian state became evident with Soulouque in power. Widely regarded as a black, illiterate dictator, Rome did not respond to the various requests made by Soulouque. In Haiti, even the mulattoes were embarrassed by the new situation. The political debate concentrated on the colour issue, the so-called struggle between the blacks and mulattoes, which erroneously identified the black class with the peasants of the south (Les Piquets), who rebelled against the owners of large estates.[4] Soulouque gained power in order to control the masses. Although he was black, Soulouque surprisingly established one of the most cruel dictatorships of the nineteenth century, after proclaiming himself emperor. Between 1847 and 1859, he practised a policy of cruel oppression of the entire population, and not only of the mulattoes as was suggested by the international press in the nineteenth century.

In this context, it was understandable that the Holy See did not want to get involved in this dictatorial regime, although we are not even sure of this. As with Boyer, Rome tried to obtain certain privileges, defending its independence from the Haitian state, under pressure from the European powers that were against the annexation of the Eastern part of the island. Soulouque could request a bishop for his church or promote the negotiations for the signing of the concordat, but there was no response from Rome. None of the great powers wanted to recognize his empire. The situation was thus favourable for intrigues.

Father Cessens, a perfect schemer, knew how to handle the Vatican and the Haitian state. In order to satisfy Rome, he opposed the priests who were not tied to Rome. Rome's problem was the constitutional church of Abbé Grégoire. In order to satisfy the Haitian government, he presented himself as being against the Roman representatives. The problem faced by the Haitian government was that of discovering international spies who were using the church to destroy Haiti's political independence. Cessens hoped finally to be ordained bishop. Rome, however, did not appoint him bishop, and he started to act as the de facto bishop, with the political approval of Soulouque.

But one cannot consider those plots by Father Cessens and other priests to gain privileges as the reason for the failure of negotiations between Rome and Haiti. Those schemes originated out of the strategy of the Haitian government and of the Holy See. It was part of the political strategy of both parties. Soulouque's fall in 1859, which was caused by pressures within the country, created favourable conditions for the signing of the concordat. President Geffrard received support from the consul of France, who was interested in sending French priests to Haiti. The concordat was signed in 1860 and was based on the text of 1842: the church could determine its own discipline and administer its property without intervention from the state. The president had the right to elect bishops and archbishops. Moreover, the parish priest and the ecclesiastical authorities had to take the oath of fidelity to the civil authority.[5]

The Significance of the Concordat

The church: an ambiguous instrument of ideological control

The Catholic Church enjoyed many privileges, but was subjected to political power. Religious congregations took charge of the educational system. Their task was to train an elite that could compete with those of European countries, in order to make the nation appear civilized. We have to question this urgent objective of the church which was supported by most members of the Haitian government and which made the church more dependent on the state.

After the ratification of the concordat, the secretary of foreign affairs stated that: "The will of the President is to establish in this country a regime of order and stability . . . Our first authorities lacked the support of a qualified clergy capable of civilizing this young nation."[6] The president of the senate spoke about the "social necessity" of the concordat and about the "moralization of all the classes of the society" through religion.[7] The Haitian government and the church agreed on this issue. Msgr du Cosquer, the first archbishop, wrote: "They surrender themselves to us, asking us to pacify the souls."

The church had a double task: civilisation and pacification. But there is more. It is not difficult to imagine that the Haitian governments faced a difficult problem caused by the many peasant rebellions. The military reaction was not successful, mainly because the majority of the soldiers were badly paid and had the tendency to side with the peasants. The newly started education system was only benefitting the elite.[8] In this context, the church could only function as the state's instrument of ideological control of the masses. In the meanwhile, the established church in Haiti enjoyed true recognition of the political independence by a European power, at a moment when they were trying to isolate Haiti from the rest of the Caribbean which remained under the control of the colonists. There is nothing more contradictory than the fact that the church was being used as a means of ideological control (internal affairs) and of acknowledgement of Haiti's independence (foreign affairs).

In order to understand this contradiction, we have to bear in mind that the Haitian governments were under pressure from the people who were demanding Catholic ceremonies. They could not ignore the "osmosis" of Catholicism and voodoo, the religion which was based on

African traditions and reinstated after Haiti's independence. Therefore, they had to take the initiative in negotiating the concordat without questioning the misunderstanding on which the establishment of the church was based. Msgr Guilloux, the second archbishop of Port-au-Prince, stated correctly, that: "The many parishes which have no priests, urgently need pastors . . . They should have their own parish priest as soon as possible."[9] Two centuries before, Father Labat had written a similar statement about the religious demands of the slaves.[10] During the nineteenth century, the voodoo religion incorporated Catholic practices with the aim of improving its own practices. Was it not a contradiction for the Haitian governments? They never wanted a church which would completely and absolutely eradicate voodoo. They only wanted to limit its practices to the country areas and to the outskirts of the city. The church was entrusted with a discourse against voodoo as the religion which caused disorder and paganism, with the aim of keeping the masses out of the political struggle. The imposition of Catholicism was a way to keep this promise alive: one day all would be civilized.[11] In order to maintain "order and stability", it was necessary to establish a church which appeared to be civilized, the only institution able to protect the reputation of the country at the international level.

Voodoo already expressed the Haitian identity, one which was unique and as such should not disappear from the international scene, despite all the attacks against the 'bad example' of Haiti in defeating slavery and colonialism. In fact, during Soulouque's period, various rumours started to appear in the international press, especially the British and the French, about the "barbarism of the black masses".[12] Soulouque's despotism was considered to be the result of a combination of voodoo and his being of the black race and illiterate. This was the reason why the Haitian governments looked for an alliance with the church as a defence mechanism against the racist attacks by the European powers, which were interested in Haiti's isolation. Consequently, voodoo would survive as the dominant religion, but without an ideological consensus. If power is especially linked to the sacred, for the Haitian masses, the sacred was linked to voodoo. Therefore, a Haitian president had to gain support from voodoo in order to justify his power. It is said that Boyer remained in power for many years, thanks to a fetish hidden in his palace and that Soulouque was invulnerable thanks to the voodoo rites that took place in his palace.

As a result, voodoo remained a clandestine practice and, at the same time, was a means of escape for the masses, a kind of maroonage and method of opposing the central power, similar to that used by the Maroons. After Toussaint L'Ouverture, the former slaves opposed the distribution of land which only benefited generals, high officials and exports, which were not under their control. Since 1826, the rural codex of Boyer stated that the peasants had to remain in the country-side; if not, they would be punished.

In light of his decision to pay the external debt to France, Boyer was totally dependent on his country. The peasants opposed his policy by organizing several rebellions. In this context, the church was entrusted with the mission to "pacify the souls" and present voodoo as the reason for social disorder. The armed groups of the south, which reached Port-au-Prince in 1843, were classified as savage groups of wizards and cannibals. Their leader Jean Jacques Aca was considered a keen follower of the voodoo religion.[13] The church had to carry out this task under difficult conditions. On the one hand, the church put its position in danger by publicly attacking voodoo; on the other hand, guided by a foreign clergy, the church provoked suspicions of serving the interests of the European powers and, consequently, the mulattoes of the elite. Was this suspicion justified? We can only answer this question by studying the ideological version of the church's history in Haiti, as it was expressed by the spokesmen of the church.

The church confronts slave traditions

This subject is discussed in the works of A. Cabon, J-M. Jan, J. Verschueren and Paul Robert. Between 1804 and 1860, the Haitian state and the "unworthy" clergy, due to the influences of Abbé Grégoire's ideas, tried to establish a national and schismatic church in Haiti. This was one of the reasons why the Vatican adopted an intransigent attitude during the negotiations with the Haitian state. Father Cabon stated that before the abolition of slavery, "the conflict between the civil and the religious authorities was a matter of principle", which was as a result of the regulations of 1781, authorizing the governor to have control over the personal behaviour of the missionaries.[14] Abbé Grégoire's influence became more apparent during the reign of Toussaint L'Ouverture. The negotiations between the Vatican and Haiti failed, due to "the ignorance of the governments with respect to the religious issue" and to "the opposition of an unworthy clergy".[15]

The Haitian government would gain the following privileges: the appointment of bishops and archbishops; the oath of fidelity by bishops and priests; official ceremonies (Te Deum). Benefits for the church and privileges for the state: an exchange system of *do ut des* between the church and the government, realizing closer harmony. Nothing became more illusory than the so-called independence of the church. The concordat became a powerful weapon in the hands of the state which did not respect the rights of the church. During the nineteenth century, the church insisted on its institutional autonomy, because it sought to structure itself as a bureaucratic power, in order to face the different new states which had emerged since the French Revolution. This revolution opposed the freedom of the church; the latter until then, had served the absolutist state and remained a royalist church both in its structure as well as in its ideology. Therefore, Haiti's independence influenced by the French Revolution, could not include the (spiritual) innocence of the church.

"The church has nothing to reconsider": Father Cabon, in making this statement, meant that during slavery the church was correct in its position concerning slavery and had nothing to do with antislavery ideas.[16] In independent Haiti and after the abolition of slavery, all of the governments had shown preference for the priests who stood for Haiti's independence and opposed slavery and racism, such as Abbé Grégoire. The official church or the Vatican had never criticized the institution of slavery. The new leaders were too well aware of the horrors of slavery and of the involvement of the church. Consequently, they considered the church a European power, an institution serving the interests of the other powers or at least an ally of the colonists. Even in Europe they could not imagine the church undertaking a new role in independent Haiti.

Indeed, the church did not act differently, after having gained the support of the French government.[17] Boyer, Soulouque and Geffrard requested priests through the consul of France. The representatives of the Vatican first paid a visit to Paris before arriving in Haiti. The Haitian state was not wrong in distrusting the church. Father Cabon was right in thinking that the Haitian government wanted to take advantage of the church. He did not know of any other church model than that of the slavery period: a church closely related to the political authorities. This was also the opinion of one of the negotiators during Boyer's government.[18] Toussaint L'Ouverture had the same opinion.[19]

The priests who were scheming against the political authorities – the representatives of the Vatican, the priests of Abbé Grégoire, those who arrived in search of riches, the suspended or false priests – shared the church's opinion, an institution which enjoyed many privileges. The divisive and ignorant attitude of the Haitian government does not explain the difficulties of the negotiation process that resulted in the concordat. The church needed the state in order to establish itself as a prestigious power, and the state needed the church in order to consolidate itself internally and externally. Nevertheless, in the concordat there were some dangerous contradictions for the state and for the church.

Therefore, contrary to the statements of Father Cabon, the Haitian government never really desired a divisive church. This would not have solved their basic problem: the recognition of their independence by a foreign power and the appearance of being a civilized country. Otherwise, we cannot explain the efforts of the different governments in search of a concordat. The Haitian state desired a church that could be used without its showing resistance. The state succeeded in its purpose, but for both the church and the state, it was a vulnerable relationship. The church was based on a European model of civilization, therefore it could not practise the acculturation of Christianity in Haiti. The theology being practised in the nineteenth century considered the church as the perfect and eternal society and consequently any attempt to Christianize the black masses was seen as a situation of alienation.

The church was later criticized, because it sided with mulattoes and with French culture, and because it practised a racist policy against the blacks. Is it possible to see the difference between the ideology and the practice of the church after the signing of the concordat?[20] Following the signing of the concordat, the church could not liberate itself from the past and the Western French culture. The church was only concerned with the "schismatic" church which was established between 1804 and 1860 in Haiti. Verschueren and Msgr Jan (according to him the schism began in 1790) shared Father Cabon's opinion.[21]

Msgr Robert, who was more concerned with the purity of the church, considered the "schismatic" period of the church between 1795 and 1864, as the source of the voodoo–Christianity confusion in Haiti. According to him, that period was a disaster for Catholicism, because the state committed abuses against the rights of the church.[22] But did it differ from the period of slavery? The only problem which the spokesmen of the church faced was the schism which was abolished because of the concordat.[23] The experiences of the church during slavery – Christianity imposed upon the blacks which led to the combination of voodoo and Catholic rites, missionaries who were slave owners in search of privileges – is not important for the church history of Cabon, Msgr Robert, Msgr Jan, and Verschueren. The "schism" was the source of all evil before the concordat.

For the people, the religious debate did not include the concordat issue. Since independence, they had been involved in the reconstruction of voodoo practices, the temples (the "ounfo"), the "lakou" (a network of families living on the same land with a patriarch as a leader and worshipping in the same voodoo temple); everything that was related to their culture was based on African traditions. Catholicism, either in its legal form (with a concordat) or in its illegal form (the "schismatic" priests) represented a foreign institution, although its rites and symbols could be used in voodoo.[24]

On the social and political levels, the problem for the elite was the issue of colour. The majority demanded new land distribution which would not favour the owners of large estates nor the foreign businessmen, especially the French. The despotism of Boyer (mulatto) or of Soulouque (a black) was believed to be a "continuum" of the slavery situation. The majority continued to take refuge in the mountains, because they wanted to escape the state's control. The church, after signing the concordat, contributed to the consolidation of the Haitian state, but this only led to an unstable balance of power.

The Church in Haiti, 1860–1915

There was a generalized crisis situation after the fall of Emperor Soulouque, whose government was the greatest disaster of the nineteenth century: twelve years of dictatorship, corruption, a desperate war against the Dominican Republic, frequent massacres of entire families of mulattoes and blacks who had been accused of plotting against the government, and an unpayable external debt to France. The new government had to face many problems after 1860. The international press in Europe and in the USA attacked, from a racist point of view, the black republic as being unable to manage its own affairs and as having the tendency to despotism.

The social and political crisis after Soulouque intensified. Elements included conflicts between generals, political groups, intellectuals, all striving for political power, as well as massacres and fires that destroyed the national palace in 1912. Eighteen black and mulatto presidents governed Haiti between 1860 and 1915, all proclaiming themselves as presidents for life, and violence always triumphed, thus ensuring that the next generation would seek revenge. Within this context of constant crisis,[25] the church consolidated and expanded its position of power after the establishment of the concordat, until the American military intervention and occupation of Haiti in 1915. Only a few historians traced this part of the church's history in Haiti, with the exception of Father Cabon,[26] who patiently described the relationship between the church and the different governments. His perspective was essentially apologetic, and his work merely became a history of bishops and priests without any reference made to the social, cultural and political life of the country.

Never before, at any time during the nineteenth century, had the church received such contradictory claims. They expected political neutrality from the church, but each political group tried to take advantage of the church. The church was entrusted with the education of the masses, but the elite was the first to receive benefits from its educational system. They asked the church to eradicate the African religious practices (particularly voodoo), but the masses were in search of sacraments which would improve their voodoo practices. More importantly, it was hoped that with the help of the church, Haiti would gain international recognition as an independent nation. How could the church respond to all those demands without losing its autonomy and without becoming a simple instrument of the Haitian state or a national church? Everything indicated that this original misunderstanding, fundamental in the negotiation process that would result in the concordat, became increasingly problematic with each new government and continued to aggravate the political crisis.

For this period of the church's history in Haiti, abundant documentation is available: bulletins, pastoral letters, synodal statements, letters and other types of correspondence between bishops and the Vatican, between bishops and religious congregations, between bishops and Haitian governments, in addition to newspapers and reviews published by intellectuals in the provinces and in the cities. All this material should be systematically studied in order to have a better understanding of the relationships of the Catholic church with the political power, the Protestant churches, voodoo, the internal conflicts within the church, and the institutional organization and doctrine related to the social problems of that period.

We can only trace some important aspects of this history as only the documents of the Fathers of the Holy Spirit in Paris are available for study. A solid and critical work should examine in detail the documentation which has been circulated in different countries (Italy, France, England, Spain, the United States and Haiti). We will present two subject areas. The first refers to the church–state relationship, in so far as the church was involved in projects of the elite who were striving for political power, or of foreign powers which were trying to reconquer Haiti. The second refers to the church–voodoo relationship, which expresses the involvement of priests and the religious in the world of the poor, their culture and their social struggles during the nineteenth century.

The church-state relationship

When the first archbishop of Port-au-Prince, Msgr Testard du Cosquer, arrived in Haiti with twenty-four priests, he was expected to establish a church on a solid and definite basis in accordance with the concordat. On the one hand, the suspicions about a separation, which prevailed from 1804 to 1860, should disappear: the suspended priests or those not in agreement with Rome had to leave the parishes and even the country. On the other hand, the church would play the role of the mediator in frequent social and political conflicts. The state would be able to maintain peace and order if it was subjected to the spiritual guidelines of the church.[27] The unconditional support of President Geffrard for the church made it possible for the church to control its own finances, the administration of the sacraments and the educational system, thus serving the interests of the élite. Only the war against voodoo, characterized as the last remaining element, would be unsuccessful without the intervention of the state. Geffrard's government regarded the concordat as an instrument which would remain in power for life. The revolts against Geffrard automatically challenged the concordat. The church, which had barely been established, entered an era of instability and conflicts with successive governments, characterizing the situation as one of persecution of the church.

The suspended priests: the first source of conflict

The first difficulties experienced by the church following the establishment of the concordat arose due to the presence of the suspended
priests, or of those who were not in agreement with Rome, but who
were tolerated by the state. Fifteen years later, this problem was almost
solved after the arrival of more Roman Catholic priests. But there was
a basic problem in the struggle against the suspended priests: the power
struggle between the church and the state.[28] After Geffrard's fall, suspended priests were serving the different political groups in several
parts of the country. Father Buscail was one of them, who was serving
Salnave and his army in the northern part of the country. In 1867, the
country was divided into three sections each governed by different
groups: one in the north, another in St Marc and the third in Port-au-
Prince. The church feared that Soulouque and his black followers
would return to power and they considered the concordat as an instrument of the mulattoes who were represented by Geffrard's government.
Msgr du Cosquer stated in a letter that the re-emergence of African
superstitions was possible.[29]

A letter from the vicar general, Jean Marie Guilloux, in 1868 condemning Father Buscail, strengthened doubts that existed within the
church based on the concordat. Other priests, such as Father Degerine,
the parish priest of Gonaives, dared to criticize publicly the political
developments of the country. The government believed that the
church was involved in this situation from the beginning. After the
triumph of Salnave's army, he opposed the destitution of Father
Buscail, his military chaplain, who provided tremendous assistance
during the war against the peasants of the north, the Cacos,[30] who had
rebelled against his government. According to Salnave, the destitution
of Father Buscail would be interpreted as public support for the rebels.
Based on the concordat, the minister of religious affairs, Demesvar
Delorme, criticized the church, referring to it as "a new power
controlled by foreign priests which was able to contradict the plans of
the state".[31] On 10 August 1867, he wrote to the vicar general that a
priest should not be involved in politics and the priest who did not
have the confidence of the head of state could not function in Haiti.
On 26 August 1867, the vicar general was called by the Council of
Ministers and they threatened to abolish the concordat if the church
continued to resist political power.[32]

On 3 December 1867, the vicar general published a document on the concordat, in which he criticized the government's accusations against the church. The conflicts became more violent. After Geffrard's fall, the Catholic authorities considered the free development of antireligious ideas in Haiti as the source of conflict with the Haitian state, especially because of the success of free masonry in the cities. According to the church, this was related to the French Revolution. The friction between the archbishop and the suspended priests should be placed within this context of true mutual suspicions between church and state. The archbishop stated that the concordat recognized the spiritual authority of the church, while the government expected the church to be an instrument of political power.

The suspended priests continued to be active, at least over the years. They managed to slander the loyal priests knowing that Rome was always ready to hear gossip. For example, if the archbishop was not an ally of the Jesuits, he was labelled as being leader of the opposition. Having been in the crossfire, Msgr du Cosquer finally suffered from paranoia before dying.[33] In one of his last letters to Cardinal Antonieli of Rome, on 10 May 1869, he made reference to a plot against his life and asked the cardinal to study his case. The suspended priests criticized Msgr du Cosquer for having violated the laws of morality and chastity. Rome was inclined to recall the archbishop, but Salnave took the necessary measures and fired the archbishop while he was abroad.[34]

It seemed that the Haitian government would soon abolish the concordat. The head of state not only took advantage of the suspended priests (as in the case of Father Buscail), but wanted to end financial support to priests and archbishops, and finally demanded a close collaboration between church and state in order to re-establish order in Haiti.[35] The archbishop was considered to be a government official. The news about the destitution of the first archbishop was first represented in the international press (Le Monde, 20 April 1869) as a separation from Rome. In Haiti, the vicar general, Msgr Guilloux, sent a letter to the clergy and the people, criticizing Salnave's decision and defending the autonomy of the church as a spiritual force.[36]

One should not believe that the Haitian church gave preference to mulattoes and not to the black political leaders. The church was against any revolutionary movement that questioned the establishment. Salnave was a mulatto and disagreed with the church, because his government promoted disorder and planned to report the archbishop and the priests to the civil authorities. Each government, invoking the nationalist ideology, wanted to take advantage of the church. As Demesvar Delorme stated, the church was seen as a state within the state, because it consisted of French priests and, consequently, was linked to a foreign colonial power. The fact that the church was easily manipulated was due to the misunderstanding on which the concordat was based. The Haitian state was in need of an ideological instrument of control over the masses. The church demanded autonomy as a spiritual force, but at the same time expected the state to pay the salaries of priests and to grant other privileges which would make them true officials of the state.

According to the church, abolishing the concordat would not resolve this controversial issue. The church should be recognized as a spiritual power above the state and henceforth should enjoy all the relevant privileges. In light of Father Buscail's appointment as military chaplain by Salnave, the clergy continued talking about the danger.[37] The church, based on the concordat, firmly defended the autonomy. In this context, the failure of the state to abide by the articles of the concordat was seen as an act of persecution of the church. The church concentrated its efforts on the defence of its rights and privileges which were not respected by the Haitian state and which were influenced by the "modern liberties" of the French Revolution. The church would not tolerate any state intervention in church affairs.[38] Several governments, even those in favour of the concordat, were unable to leave the church free and tried to manipulate this institution.

Civil laws and religious deeds: a new source of conflict

During the period of Geffrard's government, Parliament refused to accept the free administration of the parishes by the church. In 1863, Geffrard dissolved the Parliament. During Salnave's administration, the problem arose once again. It was said that church taxes were too high for the people. Salnave's fall did not solve the problems.[39] The drafting of a new constitution included Article 33 which would regulate the territorial outline of parishes and bishoprics by the government.[40] Some months later, the government declared that priests who did not request civil certificates from the parishioners would be punished.[41]

For the church, it was a clear sign of persecution, that priests could be taken to court, that there were rumours of the establishment of a national clergy and that the state had decided to control religious acts.

This strengthened the archbishop's idea that antireligious modern elements were creating a disaster in Haiti. The archbishop declared that nothing was as important as the salvation of souls.[42] To suspend baptisms or marriages in emergency cases would mean not to carry out the church's obligations. But the real source of conflict was seen in the establishment of a national clergy.

During this period, the political field was dominated by two parties, the liberals and the nationalists,[43] and both played upon the colour issue, inherited from the slave society. On the one hand, the liberals used the slogan "the most capable in power". This party was, however, led by mulattoes. On the other hand, the nationalists defended the idea of "the majority in power", thus referring to themselves as the black representatives of the Haitian masses. It was debated by the elite, the politicians and senior officials of the army. The church lost control of the situation and any initiative to mediate between the parties would have ended in the manipulation of the church.

When Salomon, a black man who belonged to the nationalist party and a former minister of Soulouque's government, became president, the proposal was made to join the church with the state. The press also began to promote the idea of the church as a state within the state.[44] A number of black intellectuals, educated in Catholic schools, were in favour of free masonry, divorce, and the church's adherence to the civil laws, and published their ideas in newspapers and bulletins. A book on the divorce issue was edited in Haiti, first published in France, producing five thousand copies. The church understood once again that a solution to the conflicts with the state during the period of Salomon's government would be rather difficult.

Finally, the Parliament ordered that the church abide by the civil laws. The church reaffirmed that its spiritual authority could not be controlled by the state.[45] The church's priority was the defence of its autonomy and the spiritual authority of a power similar to the state's. The aim of the concordat was the establishment of a privileged church that could function in Europe, but not in Haiti. The church in Europe was constantly concerned about the number of baptisms, first communions, chapels, churches, schools and religious groups. In 1868, the vicar general's report stated that Haiti had as many baptisms as a parish of France.[46] In 1870, the archbishop was happy with the quantitative growth of religious deeds, but complained about the material decrease within the church, such as the lack of priests, of money, and so on.[47]

In 1900, the church's situation was "normalized" with the establishment of several dioceses, a seminary in France, religious congregations that were in charge of the most important schools in Haiti, and with more than 150 priests working in seventy-eight parishes. In 1913, an agreement reached between the state authorized the church's administration of schools in the countryside under the supervision of the parish priest. Religious organizations which were successful in France were also founded in each parish of Haiti. A religious bulletin was printed in each diocese. The church was apparently experiencing a period of exceptional prosperity. Unity within the church was also reestablished. But the church did not succeed in increasing the number of church marriages, nor did the number of illegitimate children decrease. The other problem mentioned by the bishops in their reports was that of "superstitions", namely voodoo practices.

Confronting voodoo

One of the explicit objectives of the concordat was to remove voodoo as a superstitious heritage of Black Africa, that had survived in Haiti due to the ignorance of the masses. Since the arrival of the first archbishop and the twenty-four priests, Geffrard started a campaign against voodoo. At that time, after Soulouque's long despotic rule, Haiti was considered on the international level as a country liberated from "African barbarism". The massacre of opposition leaders, organized by Soulouque, was explained as a result of the black "instinct" symbolized by voodoo practices. It was said that Soulouque tolerated those "superstitious practices" that were organized even within the National Palace. The concordat should, thus, prove the willingness of the country to embrace civilization, which would mean the end of "African barbarism". The church was well aware of this mission which was proposed by Geffrard's government.

During the first twenty years, since the signing of the concordat, the struggle against voodoo was not the most important concern of the church. This institution was more busy organizing internal unity and external autonomy. The state planned to eradicate the "superstitious" practices in the cities which were considered embarrassing for the international image of the country. One was not sure that voodoo would disappear from the countryside, but at least it should have been possible to keep it at a distance. The presence of voodoo in the cities was one of the consequences of Soulouque's policy. The struggle against voodoo acquired a political dimension. Even for the officials of Geffrard's government, voodoo was identified with practices of witchcraft and cannibalism, which ignorant blacks engaged in during Soulouque's government. It was felt that Soulouque's power was linked with black magic practices which were used to maintain control over the people.

This situation concerning voodoo during Geffrard's government was well illustrated by the event known as "the case of Jeanne Pelée" or "the case of Bizoton". The tribunal of Port-au-Prince condemned eight persons to death, including four women, who were accused of having participated in cannibalistic rituals while practising voodoo in Bizoton, which was located near the capital. The case became a national affair. A large crowd gathered to witness the execution of the accused. According to an article published in Le Moniteur on 20 February 1864, the church had the task of attacking and eradicating the voodoo cult. One month later, on 5 March 1864, Le Moniteur published a letter written by President Geffrard, in which he stressed the importance of the struggle against voodoo, given its association with criminal practices.[48]

This letter proves once again that Geffrard's government took the struggle against voodoo seriously, applying the same measures used during slavery to African traditions. Dances, healing practices and voodoo ceremonies were all rejected. In 1900, Hannibal Price, one of Geffrard's followers wrote about the attacks on voodoo temples and the persecution of the practitioners in the countryside during Geffrard's government.[49] Voodoo was then a key issue for the Haitian state. At the end of the 1880s, the church recommenced the persecution of voodoo followers, which culminated in a national campaign against superstitious practices in 1941. The church had to first solve its problem of the suspended priests. They were administering sacraments to all the faithful and consequently, after Haiti's independence, the union of Catholic and voodoo practices was consolidated, thanks to their activities. After the establishment of the concordat, which was planned to attract the masses and to fight the suspended priests, voodoo still remained a problem for the church.

The confrontation involved the Cult of the Saints. The church authorities tried to rid certain parish churches of some of the statues of saints linked with voodoo practices. During the time of Salnave's government, the people forced the archbishop to reinstate in the cathedral a statue of the Virgin, which was removed by the parish priest. At Jacmel and in Cap, the same thing happened and provoked negative feelings among people who were opposed to the concordat. But, in the new context, the church tried to impose its authority in order to ensure the purity of the Catholic practices. In fact, nearly all Catholic ceremonies had already been influenced by voodoo. Baptism and first communions were recommended by voodoo priests; "oungan" or "mambo" masses for the deceased with the voodoo cult of the deceased and the feasts of the saints were seen as feasts in honour of the "spirits" (*lwa, anges,* or *mystéres*). Even the liturgical calendar of the church was interpreted based on the voodoo cult. Consequently, the regular institutional functioning of the church strengthened the development of voodoo practices or beliefs. After the concordat, the link between the church and voodoo became more complex.

The church attacked the so-called idolatry of the masses, supported by Salnave's government. In 1880, some parishioners of Hinche were exorcised by the bishop because they had been caught in a trance, believed to be possessed by voodoo spirits.[50] The bishop of Cap denounced the superstitious practices he found in the countryside during his pastoral visits from 1881 to 1882.[51] The church was unable to take a pastoral approach to voodoo: it considered voodoo neither a religion nor a cultural system but, rather, the expression of barbarism and ignorance. At the same time, the church was in the process of preaching Western culture. As a consequence of the church's campaign against voodoo, the church was willing to sacrifice its independence to the state. For the church, it was a struggle to promote its institutional establishment, but in truth, it was more beneficial to the political power of that period. The campaign against voodoo had a special meaning for the Haitian state.

Peasant revolts were a constant threat to the political powers. The struggle against voodoo was at the same time a criticism of the subversive meetings held by the peasants and organized without any state intervention. To keep voodoo outside of the cities was to marginalize the peasants from the rest of the nation. For this reason, the state called on the church's services to put forth the appearance of a civilized nation. At the end of the nineteenth century, several works were published in Europe and in the USA, which stated that the first black republic became barbarous because it rejected colonial powers, with special reference made to Soulouque's despotic government and to the Jeanne Pelée affair.[52] At this time, the racist ideology was in search of a scientific base and Haiti was seen as the perfect example of the so-called natural inferiority of the blacks, because the first black republic was unable to develop itself on the economic and political level.

Black and mulatto Haitian intellectuals defended Haiti's position, stating that voodoo was disappearing or that it was limited to the countryside due to the lack of education. They wrote that Haiti became civilized because of the concordat which established Catholicism as the official religion of the Haitian people. But on the other hand, the same intellectuals criticized the church, because it refused to become an instrument of the Haitian state. Louis-Joseph Janvier, a black Haitian intellectual, played an active part in defence of Haiti at the end of the nineteenth century, but he opposed the concordat.[53] Hannibal Price, a mulatto, defended the concordat as a means of civilizing Haiti and eradicating voodoo. This nationalist perspective did not question the "superiority" of the Western civilization, nor did it challenge the new colonial conquest of Haiti proposed by the racist ideology. The Haitian elite was imprisoned in its world, attached to its own interests.

The church continued with the campaign against voodoo, defending the civilization process supported by the church. In 1896, anti-voodoo leagues were created between Cap and Cayes, and in Port-au-Prince. The religious bulletins systematically criticized the Catholics who worshipped "God and Satan" at the same time.[54] The state supported the church in its struggle against voodoo, but without giving up the idea of using the church as a simple instrument of the state. In 1899, during the government of Florvil Hyppolite, the secretary of interior affairs stated that those who practised voodoo were to be regarded as criminals. At the end of the nineteenth century, politicians and generals were vying for the presidential seat. Anarchy in Haiti confirmed the negative opinion of the imperialist powers, the French, German, American. The action by Hippolite's government against voodoo, with the aid of the church, was a new attempt at controlling the masses in the cities. But it was in vain: the social and political uprisings were used by the USA to justify its military intervention and occupation, which lasted from 1915 to 1934.

Some issues

Father Cabon wrote that after the signing of the concordat, the Haitian state was the absolute master and the church did not have any rights other than those granted in the form of privileges.[55] This opinion regarding conflict between the church and the state after the signing of the concordat, distorts the facts and does not explain the conflict. On analysing the declarations, the synodal instructions, the letters and pastoral letters, we can conclude that the church reproduced the major religious problems of Europe and applied them to the particular context of Haiti. If the state did not grant privileges to bishops and priests, it was due to the influence or the ideas of the French Revolution, while the church considered itself as the only source of divine laws. Perhaps the state planned to build a secular city, considering the church as useless for the historical process. From this point of view, the church was indifferent to politics, being more interested in its own identity than in a world power that had begun to ignore its presence.

Between 1867 and 1878, all pastoral letters from the bishops dealt with these issues: the unity of the church (dated 25 January 1869), the church as protector of the revealed truth (Lent, 1875), the rights of the church (1877) and the church as an absolute necessity for the human society (Lent, 1878). Each letter was based on the papal encyclical which preceded it and was directed to the political and intellectual group that was influenced by Voltaire and other liberal ideas after Haiti's independence.[56] In fact, the Haitian state tried to establish a national church, following the example of the French Revolution.

On the eve of independence, the state became the largest owner of estates, as a result of the nationalization of the goods of the colonists. During the nineteenth century, it was a source of enrichment for generals and politicians. While the ex-slaves were expecting land distribution in favour of the poor, they became servants of a small minority of owners of large estates. As in slavery times, widespread abandonment of plantations occurred. The economic crisis which was further threatened by the return of the European powers lasted until 1860 and a real "military complex",[57] was established, one which was used to repress the peasants and to defend the privileged position of certain generals.

After 1860, Geffrard applied the same rural codex elaborated during the period of Toussaint L'Ouverture (1801) and reinforced by Boyer (rural codex of 1826), which subjected the peasant to the arbitrary will of the chief of the rural district, who gained administrative, judicial and military power. Through this system, the peasant was obliged to carry out his duties in order to produce export crops, such as coffee, and to stay in his district, leaving aside time for the planning of rebel-lions. The state never thought of developing a national economy which would serve its citizens.

Between 1870 and 1880, there were one and a half million inhabitants, 90 to 95 percent of whom lived in the countryside and were the main contributors to the state's income and to national production. However, they did not experience any improvement in their living conditions. A commercial bourgeoisie comprised of Germans, Frenchmen, Englishmen, Americans and a large group of small intermediaries were exploiting the poor peasants. The Haitian state organized the separation of the city and the rural areas as well as the protection against the demands of the peas-ants and the unemployed, that is, the peasants who sought refuge in the cities. Consequently, a distinction was made between an order of civiliza-tion and one of barbarism, the latter referring to the ignorant and "super-stitious" (voodoo practitioners) peasants.

In this context, the Haitian state was vulnerable, because it was not easy to maintain control over the peasants, who through maroonage, voodoo practices and rebellions, continued to intervene in the politi-cal arena. How could the peasants be considered the barbarous ele-ments of the country, when they were the principal contributors to the economic development of Haiti? During the nineteenth century, the Haitian state was based on this contradiction and could only be dealt with by the government through despotism. The state did not have any other importance than that of being a place where one could become rich rapidly. Businessmen and politicians were looking for lucrative deals, the bureaucracy consisted of political followers or the president and the political class, including liberal intellectuals and generals of the army, who continued to use the nationalist ideology and the colour issue in the struggle for the presidency. The political debate remained limited to the question of having a black or a mulatto as president, an intellectual or an "ignorant" general.

Each government demanded the support of the church in order to control the masses and to keep the established social structure. The acts of repression by the army or the chief of the rural district were not sufficient and the church was the only instrument which was able to control the people. We will analyse each case individually.

1. The conflict regarding the civil certificates which were indispens-able for the administering of the sacraments of baptism and marriage as well as for funeral services.

The people, in an effort to escape from the control of the state (the obligatory shifts and taxes), refused to obtain the certificates. The state urged the church to promote its civil authority, or else it would become a destabilizing factor. Each government used the same argument: the church could become a state within the state, a place of conspiracy against the government, where the racist and colonial powers were fighting against Haitian nationalism. The bishops' declarations expressed the desire of a church in search of autonomy, violated by the French Revolution. This church considered the demands of the Haitian state which had been influenced by the French Revolution as impious and heretical. This idea of the church against the Haitian state contributed once again to the evasion of the real issue, which was the exclusion of the poor peasants.

2. The problem of the state (the latter was considered as the "absolute master").

There were politicians who requested the intervention of one of the colonial powers who were trying to recolonize Haiti, in order to become president of the republic. Geffrard was the first to grant foreigners the right to own property, in contravention of the principles of national independence. Salnave presented the USA with the option concerning the Bay of St Nicolas,[58] and later each political group, with the exception of some intellectuals, sought alliance with one of the powers, by offering them a section of the national territory. The church criticized the plans regarding the annexation of Haiti to the USA, but the fear of losing its autonomy made the church more passive at the political level.

3. The struggle against "impiety and heresy", as seen in freemasonry and protestantism, and "all the sects known as socialism, communism, nihilism".[59]

In their sermons, letters and other documents, the bishops expressed their opposition to freemasonry, which was to be the enemy of the spiritual authority of the church.[60] The church sought more support and privileges from the state for fear of the increase in the number of protestants. The socialist and communist movements were characterized as "sects" that were plotting against the church and consequently against the civil authority.[61]

The church linked its own destiny with a policy of defence of the status quo. It was indifferent to the problems of social justice, as the politicians could easily take advantage of the church between 1880 and 1890. Louis-Joseph Janvier, for example, criticized the concordat, stating that the church was antipatriotic. In his work, The Republic of Haiti and its visitors (1882), he stated that it was impossible to establish a national government with the presence of Haitian priests, and that the clergy had to remain in the hands of the civil government. In a later work, The Affairs of Haiti (1885), he proposed the establishment of a Protestant and national church which would be dependent on the state, and better able to carry out the transformation of the peasantry including the elimination of social distinctions between the poor and the rich and the suppression of superstitious practices.[62]

Those were the same arguments used by Delorme against the concordat during the time of Salnave's government. The theme of a "national government" referred to the colour issue, thus reducing the social struggle to the issue of whether the president had to be black or mulatto. The bishops strengthened the position of the elite by fighting the intellectuals who were opposed to the concordat and the autonomy of the church. At the same time, the church interpreted all the social and political uprisings in Haiti as an expression of the lack of civilization, and only the church, through its education system and the campaign against the "African superstitions" (voodoo practices), could make the country civilized.

The more the church defended its neutral position and its spiritual autonomy, the more it was manipulated by the Haitian state as a structural element of the social pyramid. Its struggle against voodoo helped the state to keep the masses outside of the cities and far away from the political arena. Meanwhile, the church organized parish schools, charity works, community clinics and so on. Since 1913, social work was officially entrusted to the church.[63] According to the church doctrine of that time, charity was the only means of improving the living conditions of the poor.

The church used "créole" (the language of 95 percent of the population), especially in the countryside, but in the cities French was used. "Créole" and French indicated the social and cultural distinction, similar to the voodoo–Catholic relationship. The church accepted the social order as natural. But the Catholic schools promoted French as the language of a civilized nation, whereas "creole", was considered a dialect and a symbol of primitivism. There was not always a clear distinction between the work of the church and that of the state. This was precisely the aim of the state: to keep the masses in the countryside and to protect the rich against the uprisings of the poor. The church's fear of a national church also helped the Haitian state, because the bishops postponed, as much as possible, the creation of a national clergy. After forty years of the concordat, there were only two Haitian priests. The government would have experienced more difficulties with a Haitian clergy.

It was a Pyrrhic victory for the church during the nineteenth century. Dioceses, churches and religious congregations functioned as in Europe, with the cult's splendour displayed in the temples and chapels, dominating daily life and the collective manifestations belonging to the church. The Haitian believer felt, nevertheless, more at home with the voodoo religion than with the Catholic Church. Only later was the depth of the presence of Catholicism among the masses questioned, during the American military occupation, which used the arguments of social and political anarchy and of barbarism, due to the presence of voodoo, to justify the exploitation of the Haitian economy by the USA.

NOTES

1. Address given by the first archbishop of Port-au-Prince on 10 June 1864, quoted by Msgr J-M. Jan, *Le Cap-Haïtien: 1860–1966, Documentation religieuse* (Port-au-Prince 1972), 121.
2. See article 14 of the preliminary declaration of the imperial constitution of 1805.
3. P. Adolphe Cabon, *Notes sur l'histoire religieuse d'Haïti: de la révolution au Concordat 1789–1860* (Port-au-Prince 1933).
4. Letter from P. Percin, quoted by Cabon, *Notes sur l'histoire religieuse d'Haïti*, 397: "*Une Révolution terrible a éclaté parmi la classe noire contre la classe de couleur . . .*" (A terrible revolution erupted among the black class against the coloured class).
5. See Articles 4 and 5 of the text of the concordat:

   Art. 4: *Le Président d'Haïti jouira du privilège de nommer les archevêques et les evêques; et si le Saint-Siège leur trouve les qualités requises par les Saints Canons, il leur donnera l'institution canonique* (The president of Haiti will have the privilege of naming the archbishops and the bishops, and if the Holy See considers that they have the required qualities as stipulated in the Holy Canon, they will be given the canonical institution).

Art. 5: *Les Archevêques et les Evêques, avant d'entrer dans l'exercice de leur ministère pastoral, prêteront directement entre les mains du Président d'Haïti le serment suivant: "Je jure et promets à Dieu, sur les saints Evangiles comme il convient à un Evêque, de garder obéissance et fidélité au gouvernement établi par la constitution d'Haïti et de ne rien entreprendre ni directement ni indirectement qui soit contraire aux droits et intérêts de la République"* (The archbishops and bishops, before taking up duties as ministers, will take the following oath before the President of Haiti: I promise and swear before God and on the holy gospel, as is appropriate for a bishop, to obey and be loyal to the government established by the Constitution of Haiti and not to undertake anything which may directly or indirectly violate the rights and interests of the republic).

6. Quoted by J-M. Jan, *Le Cap-Haïtien*, 11.

7. Ibid., 13.

8. See Edner Brutus, *Instruction publique en Haïti* (Port-au-Prince 1948).

9. Quoted by Paul Robert, *L'Eglise et la première République Noire* (Rennes, France 1964), 108.

10. Jean Baptiste Labat, *Voyage aux Isles de l'Amérique, 1693–1705* (Paris 1722), Vol. II: 44: *"Ils importunent sans cesse les maîtres et les curés afin d'être baptisés: de sorte que, si on les voulait satisfaire, on emploierait des jours entiers à leur enseigner la doctrine et les prières"* (They continuously implore the masters and the priests to baptize them; they do this in such a way that, if the priests wanted to satisfy this wish, they would spend entire days teaching them the doctrine and prayers).
   For a new interpretation of the Soulouque regime, see Murdo J. Macleod, "The Soulouque regime in Haiti, 1847–1859: a reevaluation", *Caribbean Studies* 3 (1970): 35–48.

11. President Geffrard said in his speech on 19 July 1864: *"C'est à l'Eglise de continuer l'oeuvre que j'ai commencée la destruction du fétichisme et de ses futiles pratiques"* (It is the church's responsibility to continue the work that I have begun, the elimination of fetishism and of useless practices), quoted by Paul Robert, *L'Eglise et la première République Noire*, 115.

12. See for example the racist works of: G. d'Alaux, *L'Empereur Soulouque et son empire* (Paris 1856); Spencer St John, *Haïti ou la République noire*, translated from English (Plon 1886).

13. A. Cabon, *Notes sur l'histoire religieuse d'Haïti*, 390, quotes from a letter dated 7 August 1845 referring to the peasant rebellions: *"On prétend qu'ils avaient de la chair humaine dans leur macoute. La barbarie déborde"* (They claim that humanity prevails in their macoute organization. Barbaric acts abound).

14. Ibid., *Notes sur l'histoire religieuse d'Haïti*, 12.

15. Ibid., 449, 201–2: *"L'Eglise n'avait rien à réparer. La marche normale des négotiations était donc tout indiqué comme il suit: que l'Etat renonçat d'abord à tous les abus de pouvoir qu'il pratiquait en matière ecclésiastique et restituât a l'Eglise tous ses droits, qu'il offrît ensuite les bénéfices qu'il voulait assurer à l'Eglise et demandât en échange les privilèges, qu'il désirait obtenir . . ."* (There was nothing for the church to repair.

The normal procedure for negotiations was indicated as follows: that the state renounce, first and foremost, any abuse of power that it practised against the church, restore all rights to the church and that it then offer advantages to the church and demand in exchange certain privileges that it wished to obtain).

16. Ibid., 10: "En *matière d'administration ecclésiastique l'Ancien Régime non seulement reconnaissait à l'Eglise la liberté de se gouverner selon ses lois, mais encore lui prêtait son appui à cet effet. . . Malgré quelques abus inévitables, cette procédure respectait les prérogatives de l'Eglise. Les gouvernements issus de la Révolution française, même s'ils signent des Concordats avec l'Eglise, ont tendance au contraire à lui imposer leur souveraineté . . .*" (With regard to the administration of the Church, the Old Regime not only granted the Church the freedom to govern its own affairs according to its laws, but also provided assistance for this purpose . . . Despite some inevitable abuses, this procedure respected the prerogatives of the Church. Even though they had signed Concordats with the Church, the governments that were established after the French Revolution had a tendency to impose their sovereignty on the Church . . .).

17. B. Ardouin, *Etudes sur l'histoire d'Haïti* (Paris 1860), IX, 156.

18. Ibid., 151: "*Sachant le concours que trouvent les gouverneurs dans les sentiments religieux pour apaiser les troubles civils et fortifier l'esprit humain dans la soumission aux lois, en partant de la capitale pour se rendre à St Marc et dans le Nord, le Président avait invité l'abbé Jérémie à le suivre, afin de faire des prédications dans chaque ville ou bourg. Le prêtre remplit cette mission aux grés des désirs de Boyer*" (Aware of the fact that the governors depended on religious sentiment to quell civil unrest and strengthen the human spirit so that the population will more easily accept the laws, the president, on leaving the capital for St Marc and the northern region, invited the priest Jérémie to accompany him to give sermons in each city or village. The priest fulfilled this obligation, as Boyer wished).

19. Thomas Madiou, *Histoire d'Haïti* (1st edition: 1848; Port-au-Prince 1989), II, 128: "*Quant aux prêtres, il (Toussaint) leur accorda toutes sortes d'avantages. Aussi dans les églises, son nom était-il béni! Les prédicateurs, en chaire, ne l'appelait que le Papa Toussaint, le bienfaiteur de la colonie: l'influence du clergé se fit partout sentir*" (Toussaint granted all types of privileges to the priests. His name was, therefore, revered in the churches! At the pulpit, the preachers referred to him as Papa Toussaint, the benefactor of the colony: the influence of the clergy was felt everywhere).

20. Paul Robert, *L'Eglise et la première République Noire*, 83: "*Le général illettré, tiraillé entre l'instinct de dictadure et le respect des formes administratives que ses ministres cherchaient à lui imposer*" (The illiterate general, torn between his instinct to be a dictator and respect for the administrative arrangements that his ministers were trying to impose on him).

21. J-M. Jan, *Le Cap-Haïtien*, 2.

22. Paul Robert, *L'Eglise et la première République Noire*, 34: "*L'ancien Régime français reconnaissait la constitution divine de l'Eglise*" (The old French Regime recognized the divine constitution of the church).

23. A. Cabon, *Notes sur l'histoire religieuse d'Haïti*, 366: *"Heureux furent ceux d'entre les prêtres qui décedèrent avant l'établissement d'une autorité régulière, parce qu'ils n'eurent pas l'occasion de lui être rebelles!"* (Those priests who died before the establishment of a regular authority were fortunate because they did not have the opportunity to resist it!).

24. See Laënnec Hurbon, *Dieu dans le vaudou Haïtien* (Paris 1972).

25. An excellent but brief introduction to the nineteenth century in: Pierre Pluchon (ed.), *Histoire des Antilles et de la Guyane* (Paris 1982), ch. XI, "The black independence of Haiti", especially pp. 352–58; the most important work on the nineteenth century is written by Benoît Joachim, *Les racines du sous-développement en Haïti* (Port-au-Prince 1979); on the violent power struggles between 1870 and 1900; see also Alain Turnier, *Avec Mérisier Jeannis, Une tranche de vie jacmélienne et nationale* (Port-au-Prince 1982).

26. Father Adolphe Cabon wrote a fundamental work on this period: *Monseigneur Alexis Jean-Marie Guilloux* (Port-au-Prince 1929); see also, the works of J. Verschueren, *La République d'Haïti* (Paris 1948), especially vol. II, 240–92, of Msgr Paul Robert, *L'Eglise et la première République Noire*, and of Dantes Bellegarde, *La nation Haïtienne* (Paris 1938), 322–38 which summarize the work of Father A. Cabon. After one and a half centuries we do not have an important work on the history of the church in Haiti. We shall only present here a critical point of view on those published sources.

27. Letter dated 8 July 1864, quoted by A. Cabon, *Monseigneur Guilloux*, 81.

28. See letter written by Vicar General Alexis Jean-Marie Guilloux to the clergy and the faithful of the Republic of Haiti, 1868: *"Il est aujourd'hui constant que Mr l'Abbé Buscail, prêtre juridiquement frappé de suspense, exerce publiquement cette charge près de l'Armée d'Haïti, qu'il administre les sacrements et remplit les autres fonctions du Saint Ministère"* (Msgr Buscail, a priest who had been suspended by the authorities, continues to minister to the Haitian army, distributing sacraments and fulfilling other duties of the holy ministry).

29. This was the point of view of the most important newspapers of Europe on the political problems in Haiti. The newspaper *L'Univers* of 1 June 1867 wrote for example: *"On commence à croire que la dernière révolution d'Haïti pourrait bien se terminer par la restauration de Soulouque. Ce dénouement baroque prouverait que les nègres ont l'esprit plaisant"* (It is seeming more and more that this latest revolution in Haiti could conclude with the reinstatement of Soulouque. This unusual outcome would prove that blacks are agreeable). And the Paris newspaper *La Liberté* of 26 May 1869 characterized the government of Nissage Saget (a mulatto) as a *"sorte d'oasis civilisée au milieu de cette Afrique en délire"* (a sort of civilized oasis in the middle of this Africa in chaos).

30. The Cacos consisted of the peasants in the North of Haiti, who frequently attacked the cities and the capital, demanding social and political rights. It was rumoured that Salnave granted the Bay of St Nicolas (in the north) to the USA and that the Cacos rebelled against Salnave's government. Many politicians in

the second half of the nineteenth century manipulated those uprisings for their own interests.

31. Quoted by A. Cabon, *Monseigneur Guilloux*, 117.

32. Letter dated 26 August 1867: "*Vous me demandez des preuves juridiques de la culpa-bilité de ces prêtres, disait Delorme; je n'en ai pas de cette sorte à vous fournir. Les écclesiastiques n'ont plus la confiance du gouvernement dans les postes qu'ils occupent; le gouvernement exige qu'on les déplace*" ("You are asking me for legal proof of the guilt of these priests," said Delorme. "I am unable to provide you with this infor-mation. The government no longer trusts the priests who hold these positions and is demanding that they be removed").

33. Father Jules Degerine, vicar of St Thomas, narrates the last days of Msgr du Cosquer in a letter dated 13 August 1869 to Msgr Guilloux: "*Pendant les quinze jours de sa maladie, où il avait le délire une partie de la journée, il ne voyait que des assassins et des empoisonneurs autour de lui, il se disait alors persécuté par les ministres de l'Empereur qui se montraient froids à son égard*" (During the two weeks of his ill-ness, when he was delirious for a part of the day, he saw only murderers and poisoners around him. He therefore felt betrayed by the emperor's ministers who were insensitive to his plight).

34. "*Le gouvernement n'en a vue nullement le dessein de créer une sinécure pour la caisse publique au profit des ministres du culte; considérant que la première obligation faite à tout écclésiastique et notamment à un Archevêque est de résider dans son diocèse ou dans sa paroisse, sauf les causes légitimes d'absence, et qu'au surplus, une des disposi-tions dressées entre le gouvernement de la République et les Représentants du St Siège pour la bonne administration du culte catholique dans le pays, est la suppression du traitement pécuniaire convenu à tout écclésiastique en congé non renouvelé dans l'année et de trois mois. Considérant que depuis plus de deux ans, Msgr Testard du Cosquer qui avait été crée Archevêque de Port-au-Prince, a quitté la République sans avoir jamais demandé à qui de droit de renouvellement à son congé, si congé il y a jamais eu, et qu'il n'a jamais non plus entretenu avec le gouvernement, dont il est un haut fonc-tionnaire, aucune correspondance directe et régulière; qu'au contraire, depuis ce long laps de temps, il a laissé et laisse encore le pays qu'il était chargé de surveiller et d'ad-ministrer spirituellement, dans le plus complet abandon, à un moment où la guerre civile déployant ses tristes horreurs en Haiti, la voix de son premier Pasteur aurait été si puissante pour agir sur les âmes et aider l'Autorité légitime séculière à rétablir la paix et l'union dans la République, qu'une telle manière de faire de la part de Msgr du Cosquer ne peut être considérée que comme une démission de la charge d'Archevêque . . .*", *Le Moniteur 28 juin 1869* (The government does not intend to create a sinecure of public offices for the benefit of ministers of religion considering that the first obligation of all priests in general and an archbishop in particular, is to reside in his diocese or parish, except where there are legitimate reasons for absence. Furthermore, one of the provisions drawn up between the government of the republic and the representatives of the Holy See for the proper administration of the Catholic religion in the country, is the cancellation of payment to all priests

on leave; no more leave may be granted during the year and leave cannot exceed three months. Considering that for more than two years, Monsignor Testard du Cosquer, who was appointed archbishop of Port-au-Prince, left the republic without ever requesting renewal of his leave through the proper authorities [if he had even been granted leave in the first place], and that he had never maintained direct or indirect contact with the government, of which he is a senior member. And considering on the other hand, that during all this time, he has left and continues to leave the country he was to monitor and to which he was supposed to administer spiritually, in a state of complete abandon, at a time when civil war was unleashing its horrors on Haiti. The opinion of its most important spiritual authority would have been so powerful that it would have had an impact on the people's souls and helped the legitimate secular authority to re-establish peace and unity in the republic; such behaviour on the part of Monsignor du Cosquer can only be considered as an abdication of his responsibilities as archbishop, *Le Moniteur*, 28 June 1869).

35. "*Aider l'autorité légitime séculière à rétablir la paix et l'union dans la République*" (To help the legitimate secular authority to establish peace and union in the republic).

36. "*Un acte inouï qui va frapper au coeur tous les vrais enfants de l'Eglise en Haïti vient d'être publié au Moniteur de la République . . . L'arrêté du 28 juin est nul et de nulle valeur; . . . Msgr du Cosquer conserve toutes les prérogatives et les droits inhérents à sa charge d'Archevêque de Port-au-Prince: . . . il n'y a pas d'autre autorité que la sienne ou celle de ses délégués; . . . en conséquence, on ne saurait recourir au ministère des prêtres qui ne tiendraient pas leurs pouvoirs de cette source, la seule légitime . . . Je ne puis m'empêcher de vous adresser immédiatement ma protestation la plus énergique et la plus solennelle . . .*" (An unprecedented event which will have a significant impact on the true children of the church in Haiti has just been printed in *Le Moniteur* . . . The decree of 28 June is null and void; . . . Monsignor du Cosquer will retain all the prerogatives and rights inherent in his responsibility as archbishop of Port-au-Prince. There is no other authority but his or that of his representatives. Consequently, only priests whose authority flows directly from the ministry may call upon this source, the only legitimate one . . . I am forced to express to you immediately my most vigourous and solemn protest . . .).

37. Letter dated 11 November 1868, signed by all the members of the clergy.

38. "*Ne permettez à personne de régler ce qui concerne le jour et l'heure des enterrements, des services et des messes chantées; faites seul la police de votre église . . .*" (Do not allow anyone to determine the day and time of burials, services and sung masses; simply maintain law and order in your churches . . .) quoted by A. Cabon, *Monseigneur Guilloux*, 113.

39. On 11 July 1874 Thomas Madiou declared to the official newspaper, *Le Moniteur*: "*Il importe de rappeler au clergé que le mariage en Haiti comme en bien d'autres pays catholiques, est un acte que doit être d'abord célébré conformément aux articles 73, 74, 75 du Code Civil. C'est l'accomplissement des prescriptions de ces articles qui forme l'union légitime aux yeux de la loi . . . Messieurs les Curés et vicaires*

ne doivent non plus baptiser aucun enfant ni procéder à aucun enterrement si la décla-ration de naissance et celle du décès n'ont pas été faites d'abord au Conseil Communal" (The clergy must be reminded that a wedding in Haiti, as in many other Catholic countries, is an act that must be carried out in accordance with Articles 73, 74 and 75 of the Civil Code. It is compliance with the dictates of these articles which seals the legitimate union in the eyes of the law . . . priests and the vicars may not baptize any child nor officiate at any funeral service if the local council has not been previously notified of the birth or death).

40. Article 33: *"le gouvernement détermine l'étendue de la circonscription territoriale des paroisses et évêchés"*. Article 193: *"Pour bien concilier les intérêts du peuple avec ceux du culte catholique, apostolique et romain, qu'il professe le Concordat laissant à désirer, le gouvernement est autorisé à en proposer la modification dans le but de créer le plus tôt possible un clergé national"*; article 192: *"En attendant, au gouvernement seul est déféré le droit de délimiter la circonscription teritoriale des paroisses et évêchés, et de nommer les administrateurs supérieurs de l'Eglise en Haiti; lesquels à l'avenir, doivent être haitiens"* (Article 33: "The government shall determine the extent of the limit of the parishes and dioceses". Article 193: "In order to reconcile the interests of the people with those of the Catholic, apostolic and roman churches, provided that the desired Concordat is declared, the government is authorized to propose modifications to said Concordat in an effort to establish a national clergy as quickly as possible". Article 192: "In the meantime, the government shall be solely authorized to determine the limits of the parishes and dioceses and to appoint senior administrators of the church in Haiti, who should in future be Haitian nationals").

41. *Le Moniteur* published the following changes to articles 160 and 161: *"Tout ministre d'un culte qui procédera soit aux cérémonies religieuses d'un mariage, d'un baptême ou d'une inhumation, sans qu'il lui ait été justifié que les formalités de l'état-civil relativement à ces divers cas, ont été légalement remplies devant l'Officier de l'état civil compétent, sera puni d'une amende de cent piastres. Pour la première récidive, de l'interdiction de ces fonctions pour un an et trois ans au plus. Pour une seconde récidive, il sera puni de l'interdiction de ces fonctions à perpétuité"* (Any minister of religion who officiates at a wedding, baptism or funeral service, without first verifying that the formalities regarding these different situations have been legally adhered to before an officer of the relevant authority, shall be fined 100 piastres. For a second offence, he shall be banned from performing his duties for a minimum of one year and a maximum of three years. On the third occasion, he shall be banned from office for life).

42. Letter from the archbishop to the priests on 3 January 1876: *"Le salut des âmes est au-dessus des considérations humaines"* (Salvation of the soul is above human considerations).

43. But there is no difference between those two tendencies, which continued to dominate the Haitian political scene. Mulattoes and blacks were present in each group. Both were against the peasants. See recent studies: Benoît Joachim, "Sur

l'esprit de couleur", *Nouvelle Optique, Recherches haitiennes et caribéennes* 9 (1973): 149–58; Gil Martínez, "De l'ambiguïté du nationalisme bourgeois en Haiti", *Nouvelle Optique* 9 (1973): 1–32; Jean-Luc, *Structures économiques et lutte nationale populaire en Haïti* (Montreal 1976); Micheline Labelle, *Idéologie de couleur et classes sociales en Haïti* (Québec 1978); David Nicholls, *From Dessalines to Duvalier, Race, Colour and National Independence in Haiti* (Cambridge 1979).

44. "*C'est le Concordat, au dire des membres du clergé, qui favorise toutes les violations des lois, c'est le Concordat qui donne à ces disciples du Christ leur ton de hauteur et leur permet de constituer un véritable Etat dans l'Etat . . . baptêmes et mariages purement religieux ont pris des proportions colossales et par leur multitude constituent un véritable fléau . . . Le Concordat . . . compromet le berceau par les baptêmes sans état-civil, la famille par le mariage sans sanction de la loi, la sépulture par le refus injurieux qu'on fait, l'administration publique, par le antagonisme et les conflits incessants*" (It is the Concordat, according to the members of the clergy which encourages breaches of the law, it is the Concordat that gives these disciples of Christ their nobility and enables them to establish a true state within their state . . . Baptisms and marriages are on the rise and by their sheer numbers, are becoming a true scourge . . . The Concordat jeopardizes infancy through unauthorized baptisms, the family through marriage without legal sanction, the burial place through the offensive refusal to bury the dead and public administration through antagonism and ceaseless conflict). *L'Oeil* [newspaper], 15 January 1881.

45. Letter from the archbishop dated 18 October 1881: "*Il est faux que l'Eglise soit un Etat dans l'Etat, mais il est vrai qu'elle est une société réelle, parfaite et libre. Il est faux qu'elle soit un Etat au-dessus de l'Etat, mais il est vrai que les rois et les princes ne sont pas exempts de sa juridiction et que les lois humaines ne sauraient être contraires à la loi divine, dont l'Eglise est seule l'infaillible interprète . . .*" (It is untrue that the church is a state within the state, but it is true that the church is a real, perfect and free society. It is untrue that it is a state above the state, but it is true that kings and princes are not exempt from its jurisdiction and that human laws cannot be contrary to divine law, of which the church is the only infallible interpreter).

46. Report by Msgr Guilloux to Msgr du Cosquer, dated 23 March 1868 on the deeds of 1867.

47. Letter from Msgr Guilloux to Propagande Fide, dated 26 July 1870, published in the *Annales de la Propagation de la Foi*, no. 254, January 1871.

48. Letter from President Geffrard, published in *Le Moniteur*, 5 March 1864: "*La plupart de ceux qui se livrent aux pratiques, aux sortilèges, aux réunions et aux danses de la secte du vaudou tombent sous l'application de ces dispositions de la loi pénale. En conséquence, je vous invite à poursuivre sévèrement tous ceux qui, dans l'étendue de votre commandement, se livrent publiquement ou secrèment aux pratiques du Vaudou, à les faire arrêter et à les livrer à l'autorité judiciaire pour être jugés. Vous ferez aussi des recherches et des perquisitions dans tous les quartiers de votre commandement, à l'effet de saisir les objets et instruments servant aux dites pratiques et aux sortilèges et vous les ferez déposer, comme pièce à conviction au greffe du tribunal civil du ressort*"

(The majority of those who indulge in evil practices in the casting of spells in meetings and dances of the voodoo cult are subject to the provisions of the penal law. Therefore, I implore you to punish severely those who, in carrying out your duties, indulge, publicly or privately, in voodoo practices and to have them arrested and handed over to the judicial authorities to be tried in court. You will also carry out investigations and searches in all the areas under your jurisdiction and will seize all objects and instruments used in these practices and spell casting, presenting proof to the clerk of the relevant civil court).

49. Hannibal Price, *De la réhabilitation de la race noire* (Port-au-Prince 1900), 442.

50. J. Verschueren, *La République d'Haïti*, II, 334–37.

51. Ibid., III, 233–34: "*Des faits d'anthropophagie ont souvent été constatés dans ces parages, non seulement sur des personnes sacrifiées dans les cérémonies du Vaudoux, mais sur des cadavres arrachés à la tombe. Les montagnes brisées, les vallées profondes, des gorges sans issue favorisent cette horrible superstition, en permettant à ses cruels adeptes d'échapper aux poursuites et aux recherches de l'autorité*" (Reports of cannibalism have been observed in these parts, not only concerning persons sacrificed during voodoo ceremonies, but also corpses removed from their graves. Cracks in the mountains, deep valleys and never-ending gorges favour this horrible superstition, enabling its brutal followers to elude the authorities and avoid prosecution), archbishop of Cap, report of his pastoral visits in 1881–82.

52. Gustave d'Allaux, *L'Empereur Soulouque et son empire* (Paris 1856), 1; see also Spencer St John, *Hayti or the black Republic* (London 1884), especially chapter 5, "Voodou worship and cannibalism", 182–228.

53. Louis-Joseph Janvier, *Les constitutions d'Haïti* (Paris 1886), I, 281; *L'égalité des races* (Paris 1884); *Les affaires d'Haïti (1883–84)* (Paris 1885); *La République d'Haïti et ses visiteurs (1840–1882)* (Paris 1883). The thesis by Arthur Gobineau, *Essais sur l'inégalité des races humaines*, published with great success in France in 1853–55) was criticized by Anténor Firmin, *De l'égalité des races humaines* (Paris 1885).

54. See for example Msgr Kersuzan, *Conférence populaire sur le Vaudou* (Port-au-Prince 1896) and J-M. Jan, *Le Cap-Haïtien*, 301–36. See Laënnec Hurbon, *Le barbare imaginaire, Le soupçon de sorcellerie en Haïti* (Paris 1988).

55. A. Cabon, *Monseigneur Guilloux*, 98: "*l'Etat était regardé comme le maître absolu et le suprême et unique législateur, près duquel l'Eglise n'avait d'autres droits que ceux qui lui étaient gracieusement concédés*" (The state was considered to be the absolute and supreme master as well as the sole legislator; the church does not have other rights than those that were graciously conceded).

56. "*L'impiété d'une part, et de l'autre l'hérésie, se donnent la main, et s'efforcent de concert d'arrêter les progrès toujours croissants du règne de Jésus-Christ au milieu de nos populations, et de ruiner la foi dans les âmes . . . Il leur faut une doctrine positive revêtue d'un caractère de certitude absolue, seul capable de s'imposer à la conscience, et de lui donner une impulsion efficace vers le bien et d'y établir la sécurité et la paix . . . Nos populations sont catholiques par instinct et par besoin comme elles le sont par tradition et par sympathie . . . Haïti a hérité du funeste principe de l'omnipo-*

tence de l'Etat en matière religieuse et par suite de la subordination du prêtre aux autorités civiles" (Ungodliness and heresy have joined forces and are working together to halt the continuing progress of Jesus Christ's reign among our people and to destroy their faith . . . What they need is a positive doctrine which contains absolute certainty, capable of guiding peoples' conscience, of encouraging each individual to do good and of establishing security and peace . . . Our people are Catholics by instinct, need, tradition and affinity . . . Haiti has inherited the dangerous principle of the omnipotence of the state with regard to religious matters and consequently the subordination of the priest to the civil authorities), letter written by Msgr Guilloux in 1872.

57. Words of Benoît Joachim, *Les racines*, 137ff; here we present a summary of chapter 5, 115–56, a seminal work in the understanding the nineteenth century Haiti. For more details on the nature of the Haitian state, see M. Lundhals, *Peasants and Poverty: A Study of Haiti* (London 1979), especially pp. 326–34, where the author uses the concept of "soft state" to analyse the Haitian state of the nineteenth century. With respect to the exploitation of the peasants see the work of Christian H. Girault, *Le commerce du café en Haïti* (Paris 1980).

58. The American plan to take over the Bay of St Nicolas reappeared constantly after 1868. The interventions of the USA were justified, making reference to the so-called anarchy and barbarism of the blacks. This argument is present in the work of Samuel Hazard, *Santo-Domingo, Past and Present, With a glance at Hayti* (New York 1873).

59. Pastoral letter of the archbishop of Port-au-Prince on 28 December 1878.

60. Letter written by Msgr du Cosquer on 22 June 1866.

61. Pastoral letter from the archbishop of Port-au-Prince dated 28 December 1878.

62. L.-J. Janvier, *Les constitutions*, I and II, presented the same criticisms of the concordat. Many intellectuals shared the same ideas.

63. Research needs to be done on the subject of the church in relation to the poor in Haiti after 1864.

REFERENCES

Primary Sources

Documents in the Archives of the Priests of the Holy Spirit in Chevilly-Larue, France, thanks to Father Bernard Noe.

Texts of Msgr Alexis J.M. Guilloux:

Archives B-221 – Dossier B, chap. IV: on the concordat.

Archives B-221 – Dossier A, chap. VII: Actes et Statuts du second Synode diocésain de Port-au-Prince, 1872.

Archives B-222 – Dossier B, ch. III: Lettres pastorales and Instructions pastorales.

Texts of Msgr Hillion:

Archives B-222, Dossier B, chaps. II, III and IV: Lettres pastorales 1874–79, Lettres pastorales et Lettres circulaires 1880–89.

Correspondence: Archives 222-A – chap. III, Rapport du Vicaire général sur les
diocèses en 1867; chap. IV, Histoire religieuse: correspondance de Msgr
Guilloux; chap. V, Relation des évènements politiques du 26 Avril 1868 au 7
Juin 1868; chap. VII, Circulaire de Salomon
Letters and bulletins: Archives 222-B: chaps. II to VI
Extracts of newspapers from 1868 to 1902: Archives 223-A, chap. I;
Archives 225-A

WILLIAM L. WIPFLER

The Catholic Church and the State in the Dominican Republic, 1930–1960

The Church's Struggle to Exist, 1844–1929

The beginnings of the movement to free the people of Santo Domingo from Haitian domination were initiated in 1838 with the formation of a secret society known as La Trinitaria. Led by Juan Pablo Duarte, the movement organized cells throughout the Spanish-speaking community and stirred up patriotic sentiment in favour of independence. A number of Spanish and creole priests took an active part in this process, utilizing their pulpits and the limited possibilities within their parishes to recruit supporters.

Several priests were deported by the Haitian government for "fomenting discord". When President Boyer of Haiti was overthrown by a reformist movement on 13 March 1843, the first attempt was made to establish the republic. Victory seemed to be at hand, but the rapid response of the newly self-proclaimed Haitian president, Charles Herard, frustrated the rebels and forced the leaders of La Trinitaria to reorganize. Herard's persecution and increased authoritarianism stimulated greater support, and on 27 February 1844, the independence of the Dominican Republic was proclaimed. The Haitian contingents throughout the republic capitulated rapidly, and Herard led a large army across the frontier. In spite of their numerical superiority, the Haitian forces were defeated in almost every encounter. A military coup in his own country forced Herard to return, and his overthrow and the resulting power struggle relieved the infant republic of any major threat from the Haitians for almost a year.

A provisional governing junta was established on 28 February and comprised a mixed group of persons who were already identified as either "liberal" or "conservative". Political tensions that would disrupt the country for several decades appeared almost immediately. The conservatives, convinced that the Haitian threat rendered the existence of the republic tenuous, if not impossible, initiated negotiations with France to establish a protectorate. The liberals, led by the founders of La Trinitaria, were totally opposed to any foreign involvement and believed in the nation's ability to survive on its own. The matter was temporarily resolved on 9 June with the seizure of power by the liberals and the expulsion of the conservatives from the junta. Their own ability to exercise authority, however, was almost immediately destroyed as a result of dissension over the method to be used, proclamation or election, for Juan Pablo Duarte to assume the presidency. The door was open for the conservatives to regain control of the government.[1] On 12 July, General Pedro Santana, commander-in-chief of the army, entered Santo Domingo with an impressive military force, making it known that as far as he was concerned, no government had existed since the coup of 9 June. The following day he was named "Supreme Chief of the Republic with dictatorial powers in the name of the army and the people".[2]

Shortly before the liberal coup, the church had been given good reason to believe that its fortunes had changed with the coming of independence. On 11 May the governing junta had issued a lengthy decree favourable to the church in which it stated: "The Christian, Catholic, Apostolic, Roman religion, being that of the State, must be maintained in all its splendour."[3] Then, assuming the authority that had been granted to the Spanish monarchs under the "Patronato Real" (Royal Foundation) it declared: "the government elects as Archbishop . . . Doctor Tomás de Portes".[4]

General Santana delayed action on the decree from his own uninterested and impotent institution that was neither a support for, nor an obstacle to his purposes. However, the church had gained new respect among the common people because of the martyrdom and exile of a number of its priests during the Haitian occupations and the activity of the clergy on behalf of independence. As a result, public pressure made it necessary to take some measure regarding the church, so that in April of 1845, the general wrote to Rome calling attention "to the need that this Church has to be provided with a Prelate, and at the same time to request that Dr Portes' proposal for the mitre be accepted and his election confirmed".[5] Due to subsequent decisions by Santana and their approval by the congress, however, the confirmation from Rome was delayed until 1847.

On 7 June 1845, a law was approved by which "all mortgages and perpetual rents established in favour of the church were declared abolished".[6] A month later on 2 July further legislation dealing with national assets confiscated on the state's behalf, all properties that belonged to extinct religious communities, inactive churches and charitable foundations.[7] In effect, the laws were an extension of Boyer's policy and deprived the church of virtually all its income. As a balm to the enraged, the budget for 1845–46 was amended "to grant to the Prelate, a salary that would permit him to live with the decency befitting his high office",[8] but the clerics were not put off so easily. Dr José Bobadilla, brother of a secretary of state, published a widely distributed pamphlet defending the inalienability of church property by the state. Santana ordered the priest's expulsion from the republic. A mutual suspicion had been created between General Santana and the church that would break out in open conflict during his several terms in office.

In the final months of 1847, Santana's government was seriously threatened by dissension and opposition. The experience of the church had clearly demonstrated that its suffering had been greater in the past, in those periods of political turmoil when it lacked a resident superior. Rome hastened to confirm the election of Dr Portese Infante, and on 20 January 1848, he was elevated to the office of archbishop of Santo Domingo. One of his first major efforts was to convince the congress of the republic's urgent need for a centre for higher education to train its leaders. In May, the congress reestablished the Conciliar Seminary of St Thomas Aquinas as a mixed college, where students could study not only for the priesthood, but also in the fields of law, medicine and literature.[9] However, its purpose was given a limited and elitist vision: "The propagation of cultural attainment among the higher classes of society."[10] The archbishop came from that stratum of society and the thirteen men whom he would ordain in the next decade were also drawn from the privileged class. As a result, the church began to serve that class and its interests and became increasingly alienated from the mass of the Dominican people.

Santana's difficulties, caused by his own despotic use of presidential powers, came to a climax in August of 1848, when he was forced to resign. He was succeeded by his own minister of war, General Manuel Jiménez, who had engineered the undermining of Santana's power.

Unfortunately for the new president, a similar change had occurred in Haiti, and the new ruler, General Faustino Soulouque, felt compelled to emulate those earlier generals in Haiti's history who had attempted to unite the island. Soulouque invaded, pushing Dominican troops before him and leaving devastation behind. Jiménez was blamed for the defeats and was compelled to enlist Santana's support in reorganizing the military and directing the struggle. Soulouque was driven back to Haiti. Jiménez was deposed and sent into exile.

With the presidency vacant after Jiménez's expulsion, the name Buenaventura Baez appeared on the political roster. Sumner Welles described this man, who would be president of the Dominican Republic five times, in harsh terms.[11] From the beginning of his term in office, Baez recognized the value of having the Roman Catholic Church as an ally. His relations with the archbishop were most cordial. Arrangements were made for the initiation of diplomatic relations with the Vatican, aimed at signing a concordat. Public schools were required to include religious education in their curriculum. Priests were granted special privileges.[12] Finally, at the urging of the archbishop, the congress went so far as to pass legislation in 1851, prohibiting the use of bells by Protestants declaring that only the Catholic Church had that privilege.[13]

Made confident by the gains that had been experienced in a comparatively short time, Archbishop Portese and his clergy initiated a campaign aimed at the repeal of legislation that had been enacted during the French and Haitian occupations and confirmed during Santana's first term. In particular, they sought the abolition of civil marriages and the restitution of the right of persons to will their assets to the church. Their efforts, and the support of President Baez, however, did not suffice to move the congress to take action.[14]

Time had run out for Baez and once again it was General Pedro Santana's turn to occupy the presidency. Santana was inaugurated on 15 February 1853 in a peaceful transfer of power. On 27 February the anniversary of Independence, he granted amnesty to a large number of political enemies whom he had sent into exile. On 14 March he summoned Archbishop Portes to appear before the congress. As President Santana declared, he had sworn to uphold the laws of the nation and required that they be upheld. Because the clergy had formed themselves into a force of opposition that could lead the country into anarchy, he had to demand that the archbishop take an oath of allegiance to the constitution. The cleric refused and in the ensuing dispute the congress vigourously supported Santana. Unnerved, Portes referred to both the constitution and the president's advisors as heretical and asserted that it would be better to abandon the country than to take such an oath. Santana was prepared; he handed the archbishop his passport. Portes left the session a depressed and broken man.[15]

Prompted to further action by the endorsement received from the congress, the president decreed the expulsion of three of the most influential priests in the republic. The archbishop, unable to face exile, gave in two weeks later and took the oath. The emotional upheaval had been so terrible, however, that he became mentally unbalanced and retired from public life. The congress now started to provide legislation to ensure control of the church in the future, as shown by the approved decree on 13 June 1853.[16] With the revision of the constitution in 1854, the control was tightened further by a provision that "the Congress shall name the dignitaries of the Catholic Church, which shall continue being that of the state, beginning with the archbishop of the Republic".[17]

Santana resigned from the presidency and on 26 May 1856, his vice president, General Manuel de Regla Mota, succeeded him. Buenaventura Baez's fortunes seemingly improved once again. The Spanish consul, eager to continue with the negotiations for a protectorate and anxious about American, British and French aggressiveness in the same matter, persuaded Regla Mota and Santana to allow Baez to return from exile to which he had been sentenced. Then, in a successful manoeuvre, Baez had himself elected vice president, secured the resignation of Regla Mota, and assumed the presidency on 8 October 1856. An insignificant "rebellion", suppressed in a matter of hours, was blamed on Santana, who was imprisoned and then sent into exile. The relationship between Baez and the church returned to its former cordial state. But a major revolution broke out in July 1857. A new revolutionary government, a liberal and progressive movement, was formed in Santiago. After its defeat on 1 September, General Pedro Santana again assumed the presidency of the wasted and bankrupt republic.

The Roman Catholic Church was in an extremely precarious position. With the death in 1857 of Dr Elias Rodríguez, rector of the seminary, "the classrooms were nearly deserted, caused in no small part by the civil disturbances that afflicted the Republic".[18] In April 1858, the infirm Archbishop Portese Infante died. The church could count on only one outstanding personality, Arturo Meriño, a young priest who subsequently served as president of the republic and then as arch-bishop. Meriño took over the care of the cathedral and became the spokesman for the church.

Santana, however, had much more to occupy his time than concern about the church. Once again he threw himself into the negotiations to establish a protectorate. The USA, Great Britain, France and Spain continued to manoeuvre for the key position, largely motivated by pressure from private commercial and economic interests, seeking con-cessions in the republic. Faced with a number of minor but trouble-some rebellions within the threatening organization of the multitude of Dominicans whom he had sent into exile, and a small but growing opposition movement to the idea of a protectorate, Santana made an open offer to surrender the republic for annexation by Spain. On 27 February 1861 at the Te Deum celebrating the seventeenth anniver-sary of independence, Arturo Meriño attacked the proposal from the pulpit of the Cathedral.[19] On 18 March 1861, the Spanish flag flew over the Puerta of El Conde, where the struggle for independence had begun. Santana declared himself governor and captain-general and Arturo Meriño was sent to Spain as a prisoner.

In May 1861, Queen Isabel II elected a new archbishop for Santo Domingo, Bienvenido Monzón y Martín. The prelate began his work vigorously and set out to reorganize the church throughout the colony. He had little material with which to work, due to the church's impoverished state and to the few priests who were available. As a result, he turned to the church in Spain to provide the manpower nec-essary to carry out his plans. The conciliar seminary was opened once again and staffed by a Spanish rector and professors. The cathedral chapter was reformed with Spanish dignitaries occupying the posts of honour. Several churches and other institutions were reopened. These and other efforts were conveniently endowed by funds from Spain.[20] Together with the Spanish governor (Santana had angrily resigned in March of 1862 because of his eroding authority), the archbishop intro-duced regulations controlling in detail almost every aspect of life in the colony, demonstrating remarkable insensitivity to the feelings and customs of the Dominican people and the national clergy.[21]

The unenlightened and repressive Spanish rule stirred up discontent and rebellious sentiments throughout the colony. Finally, on 3 May 1865, having suffered the loss of 21,000 soldiers and the expenditure of thirty-five million pesos, "the Spanish Congress approved a decree for the abandonment of Santo Domingo, whose brief text simply annulled the decree of annexation".[22] The hard-won reconquest of independence and the "Restoration of the Republic" were ushered in with a fierce partisan struggle that would typify the Dominican political scene for fifty years. From the inauguration of the government of General José María Cabral in August of 1865 until the establishment of a government of occupation by the US Marines in November of 1916, power would change hands forty-nine times and fourteen constitutions would be promulgated. The Spanish had left a country that was in ruins.

The church was hardly in a better position. Archbishop Monzón had withdrawn with all the other Spanish authorities. He had taken with him all of the clergy who had come to Santo Domingo at his request, as well as the resources that had maintained the church's institutions during his four years there. Nevertheless, in spite of the church's penury, some members of the Dominican clergy were held in high esteem because of their contribution to the restoration of the republic. One such person was Calixto María Pina, who was appointed ecclesiastical vicar upon the departure of Archbishop Monzón, and elected to preside at the constituent assembly in October of 1865.[23] Another was Arturo Meriño, who had been exiled to Spain in 1861, and whose efforts aided "in influencing Isabel II to favour the restitution of sovereignty to the Dominican Republic".[24]

Father Meriño returned to his homeland as the party struggle began to take shape. He threw his energies into the political efforts of the "Azules" (Blues), a party that was led by persons who had fought both for independence and restoration. The "Rojos" (Reds) were largely from the business sector, the traditional supporters of Buenaventura Baez, who were ready to support him for a third time for the presidency. Baez's moment arrived when General Cabral, who had been appointed as protector of the republic in August with the support of the "Azules", suddenly tendered his resignation to the constituent assembly in October and then led a movement which resulted in the election of Baez as president. On 8 November he was sworn into office by the newly-elected president of the assembly, Father Arturo Meriño. Baez, however, did not change. An easily controlled insurrection by one of the heroes of the restoration and an "Azul", General Gregorio Luperón, was used by Baez as an excuse to hunt down his opponents, and to imprison or exile almost two hundred of the republic's most influential citizens. Among them was Arturo Meriño, who once again went into exile.

It was a simple process for the president to fill the national assembly with his own supporters, have them abolish the liberal constitution of 1865 and re-establish the repressive 1854 Constitution of Santana, and then convert the president into a dictator with power to rule by decree. The farce was too much for General Cabral, the very person who had turned power over to Baez, and he, together with Luperón and an officer in Baez's Cabinet, overthrew the government. Cabral was elected and inaugurated under the 1865 Constitution on 22 August 1866.[25]

The support of the returned exiles, mostly liberal "Azules", and the former supporters of Santana, permitted Cabral to initiate a series of reforms in some of the areas that had suffered most as a result of the chaos since the beginning of the hostilities against Spain in 1863. Principal among them were the improvement of agriculture and commerce, and the development of education. In the latter effort, churchmen once again played an important role. In November, Cabral allowed the buildings of the old monastery of the "Mercedarios" (Mercedarians), Regina Angelorum, to be used by Father Francisco Xavier Billini for the establishment of the San Luis Gonzaga College.[26] In subsequent years, Father Billini was to become one of the most significant figures in education in the Dominican Republic. In 1867, Father Meriño was appointed rector of the seminary as well as the organizer of the Professional Institute, a centre that attempted to meet some of the needs of higher education in the republic.

The opportunity given to Meriño to use his immense talent on behalf of these institutions was sharply limited as the result of a conflict between the government and the Vatican in which he was the central figure. In accordance with the constitution, President Cabral nominated Arturo Meriño to fill the vacant post of archbishop of Santo Domingo, and on 1 October 1866, the congress confirmed the proposal.[27] Unfortunately for the republic and the church, Archbishop Monzón y Martín had not forgiven the national clergy for their opposition to the proposed annexation and, with the support of the Spanish hierarchy, persuaded the pope to deny recognition of any Dominican for the high post. Rome responded to the nomination by naming a foreign priest, the apostolic vicar of St Thomas, as apostolic vicar of Santo Domingo as well. In the name of constitutional order and national dignity, President Cabral refused to accept the credentials of the new hierarch which in turn led to a virtual schism. The impasse threatened once again to leave the church bereft of a superior during a critical period in the nation's history, so that Meriño was commissioned by the government to go to Rome to argue the Dominican case.[28] The nature of his visit to the Vatican was soon converted, and he was once again exiled when the Cabral government collapsed and Buenaventura Baez regained control.[29]

Unlike the "Azules" whose principles would not permit the submission of the Dominican Church to the authority of a foreign hierarch, Baez accepted the appointment of an apostolic delegate by the Vatican.[30] But opposition to Baez exploded into a full-scale civil war. His policy of annexation, his unrestrained and arbitrary repression and his disastrous fiscal practices helped to create a coalition that finally led to his overthrow. On 2 January 1874, he fled to Caracas. Between January 1874 and October 1879, the republic had seventeen changes of administration.

The separation of the Dominican Church from the Vatican had not been overcome fully through Baez's acceptance of supervision by an apostolic delegate. To all intents and purposes, the church remained without a leader and the clergy functioned independently in their parishes. The institutions of the church, namely the seminary and schools, suffered the same disruption as those of the state. Some relief was experienced during Gonzalez's dictatorship (1874–76) when "several Catholic Churches were repaired" with government assistance,[31] but in general, the church lacked the resources to engage in more than a minimal pastoral ministry.

Arturo Meriño, having returned to the republic in 1874 after Baez's fourth rout, became parish priest in El Seibo, one of the strongholds of the "Azules" in the east, where he divided his energies between spiritual and political concerns. When in 1876, Baez manipulated himself into power for the fifth time, unleashing a wave of persecution and terror throughout the republic, Meriño ventured into the much harsher realities of the political struggle, inciting an insurrection in the eastern province.[32] The overthrow of Baez in March of 1878 inspired an attempt to reorganize the political structures, and Meriño presided over a meeting of a newly selected assembly in May, which established a twelfth constitution.[33] Conditions in the nation were still extremely unstable, however, and during the next fifteen months, six more governments would rise and fall before the country could make a serious effort to establish a democracy.

On 7 October 1879, Gregorio Luperón, bound by his own dedication to democratic principles, refused to accept the title of president of the republic on the grounds that he had not been chosen under a constitutionally regulated election. Instead, he became provisional president until a constituent assembly could revise the constitution and arrange elections. He set up his government in the northern city of Puerto Plata to emphasize his interim role. Luperón appointed General Ulises Heureaux, who had suppressed the last of the insurrections, minister of war and his representative in Santo Domingo. Meriño was once again elected to preside over the constituent assembly. With the support of these and other political friends, the provisional president carried out prodigious reforms in only eleven months. Luperón reorganized the collection of taxes and customs tariffs, adjusted the terms on foreign indebtedness and payments, paid retroactive salaries to public employees and set up a system of punctual remuneration, promoted the establishment of newspapers and offered a small subvention to assure their survival. He also established a teacher training institution for the preparation of teachers and founded other public schools throughout the country, located agricultural commissions in important centres to stimulate production, modernized the organization and equipment of the army and, most importantly, presided over the tranquil election by the people and inauguration of his constitutionally based successor, Father Arturo Meriño.[34]

President Meriño's term in office was one of unprecedented development and prosperity for the Dominican Republic, and has been described as "the most constructive and civilizing period of the history of the Republic during the nineteenth century".[35] The reforms that had been initiated by Luperón were strengthened during the next two years. Meriño encouraged the political refugees from the independence struggles in Cuba and Puerto Rico to emigrate, and with their assistance, particularly that of the Cubans, the neglected sugar industry was revived and modernized. The educational system, which was of particular interest to the president, was expanded and the Professional Institute, which had limped along uncertainly since its establishment in 1866, was expanded and granted a subsidy.[36]

The church's situation began to improve from the time of the provisional presidency of Luperón. The return of the "Azules" to power initially reopened the schism with the Vatican that had been, superficially healed by Baez's acceptance of a foreign apostolic delegate. Through the efforts of Luperón, however, the supreme pontiff was persuaded to recognize the right of the republic to nominate its archbishop, and normal relations were once again established.[37]

Understandably, the election of Meriño to the presidency solidified the ties with Rome and could only result in benefits for the Dominican church. Through his efforts, a number of charitable institutions were aided in their work and the cathedral chapter was reorganized with endowments for its support being provided from public funds.[38] But his greatest contribution was the prestige he brought to the church, having occupied the nation's highest office.

On 1 September 1882, the republic experienced its second peaceful transfer of power when President Arturo Meriño turned over the administration of government to another democratically elected Azulista, General Ulises Heureaux. Shortly thereafter, Father Meriño became the rector of the Professional Institute, reorganizing it and converting it into an effective university centre.[39] In 1883, he persuaded President Heureaux to create a medical court to "regulate the professional practice of doctors, surgeons, pharmacists, dentists and mid-wives".[40] In the following year, the institute was permitted to use the property of the old Dominican University.[41] During the same year, Meriño, in his recognized position as apostolic administrator of the diocese of Santo Domingo, reopened the seminary in order to provide facilities for the education and preparation of priests, since the Professional Institute had dropped "Sacred Letters" from the curriculum some years before.[42]

With the re-establishment of relations between the republic and the Vatican, and the confirmation of Meriño as apostolic administrator, it was natural that the "Azules" should once again submit his candidacy for the office of archbishop. This time the nomination was accepted, and on 6 July 1885, eighteen years after he was first nominated, the former president was ordained in Rome as archbishop of Santo Domingo.[43] During his prelacy until his death in 1906, Archbishop Meriño demonstrated a constant concern for the institutions of the church and particularly its educational centres. Under his direction, the seminary "began to sponsor other schools for the preparation of the youth: the Cathedral Parochial School in 1886 and St Thomas College in 1892",[44] the more advanced seminarians served as the first professors in these schools.[45] Father Francisco Billini's work was given particular support by the archbishop, and at the time of his death in 1890, the deeply respected priest had established an orphanage, an asylum for the mentally ill, a home for poor elderly people and a public library.[46]

The "Azules" party had fully supported Ulises Heureaux's election in 1882. From the beginning of his first term in office, however,

Heureaux manipulated the political scene in order to destroy the unity of the party and undermine anyone who might be a competitor for power in the future. His successor was faced with several conflicts, instigated by Heureaux himself. He divided the "Azules", by manufacturing rumours of conspiracy, engineering a rigged election, goading some of the "Azules" leaders to insurrection and then driving them out of the country. He then reinstated himself as president on 6 January 1887, and remained in power until his assassination on 26 July 1899. The church had shared in the uncertainties of the period between 1899 and 1916. The archbishop's increasing ill health and the impoverished state of the church contributed to the loss of its influence in public affairs. In 1902, the provisional government of General Horacio Vasquez promulgated an educational law that required the rector and professors of the Professional Institute to have academic degrees. Although Meriño commented that his "high investiture as Prelate freed him from the requirement" of this decree, his resignation as rector was accepted,[47] and the church ceased to have any influence on tertiary education until the founding of a Catholic university in 1962.

The parish priest of La Vega was Adolfo Alejandro Nouel, an able scholar with degrees in theology and canon law as well as a doctorate in theology from the Gregorian University in Rome, who distinguished himself as a fine orator and pastor.[48] In 1902, Nouel served briefly as president of a constituent assembly, but its work was cut short by one of the frequent insurrections that afflicted the country. Father Francisco Fantino, an Italian priest and eminent educator, joined Nouel in La Vega in 1903, and opened a small school in that community which eventually developed into the most important private institution in the central valley.[49] On several occasions during the violent strife, Father Nouel's intervention prevented the execution of prisoners captured by one of the contending forces, and the priest's reputation as pastor and peacemaker was promoted.[50]

When age and illness prevented Archbishop Meriño from fulfilling all of his official responsibilities, Adolfo Nouel was selected as coadjutor archbishop. He was ordained in October of 1904 in Rome.[51] To all intents and purposes, he assumed the authority of the office almost immediately in order to relieve the ailing Meriño, whose activities were limited to ceremonial functions. On 20 August 1906, Fernando Arturo Meriño, metropolitan archbishop of Santo Domingo, ex-president of the republic, educator and patriot, the dominant figure in the life of the church almost from the time of his priestly ordination in 1856, died and was succeeded by Nouel. The new archbishop was more ecclesiastic and less of a politician than his predecessor, but he shared Meriño's concern for the Church's role in education.

The political disorder affecting the republic since the death of President Cáceres in 1911 was of particular concern to the US government, due to its adverse effect on the payment of foreign debts being managed by the US representatives resident in the country. With the approval of Washington, they proposed, in November of 1912, that Archbishop Nouel be elected to the presidency. The warring parties agreed, a truce was called, and Nouel was elected to a two-year term by the congress.[52] Inaugurated on 1 December the president was immediately besieged by demands from both parties for favours and privileges. On 30 March after only four months in office, the congress accepted the archbishop's resignation, and the country was thrown into four more years of bloodshed that would lead to US armed intervention on 13 May 1916, and the establishment of an occupation government on November 29. The eight-year occupation of the republic has few, if any, apologists. It was a period of great humiliation for the Dominican people that was maintained by the constant display of superior military force.

Hardly had a month of occupation passed when the Roman Catholic Church experienced the arbitrary nature of the foreign military control. On 26 December, Captain Harry S. Knapp, the military governor, decreed a modification of the marriage laws, establishing civil marriage as a legal option to the traditional religious ceremony.[53] Knapp's action was a direct encroachment on the realm of church authority. But the church was too weak and won very little popular support to raise a significant protest and the law became a permanent element of the legal code.

The most difficult situation that the US occupation created for the church, however, was not in the conflict over moral authority but in the opportunity given to Protestant denominations to begin work in the republic. Up until 1919, the Protestants' presence was largely limited to the community which had settled in the Samana Peninsula during the Haitian rule and to isolated work among English-speaking sugar industry labourers in the east. No serious attempt had been made by the American churches to begin work in the Dominican Republic or in most of Latin America, prior to that time.[54]

In 1919, the Revd Samuel Guy Inman, secretary of the Protestant Committee for Cooperation in Latin America, visited Hispaniola on behalf of the denominations in order to determine the potential for mission work. His report was an unambiguous challenge to Protestants to establish themselves in the Dominican Republic, taking advantage of the conditions created by the occupation to develop their institutions.[55] In 1920, a meeting was held which included representatives of the Methodist, United Brethren and Presbyterian Churches. The Board for Christian Work in Santo Domingo was created, combining the support of five mission boards of the three denominations. The work of the mission began in 1921 under the direction of an American superintendent and with the assistance of several Puerto Rican pastors, under the name "Dominican Evangelical Church". In a very short time, however, the missionaries learned that while Inman had accurately reported the advantages offered by the military occupation, he had not taken into account the extent of Dominican hostility towards US presence. Identification with the occupation was a serious impediment.[56]

The pattern of development for the Episcopal Church was so firmly established in the first few years, that as the missionaries moved out of Santo Domingo to other areas of the country, its strategy was always related to the activities of the foreign community. As a result, when the occupation ended and some of the denominations that had been working among Dominicans, such as the Free Methodists in the Santiago area and the Dominican Evangelical Church, experienced occasional outbreaks of hostility and persecution, the Episcopal Church continued unimpeded because of its foreign image. The occupation was no longer to be the ongoing reality that many of its American and Dominican beneficiaries had hoped. In fact, because of the growing protest throughout Latin America and within the USA, President Wilson had authorized his secretary of state to develop plans for withdrawal as early as 1921, which were carried out in 1924.[57]

The church, however, was still as Inman had described it in 1919. Weak and impoverished, it made little impact on the society. In comparison, Protestant work was well financed and dynamic, and was therefore seen as a threat. With the end of the US occupation, protection that had been provided to missionaries came to an end, and Roman Catholic frustration expressed itself in occasional acts of persecution. Not infrequently, however, the missionaries themselves were to blame for losing sight "of the main emphasis of the gospel in their zeal for pointing out the errors of the Roman Catholic Church" in the hope of attracting people to their point of view.[58]

The Protestants in the Dominican Republic never faced very violent persecution like that which occurred in Colombia and other Latin American republics. The experiences were sporadic and seemed to be aimed at creating confusion or promoting intimidation. Trujillo's rise to power was a product of the military occupation. The US authorities had established the Dominican National Guard in 1917. Two years later, Trujillo was commissioned as a second lieutenant and began a rapid ascent through the ranks, becoming inspector of the First Military District when the guard was converted into the national police shortly before the withdrawal of the marines in 1924. He became chief of staff and during the next three years he reorganized the national police in order to ensure his complete control, and increased its size to such an extent that the congress proclaimed it as the national army in 1928.[59] President Vasquez, unaware of Trujillo's ambitions and convinced of his loyalty, personally elevated him to the rank of brigadier general and chief of the army. During the president's absence in the latter months of 1929, the protests against his government were skilfully transformed into an insurrection by Trujillo's agents, who were supplied with arms from the national arsenal. On 23 February the "revolution" began in Santiago. Demanding Vasquez's resignation, the "people's" army marched toward Santo Domingo. General Trujillo made no move to suppress the rebellion. Vasquez resigned.

On 30 June, the national assembly cast a unanimous vote of compliance with the travesty that had taken place, declaring the electoral process of 15 May to be legal, and Trujillo, supported by the department of the state, as the victor.[60] During the remaining weeks prior to Trujillo's inauguration on 16 August the Roman Catholic Church underwent a crisis that not only threatened its institutional existence, but would make it utterly dependent on the will of the new president. In 1929, the church had been involved in a property dispute in La Vega. When the matter was taken before the court of appeals in that city, the decision not only went against the church but the sentence negated the legal authority of the Roman Catholic Church in the republic. On 8 August 1930, just one week before Trujillo's assumption of power, the nation's supreme court upheld the lower court ruling.[61]

Thus, the church entered the era of Trujillo as a legal nonentity threatened with the confiscation of its already meagre possessions. Its structure, consisting of a single archdiocese, had not changed in four centuries, a sign of its stagnation. The archbishop, Adolfo Nouel, a man who was already weakened by illness, was unable to provide the dynamic leadership it needed in a critical period. The lower clergy, too few in number to minister adequately to the Catholic masses, were, with only a few exceptions, poorly educated, lacking in zeal and weak in morals. The church's membership, though statistically numerous, was largely unevangelized, with the lower classes superstitious and impressed by the ceremonies of their religion while the upper classes were indifferent and materialistic. It entered the era as an institution that could be ignored or manipulated.

The Era of Trujillo: The Church as an Instrument of Control 1930–1960

The desire for uncontested authority, together with a genius for organization and a complete lack of inhibitions concerning the methods for accomplishing his objectives, made Trujillo an instinctive disciple of Machiavelli (of whom the barely educated general was probably ignorant).[62] During the first two years of his first term in office, Trujillo directed an intensive campaign against those who might prove troublesome in the future. The main target of this persecution was the Progressive National Alliance, the party that had been the most outspoken in the criticism of Trujillo's candidacy and had shown the greatest political acumen during the pre-election campaign. It was eventually destroyed.

Gathering around him those who had demonstrated their loyalty from the outset, as well as a new group of "converts" from other political parties who realized the direction in which the tide was moving, the president formed his own political organization, the Dominican Party. It was officially registered with the electoral board in March of 1932 and soon began a campaign for the re-election of Trujillo in 1934. There was an immediate rush, by many who had been in the opposition, to join the party of the strongman in order to demonstrate their loyalty. Members of the congress were almost unanimous in their compliance, the extent of their submission being manifested at the end of 1932, when they declared Trujillo "Benefactor of the Fatherland" and again in mid 1933 when they granted him the rank of "Generalísimo".[63] These were the first of many titles that would be created during the years to flatter the insatiable ego of the dictator.

Those who were not convinced of the need to join the Dominican Party because of political ambition, often did so out of fear. Trujillo made very little effort to cover up the crimes and abuses committed against his opponents. They served to create an atmosphere of intimidation and paranoia in which he increased his control. The murder of General Bencosme, an influential and active leader of the Progressive National Alliance and a rich landholder, is illustrative of the method that Trujillo used to eliminate his political enemies, a method which was perfected over the course of three decades. General Bencosme had turned from political life in disgust after the election of Trujillo and had retired to his hacienda. By inventing a charge of embezzlement against him, Trujillo ordered his arrest and Bencosme was forced to flee from his home and from the army. He was finally found and executed without any attempt being made to return him for trial. Trujillo denied any knowledge of the injustice and initiated a mock investigation to find the guilty individuals. The family of Bencosme, under terrifying pressure from the authorities, was dragged into the farce as well.[64]

Merciless in his punishment of groups or individuals who might oppose him, backed by an army that was lavishly rewarded for its loyalty and supported by a singularly powerful party, Trujillo had guaranteed his re-election in 1934. The election was held with the Dominican Party presenting the only slate of candidates. In four years the generalísimo had achieved almost everything that he had set out to accomplish since 1930. The tabulation of results showed that "all the votes were 100 percent in favour of Trujillo and the rest of the slate, including senators, deputies, governors, mayors and municipal councils".[65] Furthermore, Statute 39 of the Dominican Party required that "on accepting nomination, candidates for elected offices must send their resignations in writing, without a specific date, to the Chief of the Party",[66] thus providing the dictator with a tool that nullified the concept of separation of powers contained in the Dominican constitution.

In the process of the consolidation of power, Trujillo did not overlook the Roman Catholic Church. Its obviously weak and unthreatening condition might well have tempted him to ignore it, but the astute president recognized in the church a potential of considerable utility or a future obstacle of unknown magnitude. He chose to incorporate it, to the fullest extent possible, within his own strategy of control: the church as legitimator, Trujillo as patron.[67] On 6 March 1931, he proposed a legislation to the congress that would restore to the church the legal authority of which it had been deprived the year before.[68] The bill was approved as Law 117 on 20 April and the archdiocese was prompt in expressing gratitude in the next issue of its *Boletín* (bulletin), declaring that the new law "truly establishes an eloquent proof of the judgement and prudence of the ruler".[69] Shortly thereafter approval was given for the payment of a subsidy to assist the church with its critical financial problems. A bonus was added to this in February 1932, with the creation of the Commission for the Conservation of Monuments and Relics, an agency provided with an appropriation to repair and maintain historic buildings, many of which were churches and convents.[70]

The single potential obstacle to Trujillo's hope for a complacent and legitimizing church, was the appointment of a successor to the office of the archbishop of Santo Domingo. Alejandro Nouel was virtually incapacitated by illness and age when the generalísimo was elected. As a result, the Vatican named Canon Armando Lamarche as the apostolic administrator in 1931, empowered to conduct the affairs of the church in the nation.[71] Within a year, Lamarche died and was replaced by Father Rafael Castellanos. He was a highly qualified and respected priest, a disciple of Archbishop Meriño, a former columnist in the respected journal *Criterio Católico* (*Catholic Opinion*) and a known apologist for the dignity and autonomy of the church. It was a man such as this whom Trujillo did not want to see as the new archbishop. Trujillo seized the first opportunity provided by Castellanos to disclose publicly his hostility towards the priest. "At a civic review held in Santiago early in 1933, there was a Mass, and Father Castellanos included a blessing for 'all those in authority' but did not refer to Trujillo by name."[72] The president made a big issue of the omission. The church's subsidy was suspended and the government requested that the Vatican remove Castellanos from his post. Under pressure, the priest wrote a conciliatory letter to Trujillo which appeared to have been accepted since public discussion on the matter came to an end. However, on 10 March, in an action that was calculated to impress the Vatican concerning future relations, Trujillo disregarded the existence of the apostolic administrator and had the congress appoint Alejandro Nouel as archbishop for life and adviser to the government on church affairs. A pension was also provided for the compliant and inoffensive prelate. The death of Father Castellanos in January 1934, cleared the way for Trujillo to carry out his plans concerning the church.

The skill with which the "Benefactor of the Fatherland" manipulated the political scene during his first term in office was obvious to all observers. The Vatican, through the papal nuncio, was no exception, especially after the Castellanos episode. As a result, within a short time after Trujillo's inauguration to his second term in August 1935, Ricardo Pittini was appointed and ordained as archbishop of Santo Domingo. It has been suggested that the dictator himself chose the candidate, but the allegation is difficult to prove. Nevertheless, Archbishop Pittini was all that Trujillo could have wished for in a new prelate. "From the beginning he [Pittini] sought to tighten as much as possible the relations between church and state in the Dominican Republic."[73]

The most serious charge raised against the archbishop and the Roman Catholic Church during the Trujillo era is that of the church's complicity in the creation of the "Trujillismo" cult. Carmita Landestoy lamented the debasement of her church, stating that, "They celebrate more masses and processions for Trujillo than for the Virgin of Highest Grace who is the Patroness of the Dominican Republic."[74] Had the church's representatives remained silent in the face of the massive violations of human rights that were perpetrated on the Dominican people by the regime, they would have still been vulnerable to criticism. It would have been, however, of a different nature; less harsh and bitter. Those who reproved the church's attitude, particularly the exiles, understood the potential for disaster if a weak institution chose to confront the powerful dictator. Silence might have been justified. What was impossible to accept, was active collaboration with Trujillo by the archbishop and clergy and in the face of the most scandalous acts.

The most serious and tragic event, the greatest single violation of the dignity of human life in the history of the Dominican Republic, took place in October 1937. The roots of the tragedy that has come to be known as the "Haitian massacre" unquestionably relate to the decades of turbulent relations between the republic and its neighbour. Demographic pressure and poor agricultural conditions in Haiti had prompted many Haitians to cross the artificial frontier and settle in the scarcely populated western region of the Dominican Republic. When Trujillo came to power he initiated a process of "Dominicanization" of the frontier region. On 1 September 1931, the first official gesture was made in this process with the changing of the names of "twenty-six communities, nine rivers and several streams which had previously carried Haitian names".[75]

Shortly thereafter, a contract was signed between the Dominican government and the apostolic administrator to initiate a mission, with no less than three priests, to serve in the frontier area. Through the effort of the papal nuncio, the Jesuits agreed to provide personnel, and on 4 August 1936, the Frontier Mission of Saint Ignatius of Loyola began.[76] The efficient and carefully executed persecution on 3 and 4 October 1937 contradicts the explanation offered by some that the violence was the result of the overzealous response of the military chiefs to satisfy the desires of their generalísimo. The project was planned with precision, carried out without warning and resulted in the merciless killing of almost 20,000 Haitians.[77]

For the Dominican public the whole matter remained a mystery. Rumours were rife but very little information was published. The full story was not made known in the republic until after Trujillo's death in 1961. For the church, however, this was not the case. The priests of the Jesuit mission which had been established on the frontier in 1936 were undoubtedly well informed about the massacres, if not, they had been eyewitnesses. In 1957, the Jesuits of the Frontier Mission prepared a report on their work in that difficult region. No reference is made in the body of the study to the clearly negative aspect of the process of "Dominicanization" in which the mission collaborated, the anti-Haitian element. Of course, there is no mention of the massacre.[78] The lack of critical awareness of the ethical factors inherent in their collaboration with Trujillo's Dominicanization policy and in the utilization of his religious and political ideology to justify that participation, leaves the Jesuits and the church vulnerable to the charge of complicity in one of the ugliest excesses of the regime. At the same time, however, this serves as a significant example of the legitimate role of the church, sought after and attained by the generalísimo.

It is difficult to determine how much of an impact the relationship between the church and the dictator had on the Dominican people. No adequate studies of the church's influence on attitudes toward the regime were ever undertaken, nor would they have been possible, during Trujillo's rule. For the overwhelming majority of Dominicans, the institutional church was not a significant factor in their lives. This is largely due to the fact that during this century, the republic had consistently been among the three or four countries in Latin America with the least favourable ratio of priests to people. The following information comes from statistics prepared for the Second Vatican Council.

Dominican Republic – inhabitants per priest

1912	1945	1950	1955	1960
10,000	17,300	13,500	10,500	11,000

Source: Yvan Labelle and Adriana Estrada, *Latin America in Maps, Charts, Tables* II (Cuernavaca 1968), 96.

Even these figures do not give an accurate picture, however, since a substantial percentage of the priests (31.4 percent in 1960) were occupied in nonpastoral activities such as administration, education, and so on,[79] thus elevating the people to priest ratio at the parish level to an even more critical point (14,000 to 1 in 1960).[80] As a result, the actual contact of most Dominicans with the clergy was minimal, reserved for special occasions such as baptisms, funerals or major religious festivals. A second important factor affecting the church's influence on attitudes, is the limited role assigned to the priest by the popular religiosity of the largely unevangelized masses.[81] However, the general feeling of awe and even respect toward the priest as a result of the tremendous spiritual power he ostensibly held must be considered. This was particularly strong among the rural peasants who made up more than 70 percent of the population in 1950.

Institutional developments occurred and significant material benefits were granted to the church as a result of its collaborative relationship with the regime. Historic edifices were restored. Hundreds of churches, rectories, schools, convents and other buildings were constructed and presented to the church, as well as a new seminary, several retreat centres, three cathedrals and a palace for the papal nuncio. Stipends for clergy and teachers were appropriated, religious orders were brought from other countries at the expense of the government, and appropriations were granted for special areas of work in the poor parishes, as well as for the Frontier Mission, and educational and charitable institutions. In addition to these government expenditures, Trujillo provided generous contributions to the clergy and religious personnel for their personal use or for the purchase of vehicles, audiovisual equipment, church ornaments and other items.[82] "Trujillo so favoured the growth of the church, that by the end of his era, its institutional strength . . . was equivalent to that of the church in most of the other Latin American countries."[83]

The mutually acceptable arrangement between Trujillo and the church reached its culmination in 1954, when a concordat between the Dominican Republic and the Holy See was signed. Since the earliest days of independence, every major figure who had occupied the presidency had attempted to reach such an agreement. Pedro Santana, Buenaventura Baez, José María Cabral, Ulises Heureaux and even Arturo Meriño had failed because of the social and political conditions in the republic and the reticence of the Vatican. The approval of the concordat was, therefore, a personal victory of historical significance for Trujillo. The ceremonial events finalizing the concordat took place in Rome on 16 June 1954. From the perspective of the Holy See, Roman Catholicism had been made the official religion of the Dominican state. For Trujillo, the church, with all that it represented in international prestige, had now become a department of his government. The concordat, to a considerable degree, only made official much of what was already reality. Now, however, it was a bilateral agreement between two sovereign powers that guaranteed the status of the church rather than subjecting it to the unreliable good will of the Benefactor. It is clear that the institutional church was the overwhelming beneficiary of the multiple provisions of the concordat.[84]

The ratification of the concordat carried with it, however, a liability for the church that would endure for a long period and manifest itself most vehemently after the death of the dictator. Prior to 1954, those critical of the relationship between the church and Trujillo viewed it as the result of a weak hierarchy, a poorly prepared clergy and an economically dependent institution. With the signing of the concordat, they were confronted with a tacit agreement by the supreme authority of the Roman Catholic Church, the Holy See, to ignore the injustices and crimes of the tyrant in return for privileges and material gain. For many Dominicans, the prestige of the Vatican and the pope himself were called into question for the first time. It was, perhaps, a key factor in the erosion of the church's legitimate role vis-à-vis the political structure.

Between 1954 and 1959, considerable funds from both the government and Trujillo were spent to construct and support the expanding institutional structures of the church. In September 1954, Trujillo announced the beginning of the construction of a pretentious basilica in the small rural community of Higuey, ostensibly to honour the Virgin of Highest Grace but actually as a monument to his own religiosity. Generous scholarships were established in order to support the seminarians who were studying in the republic and overseas. By order of the Benefactor, an international congress on Catholic culture was convened in Ciudad Trujillo in February 1956, as part of the celebration of the twenty-fifth anniversary of Trujillo's era. It was at this congress, attended by 150 representatives of the church from thirty-three countries, that New York's Cardinal Spellman voiced his support of Trujillo and "praised the Dominican regime warmly for its religious and anti-Communist policies".[85]

For the superstitious dictator, the events of 1 January 1959, must have seemed a particularly inauspicious way to begin the New Year. A victorious rebel force led by Fidel Castro had entered Havana that morning, forcing another defeated dictator, Fulgencio Batista, to escape to safety in the Dominican Republic. The Movement for Dominican Liberation, based in Cuba and supported by Dominican exiles in other Latin American countries and in the USA, initiated a series of programmes which were broadcast to the republic from Havana and New York. A revolutionary programme for political, social and economic change was announced. And then on 14 June 1959, an invasion was launched from Cuba with the collaboration of both the Cuban and Venezuelan governments. It was a small force. With the news of the Constanza attack, Trujillo feared the worst. He ordered the dreaded Military Intelligence Service, headed by the brutal Johnny Abbes, to investigate all those who had ever been or who were suspected of plotting against the government. Hundreds of men and women were questioned throughout the republic. Without actually identifying the clandestine group that had been organized to provide supplies to the guerrilla operation, the surveillance of suspects had paralyzed their efforts. After several weeks of bombing, strafing and massive attacks by the army, the guerrillas surrendered because of lack of food and ammunition. Many were executed immediately; several were flown back to Ciudad Trujillo and dropped from the planes into the Caribbean Sea. A few of the leaders were burned alive at the military air base. The government loudly proclaimed that the communist plot had been destroyed.

Unexpectedly and without warning, the attitude of the church began to change. It did not condemn the 14 June invasion or praise the generalísimo's decisive action. The shift to a more "neutral" position was reflected in a speech made by the bishop of Santiago, Monsignor Hugo Polanco Brito, on 25 July, just one month after the military hostilities.[86] Within a short time, one of Trujillo's most active flatterers and effusive supporters, Papal Nuncio Salvatore Siino was quietly called back to Rome. The church had seen the "signs of the times". It was preparing itself for a new stance vis-à-vis the Benefactor. For the first time in three decades the church was contemplating the possibility of exercising its illegitimate role in the Dominican political arena.

Protest and Prosecution: The End of the Era, 1960–1961

The period of greatest collaboration between the Roman Catholic Church in the Dominican Republic and Rafael L. Trujillo Molina during the years immediately preceding and following the signing of the concordat, provided the opportunity for significant structural changes in the church that would prepare it for one of the most important episodes in its history. On 25 September 1953, Pope Pius XII re-established the ecclesiastical province of Santo Domingo and created the two new dioceses of Santiago and La Vega and the Prelature Nullius of San Juan de la Maguana. Initially under the authority of apostolic administrators, three bishops were appointed and ordained for the new regions in 1956. The Diocese of Nuestra Señora de Altagracia, comprising the three eastern provinces of the republic, was founded on 1 April 1959, and its bishop consecrated on 31 May of the same year.[87] In addition to this process of the decentralization of the archdiocese and the strengthening of the hierarchy through the increase in the number of bishops and the creation of an episcopal conference, a further change reduced the dictator's direct influence on the church. The aged Archbishop Ricardo Pittini gradually surrendered the primary responsibility of the administration of the archdiocese to his Dominican coadjutor bishop, Octavio Beras. Finally, in October 1959, in anticipation of an inevitable confrontation between the church and the government, the Vatican replaced the compliant papal nuncio, Salvatore Siino, by the strong and experienced diplomat Archbishop Lino Zanini.

The regime was still shaken by the events of 1959 that were related to the invasion of 14 June. In spite of the widespread propaganda claiming a decisive victory, the repression that had been unleashed against the opposition within the republic did not succeed in destroying the widespread organization. The police and military intelligence were unable to discover the leaders and they continued to recruit new supporters, including the young members of many of the country's most important families. Then, in January 1960, the security forces learned of a plot to assassinate Trujillo. In an unprecedented action, he ordered the arrest of anyone who might be a potential conspirator. The roundup was estimated to run into the thousands.[88] Among those detained were several Roman Catholic seminarians. Many of the prisoners were subjected to relentless interrogation and cruel torture. Some died as a result of the treatment and others were summarily executed. A few faced trials that resulted in sentences of up to twenty and thirty years of imprisonment while others simply disappeared.

On 25 January, moved by public pressure and with the encouragement of Nuncio Zanini, the bishops met at the archbishop's palace to draft a joint pastoral letter to be read the following Sunday, a day when the republic's churches would be filled with worshippers celebrating the Festival of Our Lady of Highest Grace, the patroness of the nation. It was a carefully worded document that avoided a direct attack on the government, but which left little doubt regarding the bishops' opposition to the terrible repression taking place.[89] The concerted effort on the part of the bishops took Trujillo and his advisers by surprise. The nuncio had even blocked Trujillo's usual access to the church through the aged archbishop, by arranging for the Vatican to appoint Octavio A. Beras the apostolic administrator of the archdiocese of Santo Domingo and of the military chaplaincy with "full powers", effective 30 January.[90]

The government's counterattack struck at the church's most vulnerable areas: its reliance on large numbers of foreign clergy and religious personnel, its dependency on state assistance to meet its economic requirements, special legal arrangements to maintain its privileged status vis-à-vis other religious bodies and, finally, the unreliability of many who professed Roman Catholic loyalty when forced to choose between the church and the generalísimo. On 3 February Msgr Francisco Panal, bishop of La Vega, was advised by supporters that a political meeting was being organized for that night to protest the pastoral letter. In an effort to lessen its impact, the bishop broadcast a statement to "Faithful Catholics", calling on them not to participate, warning the organizers that they would be excommunicated and that responsible authorities would be denied all ceremonies normally offered on their behalf.[91] In spite of the bishop's communiqué, the rally was held in the main park of La Vega directly in front of the cathedral and was well attended. The bishop was infuriated. In keeping with the warning stated in his communiqué, he proceeded with the excommunication of those whom he held responsible for the disgraceful and sacrilegious demonstration against the Catholic Church and its hierarchy.

Elements of the government's response took shape gradually. On 4 February a scholarly bibliography entitled "Trujillo and the Church" was published in *El Caribe*, one of the government controlled newspapers. It listed fifty-eight books and articles, most of which dealt with Trujillo's favourable treatment of the church and its concerns. A few days later, the first of what would be dozens of letters from Protestant ministers to Trujillo was written, praising him for the freedom of religion that had permitted them to labour fruitfully in the Dominican Republic.[92] Then, as if to exacerbate Protestant-Catholic conflicts, the government published a letter written by Bishop Thomas Reilly, of San Juan de la Maguana, to the US ambassador Joseph E. Farland, dated 6 September 1958, in which the bishop asked, "Is the US Embassy and its personnel used as an instrument of these Protestant groups which come to this country in an open campaign of proselytism of the Catholic population?" The single comment accompanying the letter stated: "Manuel de Moya, minister without portfolio and principal assistant of Generalísimo Rafael L. Trujillo, indicated that the government's failure to suppress missionary activity partially motivated the recent Catholic Pastoral."[93]

As the public face of the campaign was revealed in the press and on the radio, church authorities began to feel the first pressures of an economic squeeze. It was clear to Trujillo and his advisors, and would become so to the hierarchy, that the long history of financial dependency was the church's greatest weakness. Just how long the church could continue in a struggle with the government should its budget be reduced or cut off completely was unknown. For the papal nuncio, however, the matter was crucial and he immediately sought to establish the legal basis for continued assistance. On 15 February the nuncio initiated four days of intense communication with Trujillo, using Vice President Joaquín Balaguer as his medium.[94] By the end of February, the bishops had not received an official response to the letter addressed to Trujillo. In an unusual move, they prepared another joint pastoral letter which was dated 28 February and ordered that it be read on the first Sunday in Lent, 6 March. The message of repentance was clearly directed to those who wielded power at the expense of others.[95]

Response to the firm stand that had been taken by the hierarchy was manifested in a new strategy that would prove to be the central and abrasive element in the struggle for more than a year. A campaign was launched to humiliate the church for its ingratitude after so many years of receiving gifts from the generalísimo. On 14 March an article that had been written sometime earlier by a Dominican priest, Zenón Castillo de Aza was published.[96] It was a superficial piece of writing, typical of the extravagant flattery that had been showered on Trujillo during his three decades of power. The difference, however, was that this article was written by a priest and it proposed that Trujillo be granted the title "Benefactor of the Church" because of all the tasks he had performed on behalf of the church. The article was printed, without comment, as the principal item on the first page.[97]

Two days later, a letter appeared on the front page of the newspaper under the headline: "Support Giving Trujillo Title Benefactor of the Church". It was signed by the president and vice president, all the secretaries and subsecretaries of state, and officials of the supreme court, the university and the Dominican Party. Not only did the letter emphatically back the granting of the title but went on to recommend the holding of a plebiscite in order to determine the will of the Dominican people on this matter.[98] The importance of this issue became apparent to Trujillo himself in a voluminous letter sent to Msgr Thomas Reilly, the North American bishop of San Juan de la Maguana. At the outset of the conflict, the question of granting the title was only one element in the strategy to force the hierarchy to retract or at least modify the criticism stated in the first pastoral letter. During the intervening weeks, however, it would appear that Trujillo's vanity led him to believe in the appropriateness of the honour and in the authenticity of popular support.

Six weeks had passed since the government authorities had issued their proposal to confer the title and had recommended the plebiscite. Trujillo decided to test the matter by forcing the new apostolic administrator, Archbishop Octavio Beras, to put forth an opinion. The prelate himself had provided the opening. In January, prior to the conflict, he had sent a letter to the secretary of state for religion, requesting that the government cover a $34,000 debt of the pontifical seminary. An unexpected reply from the generalísimo was designed to pressure the archbishop into taking a position in the face of an exasperating dilemma.[99] On the one hand, it was crucial to maintain the solidarity of the episcopal conference and the loyalty of the clergy and laity, relationships that would be seriously threatened by vacillation under pressure from the regime. On the other hand, however, the church was heavily dependent on support from the government and that was clearly in jeopardy. Msgr Beras chose a tactic of conciliation and evasion.[100] Subsequent events would suggest that the generalísimo was neither convinced nor satisfied by the archbishop's reply.

The erosion of the church's economic security and privileges to which the church was accustomed was accelerated by the bureaucracy. Government officials punctiliously adhered to the agreement established in the correspondence between the papal nuncio and the vice president regarding contracts, while cancelling every other unprotected subvention. Bishops were unceremoniously advised of the termination of diocesan budgets, institutional support, clergy stipends, housing and travel allowances, scholarship assistance and other items that had been granted over the years.[101] Although the unrelenting assault on the church's finances was the most critical front, the public attacks were a constant cause of anxiety for the hierarchy, clergy and still faithful laity. One element in the campaign, however, became almost ludicrous. The Dominican people had become accustomed to hearing Trujillo's enemies labeled as communists. The church itself had contributed to the image of the generalísimo as the great anti-communist leader of the hemisphere and the defender of Christian civilization. Shortly after the appearance of the first pastoral letter, it had been insinuated that the church was supporting its own worst enemy through its criticism of government policy. Within two months, Trujillo would move from innuendos to accusations of complicity.[102]

The public accusation against the church was actually the result of the generalísimo's loss of patience after several direct actions against members of the hierarchy failed, which embarrassed the government. The first was an attempt to assassinate, or at least wound, the aged and almost blind Archbishop Pittini. It was scheduled to take place during the celebration of the liturgy on Maundy Thursday when the church would be full of worshippers. What resulted, however, was a comedy of errors in which one of the gunmen, rather than the archbishop, was fatally shot.[103] The newspapers reported the attempt as the work of a "Colombian terrorist" who was killed by the ever vigilant national police.[104] Within two weeks, the regime was confronted with another predicament, but this time caused by the underestimation of Bishop Reilly's resourcefulness. The prelate's aggressiveness aggravated Trujillo and his advisors, and a simple bureaucratic action was devised to remove him from the scene temporarily. He was notified that his residence permit could only be renewed outside of the Dominican Republic. Reilly accepted the notification and then announced "that since he was being expelled, he would have to order certain clergy under him to leave also, which would involve closing some schools". This was certainly not the interpretation that the government wanted to have publicized, since it was already facing growing international pressure. Trujillo himself intervened to assure the bishop that the issue was all a mistake and would be corrected to his satisfaction.[105]

The papal nuncio, now considered by Trujillo to be the villain behind all of his troubles, returned briefly to Rome. The chargé d'affaires of the nunciature was summoned to the office of the Foreign Ministry on 21 May to be advised that the nuncio was to be considered *persona non grata*.[106] The public announcement, however, reflected typical Trujillo drama and a new declaration of hostilities. On 9 June the newspaper published the text of a letter to the president written by Mario Abreu Penzo, secretary of state for justice. He accused Archbishop Zanini of being "an international agent provocateur" responsible for inciting anarchy and revolution, and went on to petition, after the fact, that he be declared *persona non grata*. To that insult the secretary then added a recommendation that consideration should be given to expelling all six bishops in the interest of security.[107]

The campaign was intensified during the following months. Mass rallies were held throughout the country, advocating the granting of the title and newspapers were filled with letters of support. Public employees received strong recommendations to avoid participating in church activities. Priests were placed under surveillance and were frequently called upon by Military Intelligence to account for statements made in sermons. The consular offices of the Dominican Republic in foreign countries stopped granting visas to priests and religious personnel who were assigned to work with the Dominican Church, and dozens of those who were already in the republic were forced to leave when their residence permits expired or they were expelled on trumped-up charges. Other priests were threatened with physical harm or were victimized by humiliating pranks.[108]

The bishops met in an emergency session to strategize, but the course they had to take was unclear. The situation that had been challenged by their pastoral letter had worsened during the year, and many people still looked to the church as the one sign of hope amidst the increased repression. The international position and economic condition of the regime had deteriorated critically as the result of actions taken by the Organization of American States (OAS) in the wake of Trujillo's unsuccessful attempt to assassinate the president of Venezuela.[109] But no one would venture to predict the impending collapse. Thus, the bishops, as the pastors and bureaucrats of the Dominican Church, were torn between the desire to remain true to the principles of justice and to the hope of preserving their beleaguered institution. Furthermore, upon convening, they received two communications which added to their dilemma.

In anticipation of the bishop's meeting, the superiors of the religious orders working in the republic had prepared a letter of appeal, calling on the prelates to break their silence and offer guidance to the church.[110] The letter went on to list those things that the superiors saw as immediate threats requiring action from the bishops: the "gross" campaigns being waged by the radio and the press; the unjustified expulsion of personnel and the pending law against all foreigners; the attack on religious instruction, including the closing of church schools and the firing of clergy members who taught religion in public schools, and the pending law to establish secular education; the termination of contracts and the violation of other elements of the concordat.

The bishops, however, had received another signal. Trujillo made it known that he would be open to a gesture of reconciliation. It was made clear that the initiative had to be taken by the episcopal conference, since it was their pastoral letter that had created the conflict. In spite of the support expressed by the superiors and other clergy and the loyalty that had been demonstrated by the laity, the bishops decided to avoid even greater losses for the church and submit a declaration of surrender. On 10 January 1961, not quite a year since the heroic pastoral letter had been issued, the bishops of the Dominican Church signed a letter addressed to the generalísimo and carried it to the National Palace to be presented in a formal meeting.[111] The letter they addressed to Trujillo was almost everything he could have desired. The bishops concluded with a petition to Trujillo asking him to intercede with the authorities to put an end to the various problems being faced by the church, and specifying in diplomatic terms, those critical matters which the religious superiors had passionately detailed a few days earlier.[112]

The generalísimo seemed satisfied with the gesture. He assured the bishops: "The president and I are honoured by the visit of the prelates and we would like you go away with the impression that we are with the Catholic Church . . ."[113] His assurances were repeated in his written confirmation sent to the bishops on the following day, in which he accepted their acknowledgement of "indiscretions" and promised to solve the problems confronting the church.[114] The conflict appeared to be resolved, but at the price of profound disillusionment in many sectors of the church and Dominican society.

For Trujillo, however, there was one matter that had not been satisfactorily settled. What had begun as an effort to humble an ungrateful church, had been transformed into a crusade. He now believed that he truly merited the title of "Benefactor of the Church", and he would have it at any cost. On 16 January, less than a week after the mutual expressions of reconciliation, the president and members of the cabinet sent a letter to the members of the hierarchy suggesting that the moment was particularly propitious for them to support the initiative that had already been taken to grant the title.[115]

The church was faced with a serious dilemma. As far as the Dominican people were concerned, the hierarchy had confessed to the "errors" of some members of the clergy, had admitted its indebtedness to the regime and had made peace with Trujillo. The generalísimo's response appeared to contain the promise to refer to the church the status quo ante along with all of the benefits which it had enjoyed in the past. Nevertheless, the intentions of the government remained doubtful for the prelates, almost from the moment of supposed reconciliation.

On the very day that the bishops faced the humiliating audience along with Trujillo and his entourage, the secretary of state of the interior and religion had sent a letter to Monsignor Hugo Polanco in which he sharply criticized a priest of the Santiago diocese for refusing to offer the annual Mass in celebration of the Day of the Judiciary. The priest's decision was in protest of the continued campaign of defamation against the church being waged by Radio Caribe. The secretary vehemently denied that the attacks on the clergy could be considered as "an expression of the official voice, since they involved completely private enterprises".[116] The bishop's answer was firm and he concluded, pointing out that if the campaign continued, it would be difficult "to encourage good wishes for true harmony" among the clergy.[117] The secretary, Rafael Paino Pichardo, was provoked by the bishop's attitude and his message was clear: the only basis on which reconciliation can truly be established is through total surrender of the church to Trujillo's will.[118]

The battle lines were now defined. For both the regime and the hierarchy the question of the title had become a symbol of resistance to the generalísimo's claim to uncontested authority. On 6 February the prelates addressed their answer to President Balaguer and his cabinet. Written in terms that were cordial and yet cautious, the letter recognized Trujillo's generosity toward the church and called attention to the numerous occasions on which gratitude had been expressed. As far as the title was concerned, however, their position was simply a confirmation of that which had been taken by Archbishop Beras a year before. They wrote: "It is precisely now, on the matter that you recommended to Us, when we cannot but recognize the limit of Our power, seeing that it exceeds Our authority not only to grant but even to further this initiative since the Holy See had reserved to itself the promotion and granting of such titles."[119] Regardless of the reason given or the manner in which it was expressed, Trujillo, who believed that the hierarchy had the authority that they disclaimed, viewed the response as an act of defiance.

The persecution became overt and more intense. On 12 March the offensive was joined by Bishop Reilly, who read a bold declaration at all the masses celebrated in his Cathedral of San Juan de la Maguana.[120] A Belgian missionary priest had been deported just the day before and the prelate portrayed the action as "the latest in a long series of violations of human rights and the rights of the Church". He went on to describe the detention and beating of another priest, the intimidation of the youth of Catholic Action, the decision to dissolve some of the Catholic organizations in order to protect their members, the burning of the cathedral doors, and the presence of spies at Catholic services. Bishop Panal prepared a pastoral letter to be read in all churches of the diocese of La Vega on 26 March. Not only did he question the government's policy toward the church and attack the regime for the persecution it had unleashed, but the bishop also ordered his clergy to refrain from celebrating any religious function outside of their regular parish activities without his written permission.[121]

The church's obstinate stance was in defiance of the dictator's will, one that he had never experienced in his three decades in power. The regime resorted to every type of pressure, short of assassination, to break the prelates' resistance. An almost interminable succession of mass meetings was staged in every city and tiny village, chastising Reilly's and Panal's behaviour and demanding their expulsion. By the end of May, Trujillo had had enough. The protracted struggle with the church had contributed greatly to the weakening of his heretofore uncontested authority in the republic. Furthermore, the attack on Bishop Reilly had resulted in the presentation of a formal protest by the USA to the Inter-American Peace Commission, accusing the regime of the persecution of the church and of the American prelate, thus compounding Trujillo's problems with the OAS. On the night of 29 May the general decided to bring an end to the imbroglio in the one way he knew best. The following day, "the order went out to round up the bishops and take them to prison".[122]

Unknown to the hierarchy, the clergy and the faithful, the Dominican Church was on the brink of a disaster, not unlike those frequent occurrences that had threatened its existence during the past four and a half centuries. As in the past, however, unforeseen circumstances beyond the control of those most likely to be affected by them, intervened to bring about a dramatic change. Crassweller describes the events of 29 and 30 May as "one of those incalculable freaks of timing which so often intervene in human affairs".[123] Trujillo left the capital for his farm in the nearby city of San Cristobal several hours after making his decision concerning the fate of the bishops. Just a short distance beyond the limits of Ciudad Trujillo, his car was halted by a barrage of bullets. The generalísimo, already wounded, stepped out onto the pavement to confront the attackers. Within a few moments, he died on the highway.

On the morning of 30 May as rumours of the assassination spread throughout the republic despite the news blackout, President Joaquín Balaguer cancelled the order for the imprisonment of the bishops. According to his own declaration made in the USA in December 1964, Balaguer went further. He confronted Ramfis Trujillo and several high officials of the armed forces and threatened to resign the presidency if they went through with a plan to expel the bishops from the republic to avenge Trujillo's death. The officers withdrew their demand.[124] The persecution was over. Trujillo's era had come to an end.

NOTES

1. Hubert Herring, A History of Latin America (New York 1957), 425–26.
2. Ramón Marrero Aristy, La República Dominicana: Origen y destino del pueblo cristiano más antiguo de América (Ciudad Trujillo 1958), II, 277–95.

3. Leonidas García, *Influencia de la Iglesia Católica en la formación de la nacionalidad y en la creación de la República Dominicana* (Santo Domingo 1933), 90–91.

4. Ibid., 91.

5. Carlos Nouel, *Historia Eclesiástica de la Arquidiócesis de Santo Domingo, Primada de América* (Santo Domingo 1915), III, 15.

6. J. Lloyd Mecham, *Church and State in Latin America* (Chapel Hill, North Carolina 1934), 352.

7. Nouel, *Historia Eclesiástica*, III, 17.

8. Ibid.

9 Ibid.

10. Juan Francisco Sánchez, *La Universidad de Santo Domingo* (Ciudad Trujillo 1955), 53.

11. Sumner Welles, *Naboth's Vineyard: The Dominican Republic, 1844–1924* (New York 1928), I, 96.

12. Marrero Aristy, *La República Dominicana*, I, 365.

13. J. Marino Inchaústegui, *Historia Dominicana* (Ciudad Trujillo 1955), II, 47. Nouel also refers to the criticism made by the archbishop of the use of bells by the Protestant church in Samana, but mistakenly dates the restrictive legislation as of 5 May 1846 (Nouel, *Historia Eclesiástica*, III, 43).

14. Marrero Aristy, *La República Dominicana*, I, 369.

15. Ibid., I, 371.

16. Nouel, *Historia Eclesiástica*, III, 73.

17. Marrero Aristy, *La República Dominicana*, I, 375.

18. Hugo Eduardo Polanco Brito, *Seminario Conciliar Santo Tomás de Aquino: 1848–1948* (Ciudad Trujillo 1948), 44.

19. Marrero Aristy, *La República Dominicana*, I, 442.

20. Juan F. Pepén, *La Cruz señaló el camino, Influencia de la Iglesia en la formación y conservación de la nacionalidad dominicana* (Ciudad Trujillo 1954), 81.

21. Welles, *Naboth's Vineyard*, I, 240 ff.

22. Marrero Aristy, *La República Dominicana*, II, 97.

23. Ibid., 101.

24. Inchaústegui, *Historia Dominicana*, II, 77.

25. Ibid., 81.

26. Ibid., 82. The congress confirmed the concession of the properties on 15 April 1867.

27. Pepén, *La Cruz señaló el camino*, 80.

28. Marrero Aristy, *La República Dominicana*, II, 111–12. Also Nouel, *Historia Eclesiástica*, III, 335.

29. Pepén, *La Cruz señaló el camino*, 80. The author points out that during his years in exile, Meriño settled in Venezuela where he became vicar of Barcelona and was elected to the legislature in spite of foreign citizenship. After July 1870 he organized European opposition to an annexation of the republic by the USA.

30. Marrero Aristy, *La República Dominicana*, II, 200.

31. Ibid., 166.
32. Ibid., 184.
33. Inchaústegui, *Historia Dominicana*, II, 94.
34. Selden Rodman, *Quisqueya, A History of the Dominican Republic* (Seattle 1964), 95; Marrero, Aristy, *La República Dominicana*, II: 195-200; Inchaústegui, *Historia Dominicana*, II, 95–97.
35. Marrero Aristy, *La República Dominicana*, II, 201.
36. Sánchez, *La Universidad de Santo Domingo*, 57 and Bernardo Pichardo, *Resumen de Historia Patria* (Buenos Aires 1947), 184.
37. Marrero Aristy, *La República Dominicana*, II, 210.
38. Pichardo, *Resumen de Historia Patria*, 185.
39. Inchaústegui, *Historia Dominicana*, II, 100.
40. Sánchez, *La Universidad de Santo Domingo*, 58.
41. Ibid.
42. Polanco, *Seminario Conciliar*, 70, and Sánchez, *La Universidad de Santo Domingo*, 59.
43. Pepén, *La Cruz señaló el camino*, 81, and Marrero Aristy, *La República Dominicana*, II, 210.
44. Polanco, *Seminario Conciliar*, 71.
45. Pepén, *La Cruz señaló el camino*, 118.
46. Pichardo, *Resumen de Historia Patria*, 200.
47. Ibid., 225–26.
48. Pepén, *La Cruz señaló el camino*, 87–88.
49. Ibid., 119.
50. Pichardo, *Resumen de Historia Patria*, 239, 255.
51. Pepén, *La Cruz señaló el camino*, 90.
52. Welles, *Naboth's Vineyard*, II, 700.
53. Inchaústegui, *Historia Dominicana*, II, 131.
54. Sante Uberto Barbieri, *Land of El Dorado* (New York 1961), 66.
55. Samuel Guy Inman, *Through Santo Domingo and Haiti with the United States Marines* (New York 1919).
56. Edward Odell, *It Came to Pass: Board of Mission of the Presbyterian Church in the USA* (New York 1952), 153.
57. Robert D. Crassweller, *Trujillo, The Life and Times of a Caribbean Dictator* (New York 1966), 49.
58. Barbieri, *Land of El Dorado*, 86.
59. Crassweller, *Trujillo*, 49.
60. Inchaústegui, *Historia Dominicana*, II, 146.
61. Vetelio Alfau Durán, "Trujillo, Auténtico Benefactor de la Iglesia Dominicana", *El Caribe*, 25 March 1960, 4.
62. Howard J. Wiarda, "The aftermath of the Trujillo dictatorship: the emergence of a pluralistic political system in the Dominican Republic" (PhD diss., Univ. of Florida, Gainesville 1965).

63. Jesús de Galindez, *La Era de Trujillo* (Santiago 1956), 342–43. Hereafter referred to as *Era*.

64. Felix A. Mejía, *Vía Crucis de un pueblo* (México 1951), 48.

65. Galindez, *Era*, 65.

66. Ibid., 290.

67. Zenón Castillo de Aza, *Trujillo y Otros Benefactores de la Iglesia* (Ciudad Trujillo 1961), 216. See also Vetilio Alfau Durán, "Trujillo", 4.

68. Inchaústegui, *Historia Dominicana*, II, 187.

69. *Boletín eclesiástico de Santo Domingo*, no. 86 (May/June 1931): 153.

70. Inchaústegui, *Historia Dominicana*, II, 183.

71. Pichardo, *Resumen de Historia Patria*, 304.

72. Crassweller, *Trujillo*, 96.

73. Frank Moya Pons, "Notas para una Historia de la Iglesia en Santo Domingo", *Revista Eme Eme*, no. 6. (May/June 1973): 15.

74. Carmita Landestoy, *Yo también acuso!* (New York 1946), 37.

75. Inchaústegui, *Historia Dominicana*, II, 173.

76. Antonio L. de Santa Anna, *Misión Fronteriza, Apuntes Históricos, 1936–1957* (Ciudad Trujillo 1958), 19–21.

77. Galindez, *Era*, 374.

78. Santa Anna, *Misión Fronteriza*, ii; Introduction by Julián Robuster, SJ.

79. Yvan Labelle and Adriana Estrada, *Latin America in Maps, Charts, Tables II* (Cuernavaca 1968), 101.

80. Ibid.

81. Gary MacEoin, *Agent for Change, the Story of Pablo Steele* (Maryknoll 1973), 71–72.

82. For details of the contributions made to the church see Castillo de Aza, *Trujillo y Otros Benefactores*, 106–48.

83. Howard J. Wiarda, *Dictatorship and Development: The Methods of Control in Trujillo's Dominican Republic*, Latin American Monographs, Series 2, no. 5 (Gainesville 1968), 143.

84. The full text of the concordat is found in Castillo de Aza, *Trujillo y Otros Benefactores*, 239–57.

85. Crassweller, *Trujillo*, 325.

86. Hugo E. Polanco Brito, "Discursos y Escritos: 1934–1965", vol. I. I am indebted to Archbishop Polanco for making these and other personal papers available to me; hereafter referred to as the Polanco Archive.

87. Data on the establishment of new dioceses are taken from the Directorio de la Iglesia Católica en la República Dominicana, Conferencia del Episcopado Dominicano, January 1972. The first bishops of the four new sees were: Hugo E. Polanco (Santiago), Francisco Panal (La Vega), Thomas F. Reilly (San Juan de la Maguana) and Juan F. Pepén (Nuestra Señora de Altagracia).

88. One of the leaders, Guido D'Allessandro, escaped capture by taking refuge in the Papal Nunciature for two months. Crassweller, *Trujillo*, 372–73.

89. Conference of the Diocese of the Dominican Republic, "Carta Pastoral Colectiva del Episcopado de la República Dominicana en ocasión de la Fiesta de Nuestra Señora de la Altagracia", no. 5, *Documents from the Conference of the Bishops of the Dominican Republic, 1955–1969* (Santo Domingo 1969), 39. Hereafter this collection is cited as *Documentos del Episcopado*.

90. Crassweller, *Trujillo*, 384. See also *Newsweek*, 15 February 1960, 52, and *US News & World Report*, 15 February 1960, 23.

91. "Atención: Fieles Católicos", a transcript of the communiqué read by Mons. Francisco Panal, 3 February 1960, at the La Vega radio station, La Voz del Camu, Polanco Archive.

92. *El Caribe*, 7 February 1960. A number of the letters from Protestant leaders took advantage of the conflict to express their own criticism of the Catholic Church or to ingratiate themselves with the authorities. E.g. Kalvin J. Steward, Adventist leader, said: "The Seventh Day Adventist Church does not tell its faithful members what their political preferences must be nor does it attempt to tell governments how they should conduct the affairs of state."

93. *El Caribe*, 11 February 1960.

94. Copy of the letter from His Excellency Most Reverend Msgr Lino Zanini, apostolic nuncio, to the Excellent Dr Joaquín Balaguer, vice president of the republic, 15 February 1960, Polanco Archive.

95. Carta Pastoral Colectivo del Episcopado de la República Dominicana, con motivo de la Cuaresma (explaining the letter dated January 25), 28 February 1960, *Documentos del Episcopado*, 50–51.

96. Lent message of the Bishops' Conference of the Dominican Republic. Robert Crassweller correctly claims that the article was originally written in 1954 after the signing of the concordat and that the date was changed to 1959 for the purpose of introducing the campaign against the hierarchy. *Trujillo*, 388.

97. Zenón Castillo de Aza, *Trujillo y Otros Benefactores*.

98. "Apoyan dar Trujillo título Benefactor de la Iglesia", *El Caribe*, 16 March 1960.

99. Copy of a letter to Msgr. Octavio A. Beras, apostolic administrator, from Generalísimo Rafael Trujillo, 31 March 1960, Polanco Archive.

100. Copy of a letter to Generalísimo Rafael L. Trujillo from Msgr Octavio A. Beras, apostolic administrator, 4 April 1960, Polanco Archive.

101. Copy of a telegram to Diócesis de Santiago from the minister of the state for the interior and culture, 22 March 1960, Polanco Archive.

102. "Trujillo lamenta desunión entre los anticomunistas", *El Caribe*, 29 April 1960.

103. Crassweller, *Trujillo*, 388.

104. *El Caribe*, 15 April 1960.

105. Crassweller, *Trujillo*, 385.

106. Copy of *aide mémoire* of the minister of state in the Ministry of Foreign Affairs, 22 May 1960, Polanco Archive.

107. *El Caribe*, 9 June 1960. See also Crassweller, *Trujillo*, 387.

108. NCWC News Service dispatch, *New World*, Chicago, 9 June 1961.

109. Crassweller, *Trujillo*, 409–20, provides an excellent narrative description of the circumstances surrounding the attempt on the life of President Betancourt and subsequent action of the OAS.

110. Copy of the letter to the Excellencies and Most Reverend Prelates of the Republic from the Superior Religious Orders and Congregations in the Republic, 16 December 1960, Polanco Archive.

111. Crassweller, *Trujillo*, 389.

112. "Memorandum to Rafael Leonidas Trujillo", 10 January 1961, *Documentos del Episcopado*, 55–58. The text is also published in *El Caribe*, 13 January 1961.

113. *La Nación*, 10 January 1961; *La Información*, 11 January 1961.

114. The text of the letter is in *El Caribe*, 13 January 1961.

115. Copy of the letter to Msgr Octavio A. Beras, apostolic administrator et al., from Joaquín Balaguer, president of the Republic, et al., 16 January 1961, Polanco Archive.

116. Copy of the letter to Msgr Hugo E. Polanco, bishop of the Diocese of Santiago, from Rafael Paino Pichardo, minister of state for the interior and culture, oficio no. 640, 10 January 1961, Polanco Archive.

117. Copy of the letter to D.R. Paino Pichardo, minister of state for the interior and culture from Hugo Eduardo Polanco, bishop of Santiago de los Caballeros, oficio no. 56/61, 18 January 1961, Polanco Archive.

118. Copy of the letter to Msgr Hugo E. Polanco, bishop of the Diocese of Santiago, from Rafael Paino Pichardo, minister of state for the interior and culture, oficio no. 1385, 21 January 1961, Polanco Archive.

119. Letter to Dr Joaquín Balaguer, president of the republic, and to the members of the cabinet, stating that it was not possible to give Trujillo the title of "Benefactor of the Church", 6 February 1961, *Documentos del Episcopado*, 59–60.

120. Declaration from Msgr Thomas F. Reilly, CSSR. to be read at all masses in the San Juan de la Maguana Cathedral, Sunday, 12 March 1961, Polanco Archive.

121. In a popular play on the words "*obispo*" (bishop) and "*avispa*" (wasp) the harsh letter became known as "the Pastoral of the Wasp".

122. Crassweller, *Trujillo*, 93.

123. Ibid.

124. Victor A. Marmol, "Balaguer revela trama matar dignatarios Iglesia", *El Caribe*, no. 5839, December 1964.

THEO TSCHUY

Protestantism in Cuba, 1868–1968

The Beginnings of Cuban Protestantism, 1868–1898

Spanish rule and the privileged position of the Catholic Church prevented the introduction of Protestantism in Cuba until the late nineteenth century. However, the War of Independence, which was
accompanied by the progressive "softening up" of Spanish religious
legislation, helped to prepare the ground for the coming of
Protestantism long before Spain ceded control of the island as a result
of US military intervention in 1898.

Among the republican-minded Cubans, there were many who
wanted to replace the colonial form of religion by a new kind of
Christianity. The spiritual outlook of the impoverished middle class,
the small farmer and the tobacco worker,[1] that is those social sectors
which were determined to end the colonial rule, was undergoing profound changes. Was it possible, they wondered, to go beyond anticler-
icalism and freemasonery and fill the growing religious vacuum by
reforming the church? Cuba's "Apostle of Independence", José Martí
(1853–95), developed a few specific ideas about the church which he
wanted to see materialize in the future: it should not be an instrument
in the hands of the property-owning classes; it needed to be free of
dogmatic confessionalism and absolutist pretentions; but it would, on
the contrary, be called upon to meet the deepest of human aspirations.
Would Protestantism be the answer? Martí had long considered this
possibility, and during his exile in the USA he carefully examined the
Protestant Churches. In the end, his conclusion was negative. While
he appreciated the moral values which Protestantism had inherited
from a long-established Anglo-Saxon Puritanism, he felt, however,
that by supporting capitalism during the nineteenth century the

American churches had alienated themselves not only from biblical precept, but also from the people. The churches had become dogmatic and Pharisaic. Martí therefore doubted that this form of Christianity was capable of replacing or reforming Roman Catholicism in Cuba. More than most people of his generation, the Cuban "Apostle" perceived the ambivalence which would surround American Protestant missions coming to his homeland.[2]

As long as the Cuban War of Independence continued, the chances that Protestantism would be accepted by the Cuban people seemed nevertheless to be uniquely favourable. The revolt against a Catholic Church committed to sustaining an oppressive régime and the revulsion against a poorly motivated priesthood was general. Religious feelings, however, remained strong enough not to drive Cubans en masse into atheism or agnosticism, as had been the case with Europe's working class during the same period. But despair over the irrelevance of the Catholic Church was profound.

The Origin of Cuban Protestantism

Cuban Protestantism can be traced back to two sources, both of which had their origin in the USA: missionary work among migrants on the mainland, and the labours of Edward Kenney, an Episcopal clergyman who was called to evangelize seamen.

Many Cubans had found refuge in the USA during the severe economic crisis which affected the island during the 1850s. Many arrived in New York and other large cities of the Eastern seaboard. Thousands more fled across the Florida Straits to Key West, Tampa and Ybor City, when, after the outbreak of the rebellion of 1868, the Spanish authorities took repressive measures against the highly unionized and independent-minded tobacco workers and cigar makers. The first Protestant Cuban parishes were comprised of these émigrés. An Episcopal Iglesia Santiago (St James Church) was founded in New York in 1866. In 1873, Joseph E.A. Van Duzer, a young Southern Methodist minister, was appointed to Key West in order to evangelize the Cubans, who seemed to be open to the kind of religion "as it is understood by the Methodist Episcopal Church, South".[3] After Van Duzer's early death at age twenty-three, the Methodist Cubans at Key West encountered great difficulties in building up a congregation. Anxious to establish their Cuban work quickly, the church authorities accepted new members too rapidly. The inexperienced Cuban pastors were unable to handle the conflicts arising out of such situations and left in rapid succession. Already at this stage a fundamental issue emerged, which was to affect seriously Cuban Protestantism during the years to come: that of puritanism and moralism. How were the converts to reconcile their newly found evangelical freedom with the narrow legalism with which nineteenth century American Protestantism confronted them? These congregations nevertheless survived and became important training grounds from which religious impulses would eventually spread into Cuba itself.

An Anglican seamen's chaplaincy in Havana, established by the Protestant Episcopal Church, turned out to have even greater consequences for future Protestant work in Cuba than the migrant parishes in southern Florida. As the result of a chance visit to Havana by Bishop Benjamin Whipple of the Diocese of Minnesota, the Revd Edward Kenney from Baltimore came to Cuba in November 1871. While his mission, by the orders of the Spanish authorities, was strictly confined to English-speaking captains, sailors and permanent foreign residents, the Anglican form of worship soon met with great interest among the Spanish-speaking population. However, it was Kenney's selfless and heroic service among the sick and dying (Havana was frequently plagued with yellow fever and other epidemic diseases), which earned him the respect of those who tried to discover the source of his spiritual strength. A few years after his arrival, Kenney also took over the chaplaincy of a large sugar estate near Matanzas (with 600 workers, many of them slaves) and finally evangelized the Chinese coolies (who arrived after 1880 when African slavery was abolished). Unfortunately, Anglo-Catholic circles in the USA pressured the church authorities to withdraw Kenney from Catholic Cuba. He returned to the USA at the end of 1880, but nevertheless left behind a group of dedicated laymen.

While Kenney was labouring in Cuba, the work of the Methodists in Key West began to develop under the leadership of H.B. Someillan (1857–1921). Born in Caibarién of a family of French descent, Someillan had sought refuge in the USA after his father had been arrested for political reasons and deported to West Africa. In 1879, he received permission from the Southern Methodist Church to initiate a mission in Cuba. The armistice of Zanjón, which ended the first phase of the Cuban War of Independence, had helped to create a more tolerant political and religious situation in the island. Someillan was accompanied by an assistant pastor, Aurelio Silvera.

At this moment, a significant shift in missionary objectives occurred. In Key West, Someillan and Silvera had been content to evangelize the tobacco workers, who were generally poor and racially mixed. Once their work in Havana had been established, the two Cuban pastors decided that they wanted to convert the "more edu-cated classes", the whites. This shift in social objectives from the lower to the middle classes, would in due time have significant and perhaps fatal consequences for much of Protestant missionary work.

The new strategy did not prove beneficial then nor during later decades, and Someillan and Silvera had little success in Havana, a city in which at that time the poor predominated, by far. Moreover, Someillan remained the pastor of the church at Key West and kept travelling back and forth between the two cities. Neither of the parishes flourished, until Someillan decided to focus his attention upon Key West alone. Although it had succeeded in establishing a parish by the name of El Tabernáculo, Methodism did not gain any importance on the island until after 1898.

Protestantism takes root

The heritage of Kenney, who paradoxically had reluctantly evangelized Cubans only, turned out to be the most decisive factor in the definitive establishment of Protestantism in Cuba. After he had returned to the USA, the abandoned Cubans formed their own congregations in Havana and Matanzas. The latter congregation, which called itself Fieles de Jesus, turned out to be a real nursery for future Protestant leadership. The personalities who were schooled in this community of former slaves, tobacco workers and members of the lower middle class, were men of strong charismatic character. From the scant records we have about these people dating from the 1880s and early 1890s, it is clear that the first Cuban parishes were built around these personalities, to whom denomina-tional loyalties were secondary. These churches were communitarian fellowships, whose members gave each other strong mutual support. Such qualities were needed, because the Spanish authorities and the Catholic Church kept Protestants under tight social and political control. Protestants were suspected (usually rightly so) for their republican and revolutionary associations. Pedro Duarte, Alberto J. Díaz, Evaristo Collazo and Manuel Delofeu, who had all been leading members of the Fieles de Jesus community, belonged to that first generation of Protestants, who fought for Cuba's independence.

A visit by Bishop Young from the Episcopal Diocese of Florida in 1884, led to the recognition of the churches in Havana and Matanzas as Episcopal parishes. Young thereby disowned his church's Anglo-Catholic policies, which had driven away Kenney. He refrained however, from sending new American missionaries to Cuba. Instead, he saw to it that Duarte and Díaz received theological education in the USA, after which they became clergymen of the Protestant Episcopal Church. Upon their return to Cuba, their work expanded successfully. Within a few years, it was possible to imagine that through the ministry of the Episcopal Church, a large number of the island's population would shift their religious loyalty. The Anglican ritual, combined with the personal charisma and the revolutionary conviction of the church's leadership, seemed to provide a real alternative to those who were seeking a new political and religious way of life. In light of this, it is significant to note that it was Duarte, who, by appealing to Queen Maria Cristina, succeeded in having the Spanish government extend religious tolerance to Cuba.[4]

Presbyterianism was introduced in Cuba by Evaristo Collazo. During Duarte's absence in the USA, Collazo had taken his place as a lay leader in the Fieles de Jesus Church. In escaping arrest for his revolutionary activities, he became familiar with a Southern Presbyterian parish in the USA. Upon his return, he founded a Presbyterian congregation in Havana and another in Santa Clara. When his appeal for recognition and aid had been granted, the Board of Missions of the Presbyterian Church in the USA (PCUS) sent John Gillespie Hall, a missionary in Mexico, to Havana. Hall investigated the situation and gave Collazo a short course in theology and Presbyterian Church policy. After several weeks, and after having been successful in an examination, Collazo was ordained pastor and was officially placed in charge of the new work. The PCUS Board, nevertheless, sent missionary observers to Cuba at regular intervals, an action which Collazo apparently resented. Moreover, the visitors expressed increasing apprehension over the Cuban style of worship. Church gatherings were more like popular festivals than the well-ordered Presbyterian services to which the missionary inspectors were accustomed. Apart from this, Collazo, as an engaged revolutionary, rejected the political attitudes of the visitors, who kept speaking of the "special responsibility" which the USA (and its churches) had towards Cuba.[5]

A controversy arose when Collazo refused to accept two missionaries who arrived in late 1894, for permanent assignment. Shortly afterwards, in February 1895, when the last phase of the Cuban War of Independence began, it was the Spanish authorities who forced the missionaries to leave. Collazo, however, and a large number of his church members went underground and participated in the revolutionary war.

Methodist work also stabilized after a slow beginning. The El Tabernáculo Church flourished for a short while under the leadership of Manuel Delofeu (former member of Fieles de Jesus). Delofeu, like Duarte and Collazo, was engaged in political action. At the beginning of 1895, he was forced to flee to Key West. There he took over Someillan's pastorate (the latter had moved to another part of Florida), but kept a high position in the military network of the revolutionary army.

Between 1895 and 1898, for the duration of the last and most violent phase of Cuba's War of Independence, Protestantism on the island virtually dissolved, but several parishes, including Fieles de Jesus and El Tabernáculo, continued to function in a clandestine way.

Arrival of the North American Mission, 1898–1902

The Spanish-American War of 1898 completely changed the context and nature of Protestantism in Cuba.[6] In the first place, the US intervention ended not only 400 years of Spanish colonial rule, but it also ended the privileged status of the Roman Catholic Church, which now appeared to be facing ruin. Not only had it fully and uncritically supported the Spanish colonial state, but it was also morally decadent, although several religious orders had been doing remarkable educational work (though with a conservative orientation).

Secondly, all restrictions on Protestant missionary work were lifted when the American military forces took control of the island. Freedom of religion was later guaranteed by the Cuban constitution of 1902.

Within weeks of the Battle of Santiago de Cuba,[7] the first emissaries from the North American churches made their rounds in Cuba, in order to explore mission possibilities. They were often aided by members of the military occupation forces who belonged to the various religious denominations. Most of the Protestant military and missionary representatives involved came from the southern USA, in other words from the region which had always had a keen interest in the annexation of the island. This fact is not without significance, because in the upcoming years, most missionaries coming to Cuba were also from the

south, which was marked by its pronounced racial attitude and conservative theological outlook. Moreover, in several of the reports from
these early visitors, the hope that Cuba would undergo an
"Americanization" process was expressed. The military occupation
would be followed by a cultural transformation, which would in due
time lead to outright annexation. The "conversion" of Cuba from
Catholicism to Protestantism was to be a key element in this change-
over.[8] The establishment of the major US religious denominations is
described below.

The Methodist Episcopal Church, South

In September 1898, H.B. Someillan visited Santiago de Cuba and
Oriente Province at the request of his church's Home Mission Board.
W.K. Simpson, a Methodist chaplain from Alabama (Fifth US
Infantry), and Dr Irene Tolland, a medical doctor from Texas attached
to the occupation forces,[9] facilitated his contact with the occupation
authorities. Someillan was impressed by the readiness of these compa-
triots "to hear about the Gospel" and to learn about "anything related
to the USA". He sent an optimistic report to the Home Mission Board
about missionary possibilities on the island.

For the Home Mission Board, however, Someillan's investigations
were only a preliminary enquiry. The real task of negotiating for a
Methodist Church, was left up to Warren A. Candler, from Atlanta.[10]
Candler visited Havana and Matanzas in November 1898 with a number of other leaders from his church. He dealt directly with the occupation authorities and the leaders of the new establishment of the
rapidly growing "community" of North American businessmen and settlers who were now pouring into Cuba, attracted by cheap land and
the prospect of annexation.

Now that the legal and material basis for the extension of the
Methodist Episcopal Church, South (MECS) in Cuba was laid, R.J.
Parker, an experienced Methodist missionary in Mexico, was asked to
undertake a detailed study of the new mission field. Parker visited
Cuba in February and March 1899. His recommendations established
the mission policies which the Methodists (as well as a large sector of
the remaining Protestants) were to follow during the decades to come.
While not giving an opinion about Cuba's possible annexation, his
analysis was based on the assumption that the USA and its "liberal,
democratic." traditions, in addition to its economic interests, would

somehow remain decisive for Cuba's future. Protestantism, he felt, as the "predominating religion" of the USA, was bound to replace "medieval and retrograde" Catholicism. Parker therefore recommended that the middle and upper classes should be the target group of Methodist missionary work, because their "political liberalism" agreed with the fundamental political ideas of Protestantism. He recommended that missionary progress should take place simultaneously at three levels: (a) evangelism (preaching, revivals, and church building), (b) Sunday school work and (c) the establishment of private schools. The MECS did not wait long to implement these policies, especially because Candler soon became worried about the growing strength of socialist labour, which was a part of the nationalist reaction against the USA's imposition of the Platt Amendment and the Treaty of Reciprocal Trade, which warned that "atheism" might replace Catholicism in Cuba before Protestant missions had any chance to take effect. By the end of 1899, a dozen young and "dynamic" missionaries had arrived to participate in church construction and the establishment of schools.

The American Baptist Convention (ABC)

Although this denomination did not have any relations with Cuba prior to 1898, it decided in September of that year to engage in missionary work on the island. In November 1898, it agreed with the Southern Baptist Convention (SBC) to "divide" the new mission field into two territorial areas: the ABC "received" the eastern provinces of Camagüey and Oriente, and the SBC "took" the remaining four provinces in central and western Cuba. The American Baptist Home Mission Society (ABHMS), to whom this new extension became entrusted, was firmly convinced that, on the one hand, "Divine Destiny" had brought Cuba (and Puerto Rico) under American military control and that, on the other hand, the Cuban people were themselves calling for missionary and evangelical work. The ABHMS also believed that the Cuban people would accept such missionary work gratefully, because "the United States has not conquered the island, but has defeated its enemies and liberated its inhabitants".[11]

The first missionary designated to supervise the new Cuban work was H.R. Moseley from South Carolina, who had several years experience in Mexico. In early 1899, he paid a preliminary visit to the island's Eastern provinces, but what he saw there did not please him.

A Cuban linked to the SBC preacher, José O'Halloran,[12] had already visited Oriente Province during the second part of 1898 and established several Baptist congregations. These, Moseley thought, had not been sufficiently well constituted. He considered O'Halloran a charlatan and asked the SBC to transfer him to the western part of the island. Two American missionaries sent to assist Moseley did not measure up to his expectations either and were sent back to their home country. Moseley also complained about his fellow countrymen who were settling in Cuba. He considered their behaviour to be "an offence to their homeland and a hindrance to Christian missions". To the credit of this difficult and obstinate missionary, it must be pointed out that he was perhaps the only one of his generation who took the plight of the rural population seriously. By the time the US occupation ended, he had established the basis for several rural parishes and outposts. Moreover, he insisted from the start that the Cuban ABC (or Convención Bautista Oriental – CBOR – as it came to be called) become financially self-sufficient at an early stage. These two elements distinguished the CBOR from the other Protestant denominations from the very start.

The Southern Presbyterian Church in the US and the Northern Presbyterian Church

The PCUS was the first of the large American Presbyterian Church bodies to take the initiative to carry out missionary work in Cuba. John Gillespie Hall, who had visited Cuba during the early 1890s and had cooperated with Evaristo Collazo, returned to the island from Mexico in April 1899. During the Spanish–American War, he had read in the papers that the first American victim of the war had been a Southern Presbyterian by the name of Ensign Worth Bagley, whose cannon boat had been shelled by Spanish coastal batteries near Cárdenas. Hall felt that God was calling him to go to that city, and he asked his Mission Board for a transfer from Mexico. Upon arrival in Cárdenas, he discovered a Cuban family by the name of Torres, that had recently returned from the USA where it had become a member of the Presbyterian Church. The establishment of the mission was further aided by the presence of W.H. Forsytone, an American medical doctor attached to the occupation forces. Cárdenas had been the site of one of the most notorious Spanish concentration camps. The American doctor had cured many of the camp's former inmates and he willingly cooperated in the establishment of a Presbyterian mission in that city.

However, it was Robert L. Wharton, a young theologian and teacher, who would become the dominant figure of the Cárdenas group. Stimulated by the outbreak of the war, he applied for missionary service and was sent to that city. He engaged the mission team in a serious reflection on missionary strategy, which resulted in the following policy: (a) a school with primary and secondary levels was to become the pièce de résistance of the mission and (b) a careful evangelical effort would be undertaken, first in Cárdenas itself and later in the immediately surrounding small towns. Wharton and his team felt that there was no point in spreading the mission throughout the entire island, simply to establish a missionary presence. The school, La Progresiva, was founded on 19 November 1900. It was to have a marked effect upon Cuban Protestantism.

The Northern Presbyterian Church (PCUSA) did not, at first, initiate any missionary work in Cuba. In 1899, the Board for Publication and Sabbath School Work, nevertheless, decided to send Pedro Rioseco, an American citizen of Cuban birth, to Havana, in order to establish a Sunday school. This curious beginning led to the formation of a parish. After much uncertainty, the Home Mission Board of the PCUSA assumed the responsibility for this work. Rioseco was replaced by J. Milton Greene, a missionary in Puerto Rico. Within a short time, Greene and a number of additional missionaries, who had been sent to support him, founded several additional parishes, both in the province of Havana and in Sancti Spiritus, where thousands of North American farmers had begun to settle.

The Protestant Episcopal Church in the USA

The new beginnings of the Protestant Espiscopal Church in the USA (PECUSA) mission after 1898 were uncertain and contradictory, even though it was this denomination which before 1898 had been the first and most successful. However, even now, the obstacles caused by the Anglo-Catholic win in the PECUSA kept this church, for a long time, from establishing a coherent mission policy in Cuba. The "Anglo-Catholics" held that the PECUSA, as "one of the branches of the Catholic Church", had no right to engage in missionary activities in "Catholic" territory.

However, the events of 1898 helped to "soften up" the intransigent position of the "Anglo-Catholics". A special committee, appointed by the general convention of 1898 came to the conclusion that the "newly-acquired territories" (Cuba, Puerto Rico, Hawaii and the Philippines) had entered into a "special relationship" with the USA and therefore also with the PECUSA. The committee added that the question whether or not any missionary activity violated "ancient Catholic discipline" (based on the Council of Nicea), preventing one bishop from interfering in the affairs of another's diocese, should nevertheless be carefully examined. It concluded that such interference was permitted only in the case of "the gravest of reasons". In Cuba (and in the other countries), the committee found that such reasons did indeed exist: unscriptural communion, deviation from original Catholic teaching, forced domination (of the church) by a foreign bishop, immoral way of life of the clergy and the need for liberation from error and sin. The committee concluded that the PECUSA had not only the right but the duty to intervene!

On the basis of this radical recommendation, the general convention agreed that the PECUSA should consider Cuba to be a "mission land". Duarte, Díaz and others regained recognition as clergymen, and a missionary, W.H. McGee, was sent to Havana as a chaplain to the English-speaking colony. Even with this delay, there was no reason why the PECUSA mission, with its experienced and prestigious Cuban leadership, could not have made rapid headway again. But once again the "Anglo-Catholics" succeeded in applying their delay tactics. Having won a victory en principe, the proponents of the Cuban mission failed to obtain the election of a missionary bishop for Cuba from the general convention of 1898. They were no more successful during the next general convention in 1901. Only in 1904, after six costly years, was the first missionary bishop, Albion W. Knight, elected and sent to Havana.

The PECUSA leadership's limited grasp of the realities of the Caribbean island can be illustrated by the case of Juan Mancebo, a mulatto clergyman from Santiago de Cuba. He returned to his native city at the end of 1898, after a long absence in the USA. He noted that since the beginning of the American occupation, thousands of black Jamaicans, many of them faithful members of the Anglican Church, had arrived in Cuba. They carried out heavy work in the ports, on the sugar estates and for the US occupation forces under deplorable conditions. They received the mulatto clergyman with great enthusiasm and pleaded that he take up residence in Santiago de Cuba. On returning to the USA, Mancebo asked that he be transferred to his native city with permission to initiate work in Spanish and in English, especially among the blacks and the coloureds. Mancebo met with stony indifference from his white bishop. He had to spend several more years in the USA before he appealed in 1904 to the new missionary bishop in Havana and was accepted for service in Santiago de Cuba.[13]

Other missions

In accordance with the agreement with the ABC of November 1898, the SBC was entitled to engage in missionary work in the four provinces of Las Villas, Matanzas, Havana and Pinar del Río. However, the beginnings of this denomination in Cuba reach back as far as 1884, when W.F. Wood, a pastor from the Florida Convention, had begun to preach on the island. The Baptists, moreover, created what was probably the first Protestant day school, the Cuban-American College, in Havana. In 1893, the SBC had no fewer than five parishes and seventeen outstations in the Havana region. Developments were slow after 1898. The first missionary, C.D. Daniel, only arrived in 1901. The SBC was already at that time known for its individualistic and uncooperative attitude.

The small mission of the Quakers (American Friends) was the result of a small shipboard conversation in 1897 between Zenas L. Martin, the chairman of the Iowa Yearly Meeting and Capt L.D. Baker, one of the directors of the United Fruit Company in Boston. The latter encouraged the Quakers to begin a mission at Gibara (Oriente), where his company was in the process of being established and where it had purchased large tracts of land for sugar productions. After the war, a mission station (to which a large school was later added) was opened by Sylvestere and Emma Jones and María de los Santos Treviño from Mexico.

The Disciples and Congregationalists established missions in the province of Havana, which were composed of fewer than half a dozen local parishes. These small isolated efforts were not very successful.

From this brief outline of the establishment (or re-establishment) of the various Protestant denominations, it is evident that the Cuban founders of Protestantism had no place of leadership in the new denominational structures. Upon their return from the revolutionary war or from exile, these churchmen faced the same experience as Cuba's political and military leaders at the time of the American intervention. The island's independence, for which they had fought during thirty long and costly years, had proved to be a mirage, for the new "liberators" from the north had come to occupy and settle in the island.[14] The official church documents reflect this reality only by insinuations and vague references. More serious research needs to be done to unearth the real nature of the conflict which opposed the transferring of positions of leadership in the Cuban Church, from the older to the younger members who were inexperienced but powerful American missionaries who were coming in after 1898. In the case of the Methodists, H.B. Someillan, was not allowed to negotiate for the re-establishment of his church in Havana. This gifted preacher left the MECS in 1901 a bitter man and joined the small Congregational mission (which later merged with the Presbiterio Central). Duarte and Díaz carried on a successful ministry until 1904. They did not accept the "Americanization" of the UPUSA mission, which was undertaken by the new missionary bishop, Albion W. Knight, and went over to the Presbyterians in 1906. O'Halloran became *persona non grata*, along with Moseley and was compelled to leave. Collazo and Delofeu, who had held high posts in the revolutionary movement, remained with their respective churches (PCUS and MECS), but were not given any leadership positions. The conflict apparently did not exhaust itself in personality clashes (as the missionary reports suggested), but in differences of church style and political outlook. The original concept of Protestantism, as an instrument of freedom, democracy and church renewal, had become subverted, when it came to be used by those, who at church level, represented Cuba's new metropolitan power.

The missionaries brought about further significant shifts in emphasis, as the recommendation of R.J. Parker suggests. Prior to 1898, Protestantism had been largely "accepted" by the tobacco workers and the emerging lower middle classes, both of which were engaged in the struggle against Spain. In the new phase after 1898, the missionaries concentrated largely on winning the middle and upper classes (or the "more intelligent classes", as some of the missionaries insisted on calling them). Moreover, they concentrated on the cities, because they wanted to confront Roman Catholicism in its urban strongholds. The network of private Protestant schools, which the missionaries were now building, were largely patterned after the American school system and were to be the principal means to fulfil the new policy. The industrial workers and the vast rural population no longer figured as a target group (except in the case of the ABC missionaries).

This fundamental shift in objectives had immediate repercussions. In spite of all the (not so unreasonable) missionary expectations, no mass movement of conversions from Roman Catholicism to Protestantism had begun to take shape by 1902. The following reasons seem to account for this failure:

1. After 1898, Protestantism could no longer be identified with the cause of Cuban independence, but rather with the new imperialism from the North which had frustrated independence. In Cuban eyes, therefore, a subtle form of betrayal had undeniably taken place.

2. By an inverse process, Catholicism regained ground, despite the fact that it was making no effort to recapture the people's confidence, or, even less, to become a "people's religion". After the disappearance of Spanish rule, it simply remained the only intact institution which represented Cuba's Hispanic cultural, and therefore national identity, against the new onslaught of Anglo-American civilization. The church, unable to identify itself any longer with imperial rule, began to assume the responsibility of protecting itself against such rule. Catholicism therefore turned out to be much more resistant than the missionaries had expected.

However, as the Catholic Church was unable to grasp the missionary significance of this historical period, it still remained largely restricted to those same middle and upper classes which the Protestants had hoped to convert. Its political outlook remained completely conservative.

Building Protestant "Denominations", 1902–1940

In order to understand the place and function of Protestantism within the Cuban society of this period, it is important to recall the three basic factors which marked the life of the new "republic": (a) economic dependence, (b) political dependence on the USA and (c) the deformation of Cuban life caused by the sugar economy. The period between 1902 and 1940 can be divided into two distinct stages: the economic boom which lasted until 1920 (strengthened by the economic effects of World War I) and the economic collapse which was followed by social unrest and fascist dictatorships (Machado and Batista). An indication of the depth of the social problem is that in 1935, Cuba had 250,000 permanently unemployed people. In other words, out of a population of 3.9 million, one million were starving. Most of the remaining Cubans were constantly struggling to make ends meet, facing undernourishment and humiliation by those who were superior to them. A few thousand, however, the remnants of the ancient Spanish-Cuban oligarchy and the newly rich, all closely linked to North American economic interests, were able to live in ostentatious luxury.[15]

Growth of the Church

At the time of Cuba's "independence" in 1902, the various missions had already established their basic geographical territories. The various mission representatives met at the beginning of 1902 in Cienfuegos during an "evangelical conference", where the now established geographical distribution was ratified:

(a) the Methodists "occupied" all of the provincial capitals and some of the other major cities;

(b) the Baptists had divided the island into two geographical areas – from the PCUSA to the provinces of Havana and Las Villas and from the PCUS to Cárdenas and its surroundings;

(c) the PCUSA mission resumed its work in Havana and Matanzas (later it would, like the Methodists, establish its congregations in all provincial capitals); and

(d) the remaining smaller missions restricted themselves to certain localities (the Quakers to Gibara, Oriente, and the Congregationalists and Disciples to the Province of Havana).

Except for minor changes, the basic denominational distribution and structure would henceforth remain unchanged. The only significant alteration came when, after 1920, the various North American fundamentalist denominations that had broken away established their own, competitive missions in Cuba. After World War II there was also a growth of national Cuban Pentecostal congregations. Apart from this last group, however, the American denominational system was introduced to the island virtually unchanged. Moreover, in nearly every case, the Cuban branch denominations were placed under the administration of the Home Mission Boards and integrated into the internal US church structures (for example, the Cuban Methodists came under the jurisdictional supervision of the Episcopal diocese of Georgia and Florida, and the Presbyterians, at first only the PCUSA mission in Havana, became attached to the synod of New Jersey). This arrangement remained in force long after it had become clear that Cuba would never become a territory of the USA, as had its neighbour, Puerto Rico.

The church's statistical data of the period generally have only a relative value. In Cuba, as in the rest of Latin America, Protestant policy governing membership records followed two conflicting patterns. On the one hand, the churches were anxious to point to rapid membership growth in order to verify their claim that they were overcoming a "decadent" Roman Catholicism. On the other hand, Protestantism also became concerned about whether exaggerated membership figures included too many inactive or indifferent (secular) members. This second preoccupation reflects the "free church" tradition coming out of the English Reformation and pietism (where the "folk church" principle is rejected in favour of the church as the community of the "elect" or the "saved"). The PECUSA (or Iglesia Episcopal – IP), which came out of the Anglican State Church tradition, took a more generous view of membership statistics than either the Iglesia Presbiteriana (IP) or the Baptists. The MECS (Iglesia Metodista – IM) stood somewhere in between.

Most of the Protestant missions nevertheless, grew at a rapid pace during the first decade of their existence (though not in the form of a mass movement as the early missionaries had at first expected). The MECS membership went up from 443 members in 1902 to 3,185 in 1910. The ABC mission grew from 543 in 1905 (when it first began to keep records) to 2,218 in 1910, and the PECUSA mission from 463 to 1,440 during the same period. After 1910 growth declined considerably. In 1920, Cuba had 4,510 Methodists, 1,939 (CBOR) Baptists, 3,000 Presbyterians and 2,005 Episcopalians. After 1920 growth declined further, and during the 1930s, several of the denominations declined in number. In 1940, there were 5,687 Methodists, 4,205 (CBOR) Baptists, 2,491 Presbyterians and 5,649 Episcopalians. The preparatory documents for the evangelical conference of Panama in 1916 included what was perhaps the only comprehensive set of statistics between 1902 and 1940. According to that list, Cuba had at that time 15,639 Protestants, who were distributed throughout 179 parishes and belonged to nine different denominations. They were served by 158 missionaries and 200 national fellow workers (ordained and laymen).[16] If we assume that between 1915 and 1940 the number of church members roughly doubled, Cuba must have had between 30,000 and 35,000 Protestants by 1940 and more, perhaps, if we add a statistically unknown number of adherents of the fundamentalist sects.

The relative low number of Cuban Protestant members (which, contrary to earlier hopes, became almost exclusively restricted to the lower middle class) does not convey the fact that the major impact Protestantism made was through its schools. Throughout prerevolutionary Cuba, many local churches created day schools as a source of extra income, but also in order to help compensate for the deficiencies of the state's educational system. The top league of these schools vied with some of the best Catholic private schools. While they did not produce many converts, these schools nevertheless did help to create a favourable climate for Protestantism among the Cuban élite. These schools did, after all, facilitate entry into the American university system for their alumni, something which was indispensable if the student planned a career within one of the American business corporations active in Cuba or in a Cuban firm which did business with the USA (which they all did). Among the top Protestant schools were: Candler College, Havana (Methodist), Colegio de la Luz, Havana (Episcopal), La Progresiva, Cárdenas (Presbyterian), Irene Tolland College, Matanzas (Methodist), St. Paul's College, Camagüey (Episcopal), Pinson College, Camagüey (Methodist), Eliza Bowman College, Cienfuegos (Methodist), International College, El Cristo (Baptist), Sarah Ashburst School, Guantánamo (Episcopal) and the Friends' College, Gibara (Quakers).

Among further developments within Cuban Protestantism during the period from 1902 to 1940, the restructuring of Presbyterian and Baptist work requires special mention. In 1918, the Presbiterio Havana (which had grown out of the mission originated by Rioseco and Greene) and the Presbiterio Central (emerging from the PCUS mission directed by Wharton) were merged into one Presbiterio Central, also called the IP. The small Congregational and Disciples missions were added to this new denomination. By 1923, this development caused a merger also among the various supporting mission boards in the USA, when these joined together to form the Presbyterian Board of National Missions (which also administered similar United Churches in Puerto Rico and the Dominican Republic). Over the

245

years, the new IP built up a remarkable inner cohesion, and it became comparable in size and significance to the other larger denominations. From the start, the ABC mission (beginning with H.R. Moseley) developed a mission pattern distinct from that of the other churches:

(a) following the Baptist tradition, each local congregation became autonomous and financially self-reliant;
(b) likewise, the CBOR Convention began to take over full responsibility at an early stage, while the ABC missionaries were reduced to the role of advisers with little or no financial role;
(c) in 1920, the Convention formed the Cuban Baptist Home Mission Society, which helped to extend Baptist work into new regions.

While this independence from the American mother church resulted in severe financial problems for the Cuban Baptists, they integrated themselves much more readily into Cuba's social fabric. They were, as was mentioned above, the only denomination which penetrated the rural areas.

Theological self-understanding

On the face of it, the theological self-understanding of Cuban Protestantism of the period does not vary from that of the American mother Churches (English Reformation, modified by Pietism, the Enlightenment and the "American experiment"). The theological schema transmitted by the missionaries focused on the following basic ideas:

(a) the need for individual conversion (with repentance and forgiveness of sins);
(b) leading a moral life (or a life of holiness, according to Baptist and Methodist terminology);
(c) joining a congregation and active participation (fellowship and mutual aid);
(d) the need for evangelism (witnessing by word and way of life);
(e) withdrawal from the "secular", which is considered evil.

This theological schema was simultaneously defensive and triumphalistic: defensive against the all-pervading religious and cultural influence of Roman Catholicism (and the "world" connected with it), and triumphalistic in helping to overcome Catholicism. In due time,

Cuban Protestantism therefore developed its own areas of focus, whose base was an exaggerated anti-Catholicism (to be sure, the continued attempts of the Catholic hierarchy to recuperate its privileged position did nothing to make Protestants think differently), which was tied to a legalistic moralism, a clericalization of the churches and a readiness to adopt a theological fundamentalism, which the missionaries brought to Cuba at the time of World War I.[17]

Three problems resulted from this fateful theological development within Cuban Protestantism:

(a) The massive rejection of the "secular" produced a large-scale lack of understanding of the country's serious social problems. This thinking in particular prevented an understanding of the root causes of social and economic underdevelopment. Only during the 1930s, did it become clear to some of the more open-minded churchmen that drinking, gambling and prostitution (three evils which were always attacked by the churches) were the result of deeper problems, which could not be eliminated by the simple call for individual conversion.

(b) The pronounced anti-Catholicism (supported, in part, by the association of [freemason] pastors and leading laymen), prevented the development of any serious ecumenical understanding. Beyond individual conversion and the act of "joining a church", little was offered which could lead to a wider concept of the visible Church of Jesus Christ. While the denominations usually presented themselves as pragmatic organizations of convenience (or as "branches" of the universal Church), each, nevertheless, maintained a sense of jealous autonomy and was wary of all and any cooperative venture.

(c) Accordingly, liturgical life was little developed in Cuban Protestantism. Holy Communion was taken infrequently and contained little concrete meaning, except in an uncertain, symbolic way. An exception must of course be made in the case of the IP, which maintained a rich liturgical life in the Anglican tradition. Also baptism by immersion, as practised by the Baptists (often in a river or on the open sea shore) usually made a great liturgical and symbolic impact.

But by and large, Cuban Protestantism generally lacked real liturgical dimension. It was a true child of Anglo-Saxon revivalism, transplanted into a cultural setting marked by Catholicism, which it rejected.

Political and social concepts

As was pointed out, during the early years after the creation of the
Cuban "Republic", the missionaries were convinced that their work
was part of the overall political responsibility which the USA had
assumed for the young state. They did not understand that Cuba's revolutionary restlessness and rebelliousness against the American "*diktat*"
of the Platt Amendment and the subsequent military and political
interventions, was not the result of "Latin irresponsibility" or inborn
"revolutionary tendencies", but an expression of the desire for true
independence and self-reliance. Therefore, the missionaries transformed the original anti-Catholic concept of Protestantism of being a
guarantor of political liberty in the face of "oppressive" and "retrograde" Catholicism, into an antirevolutionary notion: Protestantism
was the "democratic bulwark" against socialism and bolshevism!
Bishop Candler first developed this idea before the annual conference
of 1901, when a series of political strikes was spreading across the
island, and he kept returning to this theme in later years. Wharton
and Moseley practically said the same thing. Wharton, when founding
La Progresiva, believed that one of the main goals of this school
should be to "infuse a democratic spirit" into the minds of young
Cubans. After the Russian Revolution of 1917, missionaries (and by
now also the nationals) once again upheld the equation of
"Protestantism = Democracy = Anti-Communism". We are not sur-
prised that this theme resurfaced during the revival campaigns after
World War II (accompanying the Cold War) and during the heated
debate on the nature of the Cuban Revolution after 1959. Neglecting
the reality of political and economic dependence, the missionaries
were convinced that Protestantism not only promoted democracy, but
economic progress as well. They reasoned that as soon as a majority of
Cubans had embraced Protestantism, they were not only immune
against the revolutionary virus, but they would become imbued with
the spirit of "free enterprise" and would tear themselves away from the
"Latin lethargy" inherited from Roman Catholicism, which they considered to be the main cause of economic underdevelopment.[18]

However, during the long and bitter crisis of the 1920s and 1930s,
it became increasingly difficult to maintain this facile, individualistic
approach to social problems. Already at the beginning of 1926, Quaker
missionary Sylvester Jones, made a passionate plea to Cuban
Protestants to apply the insights of the World Conference on Life and

Work, which had taken place in Stockholm during the previous year. He outlined what the "Christianization of society" might mean when applied to Cuba.[19] This kind of language, partly inherited from the USA's "Social Gospel" movement, was not understood at that time. Most missionaries, because of their fundamentalist inclinations, were opposed to the "social gospel". The first significant moment of Protestant reflection on Cuba's social, economic and political reality came in 1933, when the dictator Machado fell and the USA threatened another intervention (in the end replaced by Sumner Welles' "mediation"). Within the IP, a Protestant movement began to spread, which rejected the continuous domination of the island by the USA.[20] The movement spread rapidly to laymen of the other churches, and some kind of an ecumenical lay movement was formed. It not only demanded basic structural reforms in society but assumed anticlerical and antimissionary attitudes. With the political repression, initiated by the new dictator, Batista, and the internal pressures operating within each denomination, this lay movement was shortlived. However, for a few short weeks in 1933, it succeeded in tearing apart that cloth of silence which had been spread over Cuban Protestantism since 1898, revealing a mass of social and spiritual suffering.[21]

Ecumenical beginnings

As a result of the theological problems described above, ecumenical beginnings were difficult and slow. The absurdity of reproducing American denominational divisions (each coming out of a specific sociological and theological conflict) in another country, was felt by many from the very start. But as long as no signs of encouragement to overcome the problem came from the mother churches, little could be done within Cuba itself. And though in 1908 the mainline American denominations formed the Federal Council of Churches (later, the National Council of the Churches of Christ in USA) under the impact of the "social gospel" movement, most missionaries deliberately refused to bear the consequences for the churches in Cuba. Preferring to believe the accusations made by fundamentalists about the assertions of their own denominational leadership, they suspected the new ecumenical bodies of "modernism" (a socially oriented theological liberalism), from which they fully intended to protect the new Cuban churches. Thus, the first generation of national church leaders had no opportunity to come to a conclusion about the various opposing theological currents in the USA, not to speak of those in the world at large. The ecumenical development in Cuba must be understood in the light of this peculiar and, thus far, little researched aspect of church dependence.

The most important attempt to establish some ecumenical order in Cuba came in relation to the already mentioned Latin American Evangelical Conference of Panama in 1916. The conference leader, John R. Mott, had already placed his considerable organizational talents at the disposal of the International Missionary Conference of Edinburgh in 1910. He believed that the mission boards would rationalize and dynamize their sterile denominational missionary methods when faced with a commonly elaborated serious social and spiritual analysis of each country. Such an analysis was also developed for Cuba.[22] Under the impact of the conference, the Cuban missionary leadership (among whom were J. Milton Greene and Episcopal bishop Hiram Hulse), agreed to re-examine the location of Protestant schools, consider a joint publications programme, the creation of a common theological seminary and the establishment of a dynamic programme of evangelism. For follow-up purposes, they even formed a conference committee, which would work closely with the newly created Committee on Cooperation in Latin America (based in New York) and seek to implement the ideas emerging from the Panama Conference Committee. However, following secret instructions from the MECS (which at that moment was fully engaged in the divisive struggle over fundamentalism), the Methodist missionary leadership in Cuba refused to cooperate with the other churches and the conference committee fell apart. Not until decades later were some of these concerns realized (for example, the United Theological Training School was formed in 1946). The shock of the 1916 disaster remained so deeply entrenched that over the next twenty-five years no further joint efforts were undertaken. An exception, however, is the Movimiento Cívico Social Evangélico mentioned above, but that body obviously did not have the blessing of the church authorities.

The Coming of the Revolution, 1940–1958

The establishment of the Cuban Council of Churches

The adoption of a new constitution in 1940, prepared by Batista, coincided with a new beginning in Protestant life. The missionary generation had largely disappeared and a first generation of Cuban nationals was assuming responsibility.

The visit of John R. Mott in April of that year gave an impulse to the establishment of the Cuban Council of Evangelical Churches (CCEC). The first secretary was, ironically, S.A. Neblett, a Methodist missionary who had been instrumental in undermining the conference committee of 1916. All the major churches became members, with the exception of the CBOC (sprung from SBC missions). The CCEC was, nevertheless, an instrument of limited use. Its seven commissions restricted themselves to common efforts in evangelism, education, youth and social action. Of the three "classical" bases of ecumenicity (Faith and Order, Church and Society, and Missions and Evangelism), only the third became a constitutional part of the new council. The dimension of church and society was only lightly suggested by "social action". Faith and Order as a concern was absent. At least, however, through the CCEC, Cuban Protestantism had at long last found a common forum of encounter and a visible joint instrument for facing the government authorities and the public at large.

The Problem of Dependence: J. Merle Davis' Church Study, 1941

A second significant event was the visit of J. Merle Davis from the International Missionary Council to Cuba. The Cuban delegate to the World Missionary Conference of Madras (1938), Presbyterian pastor Ferreol J. Gómez, had invited the IMC to do a study of the economic base of Cuban Protestantism in order to help it overcome its dependence upon the churches in the USA. In a remarkable study, Davis examined Cuba's deformed sugar economy and investigated the problem posed by the establishment of a middle class church system in a poor, underdeveloped country. Following are some of the specific problems whose existence he noted.

(a) Economic dependence upon the USA
The churches, he felt, reflected the overall situation of the country. In spite of the economic restrictions under which the Cuban pastors laboured, the poverty of the church members was such that they could neither support their pastors nor pay building maintenance and other

251

costs. This meant that the Cuban churches had no alternative but to continue to depend upon their American mother churches for their financial survival.

(b) Economic differences

The Cuban pastor was conscious of the high economic level in the nearby USA and of the salary differences between himself and the missionary. This awareness made him doubly aware of his poverty and weakened his effectiveness.

(c) *Tradition and practice of Roman Catholicism*

Cubans had not been trained by Catholicism to give financial support to their church. As the Protestants had no wealthy middle and upper class in their midst, the difference caused by lack of donations had to be compensated by support from the mission boards.

(d) *Loss of youth*

This was the most serious problem which Davis saw. Due to the higher education of Protestant young people, the churches were continuously drained of their best leadership potential. Educated young people usually had no desire to be further associated with congregations whose pastors were poorly educated and who discouraged them by their excessive moralism.

(e) *A divided church*

The divisions of Protestantism not only hindered its witness; but it also meant that most local churches were too small and therefore even financially weaker to support their pastor. Their expensive clerical super structure was too heavy a burden to bear.

(f) *Spiritualism*

The dry and puritanical forms of worship which had been imported by the missionaries were increasingly rejected by those who wanted to see a more lively and participatory style of worship. Hence many Protestants were turning to spiritist groups and to Pentecostalism (in which Davis saw a threat).

Davis proposed two solutions to this growing dilemma:
(i) Protestantism should give up its urban, middle class programme and concentrate on the poor, unchurched rural areas. There was little

point in a parish competing with a well-entrenched urban Catholicism and with other Protestant churches. Moreover, through gardening and farming the pastors should be encouraged to find a supplementary income. Through his new activity he would come closer to the rural population and also provide a social and educational impulse to this utterly neglected population sector.

(ii) The small competing parishes should unite.[23] Needless to say, neither the Cuban church leadership nor the mission boards heeded Davis' sensible advice.

Ecumenical enthusiasm

In 1942, a Kirchentag-like event, the convención magna of Cárdenas, gave a new impulse to the Cuban ecumenical movement. It was reminiscent of the Movimiento Cívico Social Evangélico of 1933. For several days 300 pastors and laymen came together in an ecumenical "outpouring" of the spirit which completely broke down all denominational barriers. It was an event which remained engraved for a long time in the memory of the participants. The cautious CCEC received several resolutions from the convención magna, which included demands for the creation of a united theological school, a joint student home in Havana, joint Protestant book stores and a Protestant university. Cárdenas at least helped to advance the realization of the United Theological Seminary, which became a reality in 1946.

The problem of theological education

The demand of the convención magna pointed to one of the most difficult problems of divided Cuban Protestantism. Although each mission had from the beginning emphasized the need for good theological training, no school of any significance was created. This was in marked contrast to the large financial and personnel resources which were invested in church buildings and, above all, in the church related "colegios" (schools).

The early mission of the MECS suffered from the ambivalence with which American Methodism regarded theological education at the turn of the century. Most pastors had no more than a college education, followed by an "on-the-job" theological training supervised by older colleagues. Even this informal approach posed problems when applied to Cuba, where most candidates for the ministry did not have more than rudimentary primary school education. In 1914, Candler College established a theological department. But as its students were also given the task of providing pastoral care to the other students (which included the holding of prayer services and controlling the use of tobacco and alcohol), this solution proved to be untenable. Moreover, virtually no theological literature existed in Spanish, and the students first had to learn English in order to understand their textbooks. In 1931, the theological department was transferred to Pinson College in Camagüey, and in 1943 it was moved back to Havana, where it was called upon to serve church congregations on weekends and to prepare radio sermons. These practical requirements prevented most students from obtaining a solid academic theological education.

The IE solved the problem differently. In 1907, after Bishop Knight's short-lived attempt to create a theological training school in Jesús del Monte near Havana, most of the candidates for the ministry were sent to the USA. In the IP, theological education was part of the work done by missionaries. In 1921, H.G. Smith undertook the tutelage of future pastors, in general education and theology. In 1926, the IP engaged in conversations with the IM for a joint theological education programme, which remained inconclusive. During the late 1930s, the IP began to send its students to the newly established United Theological School in Puerto Rico. Theological training was even more informal within the CBOR. Due to the fact that the general educational level of its pastors was poor, the CBOR initiated an annual four-week training course in 1909. New candidates, however, were generally required to attend a three-year course at the Department for Education and Theology of the International College in El Cristo. However, even this promising experiment did not last. After the outbreak of the economic crisis in 1920, the number of candidates for the ministry declined, and in 1933, the theological sections of the department at El Cristo were closed down. The CBOR hesitated to send its theological students to the Interdenominational Seminary in Puerto Rico, because it feared that the seminary's urban and middle class atmosphere would have a negative effect on its students. Many of the Baptist students preferred to attend the theologically conservative, if not fundamentalist, Los Piños Nuevos Bible School near Placetas, which had been founded by former Presbyterian pastor B.G. Lavastida, under the auspices of the West Indies Mission (later Asociación Evangélica). The fact that this largely self-sustaining Bible school was located in a rural setting had the advantage of ensuring that the student did not become alienated from his mainly modest small town or rural background. In fact, it is probable that this kind of school would have responded far better to the needs of Cuban Protestantism than most of the other unsatisfactory experiments in theological education.

In 1946, the proposal made at the *convención magna* at Cárdenas began to bear fruit, when the Seminario Evangélico de Teología (SET) opened its doors in Matanzas. It was supported jointly by the IM and the IP and, from 1951, by the IE as well. The rector was Alfonso Rodríguez Hidalgo, a Presbyterian graduate of Princeton Theological Seminary. The "bachillerato" (school-leaving examination) was generally required for entry. The programme followed the pattern of theological training in the USA. Education for the pastoral ministry lasted three years while a parallel course for women specializing in Christian education lasted two years. At its peak, in the mid 1950s, SET was host to between sixty and eighty students from all over the Caribbean and Central America.[23] In 1949, CBOR founded its own theological seminary near Santiago de Cuba. In addition, there were six Bible schools. In 1952, all of these theological training centres had 400 students, who were taught by a surprising seventy teachers, mostly North Americans.

The reawakening of the social conscience

Even though Cuban Protestantism (and its mother churches) had not taken up the ecumenical and social challenges made by J. Merle Davis in 1941, he had helped to create a certain unease with respect to the rural problem. However, because the Cuban churches were unable to rid themselves of their dependence on the USA, they once again turned to the mission boards and missionaries to provide funds and personnel for work in rural areas. One of the major projects was the Escuela Agricultural e Industrial in Oriente, which was organized in 1945 by the IM on land ceded near Mayarí by the United Fruit Company. Going beyond the Los Piños Nuevos Bible School, the IM hoped to provide a sound agricultural training opportunity for rural congregations, whose members would undertake a technical extension service. The results were disappointing because the IM, which had not done any detailed studies of Cuba's countryside, did not understand the socially destructive nature of latifundism and rural poverty. Once the Escuela had trained a number of young people, they resolutely turned their back on rural Cuba and headed for the cities.

Of greater significance perhaps was the extension of the Frank J. Laubach literacy campaign into Cuba. Laubach's ideas were enthusiastically taken up by Presbyterian pastor Raúl Fernández Ceballos, who in 1949 became general secretary of the CCEC. His literacy classes brought him into direct touch with rural poverty. During the 1950s, local churches in 117 cities and towns participated in this campaign. Among the denominations, the IP and the CBOR became particularly involved. The literacy campaign provided the CCEC with a firmer purpose and greater visibility.

Signs of insecurity

In 1948, Cuban Protestantism began the celebration of its fiftieth anniversary (the work of the Cuban pioneers between 1868 and 1898 was apparently not taken into consideration!). The celebrations were to last four years, that is, until 1952. During the conception and planning of the celebrations, the growing confusion and insecurity within Cuban Protestantism became more obvious. As no new guiding concept was apparent, the church leaders had to fall back on the ideas of yesterday. The celebration coincided with the emergence of evangelist Billy Graham, whose mass evangelical campaigns (coupled with modern mass media techniques) were sweeping across the USA. Soon the main denominations, concerned about these successes, imitated Billy Graham's techniques, and it was not long before dozens of North American preaching teams descended upon Cuba. The Methodists and Presbyterians, in particular, welcomed these visitors, to whom they looked desperately for help in order to get the churches on the march again. The IM prepared ambitious but unrealistic plans for new membership and finance which were never realized, although the total number of Protestants did increase during the 1950s. Inevitably, the traditional pattern of missionary Protestantism was re-emphasized (personal conversion and piety, abstinence from smoking and drinking, and so on) at the very moment when Batista inaugurated his second dictatorship (1952), which led directly to the revolutionary war. These evangelical campaigns therefore, had a disastrous effect, because they reinforced the social isolation of Cuban Protestantism at the very moment when Cuban society was desperately searching for new and more viable forms of life.

Protestantism and political conflict

The form of conservative missionary (or triumphalistic, pietistic) Protestantism, however, was already becoming a relic, when it last manifested itself during the 1950s. The other, "Cuban" form of Protestantism, that of the pioneers of the late nineteenth century, seemed to re-emerge as a result of the revolutionary war led by Fidel Castro. It had somehow survived the sombre years since the American intervention of 1898 (appearing briefly in 1933, in the form of the Movimiento Cívico Social Evangélico). It must also be added that the American mother churches were beginning to change their own social and theological thinking during the late 1950s, as if in anticipation of the American racial conflict of the 1960s and of the disaster of the Vietnam War. Nevertheless, the rethinking among the USA mother churches came too late to have any impact on their relations with the Cuban sister denomination.

One of the first signs of change was the creation of the Movimiento Social Cristiano (MSC), which was founded within the IM in 1946, it became part of the CCEC in the same year. Its founder and leader was Methodist pastor Manuel Viera Bernal. Inspired by the Social Gospel movement and the Stockholm Conference of 1925, the MSC's fundamental hope was the "Christianization of Society". In a manifesto published in 1955 (the year in which Fidel Castro laid the foundation of the Movimiento del 26 de julio – 26 July movement) the MSC called for social reform in fourteen specific areas, which ranged from abolishing the state lottery to land reform and the creation of production and sales cooperatives.[24] This document established some kind of a bridge between the more traditional Protestant ideas for a "moral" society and a socialist reform catalogue. Although a few local cooperatives were founded under Viera's guidance, the MSC never undertook a serious social and economic analysis, and barely questioned the overriding problem of the political and economic control which the large North American transnational corporations exercised over the island. All of the statements of the MSC therefore were marked by a certain vagueness and "foreignness". It nevertheless gave the churches important ideas for a new social thinking.

For a number of church leaders, however, the decisive breakthrough moment came with the second *coup d'état* led by Batista in March 1952. Raúl Fernández Ceballos was at that time still general secretary of the CCEC and Rafael Cepeda, another Presbyterian pastor, was president. The two men formed a politically astute team, and during the next few years, they travelled throughout the island, often at great risk, persuading other Protestant leaders and local parishes to align themselves in the struggle for Batista's overthrow. Thanks to this effort, Cuban Protestantism was largely able to resist the dictator's temptations. He tried to buy their support through gifts, preferential treatment and decorations. Fernández' Church at Calle La Salud in Havana became an important point of underground liaison between the capital city and the guerrilla army in the Sierra Maestra (Oriente). Another Presbyterian pastor, Mario Llerena, was for a while the representative of the Movimiento del 26 de julio in the USA. One of the most remarkable Protestant revolutionary leaders was a young and devout Baptist from Santiago de Cuba, Frank País, who, with his brother Josué, directed the revolutionary war after Fidel Castro himself. País, the son of the Baptist pastor Francisco País and his wife Rosario, was a teacher and a student of theology. In December 1956 he led an underground uprising in Oriente and wrested military control of Santiago de Cuba from the Baptista forces for three days. He gave logistic support to Castro's guerrilla army after they had settled themselves in the Sierra Maestra. During the summer of 1957, Frank and Josué País were killed in a surprise attack by the Batista police. Frank was twenty-three years old at the time.

Fidel Castro was fully aware of the great contribution which Cuba's Protestant minority was making to the revolutionary war.[25] Thus, when the Catholic archbishop, Pérez Serantes of Santiago de Cuba, offered to send military chaplains to the guerrillas in 1957, the revolutionary leader did not accept until he was assured that the Protestant community was also ready to provide a military chaplain for his partisans.[26] Castro held the CBOR Baptists in particularly high esteem, and it was one of the Baptist leaders, José González Seisdedos, who, at the end of 1958, negotiated the surrender of Santiago de Cuba, which led directly to the downfall of the Batista regime.

Revolution and Crisis, 1959–1961

Protestantism was, nevertheless, little prepared to accept the socialist Cuba of marxist orientation, which began to emerge three years after the revolutionary takeover. However, the existential crisis of 1961 cannot be explained simply by the "fear of Communism" which resulted in such a massive emigration of Protestants to the USA. The main reason lay in the still unresolved dependence of Cuban Protestantism upon the mother churches in North America. Clearly, a dependent church was an anachronism in a society which had given up capitalism as a social and economic system and which had cut itself off from the USA.

The end of an era

In order to understand the extent of the change which befell Cuban Protestantism between 1959 and 1961, it is important to review once more its position at the time of the revolutionary takeover.

It is difficult to estimate the number of Protestants at the beginning of 1959. Most of the Protestant estimates at that time suggested a figure of 300,000 (some went as high as 500,000!). However, an estimate prepared by Maruja Olmo Muñoz on behalf of SET indicates that, according to church statistics, there were 52,320 full church members in 1952, distributed among twenty-two denominations. An examination of a few denominational statistics suggests an annual growth rate of 2.5 to 3 percent, which corresponds to Cuba's average population increase during that period, so that by 1959 the total Protestant membership must have stood at about 60,000. By multiplying this figure by three, as is customary among Latin American Protestants, we arrive at a total of 180,000 for the Protestant community (which includes children, membership candidates and friends, in addition to the full members). According to Olmo, there were 112 Protestant day schools (a number which probably did not vary greatly throughout the 1950s), to which Candler University, founded in 1957 from Candler College, must be added.

In 1959, after nearly two decades had passed since the visit of J. Merle Davis, the problems of Cuban Protestantism remained virtually unchanged. The former rector of the CBOR Theological School in Santiago de Cuba (later the general secretary of the CCEC), Adolfo Ham Reyes, when reviewing the situation of Protestantism at the time of the victory of the revolution, emphasized again that dependence was the main issue. He specifically mentioned the following factors:

(a) The organic structure of the Cuban churches was exactly the same as that of the mother churches in the USA.
(b) Most of the church properties were kept in the name of the North American mission boards (except those of the IE).

(c) In most cases basic decisions were made in the USA.

(d) The number of foreign missionaries remained unusually high (at the IM they represented 30 percent of the entire clergy). Compared with Cuban pastors, their standard of living was much higher and this created much tension.

(e) The theological training of the Cuban pastors was deficient, as a result of the inadequate education of the missionaries (or missionary teachers). Cubans who were educated abroad were unable, after their return, to adapt their knowledge to suit the Cuban situations.

(f) The dependence of Cuban Protestantism after fifty to sixty years took many forms and not only financial. The mother churches set the pace in terms of theology and ideology as well.[27]

Reaction of Protestantism to the victory of the revolution

Triumph, joy and enthusiasm were the initial reactions of the Protestants when Batista was overthrown on 1 January 1959. The new revolutionary government seemed to respond to everything the Protestants traditionally held dear: the restoration of civil liberties and a dedication to "cleanse" Cuba of gambling, alcoholism and prostitution. The long desired symbiosis of Protestant and political ideals seemed to have taken place. On 7 February 1959, a large public thanksgiving service was held in Havana to give expression to this joy. Later, in May, Raúl Castro (Fidel's younger brother) and his wife, Vilma Espín, received a Bible from Protestant leaders during a ceremony at Candler University. When the Catholic hierarchy suggested that the new government reintroduce religious (Catholic) teaching in public schools, Protestants were eminently satisfied when Fidel Castro reassured them that public schools would remain under secular control.

Now that its expectations were satisfied, Protestantism had not much more to offer to the public debate on the future of Cuba, which began during the spring of 1959. Already, the first round of land reform (which divided the large estates) was causing dismay in the USA, and at the same time the Catholic hierarchy added to the beginnings of North American pressures by warning Cubans against the danger of communism and atheism. The Protestants at that time indignantly defended the revolutionary government against such warnings and reaffirmed their support. But little more was said. The CCEC, somewhat embarrassed by this lack of precision in Protestant thinking, asked the MSC to prepare a statement. A document was presented to the CCEC in May 1959, but it simply repeated earlier recommendations that the society be "Christianized" (which was evidently no longer possible), in order to promote cooperation and establish a better welfare system (which the new government had already started). The CCEC, not satisfied, demanded that the MSC make a greater effort, not realizing that this commission had reached its ideological limits and could make no new suggestions.[28]

For the time being, the CCEC nevertheless became active in relief action in Oriente, which was to be its last social action programme before Cuba definitively became a socialist country. This action was backed by the Church World Service (CWS), the overseas relief arm of the National Council of the Churches of Christ in the USA. A careful analysis was made of the emergency situation in some of the regions devastated by the revolutionary war (Gibara, Mayarí, and so on), where over 50,000 persons lived in great despair. This action was carried out over a one-year period (it included the provision of food and medical supplies). Moreover the IP (with the help of its mother churches) established a rehabilitation centre at Sagua de Tánamo for 300 war orphans, which also helped in the reconstruction of the surrounding villages.

Through this and other actions (the IM became involved in social action in the Sierra Maestra), Protestant leaders took a renewed interest in the fate of the rural population. Already, the land reform promoted by the revolutionary government was bringing hope to this hitherto abandoned social sector. The CCEC Assembly of November 1959, passed a resolution that recommended that its member churches approach the rural areas seriously. It supported the government's land reform programme and proposed that both the World Council of Churches and Agricultural Missions (another department of the National Council of the Churches of Christ in the USA) carry out studies on the rural areas on behalf of the Cuban churches. Theological education was to be adapted correspondingly, and a conference on rural problems was to be convened. Few, if any, of these recommendations were put into practice. However, the conference on rural problems was held in April 1960. But by that time, the government's land reform programme had advanced further. State farms and large cooperatives had largely replaced the former large private land holdings, and schools and medical centres were established throughout the island. The CCEC Assembly resolutions were not of use, when finally approved, due to other events that had already taken place. The church conference on rural problems bitterly disputed over whether or not the revolution had become "communist" in nature. Protestantism had now definitively missed its opportunity for a prophetic ministry in Cuba's vast rural areas!

The ideological struggle 1960–1961

The conference on rural problems marked the beginning of the debate within Protestantism over the ideological nature of the Cuban Revolution. It was a complex discussion, but by the end of 1961, it had shaken the basic presuppositions of Protestantism's existence.

During the first stage, many Protestant leaders felt obliged to defend the revolution against accusations of "communist infiltration" which were made by the US government and the Catholic hierarchy. In July 1959, the CCEC said that these accusations were untrue and that they were hindering the "traditional good relations" between North America and Cuban peoples. They said that the Cuban Revolution was indeed socialist, but it had nothing to do with communism. For several months, various churches, schools and individuals made the same assertion. More and more, however, it was admitted that there were communists in Cuba who would have loved to assume power, but that they would not be given any opportunity, because this would be against the will of the people. At this stage, the old argument that Protestantism was a "bulwark" against "antidemocratic" forces was resurrected, and this time it was clearly directed against "communism".[29] Indeed, by the end of 1959, Protestants no longer insisted that communism did not influence the Cuban revolutionary process, and during the first half of 1960, it became clear to the church leadership that they had to make a choice. At that time, three options were open to them with regard to a Marxist oriented socialist society: (a) adopting a positive attitude, (b) rejecting this form of society or (c) adopting a cautious neutral attitude. The struggle between positions (a) and (b) continued until the end of 1960 and well into 1961. Position (c) developed slowly, after the proponents of position (b) chose to surrender instead of fighting and went into exile. Raúl Fernández Ceballos and a few others became proponents of position (a). Fernández became convinced that what was important, was not whether the Cuban Revolution was "communist", a debate which he considered irrelevant and futile, but whether it was remaining faithful to its original intention, namely to end social misery and political and economic dependence on the USA. The revolution had, in his mind, passed this crucial test, and therefore he decided to support it. It must not be forgotten that in 1960, the concept of "liberation theology" or any other "Third World" position among the churches had not yet been developed. Fernández took his courageous position despite an ambience marked by the Cold War and general anticommunism sentiments among the churches. The government asked Fernández, in view of his long experience with the Laubach literacy campaign, to help prepare the major illiteracy eradication campaign of 1961 (which by the end of that year had virtually eliminated this great obstacle to development).

A massive and perhaps well-meaning campaign was undertaken through the churches to "save Cuba from communism".[30] The Committee on Cooperation in Latin America (CCLA) dispatched to Havana many booklets entitled Christian Handbook on Communism for distribution by the CCEC. This booklet which had been published in 1952 by the Committee on World Literacy and Christian Literature, described Soviet atheism and the Stalinist church persecutions from a North American point of view. A number of visitors followed, warning the "native" Cubans against the dangers of communism. This concerted effort which lasted throughout 1960, did achieve some measure of success, because in November of that year during the CCEC assembly, the MSC launched a sharp attack against "communism", repeating the main arguments of the handbook, and saying that Christianity and communism were squarely incompatible and could not live side by side. The CCEC Assembly adopted this text. It also replaced Fernández and Cepeda by a politically conservative group headed by Cecilio Arrastía (IP) and Manuel Viera Bernal (IM). The MSC moved decidedly to the right and into political opposition. It gave up its advocacy of "socialist" measures and began to defend "private property" and "personal freedom". In a theological reflection upon this historical moment, Sergio Arce Martínez (IP), thought that Cuban Protestantism was now, in the midst of a socialist revolution, adopting a position of "liberal individualism" and defending the "moral value of the bourgeoisie". He argued that the traditional emphasis on individual conversion and the maintenance of a strict moral code of ethics had prepared the road which led to this particular political line, which now made Protestantism an unwitting tool of the international forces of counterrevolution.[31]

Emigration

The conservative leadership which took over the CCEC in November 1960 undoubtedly assumed that the USA would not tolerate a "communist satellite" on its doorsteps for very long. When, therefore, the Bay of Pigs invasion of April 1961 failed (and the Soviet Union warned the USA against any further attempt to attack Cuba), and when this event was followed by a closing down of all private schools (1 May 1961), this leadership found itself in a precarious position. In quick succession, Arrastía, Viera and Rodríguez Hidalgo (rector of SET) abandoned the country and migrated to the USA. This was the signal for thousands of other Protestant pastors and laymen to do likewise. The closer a church was connected with and dependent on a North American mother church, the larger the number of its adherents seeking exile (this was especially the case with the IM and the IE).[32] Thus, of the entire Methodist clergy at work in Cuba in 1961, only two members were left by 1964. They were followed by perhaps half of the entire IM Church membership. The IP lost half of its pastors, and 85 percent of all seminarians at the SET followed their rector abroad, as did the majority of the teachers of the former Protestant schools. In Miami, CWS organized a large "refugee" operation.[33]

The arrivals from Cuba usually received much publicity. Between 1961 and 1963, CWS flew the exiles to the interior on no less than sixty-three "freedom flights". Most Protestant exiles, however, remained in Miami or went to other Gulf ports (including Puerto Rico), where many of them became involved in countless plots against the revolutionary government. It is estimated that 30,000 Cuban Protestants went abroad during and after 1961. If we are to take the statistics provided by Maruja Olmo as a starting point, however, a much larger number, perhaps 100,000, abandoned the churches without going abroad, because new membership estimates carried out during the mid sixties suggested that the entire Protestant community had at the most 50,000 adherents. What J. Merle Davis, as far back as 1941, had felt to be the greatest threat to Protestantism, namely large-scale abandonment by its youth, had now come true. The revolutionary enthusiasm, and educational and work opportunities in a new, egalitarian society, were draining Protestantism's best and most highly qualified leadership.

Later Developments

Cuban Protestants remained in a state of shock during most of the six-ties, but slowly reflection began to set in, first within small groups and then at a more general level. In the first place, although the churches were stripped of their schools and social projects, they were not perse-cuted, as the earlier propaganda had wanted Cuban Christians to believe. Second, there were many who discovered that the revolution-ary process itself was a very important theological event. Had not scripture always stressed the importance of human community and placed great emphasis on the need for work as part of human self-real-ization? Did not the churches have a new and unique opportunity for proclaiming the gospel of Christ, now that they had liberated them-selves from the degrading state of financial, theological and ideologi-cal dependence? Slowly and painfully, a new and more profound sense of Christian mission in a socialist society was born. This process, while not readily accepted by all, was aided by a number of factors: (a) through the mental change caused by the Second Vatican Council (1962–65), relationships between Protestants and Catholics were changed profoundly; (b) the various denominations became indepen-dent of their US mother churches; (c) the Cuban churches began to make contact, initially through the World Council of Churches and later directly, with churches in other socialist and Third World coun-tries, and new theological trends; (d) the Latin American liberation theologies began to have an influence in Cuba also. In a new and unexpected way, therefore, the gospel of Jesus Christ was being inter-preted differently in Cuba.

NOTES

1. The profound economic crisis during the middle of the nineteenth century drove these social groups into poverty and therefore into rebellion against Spain. The small wealthy upper class temporarily "solved" the problem by calling in American capital and technical know-how (sugar production). However, in the end Cuba was drawn into the economic and political orbit of the USA. The American military intervention simply finalized a process which had started decades earlier.

2. José Martí, *Obras Completas* (Havana 1931), XVII, 170; XXVI, 222; XXX, 1245; XXXIII, 195.

3. Annual report of the Board of Missions of the MECS, 1 June 1875, 70f.

4. The liberal Spanish Constitution of 1876 had introduced religious tolerance. War conditions in Cuba and the resistance of the conservative colonial administration had prevented the full application of the constitution on the island. Religious tolerance was again abolished in 1895, after the outbreak of new hostilities.

5. Before 1895, American commercial penetration into Cuba, at that time still a Spanish colony, advanced rapidly. The reports of these Presbyterian missionary visitors reflect their belief that Spain would soon be compelled to cede Cuba to the USA. This growing American threat induced José Martí and the rest of the revolutionary leadership to renew quickly the independence war in order to forestall such an American takeover. Collazo apparently recognized the same pattern in his relations with the Southern Presbyterians.

6. As the study of Robert Mackenzie, *The Robe and the Sword* (Washington, DC 1961) shows, American Protestantism fully supported President McKinley's interventionist policies. Many church leaders felt that US imperialism, aimed primarily toward Latin America and Asia, was "preparing the way for the Gospel". Accordingly, 1898 was the year during which foreign missions became predominant concerns of the churches.

7. The decisive Battle of Santiago de Cuba took place on 1 July 1898. The armistice was agreed upon on 17 July. The Paris Peace Treaty, in which Spain ceded Cuba, Puerto Rico, the Philippines and the Mariane Islands, was signed on 10 December 1898. All Spanish authority over Cuba ended on the last day of that year.

8. There was of course no coordinate plan between the US military forces and the Protestant churches on how Cuba was to be annexed. However, the idea of annexation was generally accepted in the southern USA. In the end this scheme was frustrated, partly because of strong Cuban resistance, partly because northern liberal politicians and midwestern farmers (sugar beet growers) opposed the strengthening of southern agrarian regionalism.

9. Dr Tolland performed remarkable health work among the Cuban civilian population, whose health was ravaged by war conditions. She caught yellow fever and died at the end of September 1898 (during Someillan's visit). The Methodist missionaries later dedicated a girl's school in Matanzas to her memory.

10. Candler came from an influential Georgia family. His brother Asa was the founder of the Coca Cola company and became state governor and senator in Washington, DC.

11. *Baptist Home Mission Society Monthly*, January 1902, 2.

12. O'Halloran had originally belonged to the Episcopal parish in Havana. As a result of his revolutionary involvement, he had to flee to the USA, where he joined a SBC church. After the end of the hostilities, he preached and baptized in Oriente before the arrival of Moseley and became very popular.

13. Mancebo, as a ten-year-old orphan, had made the acquaintance of Edward Kenney. At that time he already wanted to become a pastor in order to help the black people of Santiago de Cuba. Kenney helped Mancebo to obtain an education and, later, theological training. The long war and the bishop's indifference kept him in the USA far beyond his wishes. Mancebo died of old age in Santiago de Cuba in 1951.

14. The price for "independence" in 1902 was paid through territorial concessions (Guantánamo), the right to intervention (both laid down in the Platt Amendment) and the Reciprocal Treaty of Commerce, which opened Cuba to full economic penetration.

15. Julio Le Riverend, An Economic History of Cuba (Havana 1967), 234.

16. Christian Work in Latin America, reports and documents on the Congress of Christian Work in Latin America, Panama. February 1916 (New York 1916), II, 270.

17 "Fundamentalism" from The Fundamentals: A Testimony to the Truth, an article series which was published in the USA in 1910–12. This theological school (a neo-Calvinist response to the "social gospel") believed in: (a) the verbal inspiration of the Holy Scriptures; (b) an unquestioned belief in the Holy Trinity, including the virgin birth and the divinity of Christ; (c) the fall of Adam and the personal conversion of the individual through the vicarious sacrifice of Jesus Christ; (d) the bodily resurrection of Christ and his bodily ascension into heaven; (e) the immediate return of Christ to earth; (f) eternal life in the heavenly paradise for the saved and in hell for the lost. By 1920, most of the major US denominations (with the notable exception of the SBC) had formally rejected fundamentalism, which resulted in the break-off of several new denominations, such as the Free Methodists, the Church of the Nazarene, and the formation of independent "faith missions". Moreover, even among the major denominations there were countless pastors and congregations of fundamentalist persuasion, particularly in the southern and western USA. Many missionaries came from these backgrounds, which explains why fundamentalism gained a strong foothold also in Cuba.

18. The notions expressed by Max Weber in Die protestantische Ethik (Tübingen 1920), were frequently echoed in missionary literature.

19. He gave a speech in the Episcopal Cathedral of Havana.

20. It must be remembered that several of the outstanding Protestant revolutionaries of 1868–98, such as Collazo, Duarte and Diaz (including the nationalist oriented Someillan), had found refuge within Presbyterianism. During the 1930s the memory of these leaders was still alive in the IP.

21. The basic text of the Movimiento Cívico Social Evangélico was published in the Heraldo Cristiano in November 1933.

22. Christian Work in Latin America, I, 164. Society was only lightly suggested by "Social Action". Faith and Order as a concern was absent. At least, however, through the CCEC, Cuban Protestantism had at long last found a common

forum of encounter and a visible joint instrument for facing the government authorities and the public at large.

23. J. Merle Davis, *The Cuban Church in a Sugar Economy* (New York and London 1942).

24. Actas CCEC, *Manifiesto a los Evangélicos*, Minutes of the general assembly of the CCEC, November 1955, 1.

25. Among the victims of the Batista terror were a number of young people belonging to the emerging young Protestant intellectual elite, such as Omar Ranedo Pubillones (IE, Guantánamo), Oscar Lucero (CBOR, Holguín), Marcelo Salado (IM Pinar del Río) and Esteban Hernández (IP, Cárdenas). Several of these individuals were connected to the Protestant schools.

26. They were CBOR pastors Víctor Toranzo and Luis Herrera.

27. Adolfo Ham, "Non-Theological Factors", in *Religion in Cuba Today*, edited by Alice Hageman and Philip Wheaton (New York 1971).

28. The MSC statement published in November 1960 (and adopted by the CCEC Assembly) was formally a fulfilment of the CCEC request of May 1959. In terms of content, however, it obviously was not!

29. Such was the impression of Arthur L. Miller, the moderator of the United Presbyterian Church in the USA after a visit to the island in late 1959. He restated to Cubans the traditional belief that Presbyterianism in particular had been a key instrument in the creation of modern liberal democracy.

30. This church campaign, it must be recalled, coincided with the enormous propaganda effort of the US mass media against the Cuban Revolutionary Government and with military preparations for the ill-fated Bay of Pigs invasion of April 1961. The following question must therefore be raised: to what extent did the American establishment attempt to use the churches and the mission societies for its own political purposes (as it did during the war of 1898)?

31. Sergio Arce Martínez, "Un analisis crítico", *Mensaje* (October–December 1974): 2.

32 The part of Protestant membership going into exile usually belonged to the middle class, coinciding at that time with the general movement of that class out of Cuba.

33. During the early and mid sixties, the Cuban refugee operation consumed no less than one-third of the CWS budget.

Annotated and Chronological Bibliography

The study of the Caribbean as a region
Cahnman, Werner J. 1943. "The Mediterranean and Caribbean regions: A comparison in race and culture contacts". *Social Forces* 2: 209–14.
Wagley, Charles. 1960. "Plantation America: A culture sphere". In *Caribbean Studies: A Symposium*, edited by Vera Rubin, 3–14. New York.
Mintz, Sidney. 1965–66. "The Caribbean as a socio-cultural area". *Cahiers d'Histoire Mondiale*, 9: 812–38.

The study of the Caribbean in historical perspective
Bosch, Juan. 1970. *De Cristóbal Colón a Fidel Castro. El Caribe, frontera imperial.* Barcelona.
Williams, Eric. 1978. *From Columbus to Castro: The History of the Caribbean, 1492–1969.* 5th ed. London.
Pierre-Charles, Gerard. 1981. *El Caribe contemporáneo.* Mexico D.F.
The work of the first historian of the Caribbean, Bartolomé de Las Casas, is important in that it narrates the first confrontation between the conquerors and the natives of the Caribbean from 1492 to 1521: *Historia de las Indias*, finished in 1561, edited for the first time in 1875, and republished by Fondo de Cultura Económica, 3 vols. (México 1951). For an interpretation of the life and work of Las Casas, see the most recent work of Gustavo Gutiérrez. 1992. *En busca de los pobres de Jesucristo: el pensamiento de Bartolomé de las Casas*, Salamanca.

The history of the ideas in the Caribbean
Lewis, Gordon K. 1983. *Main Currents in Caribbean Thought: The Historical Evolution of Caribbean Society in its Ideological Aspects, 1492–1900.* Baltimore-London.
Pierre-Charles, Gérard. 1985. *El pensamiento socio-político moderno en el Caribe.* México D.F.

The history of religions in the Caribbean
Bisnauth, Dale. 1990. *History of Religions in the Caribbean.* Kingston, Jamaica.

THE HISTORY OF CHURCHES IN THE CARIBBEAN

The Church in the Spanish Caribbean in the sixteenth century
Lopetegui, L., and F. Zubillaga. 1965. *Historia de la iglesia en la América española, desde el descubrimiento hasta comienzos del siglo XIX: México, América Central, Antillas.* Madrid.
Dussel, Enrique. 1970. *Les evêques hispano-américains, défenseurs et evangélisateurs de l'indien, 1504–1620.* Wiesbaden.
Dussel, Enrique. 1979. *El episcopado latinoamericano y la liberación de los pobres, 1504–1620.* México, D.F.
Dussel, Enrique. 1983. *Introducción a la historia general de la iglesia en América Latina,* I/1. Salamanca.
Prien, Hans-Jürgen. 1985. *La historia del cristianismo en América Latina.* Salamanca.
Meier, Johannes. 1991. *Die Anfänge der Kirche auf den Karibischen Inseln.*
Die Geschichte der Bistumer Santo Domingo, Concepción de la Vega, San Juan de Puerto Rico und Santiago de Cuba von ihrer Entstehung (1511/22) bis zur Mitte des 17. Jahrhunderts, Neue Zeitschrift fur Missionswissenschaft, Immensee.
Dussel, E., ed. 1992. *The Church in Latin America 1492–1992.* New York.
Several authors including M. Rodríguez, J. Meier, A. Lampe, L. Hurbon and R. Gómez Treto wrote about the Caribbean.

Churches and slavery in the Caribbean
Jakobsson, S. 1972. *Am I not a Man and a Brother? British Missions and the Abolition of the Slavetrade and Slavery in West Africa and the West Indies, 1760–1838.* Uppsala.
Zeefuik, K.A. 1973. *Hernhutter zending en Haagse Maatschappij 1828–1867, Een hoofdstuk uit de geschiedenis van zending en emancipatie in Suriname.* Utrecht.
Bolt, C., and S. Drescher, eds. 1980. *Anti-slavery, Religion and Reform: Essays in Memory of Roger Anstey.* London.
Gisler, A. 1981. *L'esclavage aux antilles françaises (XVIIe–XIXe siècle): contribution au problème de l'esclavage.* Paris.
Goodridge, S.S. 1981. *Facing the Challenge of Emancipation: A Study of the Ministry of William Hart Coleridge.* Bridgetown, Barbados.
Turner, Mary. 1982. *Slaves and Missionaries: The Disintegration of Jamaican Slave Society, 1787–1834.* Urbana.
Beozzo, J.O., ed. 1987. *Escravidao negra e História da Igreja na América Latina e no Caribe.* Petrópolis.
Lampe, Armando. 1989. "Iglesia y estado en la sociedad esclavista de Curazao". *Anales del Caribe* 9: 75–124.
Laviña, J. 1989. *Doctrina para negros.* Barcelona.
Laviña, J. 1991. "Iglesia y esclavitud en Cuba". *América Negra* 1: 11–29.
Lampe, Armando. 1991. *Descubrir a Dios en el Caribe.* San José.
Oostindie, Gert. 1992. "The enlightenment, Christianity and the Suriname slave". *Journal of Caribbean History* 2: 147–70.

The social history of the Catholic Church in the Caribbean
(a) Spanish Caribbean
Campo Lacasa, Cristina. 1977. *Historia de la Iglesia en Puerto Rico (1511–1802)*. San Juan.
Wipfler, William. 1980. *Poder, influencia e impotencia: la iglesia como factor socio-político en República Dominicana*. Santo Domingo.
Pérez Memén, Fernando. 1984. *La iglesia y el estado en Santo Domingo (1700–1853)*. Santo Domingo.
Pérez Memén, Fernando. 1985. *El arzobispo Fernando Carvajal y Rivera: un crítico de la política española y otros ensayos históricos*. Santo Domingo.
Rodríguez León, Mario A. 1985. *Iglesia y sociedad en Puerto Rico, 1508–1814*. Bayamón.
Silva Gotay, Samuel. 1985. "La iglesia católica en el proceso político de la americanización de Puerto Rico". *Revista de Historia* 1: 102–20; 2: 168–87.
Gómez Treto, Raúl. 1987. *La iglesia católica durante la construcción del socialismo en Cuba*. San José. (English edition: *The Church and Socialism in Cuba*. New York 1988.)
Kirk, John M. 1989. *Between God and the Party: Religion and Politics in Revolutionary Cuba*. Tampa.
1990. *La religión en la cultura*. Estudios realizados por científicos cubanos. Havana.
Pruna Goodgall, Pedro M. 1991. *Los jesuitas en Cuba hasta 1767*. Havana.

(b) Dutch Caribbean
Vernooij, Joop. 1974. *De Rooms Katholieke Gemeente in Suriname vanaf 1866*. Paramaribo
Vernooij, Joop. 1989. *Indianen en Kerken in Suriname*. Paramaribo.
Lampe, Armando, et al. 1991. *De kracht van ons erfgoed*. Oegstgeest.
Lampe, Armando, ed. 1991. *Kerk en samenleving op Curaçao*. Willemstad.
Boudewijnse, B., H. Middelbrink, and Ch. van de Woestijne, eds. 1992. *Kerkwandel en lekehandel, De Rooms-Katholieke Kerk op Curaçao*, Amsterdam.

(c) British Caribbean
Caldecott, A. [1898] 1970. *The Church in the West Indies*. Reprint, London.
Harricharan, John T. 1981. *The Catholic Church in Trinidad, 1498–1852*, Vol. 1. Port of Spain.
Johnson, Wallace R. 1985. *A History of Christianity in Belize: 1776–1838*. New York, London.
Osborne, Francis J. 1988. *History of the Catholic Church in Jamaica*. Chicago.
Caribbean Quarterly. 1991. "The social teaching of the Church in the Caribbean", *Caribbean Quarterly*, 37, no.1.

(d) French Caribbean
Du Tertre, J-B. [1661–1667] 1978. *Histoire générale des Antilles*. 2 vols. Reprint, Fort-de-France.

CEP. 1983. *Haití, Opresión y resistencia, Testimonios de cristianos*. Lima.

Hurbon, Laënnec, ed. 1989. *Le phénomène religieux dans la Caraïbe: Guadaloupe – Martinique – Guyane – Haïti*. Montreal.

Association des Amis du Père Aristide. 1988. *Quelque chose a changé en Haiti*. Montréal

Petit–Monsieur, Lamartine. 1992. *La coexistence de types religieux différents dans l'haïtien contemporain*. Immensee.

Greene, Anne. 1993. *The Catholic Church in Haiti: Political and Social Change*. East Lansing.

The history of protestantism and ecumenism in the Caribbean

Hartog, J. 1969. *Mogen de eilanden zich verheugen, Geschiedenis van het protestantisme op de Nederlandse Antillen*. Curaçao.

Braithwaite, J.A., ed. 1973. *Handbook of Churches in the Caribbean*. Bridgetown, Barbados.

van Raalte, Jan. 1973. *Secularisatie en zending in Suriname*. Wageningen.

Williams, Eric. 1973. "Some historical reflections on the church in the Caribbean". Port of Spain.

Tschuy, Theo. 1978. *Hundert Jahre Kubanischer Protestantismus (1868–1961)*. Versuch einer kirchengeschichtlichen Deutung, Frankfurt am Main.

Hamid, Idris. 1980. *A History of the Presbyterian Church in Trinidad, 1868–1968: the Struggles of a Church in Colonial Captivity*. San Fernando, Trinidad.

Lockwood, George A. 1982. *El protestantismo en Dominicana*. Santo Domingo.

Silva Gotay, Samuel. 1983. "La iglesia protestante como agente de americanización en Puerto Rico, 1898–1917". In *Politics, Society and Culture in the Caribbean*, edited by Blanca G. Silvestrini, 37–66. Selected papers of the XIV conference of the Association of Caribbean Historians, Univ. of Puerto Rico, San Juan.

Cepeda, Rafael, ed. 1986. *La herencia misionera en Cuba: consulta de las iglesias protestantes en Matanzas*. San José

Rodríguez, Daniel R. 1986. *La primera evangelización norteamericana en Puerto Rico, 1898–1930*. México D.F.

Cuthbert, R. W. M. 1987. *Ecumenism and Development: A Socio-historical Analysis of the Caribbean Conference of Churches*. Michigan.

Alvarez, Carmelo, ed. 1989. *Cuba, Testimonio cristiano, Vivencia revolucionaria*. San José.

Griffiths, Leslie J. 1989. "Le protestantisme en Haïti avant le Concordat". In *Le phénomène religieux dans la Caraïbe*, edited by Laënnec Hurbon, 95–110. Montreal.

Mensaje, no. 4 (Havana) 1991. Celebrating 50 years of the Cuban Ecumenical Council.

Mangru, Simon. 1993. "The role of the Anglicans in the evangelization of the East Indians in British Guiana". *History Gazette* 57, Univ. of Guyana.

On the issue of a Caribbean theology

Hurbon, Laënnec. 1972. *Dieu dans le vodou haïtien*. Paris.

Hamid, Idris, ed. 1973. *Troubling of the Waters*. San Fernando.

Hamid, Idris, ed. 1977. *Out of the Depths*. San Fernando.

Owens, J. 1979. *Dread: The Rastafarians of Jamaica*. Kingston.

Erskine, Noel Leo. 1981. *Decolonizing Theology: A Caribbean Perspective*. New York.

Watty, William W. 1981. *From Shore to Shore: Soundings in Caribbean Theology*. Kingston.

Mulrain, George Mc. D. 1984. *Theology in Folk Culture, The Theological Significance of Haitian Folk Culture*. Frankfurt am Main.

Smith, Ashley. 1984. *Real Roots and Potted Plants: Reflections on the Caribbean Church*. Mandeville, Jamaica.

Arce, Sergio. 1985. *Church and Socialism: Reflections from the Cuban Context*. New York.

Lampe, Armando. 1986. "Entre la religiosidad popular y la resistencia popular no hay contradicción (una perspectiva antillana)". *Cultura negra y teología*, 171–76. San José.

Lewis, R., and P. Bryan, eds. 1988. *Garvey: His Work and Impact*. Mona.

Rivera Pagán, Luis N. 1989. *Senderos teológicos: el pensamiento evangélico puertorriqueño*. Río Piedras.

Davis, Korthright. 1990. *Emancipation Still Coming*. New York.

Aristide, Jean–Bertrand. 1991. *In the Parish of the Poor: Writings from Haiti*. New York.

Chevannes, Barry. 1991. "Towards an Afro-Caribbean theology: Principles for the indigenization of Christianity in the Caribbean". *Caribbean Quarterly* 1: 45–54.

Kirton, Allan F. 1991. "Current trends in Caribbean theology and the role of the Church". *Caribbean Quarterly*, no. 1: 98–107.

Aristide, Jean–Bertrand, with Christophe Wargny. 1993. *Aristide: An Autobiography*. New York.

New religious movements and African cults in the Caribbean

Simpson, George E. 1970. *The Religious Cults of the Caribbean: Trinidad, Jamaica and Haiti*. San Juan.

Hurbon, Laënec, with Dany Bébel–Gisler. 1975. *Cultures et pouvoirs dans la Caraïbe: langue créole, vaudou, sectes religieuses en Guadeloupe et en Haïti*. Paris.

Lewis, Gordon K. 1978. *Gather with the Saints at the River:The Jonestown Guyana Holocaust*. San Juan 1979.

Massé, R. 1978. *Les adventistes du septième jour aux Antilles françaises: anthropologie d'une espérance millénariste*. Montréal.

Estevan Deive, Carlos. 1979. *Vodu y magia en Santo Domingo*. Santo Domingo.

Thomas-Hope, Elizabeth, ed. 1980. *Afro-Caribbean Religions*. London.

Williams, K.M. 1981. *The Rastafarians*. London.

Lampe, Armando. 1987. "Los nuevos movimientos religiosos en el Caribe". In *Los movimientos sociales en el Caribe*, edited by Gérard Pierre-Charles, 335–65. Santo Domingo.

Hurbon, Laënnec. 1989."Les nouveaux mouvements religieux dans la Caraïbe". In *Le phénomène religieux dans la Caraïbe*, edited by Laënnec Hurbon, 307–54. Montreal.

Laguerre, Michel. 1989. *Voodoo and Politics in Haiti*. London.

Chevannes, Barry. 1990. "Rastafari: Towards a new approach". *New West Indian Guide*, nos. 3–4: 127–48.

Arguellos, A., and I. Hodge Limonta. 1991. *Los llamados cultos sincréticos y el espiritismo* (Estudio monográfico sobre su significación social en la sociedad cubana contemporánea). Havana.

Desmangles, Leslie G. 1992. *The Faces of the Gods, Voodoo and Roman Catholicism in Haiti*. Chapel Hill and London.

Brandon, George. 1993. *Santería from Africa to the New World: The Dead Cell Memories*. Bloomington.

Houk, James. 1993. "The role of the Kabbalah in the Afro-American religious complex in Trinidad". *Caribbean Quarterly*, nos. 3–4: 42–55.

Glazier, Stephen D. 1993. "Funerals and mourning in the Spiritual Baptist and Shango traditions". *Caribbean Quarterly*, nos. 3–4: 1–11.

Kremser, Manfred. 1993 "Visiting ancestors: St Lucian Djine in communion with their African kin". *Caribbean Quarterly*, nos. 3–4: 82–99.

van Dijk, Frank Jan. 1993. *Jahmaica: Rastafari and Jamaican Society, 1930–1990*. Utrecht.

Littlewood, Roland. 1993. "The divine feminine among Trinidad's Earth People: Appropriation and reinterpretation in Spiritual Baptist visions". *Caribbean Quarterly*, nos. 3–4: 56–72.

Polk, Patrick. 1993 "African religion and christianity in Grenada". *Caribbean Quarterly*, nos. 3–4: 73–81.

Pollak–Eltz, Angelina. 1993. "The Shango cult and African rituals in Trinidad, Grenada and Carriacou and their possible influences on the Spiritual Baptist". *Caribbean Quarterly*, nos. 3–4: 12–26.

Taylor, Ian A. 1993. "The rite of mourning in the Spiritual Baptist church with emphasis on the activity of the spirit". *Caribbean Quarterly*, nos. 3–4: 27–41.

Villamán, Marcos. 1993. El auge pentecostal (Describes the Pentecostal movement in the Dominican Republic). México.

Warner–Lewis, Maureen. 1993. "African continuities in the Rastafari belief system". *Caribbean Quarterly*, nos. 3–4: 108–23.

Guano, Emanuela. 1994. "Revival Zion: An Afro-Christian religion in Jamaica". *Antropos* 89: 517–28.

Murphy, Joseph M. 1994. *Working the Spirit: Ceremonies of the African Diaspora*. Boston.

Savishinsky, Neil J. 1994. "Transnational popular culture and the global spread of the Jamaican Rastafarian movement". *New West Indian Guide* 3/4: 259–82.

Chevannes, Barry. 1995. "Revivalism and identity". In *Born Out of Resistance: On Caribbean Cultural Creativity*, edited by Wim Hoogbergen, 245–52. Utrecht.

Glazier, Stephen D. 1995. "New religious movements in the Caribbean: Identity and resistance". In *Born Out of Resistance, On Caribbean Cultural Creativity*, edited by Wim Hoogbergen, 253–62. Utrecht.

Index

Contributors

Johannes Meier, Professor at the University of Mainz, Germany

Keith Hunte, Principal and Pro Vice Chancellor of the University of the West Indies, Cave Hill, Barbados

Armando Lampe, Lecturer at the University of Quintana Roo, Mexico

Laënnec Hurbon, Member of the Centre national de la recherche scientifique, Paris

William L. Wipfler, currently works in the Office of the *Anglican Observer* at the United Nations

Theo Tschuy, author of *Hundert Jahre Kubanischer Protestantismus (1868–1961): Versuch einer kirchengeschichtlichen Deutung*, Frankfurt/Main 1978

CPSIA information can be obtained at www.ICGtesting.com
Printed in the USA
BVOW03s0329261113

337311BV00007B/93/P